WHITE KNUCKLES

WHITE KNUCKLES

THE LIFE AND MUSIC OF GARY MOORE

MARTIN POWER

OMNIBUS PRESS

London / New York / Paris / Sydney / Copenhagen / Berlin / Madrid / Tokyo

Contents

AUTHOR'S NOTE

I first saw Gary Moore on stage with Thin Lizzy at London's Hammersmith Odeon in April 1979, during one of his brief, if spectacular spells with the band. I don't recall the exact date, but Monday 23 sounds about right.

As guitarists went, though only a teenager, I'd seen some good ones: Scott and Robbo with Lizzy the year before. Alex Lifeson with Rush. Then there was Edward Van Halen at north London's much-missed Rainbow theatre, where I genuinely thought I'd witnessed the second coming.

But Gary Moore was different. For a start, unlike Eddie or Alex, he didn't smile much. In fact, I don't recall him smiling at all. What I do recall was a shock of black hair flying here, there and everywhere; a body hunched over the guitar, shoulders frozen, head at the oddest of angles. Then there was that face. Moore looked like he was in agony – or ecstasy. Possibly both.

Yet, when you stopped looking and started listening, Gary Moore made perfect sense. He played like his very life depended on it, every note drawn from some intense, emotional reservoir deep inside. Moore could play slow and sweet, or sharp and fast. So fast, in fact, that when he let fly with that super-speed reel in the middle of 'Black Rose', it sounded like he could play just about anything.

I was hooked. Forty years later, I still was. I became an avid follower of Moore's career from that night in Hammersmith to his untimely death in February 2011, so when Omnibus Press asked me to write a book about him, I really wasn't going to say 'No'.

To the book, then.

First and foremost, it's a book about Gary's music: the rock, the prog, the metal, the ballads – even that flirtation with breakbeats back in 1997. Moore lived and breathed music, so when writing a book about him, music's the starting point.

At the heart of Gary's music was the blues. A curious, beguiling thing, the blues hooked onto Moore when he was young. It gave him heroes and purpose, songs and ultimately riches, and it didn't let go of him until he was done.

The blues also provided a fitting backdrop for Moore's life and times, which in some ways ran like the lyrics to one of those old Willie Dixon tunes he so loved. Good times, bad times, money troubles, woman troubles. As the saying goes, 'Trouble ahead, trouble behind'. From the love affairs and youthful misadventures to the emotional and physical scars left in their wake, the blues and Gary Moore walked hand in hand and they fed into the very fabric of his being.

Friendship was also a great mainstay in Moore's life: Rory Gallagher, Peter Green, George Harrison, the mighty Philip Lynott. What those friendships meant to him, what they brought to his music, the complexities they presented – and certainly in Lynott's case – how they were tested to breaking point and back again.

Finally, one should never forget Moore's guitars. As with his relationships, some of them stayed with Gary until the very end, while others went on their way in search of new horizons. But all were loved, each had their own story, and those stories are presented here.

Back to Hammy Odeon in '79. For whatever reason, though some gigs have come and gone, lost in time, alcohol or failing memory, I can still see Moore clearly on stage that night: fingers blazing, knuckles white, notes spitting all over the place. Lynott introduced him as 'The Belfast Whiz Kid', and he was right. Gary Moore was a whiz kid, and as it turned out, a lot more besides: musician, guitarist, singer-songwriter and, for some at least, a bit of a legend.

Martin Power
March 2023

PART ONE:

1952 – 1971: Belfast, Dublin, London

'If I didn't think I had something, I wouldn't have been doing it . . .'
Gary Moore

CHAPTER ONE

Got The Bug

It looked 'like fairyland'.

As phrases go, this one seemed pretty harmless. Conjuring up images of winged sprites, enchanted forests and dancing fireflies, 'fairyland' sounded positively chipper, in fact. But Belfast's Blitz survivors weren't describing some magical kingdom or otherworldly paradise when referring to this particular fairyland.[1] Instead, they were reliving the memory of hundreds of German flares illuminating the night skies above the city in April 1941, these awful little lights creating a pathway for the Luftwaffe to follow as they flew in to bomb the 'pearl of the north'.

Over the course of April and early May, fairyland would be repeated three more times, the raids killing nearly 1,000 people, while razing over 50 per cent of Belfast's housing stock to the ground. Of a population totalling some 415,000, a quarter were made homeless, while the shipyards and aerospace industries that fed the port city – both economically, and sometimes literally – were also heavily bombarded. Originally deemed

---

1 Alec Murray and his fellow witnesses' account of the Belfast city bombings was published in the *Belfast Telegraph* on 18 April 2016 as part of a fine article by journalist Linda Stewart entitled 'Belfast Blitz: Recalling the fear, death and horror of nights Nazi warplanes bombed city'.

too distant from Nazi positions to constitute a legitimate target for military action[2], Belfast was now second only to London in terms of damage sustained and loss of life during a single raid. Bombed, bruised and battered, the city had taken a terrible hit, and one that might be hard to come back from. So much for fairyland.

Fast forward ten years and Belfast was back on its feet. The pounding the city took during the Blitz inadvertently aided in its future recovery, those nightly bombing raids highlighting the need for more nautical and aviation-based solutions to bolster the Allied war effort. Belfast's mightiest shipyard, Harland & Wolff – builders of the ill-fated, if immortal *Titanic* – dusted off the damage done by the Luftwaffe and set to work by returning the favour in kind. Conducting repairs on over 3,000 vessels, the company's 35,000 employees manufactured six aircraft carriers and two cruisers as well as vital components for tanks and artillery over the next four years. In fact, by the time conflict ended on 2 September 1945, Harland & Wolff and aerospace manufacturers, Short Brothers, had not only provided the allies with ships and planes to help win the war, they also helped bolster the backbone of Belfast's economic future for much of the coming decade.

All in all then, there were worse times to be a resident of the city than the early fifties. Unlike the British mainland, where the likes of Birmingham, Liverpool and Coventry were still experiencing the grim realities of cavernous bomb craters and post-war rationing, Belfast had already turned a corner of sorts, its recent efforts and still robust ship-building trade creating a cushion of relative prosperity around at least some of its inhabitants. That said, progress wasn't universal, nor social conditions by any means perfect. Unemployment and a lack of council housing continued to blight areas of the city, even if the recent introduction of the 'welfare state' helped alleviate at least some of the problems faced by the poor. Gaslight rather than electricity was responsible for

---

2 At the start of the war in September 1939, Belfast was deemed too far from German military positions to be attacked, so little effort was made to fortify its defences. However, when the Nazis occupied France in June 1940, distance was no longer an object. After reconnoitring Belfast in the winter of that year, the Luftwaffe deemed it 'the worst defended city in the UK', and made plans to bomb it the following spring. With just seven anti-aircraft guns to protect itself, Belfast proved a horribly easy target for the 200 enemy planes that circled the skies over the river Lagan in April and May of 1941.

brightening many streets at night, while an equal proportion of horse-drawn carts and cars travelled on the roads leading into Belfast's centre. Radio was still the primary means of family entertainment, though like everywhere else, television would cast its spell soon enough.

There were darker political hues. Always present and of concern was the continuing divide between Belfast's Protestant and Catholic communities. Simmering away like a watched pot for nearly four centuries, neither the partition of Ireland in 1921 nor the subsequent creation of the province of Northern Ireland had quelled cries of discrimination or inequality from certain quarters. Yet, each time in recent years things had threatened to truly boil over into sustained violence, the source of the heat died down again. Of course, that would all change, and in ways often too awful to contemplate. But in 1952, Belfast, Derry, Armagh and the rest of the North at least had the chance of enjoying relative harmony, where the dissonances present in the background were temporarily drowned out by sounds of progress. Not exactly paradise then, but a damn sight better than what was happening a decade before.

It was into this place and time that Robert William Gary Moore was born at Belfast Royal Maternity Hospital on Friday, 4 April 1952. By all accounts, the weather was mild for the time of year, though it rained in the afternoon. 'Typical bloody Belfast,' ran one old, but familiar saying. Like his father and grandfather before him, the newborn was given the first name 'Robert', though in reality, he would always be known as 'Gary' by family and friends. Gary's mother, Winnifred ('Winnie') was the daughter of Robert and Margaret Gallagher, the former a heating and insulation engineer at the omnipresent Harland & Wolff, where he had reportedly worked throughout the bombing raids of the forties. A musical family, both Robert and Margaret were keen singers, while their five children, including William, Ruby and Elle, also had no trouble carrying a tune. Indeed, youngest daughter, Phylis, was a fine pianist, and known for the sweetness of her singing voice.

Gary's dad, Robert Moore (or 'Bobby' to his friends) was from another long-standing East Belfast family, and like Winnie's parents, of Protestant faith. Bobby's own father, Robert, did not earn his living in the shipbuilding

5

trade, however. He was a well-known local businessman, whose early experiments in newspaper vending had developed into a successful bookmaking enterprise, with several profitable offshoots thereafter. Lively, hard-working and what locals refer to as 'a character,' Robert's achievements ensured that he, his wife Margaret and their four children – Philip, Nancy, Kathleen and Bobby – enjoyed a comfortable lifestyle bereft of any real financial woe.

The infant Gary also benefited from the stability of both these family strands, even if his earliest years were punctuated by several house moves around the East Belfast area, a situation less than ideal for any young couple at the start of their marriage. Yet when Bobby's parents left their familiar Eastside surroundings for a new address in a more suburban part of the city, it was their son and his wife that moved into their former home. In the meantime, Gary continued to be doted on by various combinations of aunts, uncles and grandparents, while his mother kept house and Bobby worked both as a newsvendor and in the betting trade alongside his father. Like Robert Moore Sr., however, Bobby did not appear content with having just one string to his bow, and was soon pursuing business opportunities of his own.

By the time Gary was five, Bobby and Winnie had laid down proper roots, purchasing a solid-looking three-up, two-down semi-detached house at 44 Castleview Road in the Knock district of East Belfast. Located in a quiet, residential neighbourhood, the Moore's new home was defined by its proximity to the playing fields of Abbey Park, and perhaps more notably, the luxuriant grounds of Stormont Castle, then serving as the official residence of the Prime Minister of Northern Ireland. If nothing else, the estate agents' details must have read impressively. Unfortunately, the family move coincided with the beginning of a less pleasant chapter for Gary, when he became a pupil at nearby Strandtown Primary School.

Having just celebrated its 25th anniversary, Strandtown boasted a fine academic record coupled with enviable sporting and music facilities. Gary, on the other hand, appeared unimpressed by any of the subjects on offer, and preferred to stay at home whenever he could. It appears Moore's frequent absences from class had little to do with a dislike of reading, writing or arithmetic. Instead, they were more likely the result of horseplay from older pupils at Strandtown, and perhaps elsewhere. Moore seemed to confirm the bones of the story in later life. 'I'd be the one dumped in the river,' he told the author Harry Shapiro, '. . . the one the other kids picked on.' Though the situation appeared to resolve itself Gary's experiences did leave their mark, creating possible issues of self-esteem that hung around into early adolescence. It might also have soured his viewpoint of academia. 'Once, for about five minutes, when I was about six, I really wanted to be a journalist,' he told Planet Rock of his formative aspirations. The notion quickly passed.

If Gary was experiencing some difficulty finding his feet beyond the family nest his father Bobby, on the other hand, was making impressive strides. An intelligent, well-dressed and confident young man, Bobby Moore was also a natural raconteur, capable of spinning a yarn with the best of them. This gift for sharp suits and even sharper storytelling made him a natural fit for running the show at the Queen's Hall ballroom. 'My dad used to manage the Queen's in Holywood,' Gary told VH1. '[He'd] promote dances there at the weekends.'

Some 10 minutes' drive from the family's home in East Belfast on the coastal strip to Bangor, Holywood was a pleasant port town with a seventeenth-century Dutch maypole curiously placed to mark its commercial centre and a fine, sandy beach for those seeking a swim. For those seeking a drink and a dance, there was the Queen's Hall, and Bobby tended it well. Offering both locals and 'blow-ins' a chance to twist the night away to a selection of Top 40 hits performed by one of several hundred showbands then monopolising Northern Ireland and the Republic of Ireland's entertainment scene[3], the Queen's Hall sometimes served as a home away from home for the larger Moore clan. In addition

---

3 Showbands were typically six or eight musicians strong, with a repertoire that included everything from waltzes and rock'n'roll to Irish folk, Dixieland and on occasion, even comedy routines. Displaying an impressive ability to hear a Top 10 hit and then be able to play it to a packed house five minutes later, showbands were often accused of excessive cheesiness. But good ones – like Clipper Carlton or The Melody Aces – could raise the roof of any dancehall.

to Bobby's role as promoter, manager and 'master of ceremonies', there were visits to the hall from close friends and extended family. His wife Winnie was also a regular presence, helping out wherever she could. Given the Moore family's attachment to 'the Queens', it was only fitting that Gary would make his first public mark within its walls. But not just yet.

For now at least, he was content with a busy social diary based around soccer matches and rock pools, both of which could be easily found in two at his favourite places: Glentoran Football Club and the nearby seaside. In the former case, Winnie's father, Robert, would often take young Gary to games at the weekend, with Glentoran their team of choice. Based at The Oval (near Strandtown primary school), 'The Glens' had much to commend them, winning recent back-to-back premiership titles, as well as once boasting a genuine footballing superstar, Danny Blanchflower, among their ranks. Indeed, Blanchflower's captivating performance in Northern Ireland's national team at the 1958 World Cup had transformed every Belfast child into a wannabe footballer, including Gary Moore. A fine way for Robert Gallagher and his grandson to spend quality time together[4], these soccer-based bonding sessions remained a fond memory for Gary, even if his early fascination with the beautiful game was soon replaced with matters of hands rather than feet.

Other spots where the youngster felt totally at ease were local seaside resorts such as Donaghadee, Portrush and in particular, Millisle, where the Moore family had a holiday home. Blue sky alternatives to the suburban sprawl of Castleview Road, the likes of Millisle were all clear water, clean beaches and snappy amusements, their remit to provide fun, food and the occasional frolic for those visiting from the city of Belfast. In fact, one story has it that Gary's skin would tan so deeply in the summer sun, 'he could have passed for Spanish!' Whatever the case, Moore

---

4   Another local lad who attended matches with his grandfather at Glentoran in the late fifties was George Best. Six years older than Gary Moore, Best would later become a footballing legend for both Northern Ireland and Manchester United, and is still regarded as one of the world's finest ever players. After a life marred by alcoholism, George passed away in 2005 at the age of just 59. 'I spent a lot of money on booze, birds and fast cars,' he once said with typical good humour. 'The rest I just squandered.'

dearly loved his trips to the sea. 'What great summers I remember down around Millisle and Donaghadee,' he later told the journalist Eddie McIlwaine. 'Fishing trips . . . at Portrush [or] riding the hobby horses in Barry's Amusements. Every time I hear an Ulster accent, I want to talk about Millisle and the Port. My childhood was full of happiness at those holiday resorts.' Only an hour or so from Stormont, Moore would make Millisle, or 'Shankhill by the Sea' as it was sometimes cheekily called, a home away from home in later years, finding respite there when the walls started closing in on him in East Belfast.

If the football matches and seaside trips provided Gary with able distractions from any sense of unease he might have felt at school, there was another, even more valuable salve he could apply as and when required. 'There was never a time in my life when there wasn't music around me,' he later said. 'It was always there.' Surrounding Moore like a warm blanket since infancy, music was present in his mother's singing around the house, the piano-playing of his aunt and a central theme of many family gatherings. In short, anywhere the family congregated, music soon followed. Winnie's dad had even taught his grandson the rudiments of the mouth organ, though Gary failed to bond with it in any mean- ingful sense. His father Bobby's drum kit, however, was another matter entirely. 'My Dad used to play drums,' Moore later said, 'and there were bits of kit all over the house.' Left to his own devices, one imagines Gary raised merry hell on the snare until his experiments with rhythm were brought to a swift close by one or other of his parents.

Away from the skins and sticks, Bobby's record collection also truly pricked Gary's ears. 'When I was about five, my dad was really into Elvis Presley,' he told *Record Collector*. 'He brought home loads of jukebox singles [and] I was really into that sound.' As were millions of others. Pink of suit, blue of suede shoe and possessed of a 'Black man's voice in a white man's body', Presley was then at the vanguard of a new movement called 'rock'n'roll', its seeming mission to outrage the old while simultaneously delighting the young. In this, it proved spectacularly successful, with performers such as Chuck Berry, Little Richard, Jerry Lee Lewis and Elvis offering a sexually charged, hyper-electrified and very American alternative to the gentler orchestral fare then wafting through Britain's post-war dancehalls. Part blues, part country and with a pumping backbeat at its heart, even if Gary didn't understand the lyrical innuendos flying all around him, this brash, wild-eyed gumbo of a music must still have been unutterably thrilling. However, it wasn't the sound of Elvis Presley that called Gary towards the lights of the concert stage. That honour went instead to the girl with the giggle in her voice.

As years go by, the mind can play tricks. Facts and figures, events, even outcomes all risk being distorted or lost in the passage of time. Yet, on those occasions Gary Moore was asked to recount his first public appearance, the version of events he told remained admirably consistent, with several key elements always present within the story: a child and his father, a tune and a chair, and perhaps of greatest importance, an audience there to watch the tale unfold. '[My dad] used to have those showbands at the dancehall on a Saturday,' Moore told VH1 in 1997. 'Old fat guys in pink suits playing . . . Top 40 stuff. Anyway, I used to go along with him when I was about five or six and watch these bands. At that age, it was amazing to see anyone playing an instrument live. But one night, my dad actually put me on the stage [to] sing a song. I couldn't reach the microphone so he stood me on a chair . . .'

The song in question was 'Sugartime', a slight, if likeable trad-pop confection performed by Alma Cogan, whose 'giggling', if incredibly powerful voice had recently made her the UK's highest paid female singer. All candy-coated melody lines and honeyed choruses, 'Sugartime' was Cogan's thirteenth Top 30 hit of the fifties, reaching number sixteen in the British charts on 22 February 1958, only a matter of weeks after Moore's sixth birthday. Though not exactly an Elvis-style rocker, the song's saccharine charm surely appealed to any youngster discovering music for the first time and Gary had probably sung along whenever it popped up on the family radio.

However, the question of *why* Bobby Moore thrust his son on a chair and had him perform 'Sugartime' to the good people of the Queen's on a busy Saturday evening remains more intriguing. Perhaps he felt the boy needed his confidence bolstered. Maybe he had a strange presentiment that the stage was where the child was meant to be. It might just have been a little mischief-making to pass the time. We'll never know because unlike his son, Bobby reportedly had no memory of the incident. But whatever the cause, when young Gary Moore finished singing 'Sugartime' to the whoops and cheers of the appreciative weekend crowd, the die was well and truly cast. 'I was terrified [getting up there], but that was it,' Moore later smiled. 'I'd got the bug.'

There was no going back now.

With Gary Moore's ear for music publicly noted and enthusiastically received by the clientele of the Queen's Hall, one might have thought his father Bobby would turn 'Sugartime' – or at least a variation of it – into a regular event. Not so much. Young Gary continued to attend weekend dances with his parents, and avidly watch showbands from the audience. According to some reports, he even stepped on stage for a moment or two to sing along with a tune, his dad introducing him as 'Little Gary'. But it would be four more years before Bobby Moore provided another truly meaningful nudge towards the world of music. This one had profound consequences. 'My dad came home from work one Friday [when] I was ten,' Gary later recalled to the Belfast author Stuart Bailie. 'He said "Would you like to learn how to play guitar?" My attitude was "Well, I've tried everything else and I'm rubbish at it, so yes, I'd love to learn the guitar." To be honest, all I'd ever thought about since going to the Queen's Hall was the guitar.'

The guitar in question was a Framus acoustic cello body, which Bobby had bought from showband acquaintance Jackie Milligan for £5. German-made and 'fair sturdy', the instrument resembled more a double bass than a standard six-string. 'It was nearly as tall as me,' Moore said without any great exaggeration. On hand to help was former owner Milligan, who kindly showed Gary the chord of 'A' as a sweetener. 'That was it for formal training,' Milligan later joked – and then handed it over to the boy to see what happened. Moore was truly smitten. 'I fell in love with the guitar straight away,' he said. 'For some reason, I just felt right at home with it.'

At first, Bobby and Winnie Moore were keen to place some academic structure around Gary's engagement with the Framus and found him a tutor. Unfortunately, it didn't go quite as planned, with teacher and pupil soon butting heads over Moore's rendition of his favourite new band's signature tune. 'I went to a tutor but he only taught me a chord (or two),' Moore later said. 'I learned 'Wonderful Land' by The Shadows, but he said I played it all wrong, [so] I never went back.' An experiment involving another instructor, a piano and the rudiments of musical theory achieved similar, disappointing results. 'Musical theory? Oh no, and I'll tell you why,' Moore told *Guitare Et Claviers*. 'I tried to learn when I was first starting out, but the teacher never turned up. I'd be there on Saturday morning, and he didn't show. And the next Saturday morning, I didn't show up. So, I just thought "I'm not destined for musical theory".'

Like many a trainee guitar god before and after him, Gary's impatience with the world of crotchets, minims and demisemiquavers was in keeping with both his age and temperament. Having recently acquired something he could truly call his own for the first time, the idea of then being forced to study it like a mathematics textbook spoiled all the fun. 'I'd worked out the higher you go on the neck, the higher the notes, and the lower you go, the lower the notes,' he later said. 'And once you've worked that out, you're halfway there!' Evidently, 10-year-old Moore was already au fait with one of the great cornerstones of guitar lore: 'There's a reason they call it "guitar playing" and not "guitar work", you know.'

Though Moore later made light of his early experiments with guitar, his devotion to the instrument – even in these formative stages – was total. Indeed, there are reports of the youngster lugging his Framus up and down Castleview Road and nearby Abbey Park, the guitar either hanging from a strap around his neck or in its case, ready to be opened at a moment's notice. 'God, I looked really weird carrying the case down the street,' he confirmed. And on the occasions when Moore had to leave the acoustic behind such as school, he was still dreaming of strings and picks at his desk. 'I'd be sitting in class on a Monday morning, and I'd just have a guitar going through my head, going round and round all the time,' he told the BBC.

Still, before Moore could truly get to grips with the business of transferring what he heard inside his head onto the fretboard of his guitar, there were several hurdles to negotiate. Having rejected the idea of learning music theory from a qualified teacher, he had no choice but to work out tunings, chords and melodies on his own. Thankfully, he proved a natural. 'Well, I just learned [music] by ear,' Gary said. 'Sometimes I regret that [I didn't study formally], but then, sometimes I don't.' In fact, his ability to hear complex note and chord progressions and then play them back almost instantly became the stuff of legend. 'All you had to do was play it to him once and he had it,' one future acquaintance confirmed in 2020. 'It was actually scary to watch.'

The second impediment to Moore's progress was potentially more difficult to overcome, with the left-handed youngster actually playing 'a right-handed guitar'. To some, the idea of having to work things out in reverse might have put them off learning the instrument forever. Not so Gary. Knowing no better, he simply got on with it. Indeed, the situation seemed to work to his advantage.[5] By having his stronger hand responsible for fretting, it allowed the luxury of bending notes harder and further, while also providing him with the bones of a deep, soulful vibrato that would pay handsome dividends in years to come.

While there was one last restraint that would need loosening before he could truly achieve escape velocity on the instrument, Moore's ravenous appetite for all things guitar continued unabated throughout 1962. Between the stash of Elvis singles, the family radio pumping out a daily soundtrack of tunes to strum along with and Moore's newfound fascination with The Shadows' bespectacled guitarist Hank Marvin – 'Oh yeah,' he later confirmed to *Marshall*, 'I loved Hank. He was *it*,' – the boy was positively awash in new sounds and styles. 'But if you're in love [with a musical instrument], learning how to play it is no big chore,' he later said. Yet, however much Moore loved the swimming tones of Marvin's Fiesta Red Fender Stratocaster or Scotty Moore's rockabilly-style twanging with Elvis Presley, he was about to have his head turned

---

5 Gary Moore was not the only left-handed guitarist to learn on a right-handed instrument. Other notable examples include Dire Straits' Mark Knopfler, Black Sabbath's Tony Iommi, Deep Purple/Dixie Dregs' Steve Morse, Aerosmith's Joe Perry, Dragonforce's Herman Li and the late, great Duane Allman.

completely by four brand new kids on the block. 'Absolutely,' he enthused to BBC Radio 1 in 1990, 'along came The Beatles . . .'

Like many of a certain age, Moore's first real engagement with The Beatles came on 13 October 1963 when they performed four songs on ITV's flagship entertainment show, *Sunday Night at the Palladium*. Materialising like young besuited gods on the Moore family's TV set, Gary was struck dumb by the sight and sound of The Fabs. Once he recovered his composure, Moore set about gathering as much information about the band as he could, with particular attention paid to their ruminative lead guitarist George Harrison. 'There was such a melodic quality to the Beatles' songs,' he later told VH1. 'And George's solos were little compositions within those songs. He was always thinking of something different. I mean, listen to the solo on 'A Hard Day's Night', for instance. It really is genius . . . eight bars of genius as opposed to three hours of nothing.' Unbeknown to Moore at the time, he would one day tell Harrison precisely that in person.[6]

If Alma Cogan inadvertently led Moore to take the stage and Hank Marvin introduced him to the possibilities of what a guitar might sound like in the right hands, then The Beatles finally provided Gary with the impetus to try performing at a concert with a group of his own. 'To be honest,' Moore told *Guitar Heroes*, 'I'd been playing guitar in public quite a lot by then.' In fact, since acquiring his acoustic, it was almost impossible to stop Gary Moore playing in public. Aside from striking up tunes for the locals of Castleview Road, Moore had finally found a way of smuggling the instrument into school with him, where he would take requests for songs at lunch break. From 'Heartbreak Hotel' and 'Wake Up Little Susie' to 'Apache' and 'Love Me Do', Moore was a regular walking jukebox.

Taken at face value, one might have thought Moore was just showing

---

6 According to Moore, he only had to wait a couple of weeks before seeing The Beatles in person. 'I actually went to see The Beatles when I was eleven in Belfast on my own,' he later confirmed to *Sounds*' Pete Makowski. 'You couldn't hear them because all the girls were screaming and I was jumping up and down to catch a glimpse of them because I was so little!' Gary likely saw the Fab Four at Belfast's Ritz Cinema on Friday, 8 November 1963, where they appeared as part of their 'Autumn Tour'. How the 11-year-old managed to get into the venue unaccompanied remains a puzzle.

off. Yet, at risk of falling prey to cod psychology, there was probably a less ego-driven, more pragmatic reason for his behaviour. Now on the cusp of adolescence, Gary was still prone to bouts of faltering confidence, probably caused by those early, negative experiences at primary school. There were other niggles to contend with. Never the sportiest of boys, he now seldom played football with the other lads, preferring instead to spend his nights hunched over the fretboard at home.[7] No great surprise there perhaps, but it surely set him apart in the eyes of his peers. Small and somewhat overweight for his age – his nickname at the time was the distinctly unimaginative 'Fat Gary' – Moore's academic record was average too, with the boy known to his teachers and fellow pupils as a bit of a dreamer. A recent move to the larger Ashfield Boys' High School can't have helped settle his nerves either. Of course, in the overall scheme of things, these setbacks were small beer. A new friend or two here, a growth spurt there and 12 months later, all might be well with the world. But at the time, Gary appeared acutely aware of these traits of character and physique, and how they might be perceived by those around him.

Thankfully, his growing prowess on guitar offered a way out. Part conversation-starter, part social shield-come-security blanket, the instrument gave Moore a new way to conduct business with the world, helping smooth away any potential awkwardness and replacing it with a song. Realistically, he was never going to be class president, an astronaut or professional footballer. But Moore's ability to knock seven bells out of six strings provided its own form of both protection and projection. Crucially, it also acted as a clarion call to those as obsessed by music as he was. It was now time to meet these curious folk and form a union.

---

7 On one of the few occasions Moore was spotted at 'The Field', it inevitably involved a guitar and a song. According to *Belfast Telegraph*'s Ivan Little – who grew up in the area – he watched young Gary perform the old Loyalist standard 'The Sash . . . ' at the annual July 'Eleventh Night' celebrations marking King William of Orange's historic victory over Catholic forces at 1690's Battle of the Boyne. 'The first time I ever heard Gary play his acoustic guitar was around the scrawny little Eleventh Night bonfire that us cocooned kids from the leafy suburbs built on The Field,' said Little in 2011.

CHAPTER TWO

Escape Velocity

Since acquiring his first guitar in 1962, Gary Moore had roamed his little corner of East Belfast like a wandering minstrel, banging out tunes to anyone with the time or inclination to listen. School playgrounds. Eleventh Night bonfires. Wherever there was a crowd, Moore might be found happily strumming away on his Framus acoustic guitar. Yet, after seeing The Beatles perform wonders on TV, 11-year-old Moore's head had turned from life as a solo artist towards forming a group of his own. The issue now was finding people who shared his vision.

To Moore's credit, progress was swift, though to begin with the band of his dreams was more 'dynamic duo' than 'fab four'. Teaming up with fellow guitarist and Ashfield pupil Bill Downey, Gary began performing Beatles and Everly Brothers covers at garden parties and scout halls around East Belfast. Once up and running, it was only a matter of time before the pair attracted the interest of other young musicians, with local bassist Robert 'Berty' Thompson and drummer Robin Lavery soon swelling the ranks to that of a quartet. With the line-up now mirroring their Liverpudlian heroes and the prospect of several real concerts on the horizon, a band name was required. Again, The Beatles proved an inspiration. After a brief flirtation with the fetching, if sardonic Dead Beats, the group settled on The Beat Boys.

The Belfast music scene that Moore's brand-new outfit found itself about to join in the spring of 1964 was undergoing a small, but significant revolution. Just a year earlier, the city was still in thrall to showbands for much of its light entertainment, these stalwarts of the dance halls providing the only soundtrack for youth to actually do their dancing to. But since Messrs Lennon, McCartney, Harrison and Starr began dismantling what previously constituted notions of pop, demand in Belfast for young, homegrown substitutes to ape the Mersey sound had risen quickly. Like their London and Dublin counterparts, Belfast's hipsters were also on the trail of surly American blues-influenced acts in the style of The Rolling Stones and The Yardbirds to satiate their musical appetites. They would arrive soon enough.

In fact, over the course of their 18-month lifespan, The Beat Boys regularly jostled with numerous Merseybeat and Stones clones who appeared like hairy apparitions throughout Belfast's music venues. At first, they had stayed close to home, 'We debuted at my father's ballroom during a break in the showband's act,' said Gary. But the quartet soon made their way into the city centre, performing at venues such as Betty Staff's dance studio and (if reports are correct) the legendary Boom Boom Room[1], where they supposedly supported resident headliners The Banshees. One story even had the quartet aboard a train, bashing out tunes for passengers as they made their way home. Aided by a watchful Bobby Moore every step of the way: chauffeur, road manager, costumier, even bouncer, one imagines. The Beat Boys seldom played more than six songs. But those who saw the group were unlikely to forget them in a hurry.

With Gary Moore, not yet 12, and Phil Downey, the old man of the

---

1 Something of a Belfast institution, The Boom Boom Room not only played host to local acts, but also a number of high-profile imports including Gary's favourite rhythm guitarist Joe Brown and his band The Bruvvers, Welsh musical icon Tom Jones and the wonderful, pants-ripping P.J. Proby. However, as with many of Gary's earliest appearances, finding concrete proof of The Beat Boys' performance at the Boom Boom Room is extremely difficult.

band at 14, The Beat Boys were preposterously young, even for the pop game. Still, with their apple cheeks, matching tops, chinos and yacht shoes, at least they looked the part: 'Four pudding bowl haircuts all up dressed in little red shirts!'[2] Thankfully, the sound The Beat Boys made seemed to draw a positive response. Using Swinging Blue Jeans, Kinks, 'but mostly Beatles covers', to inform their set (Gary learned the tunes straight from the radio and then taught them to his bandmates), the quartet supplemented their gig or two a week with talent contests around Belfast. The story goes that they never lost. Given their age, judges probably feared a collective tantrum.

Another win for Moore at the time was the acquisition of a new guitar. This one was electric. 'It was a Rossetti Lucky Squire semi-acoustic with f-holes,' he told *Guitare Et Claviers*. '[But] nobody could play it because of the height of the strings except me.' With an action[3] so vertiginous, the guitar's strings 'sat about a foot above the fretboard,' Moore's new, Dutch-made Rosetti had already marked itself out as a difficult beast to master. Sadly, the instrument's finger-crippling action was only the start of his woes. 'Oh, that guitar was fucking horrible,' Moore recalled. 'I was playing in a club one night and the back fell off.' Despite these difficulties, one senses Moore fought tooth and nail to keep the Rosetti in playable condition, as it finally allowed him to plug into a much-coveted Vox AC30 his father had recently commandeered from one of his showband contacts. Gary could now emulate George Harrison by banging out Beatles riffs using much the same amplifier as his hero.

Given their tender age, continuing school commitments and the ever-present threat of a worried parent or two stealing their son back from the perils of showbusiness, The Beat Boys were never destined to last. The first to depart was drummer Robin Lavery, who was in turn replaced

2 While photographs confirm that three of The Beat Boys – including Gary – had pudding bowl cuts, drummer Robin Lavery's hairdo was something else altogether. Smoothed back from his forehead and almost running down to his shoulders, Lavery's cut (or lack thereof) was pretty daring for early sixties Belfast, or anywhere else, really.

3 A guitar's 'action' refers to the height of the strings above the fretboard. If the action is very high, as was the case with Gary's Framus and Rosetti, the instrument can be extremely hard to play.

by another local lad, Robert 'Robbo' Wilkinson.[4] Wilkinson brought with him a bold new image for The Beat Boys (a side parting in his hair), and the quartet even switched from their trademark red shirts to a more regal blue in order to mark his arrival. But by late 1965, and despite reports of a step up to some bigger, more diverse venues such as Bangor's Pickie Pool and the Grove Theatre on Belfast's Shore Road, the game was up and the band was over.

For Gary Moore, life in a pop group had been a learning experience. Aside from the initially terrifying act of playing in front of a paying audience, he had, in a small but important way, been allowed to step behind the curtain of the music business. From temperamental guitars, dropped picks and broken strings to unpredictable acoustics, buzzing PA systems and confused punters, Moore witnessed much that could go wrong at the average show. None of it seemed to put him off. Instead, his inquisitive nature often found him conducting backstage inquisitions with other, older performers in an effort to broaden his own musical knowledge. If Moore liked a particular song, harmony or guitar effect, he would ask how it was done or what was used to create it. In this way, he collected valuable intelligence on nascent reverb and echo units, 'Brilliance channels and Top Boosts,' all of which fed back into his own playing. 'He was gathering information like a spy,' a friend later quipped.

Following the demise of The Beat Boys, Gary Moore went to ground for a time, seemingly content to practise guitar at home rather than play it on stage. At one point, there was talk of a new band, 'The Substitutes', with drummer Johnny Crawford and bassist Sam Cook. But it seems to have come to naught. Yet, within months, Gary was back in the game again, pursuing a new opportunity provided by former bandmate Bill Downey. Unlike Moore, Downey had wasted little time in finding another group when The Beat Boys folded. Joining promising local (and slightly older) outfit The Spartans, Downey's latest band were chancing their arm on Belfast's ever-busy talent contest circuit. Score a win, and they could

---

4 As well as being a capable drummer, Robert Wilkinson was also a gifted cyclist, going on to become a championship motorcycle scrambler. In some accounts of The Beat Boys story, Wilkinson is actually listed as the band's first drummer. However, given some of those early photos, Robin Lavery appears to have got there before him.

double their concert pulling power while simultaneously upping their appearance fee. Knowing that a player of Moore's calibre would further boost the act's chance of success, Downey asked him to come on board.

The group Moore joined did not last long. Shedding and gaining members by the day, The Spartans reportedly managed to transmute into The Barons[5] while still competing in the early heats of the Bangor Beat Talent Show. Indeed, they acquired a promising lead singer – 'Handsome' Peter McClelland – just in time for the televised finals. Even by the standards of the most unpredictable teen pop combo, this was impressive stuff. Unfortunately, not impressive enough for the judges, who chose to award first prize to another group. Still, despite their chaotic birthing process, The Barons amassed a small, if devoted following, thanks in part to a natty line in Beatles covers and Peter McClelland, whose towering stage presence 'reputedly . . . drove all the girls wild.'

While Gary Moore was no doubt aware of the attention being lavished on McClelland at Barons concerts[6], his mind was on other things, specifically the brand new Olympic white Fender Telecaster now welded to his fingers. First spotting the instrument staring back at him from the window of Crymbles' art nouveau shopfront in Belfast city centre, Moore couldn't believe a real Fender guitar had made its way to Northern Ireland.[7] 'Only three Telecasters [came into Belfast],' Gary later told *Guitar World*'s Steve Rosen. 'Two were spoken for, but I got the last one.' It wasn't easy. Before Gary could get his hands on this rarest of birds, he had to persuade his father to pay for it. At £180, the Telecaster wasn't

---

5 At one time or another, The Spartans/Barons reportedly featured (among others) Alan Moffett, Dennis Bell and Brian Smith on drums, while Brian 'Barney' Cruthers and Sam 'The Substitutes' Cook took care of bass guitar. A keyboard player, Brian Scott, also appeared with the band for a little while.

6 According to journalist Ivan Little, Pete McClelland's extraordinary effect on female audience members might not have been all it seemed. '[The Barons'] drummer Alan Moffett . . . told me [their] manager would pay girls at dances to stand at the front of the stage and mob big Pete in the hope their fervour would be contagious and whip up others to follow suit.' In other news, Pete McClelland's son Mark went on to form successful Scots/NI rockers Snow Patrol.

7 American-made guitars by the likes of Fender and Gibson were still extremely rare items in the UK and Ireland during the early 1960s, with European budget brands such as Rosetti, Goya and EKO much more available options.

cheap. Yet, again sensing his son really might go somewhere with 'this music thing,' Bobby Moore signed the hire purchase forms (24 payments over two years) and Gary had his prize. 'My dad always stood behind me and my music,' he later told YLE TV, 'and my parents never tried to stop me from pursuing it. They knew it would be right for me.'

All well and good, but Moore's new Fender Telecaster represented a serious commitment from father to son. Still only 14, Gary now had a professional instrument and would be expected to do something with it.[8] It turned out the guitar itself was willing to lend him a hand. Unlike the unwieldy Framus or surly Rosetti, Moore's Telecaster came with thinner gauge strings and – miracle of miracles – a manageable action. 'I used to have these incredibly heavy strings and high action before [the Tele], because I didn't really know any better,' Moore later said. 'But that ignorance helped actually strengthen my fingers. So, when I finally got a good guitar, I took off . . .' He wasn't joking. Previously constrained by low-budget technology and the laws of physics, the Fender's buttery maple neck and lighter strings now allowed Moore's fingers to fly up and down the fretboard. Over time, he would hone this ability to a truly frightening level.

Unfortunately, speed didn't solve his problem with The Barons. Despite a decent enough gigging schedule supporting showbands at the Queen's Hall while also appearing under their own steam at church halls, youth clubs and elsewhere, the group were done by the spring of 1967. There was no one to blame. With the majority of the quintet either having already left school or on the cusp of leaving, the real world had got in the way and steady jobs with steady incomes were now the order of the day. Of course, this left Moore, still at Ashfield Boys, still only just 15, at a loose end. Not much of a problem as it turned out: he had just found 'God'. 'I went around to my friend [Graham McFarlane]'s house on a Sunday afternoon and heard the *Blues Breakers* . . . album with John Mayall and Eric Clapton,' he later told *Marshall*. 'That was it, no turning back. I borrowed it of course, for six months, [and] played it so much there was nothing left in the grooves to give back.'

---

8 According to one source, Bobby had Gary depping with Queen's Hall showband regulars Dave & The Diamonds for several gigs to help pay off some of the Telecaster's costs.

In a world now happily saturated by the influence of blues and its derivatives, it is difficult to explain the impact *Blues Breakers with Eric Clapton* had on guitar players in general, and Gary Moore in particular. Essentially a recorded snapshot of former Yardbirds guitarist Eric Clapton's[9] brief tenure with fellow Delta devotee John Mayall's latest band, the 'Blues Breakers' of the title, the album announced a new, thrilling stage in the development of the British blues movement. So combustible was Clapton's playing on *Blues Breakers . . .* that within weeks of its release in July 1966, an enterprising wag spray-painted the legend 'Clapton Is God' on a wall in Islington, and the age of the guitar hero truly began. 'The *Blues Breakers . . .* album revolutionised guitar playing,' Gary later confirmed to *Guitar Presents*, 'and Eric was hugely important in the evolution of guitar.'

Another reason *Blues Breakers . . .* resonated so deeply with Moore and others was the tone and equipment Clapton deployed when recording the LP. While with the Yardbirds, 'EC' had favoured a waspish, almost curt lead guitar attack created by his use of a Fender Telecaster and Vox AC30 amp (as evidenced, both popular tools of the trade at that time). But the recent purchase of a 1959/60 flame top Gibson Les Paul Standard and a 45-watt 2x12 valve combo by new British amplifier manufacturers Marshall changed all that. Unlike the twangy but quickly decaying tonalities produced by his Tele/Vox combination, Clapton's humbucker-assisted Les Paul and distorted Marshall amp created a thick, fluid-sounding sustain that allowed Eric to stretch notes languidly into the musical ether rather than having them perish almost immediately. Warm, seductive, yet still biting, it became known as his 'woman tone'.

---

9 Surrey-born, prone to leaving bands at the drop of a hat but still destined to become rock guitar's first superstar, Eric Clapton was just 21 when he teamed up with John Mayall. A sometimes-troubled soul who grew up believing his biological mother was actually his sister, Clapton found solace in the blues as a teenager, focusing his attention on learning guitar in the style of his heroes Big Bill Broonzy, Robert Johnson and Freddie King. By 19, he had joined 'Surrey Delta' bluesmen The Yardbirds where his snappy, authentic lead lines and crisp chord work won him a devoted following. Signed to Columbia/Epic in 1964, The Yardbirds recorded the pop-flavoured 'For Your Love' as their second single. However, Clapton saw the tune as a betrayal of their blues roots and promptly quit. Thankfully, it all worked out. The Yardbirds got a Top 10 hit while Eric linked up with Mayall, drummer Hughie Flint and bassist (and future member of Fleetwood Mac) John McVie in Blues Breakers.

Moore was in love. 'That tone on *Bluesbreakers* . . . changed the sound of guitar playing overnight,' he later said. 'It was the first time I'd heard a Les Paul through a Marshall played at concert volume and [that combination] has remained the standard.' The solos too, made Moore's heart skip a beat. 'Every one of Eric's solos on *Blues Breakers* is a classic,' he enthused. 'Each one was a little motif, a tune that could be sung.' Quite right. From his note-perfect homage to Freddie King on the combustible 'Hideaway' to the fervid lead lines peppered throughout John Mayall's self-penned 'Key to Love', Clapton was on fire throughout *Blues Breakers* and the UK public were quick to respond, pushing the album to number six in the charts. Soon enough, young Eric would have them revelling in an even more progressive iteration of the form. But for the time being, he and Mayall remained the John the Baptist and Guitar Jesus of the British blues boom. 'Just listen to *Blue Breakers* . . . track one, side one, Eric playing Otis Rush's 'All My Love',' Moore later told Planet Rock. 'I'd never heard . . . a guitar being played so passionately. It changed my life forever.'

Electrified by Eric Clapton's game-changing performance with John Mayall, Gary Moore's next steps confirmed the depth of his obsession with the new progressive blues and the lengths he would go to play them. While spending 1967's 'summer of love' living at his family's holiday home near Millisle beach following the break-up of The Barons (and a possible argument with his dad), Moore became friendly with a well-regarded local covers outfit called The Suburbans. Then rehearsing at the local Masonic Hall on Main Street, the group had reportedly specialised in American-themed pop and rock'n'roll. Not anymore.

Staging what appeared to be a one-man blues coup d'état, Gary reset the band's musical direction with a song list comprised of Clapton-themed workouts, harder edged Yardbirds material and a couple of new tunes from the blues' outer limits. In fact, the only music he seemed attached to that didn't feature shaggy-haired young men from Surrey playing loud variations on the pentatonic scale were arch mods, The Who. 'Jesus, The Who really meant it,' Moore said. 'I saw them at the Ulster Hall when I was 14 and I came out of there feeling like I'd been in a fight. My friends and I were almost shaking having watched these guys put out so much energy. In a way, they were like the first punk band.'

Wilful, destructive, but always artfully entertaining, The Who's penchant for grand theatrical gestures coupled with high-energy performance played straight into another of Moore's growing interests of the time: showmanship. Once a youngster wracked with issues of self-esteem, his confidence had grown steadily with each passing year and band he joined. This was now apparently reflected in his onstage antics. At first, the depth of Moore's ambitions were limited to an extended solo here and there with The Beat Boys. But by the time he decamped to Millisle and started gigging with these 'New Surburbans', nothing appeared off the table: from playing the Telecaster 'with his mouth' to duck-walking Chuck Berry style across the boards whenever the mood took him, Gary was becoming quite the showman. 'He was quite good at the drums as well!' laughed one local on the Belfast Forum website. 'Music is just a language and the more you know, the better you'll be able to communicate,' Moore once said. By the summer of 1967, he had learnt it didn't hurt to jump around a bit either.

With his days spent by the beach and his nights spent playing 'mad blues', Gary Moore appeared to have Millisle in his proverbial pocket. However, while money could be made gigging at clubs around the resort and its surrounding areas, it was still a far cry from Belfast's busier, vibrant and more financially profitable music scene. With his last school year now in sight and the teenager fast heading towards his sixteenth birthday, decisions would soon have to be made regarding the future. But Moore seemed to have no doubt as to where that future lay. 'Since I was a child, music led me and I just followed it,' Gary later told VH1. 'It always took me somewhere new and it was always been a big adventure.'

The next stage of said adventure found Moore returning permanently from Millisle to the shadow of Stormont and straight into the arms of yet another new band. Comprised of Gary and two like-minded schoolmates again from Ashfield Boys, Colin Martin on bass and Dave Finlay[10] on drums, the group's name didn't take too long to come up with. 'We called ourselves Platform Three,' Moore joked to *Record Collector*. 'There

---

10 Though reports have him as 'Dave Finlay', one source states that Finlay's first name was actually 'Dean'.

were three of us and there was a railway station we played at. Not just a clever name, you see . . .' Very much the veteran of the band, Gary again had first dibs when it came to picking material for the trio to cover. This time, alongside his favoured palette of *Blues Breakers* standards, Moore added some tasty new morsels he first dabbled in while playing around Millisle, including a brace of tunes by Jeff Beck-period Yardbirds, Eric Clapton's latest enterprise, Cream and a promising young trio called 'The Jimi Hendrix Experience'.

Looking back, Gary's choice of cover material was right where 'progressive music' was heading, and featured the latest batch of guitar icons intent on getting it there. As importantly, these musicians and their songs also presaged Moore's own direction of artistic travel for much of the coming decade. In the case of Jeff Beck, Moore had been on the case for a while. A self-confessed 'moody sod' who replaced Clapton when he walked out of The Yardbirds, Beck was arguably even better than his predecessor. Fleet of finger, madly experimental and with a lyrical style all his own, Beck had taken The Yardbirds to new heights throughout 1965/6, allowing the group to extend beyond their bluesy origins and embrace Indian, jazz and even psychedelic colours. 'I actually got the idea of buying my Fender Telecaster [after] seeing Jeff play one,' Moore later enthused to *Guitar World*. 'He was the first person to play in that Indian style . . . [and] make the guitar sound like different instruments. No one else was doing that. He definitely changed my approach to playing.'

By choosing to cover Clapton and Cream, Moore was again reconfirming his love affair with the now former Blues Breakers' guitar style, even if Moore couldn't quite understand why Eric had exited that band so quickly after joining them. 'When Eric . . . formed Cream, I really couldn't believe it,' he told *Classic Rock*. 'I couldn't believe he'd leave a group as good as Blues Breakers.' The answer was simple enough. In a pop scene now swimming in innovation and delicious novelty – one only had to hear The Beatles' *Revolver* and The Beach Boys' *Pet Sounds* for the proof – musicians everywhere were eagerly de-mooring from their previous incarnations to embrace new and ever more serious forms.

Given this rapidly evolving crucible of activity, it made sense for the always restless Clapton to do the same. So, when the chance came to team up with former Graham Bond Organisation bassist Jack Bruce and drummer Peter 'Ginger' Baker and take 'blues to another place completely,' it proved impossible to resist. 'When we started to play together,' Clapton said of Cream's first rehearsal in the summer of 1966, 'it all just turned to magic.' Indeed, it did. By Christmas that year, Cream's debut album, *Fresh Cream*, was number six in the UK charts and Gary was frantically learning their songs to cover with his latest band. As was so often the case, Moore would return to those tunes and the men who recorded them many times in years to come.

The final candidate unknowingly providing material for Gary Moore's new set list with Platform Three was 24-year-old American guitar super-hero Jimi Hendrix. 'The first time I heard Jimi, he absolutely terrified me,' Eric Clapton later said, 'Nobody had ever approached guitar like that.' Jeff Beck felt the same. 'It was like a sheer physical assault on the guitar,' he said. 'Jimi looked like an animal, played like an animal and everyone went fucking crazy. I just thought "Right, I'll become a postman".' Discovered by British model/scenester Linda Keith at a Manhattan nightclub, and whisked away to London by ex-Animals bassist turned business manager Chas Chandler in September 1966, it took Hendrix only four months to form a band and have a UK Top 10 hit with the era-defining 'Hey Joe'. Given his depth of talent, it's surprising it took that long.

Soulful singer, writer of world-class songs and with a charm that could seduce most any audience, Hendrix was also the preeminent rock guitarist of his age. From smooth comping chords and angelic melody lines to screaming solos and a daring, occasionally deranged use of the tremolo arm, it was all in Jimi's musical kitbag. Indeed, if Eric Clapton had super-charged the blues and Jeff Beck taken them to India and back, then Jimi Hendrix was intent on firing them into the farthest reaches of the cosmos. 'Hendrix was so astounding, so far ahead of his time and just a great bridge between past and present,' Moore later observed to the TV channel Sol Música. 'But then, all these guys all had their own character. It wasn't a time of clones. Jeff, Eric and Jimi all sounded so different from each other.'

Armed with three marvellous sources from which to pilfer and another waiting patiently in the wings, pending a proper introduction in Chapter Five of this book, Moore now had the tools to offer Belfast crowds the closest thing they would get to a 'Guitar Heroes' Greatest Hits' show. He succeeded admirably. Setting Platform Three up as a power trio in honour of Cream and Hendrix's Experience, Moore led from the front with a performance that found him bending notes through the prover-bial roof (Clapton's take on Howlin' Wolf's 'Spoonful'), rattling up and down the fretboard like a lusty ferret (the instrumental 'Beck's Boogie') and sounding the spooky, 'devil's chord' that introduced Jimi's 'Purple Haze' with his teeth.

This musical metamorphosis was reflected in Moore's rapidly changing physical appearance. The puppy fat that had dogged his early years was now fast falling away, while the shock of black hair that framed his face grew ever longer, the ends soon to sail past his collarbone and stay that way for a decade at least. And then there were the clothes. Taking his cue from the nascent hippie movement in the American west, Moore was now an avid wearer of baseball boots and sandals, with a natty side line in military great coats, granny glasses and flared jeans. The times, as they say, were changing. So was Gary Moore.

Another subtle, but important change was reflected in Moore and Platform Three's choice of venues at which to perform. In the past, Moore relied on using the Queen's Hall as a base of operations. After all, he knew the management there quite well. Come 1967, however, and the net was thrown a little wider. In addition to the likes of Clarke's snug ballroom on Upper Donegal Street, the trio also performed at larger dance halls such as the Fiesta and Sammy Houston's. 'I was always doing gigs in dance studios like Sammy Houston's, Cecil Clarke's and Betty Staff's,' Gary later quipped to journalist Eddie McIlwaine. 'But for all those dance teachers, I still can't waltz or quickstep!'

Yet, the biggest step up for Moore and Platform Three came when the band secured an occasional spot at Belfast's premier rhythm and blues venue, the Maritime Hotel. Born a Royal Irish Constabulary police station before later being converted into a British sailor's hostel, the Maritime had played host to many forms of entertainment over its lifetime. But

27

in April 1964, things had changed radically when a blues-themed night began on the venue's first floor. Officially inaugurated by soon-to-be local legends Van Morrison and Them, 60 people were in the audience for week one. Seven days later, that number had risen to 150. Within a month or so, they were turning them away at the door. 'Once some of the other bands came along to start playing,' Them guitarist Billy Harrison later confirmed, 'the blues scene in Belfast just exploded.'

When Gary Moore finally got to play the Maritime with Platform Three in late 1967, it wasn't even known by that name any more, having become 'Club Rado' to better suit the times. According to Moore, whatever it called itself, 'Rado' was never the most salubrious of locations. 'Club Rado [was] a real rough place,' he told *Guitar World*'s Harold Steinblatt. 'Gangs would hang around after the shows and ask if you had any spare change. If you said "Yes", they'd take it and beat you up. If you said "No", they'd take it and *then* beat you up.' Despite having to run the gauntlet at Rado each week, Moore remained philosophical. 'When I was growing up,' he later said, 'everyone in Belfast seemed to love seeing the blues. So when my time came, I was determined to do my bit too.'

Many others were too. Following in the footsteps of Them, a plethora of promising R&B acts joined Platform Three in calling the Maritime/ Club Rado their temporary home throughout the mid-late sixties, including The Mad Lads, The Interns, The Few and The Deltones (more of them later). But perhaps the biggest draw at the venue were a young group from faraway County Cork named Taste, featuring future guitar great Rory Gallagher. As with Beck, Clapton and Hendrix, Gary Moore immediately recognised talent when he heard it. 'Rory wasn't insecure about his playing, [because] he knew he was good,' Moore later told *Hot Press*. 'And we all knew how good he was. Rory had a real charisma and presence about him on stage. As soon as he put the guitar on, there was a connection [with the audience].'

Despite being three years younger than Gallagher, Moore struck up a genuine friendship with the man they were soon calling 'The Check Shirt Wizard', the two swapping tips, tunes and even guitars each time Platform Three supported Taste at the Rado. 'We used to lend each other our guitars because we couldn't afford spare strings,' Moore laughed to writer Brian Holland. 'There was a lot of camaraderie there. He was a beautiful guy, Rory. When he first came up to Belfast, he was very, very nice to me and very kind. I was just a kid when I used to open [concerts] for him.' Forged in 'the music we loved and the blues we played', Moore and Gallagher's friendship would continue for decades.

With a thumbs up from Gallagher, a semi-regular spot at Club Rado, and featuring one of Belfast's better rhythm sections in Colin Martin and Dave Finlay, Platform Three were the most promising act Gary Moore had yet put his name to. But as before, things ground to a halt before they were really allowed to take off. By the spring of 1968, Moore had left school and reportedly taken a job as a warehouseman, while his bandmates were busy timing their run for possible places at university, college or elsewhere. Again, the real world came calling and the group stopped performing as a result. 'All I wanted was to play the blues,' Moore later said. It just wasn't going to be with Platform Three.

Having spent nearly five years tearing around stages in Belfast, Millisle, Portaferry and beyond, it was easy to forget that Gary Moore was still just 16 years old. A prominent fixture on the city's music scene, his face was well known to club owners, fellow performers and audiences alike. Routinely described as 'Northern Ireland's Finest Guitar Player', albeit on posters designed by his bandmates, the teenager's talent was unquestionable. Yet here he was, supposedly moving boxes while playing the odd gig for a few quid a week. Worse, relations with his dad Bobby had become testy, and Gary often found himself visiting various friends, aunts and uncles for a change of scenery.

Lacking a regular gig, routinely butting heads with his father and still owning neither a Gibson Les Paul nor 'bloody Marshall amp', if there was a plan, now was the time to enact it. In Moore's world, however, strategies were for generals. 'No, there was never a game plan, really,' he later told the BBC. 'It was always about being the best musician I could be.' A commendable enough ambition. Though if he seriously wanted to pursue being a musician for the ages, Moore needed to find the right band to help him do it. Try as he might, he just couldn't locate them in his hometown. Still, one piece of advice first received from his dad, then reiterated by most every performer he met, kept coming back to him in slow, steady waves: 'If you really want to get on in the music business, you'll have to leave Belfast.'

So he did.

CHAPTER THREE

Where The Action Is

The author Mark Kurlansky called 1968 'The year that rocked the world'. That might seem a tad dramatic, but Kurlansky really wasn't exaggerating. Within the space of 12 volatile months, mass protests, military escalations and political assassinations became almost normal events across the globe, as citizens sought to reshape the values and sometimes even the geographical boundaries set around them. From the tragic murders of civil rights activist Martin Luther King and US Presidential candidate Robert Kennedy to escalating tensions in Vietnam and the invasion of Czechoslovakia, all was uncertainty. Student riots in Paris. 'Black Power' at the Olympic games. Even the reliably priapic Mick Jagger stopped crowing about his little red rooster long enough to warn us about fighting in the streets.

Of course, Dublin needed few lessons when it came to guns, revolution or civil unrest. At the centre of the war against British rule during the Easter Uprising of 1916, the city had seen hundreds die and thousands more injured. Six years later, and once again the knives were out as the freedom won from Great Britain and the establishment of a new republic threw the country and its capital into a bitter civil war. As before, much of it was fought on Dublin's streets. The violence eventually settled. Sadly, the financial uncertainty that followed did not. By the fifties, both city and nation were haemorrhaging youth in waves, as 18 to 25-year-olds emigrated to the UK, Europe and America in search of work they could not find at home.

Come 1968, however, and changes were afoot. Jobs were coming back, young people were everywhere and a good time was being had. And even if the Republic of Ireland and Dublin were still 'run by the church and the bloody government in that order,' light was busy forcing its way through the cracks in the form of a rich counterculture and vibrant music scene. From clubs such as the Flamingo, Moulin Rouge and the Apartment to bands like Orange Machine, Purple Pussycat, Watchtower and The Action, Dublin was determined to not let London, Los Angeles and San Francisco have all the fun.

At the forefront of this new 'Dublin Vibe' were Skid Row. Taking their cue from influences as disparate as The Animals, The Byrds, The Beatles and Jimi Hendrix, the quartet was the brainchild of Limerick-born Brendan 'Brush' Shiels. An affable if determined fellow, Shiels had been quite the footballer in his youth, though an all-consuming love affair with music saw him throw in a contract with Bohemians FC after hearing the bass solo on Oscar Peterson's glorious, gambolling 'Night Train'.

As fanatical about learning how to play the instrument as he had been about soccer, Shiels practised his way into various country and western outfits before coming to rest aged 19 in Dublin soul act The Uptown Band. Formed from the ashes of Shiels' favourite group Rock House, The Uptowns were managed by Ted Carroll, a man then best known for starting Ireland's first beat club – 'Well, R&B, really' – on the pebbles of Killiney Beach near Dublin in the summer of 1962. 'There were these wonderful tea rooms that were built on stilts over a beach in Killiney,' Carroll said in 2020. 'So, right there was a fantastic summer night venue.'

Within months of the successful Killiney experiment, Carroll had extended his portfolio to that of both promoter and agent: he left his day job at the bank and settled into artist management with Shiels and The

Uptown Band. Or so he thought. 'Well, I ended up managing them for a while, until I was deposed by a guy called Harry Mooney who claimed to have better contacts and could get them better gigs. [But] Brush didn't like him, and soon left to form another band. That was Skid Row.'

Given his recent deposition, one might have thought Carroll would steer clear of Shiels. Quite the opposite, in fact. '[At that time] Brush worked in a jam factory but he was a good bass player . . . and really wanted to get his own thing going,' Carroll confirmed. 'Brush was quite ambitious, observant and aware of what might trigger success. He also worked very, very hard. And he wasn't flaky. Brush was dependable. If he said he'd do it, he'd really do it, and that was important. I was from a middle-class south Dublin background and Brush was from working-class north Dublin. But we got on, communicated well and liked the same kind of music. We were . . . aligned.'

The rules of that alignment were drawn up during the summer of 1967 when Shiels started pulling together the musicians that became Skid Row. First in was guitarist Bernard 'Ben' Cheevers, a gifted player whom Brush had previously worked with in country showband Brian Rock & The Boys. Following closely behind was Nollaig 'Noel' Bridgeman. Like Cheevers, Bridgeman was a skilled musician with a background in both accordion and clarinet. He also liked to hit things very hard with sticks. 'Ha! Well, I got my dad to buy me a set of drums, then drove him crazy playing them,' he later told journalist Johnny Hyland.

A fan of Shiels since seeing him perform in The Uptown Band, Bridgeman was delighted when the bassist started dating his next-door neighbour (Shiels' future wife) Margaret. Hatching a cute plan Noel would practise loudly with his windows wide open whenever Shiels was on the scene. 'I wanted to impress him.' It worked. Shiels came knocking, a friendship was formed and Bridgeman found himself drumming in Skid Row. With players in place, Shiels now set about finding a singer for his new group. He wasn't seeking vocal perfection, however. Just a 'good-looking frontman with some real charisma'.

Enter Philip Lynott. Though people called him 'Phil' or 'Philo', he liked to be called Philip, so that's what we'll call him here.

Not a legend quite yet, but busy doing the groundwork nonetheless, Philip Parris Lynott was lanky, handsome and 18 years old. He was also the former singer of The Black Eagles[1], who for a while at least were something of an institution on Dublin's mid-sixties beat club scene. 'The Black Eagles supported a band I was promoting called The Mad Lads (around 1966, 1967),' recalled Carroll. 'I remember The Eagles got out of this van and they were all wearing flared jeans with little bells tied to them. God almighty. But you know, they were really good! They played Yardbirds, Small Faces and Who stuff. And that was the first time I'd seen Philip Lynott.'

Like his fellow Eagles bandmates, Lynott had been brought up in the resolutely working-class area of Crumlin, on Dublin's south side. Yet his background was a little more complex than the average Crumlin boy or girl. Born in West Bromwich, England in 1949, Lynott was the 'love-child' of his mother Philomena Lynott and Cecil 'The Duke' Parris, a charming man from British Guiana she met at a dance hall when he was seeking work in the UK. Their affair proved memorable but brief: Philip was brought up by his grandparents Sarah and Frank in south Dublin while their daughter Philomena continued working in northern England.

A black, only child raised by aged relatives in a white, working-class, Irish neighbourhood during the early fifties, one might conclude Philip Lynott had it tough. And sure enough, there were times when he faced his fair share of racism and stupidity. Yet, Lynott's genetic gifts and essential otherness had its advantages. As genial as his mother, as charming as his father and as hard as nails when the occasion warranted it, Lynott was soon to become one of Dublin's leading 'faces' – a fact only redoubled when he started singing in The Black Eagles. 'Philip was tall, thin, striking and exotic,' said Carroll. 'There were very few black men in Dublin at that time, perhaps some students at Trinity College or at boarding school. But you see, Philip was born and bred in Dublin, with

---

1 A covers band comprised of brothers Frankie (rhythm guitar) and Danny Smith (bass), Alan Sinclair (lead guitar), singer Philip Lynott and drummer Brian Downey (more of him later), The Black Eagles gigged throughout 1965 to 1967. Sadly, no recordings of the band exist. More's the pity, as they were meant to be pretty good.

an accent to match. He was very popular, and the fact he was black didn't create any problems on a social level. Plus, he was very, very, very good at pulling girls.'

Brush Shiels was aware of both Lynott's charm and musical potential. Having seen The Black Eagles before they folded in mid-1967, he had tried to contact him about joining The Uptown Band. 'But in those days, not everyone had telephones and when we went over to try and see him on the other side of town, we missed each other.' On this occasion, however, Shiels and Carroll got their man, with Lynott joining Skid Row just in time for the band's first rehearsals in late September 1967.

Accompanying Skid Row's new vocalist on his latest adventure were Frank Murray and Paul Scully – two teenage friends Philip had met while fronting The Black Eagles – and who were now appointed as Skid Row's official road crew. 'Frank and I used to duck off from school and go over to see Philip at his granny's house,' said Scully. 'You see, she brought him up while his mother was away managing a hotel in Manchester. Anyway, while we were there, we'd play records and just talk. He'd listen to everything, from Frank Zappa to Frank Sinatra. Even at that age, Philip was amazing.'

Right from the off, Skid Row were eager to prove their artistic credentials, a fact underlined by the quartet's earliest shows in Dublin clubs such as The Flamingo and The Scene. Drawing on a canny set list that included novel takes on The Byrds' 'Eight Miles High', various Animals songs and many a Beatles tune, the group were also partial to prolonged jamming. Indeed, Shiels, Cheevers and Bridgeman were so given to entering the musical stratosphere without notice that Lynott bought an echo unit so he could make odd noises of his own until the others returned to the tune at hand. Another wheeze employed by Skid Row in their early days was a truly outré light show that combined psychedelic patterns projected behind the group with grainy film footage[2] of Pope Pius XII going about his religious business. This was not your average showband.

---

2 Brush's friend 'Little Mick' Flanagan was apparently responsible for unearthing the film of Pope Pius XII, though over time, his ambitions with a camera provided Skid Row with some even more intriguing visual effects.

Though such imagery raised a Catholic eyebrow or two on the occasions Skid Row ventured outside Dublin's hipper nightspots – 'Skid would leave Dublin,' laughed Paul Scully, 'and then take a little tour, [performing for] these poor, bewildered people in the country' – it did not impede the band's progress. 'Skid Row's first gigs were booked for November [1967] . . . and they became very popular very quickly,' confirmed Ted Carroll. 'Every gig they did, they got rebooked. In fact, by the early spring of 1968, Skid Row had become Ireland's top group.' This fact was rubber-stamped during the summer of that year when the band topped the annual poll of Ireland's best-selling entertainment magazine, *New Spotlight*.

Yet it was at precisely this time that guitarist Bernard Cheevers handed in his notice. As proven over previous months, Cheevers was a talented player and one particularly adept at using the wah pedal to enhance Skid's extended onstage jams. That said, he was equally good when operating a wire stripper, a fact confirmed when his daytime employers Guinness awarded him the title Electrician of the Year for 1968. 'Bernard was already a qualified electrician and Skid Row were very much still a part-time band [for him] at that point,' said Paul Scully. 'Anyway, he was getting married to his girlfriend, looking for security, [and] looking back now, you can't really blame him [for leaving]. Guinness was like the civil service back in those days. They really looked after their employees and people craved a job with them.' Fine and dandy for Bernard then, but less than ideal for Brush and co. 'Maybe,' Lynott later laughed, 'but then the whiz kid turned up . . .'

Since the demise of Platform Three in mid-1968, Gary Moore had not been idle. There was the continuing job at the warehouse, though one suspects he gave little, if any thought to it. Some talk had also taken place within the family about a return to education, possibly an apprenticeship of some kind, maybe even at Harland & Wolff. But again, Moore wasn't really listening. When it came to music, however, he remained all ears. Aside from a growing record collection, with more Beck, more Hendrix, more Cream and one or two bluesy surprises we will return to, Moore had thrown in his lot with several other groups, sometimes voluntarily, sometimes not. In the case of showbands like The Outlaws and The Raydots, Moore's participation was likely to be the result of his father Bobby offering his services when such acts turned up at the Queen's Hall a guitarist short. Once, Gary would have done it willingly (or to at least pay back some of the money Bobby spent on that brand new Telecaster). But as his hair had grown longer, his flares wider and his tastes more progressive, the 16-year-old now found depping for 'The Top 40 boys' onerous rather than exciting.

Yet when it came to Moore's own choices as to where he plugged in his guitar, it was again something of a mixed bag. According to various reports, Gary had a brief dalliance with blues/R&B combo The Deltones during the early summer of 1968, even performing with the band once or twice at Club Rado before moving on again. There may have been another, short-lived affair with teenage popstrels The Aztecs, though the group's resolutely chart-friendly set list make that seem unlikely. Shades of Blue, The Stratatones and Five By Five are three further acts Moore's name has been linked to during the same period. However, there was no denying his association with local heroes The Method. After all, it was Gary's blink-or-you'll-miss-it time with the Belfast band that set him on a path out of the city and on the rocky road to Dublin.

Fronted by singer/guitarist Dave Lewis who began his own career aged 12 as 'The Boy with the Golden Voice' on Belfast's social club scene, The Method were originally a promising R&B-influenced act playing Motown and Stax hits. Yet like many around them, the group soon gravitated towards performing the progressive blues of Clapton, Beck and Hendrix. By late 1967, The Method had become very good at it, a combination of strong musicianship, Lewis's soulful vocals and shrewd management courtesy of George Meehan securing them a plethora of bookings, not only in their native city but south of the border in the Republic too.

Hence, when Dave Lewis was hospitalised following a car accident and the band's residency at a key Dublin nightspot put in peril as a result, decisive action was required. In a move Gary Moore later likened to 'a kidnapping' The Method's remaining members[3] tracked the guitarist down

---

3 In addition to Dave Lewis, The Method comprised at one time or another Dave Hanna on bass, Nigel 'Nidge' Smith on bass and Wilgar Campbell on drums, among others. Campbell later went on to play with Gary's friend Rory Gallagher, featuring

to a park in Belfast city centre one Sunday afternoon in mid-September 1968 and told him about their problem. After a nod or two of agreement (Moore already knew and liked Lewis), he found himself herded into the back of a transit van and on the way to a new life.

The band's destination was Club A Go Go. A small, but atmospheric 'beat joint' in Sackville Place, and only a stone's throw from Dublin's busy O'Connell Street, the Go Go had a reputation for putting on strong groups with a bluesy edge. No folk or country and western here, the Go Go was all about providing a suitably progressive show for the city's more discerning musical clientele. 'The music these people were interested in just wasn't catered for by the mainstream,' said Irish author Daragh O'Halloran of Club A Go Go's typical punter. 'You just wouldn't hear it on the radio.'

Gary Moore fitted into this ethos rather well. Though several songs short on their set list due to lack of rehearsal time, both the band and their temporary guest of honour had played 'a blinder' at the club, with Moore blasting his way through Blues Breakers and Cream covers before an appreciative city audience.

Standing discreetly among them and watching Moore like hawks were Skid Row's road crew, Frank Murray and Paul Scully. Alerted earlier in the evening that 'a guitar genius was cutting heads at the Go Go', the pair had scurried along to the club to see what the fuss was about. Nearly 52 years later, Scully was still in shock. 'Skid were doing a gig on one side of O'Connell Street [at Club 72], and we walked over to the Go Go to see Gary,' he said in 2020. 'Now, I'm really not exaggerating here. Everyone's jaw just dropped. The *Blues Breakers* album . . . he was playing those songs note for note. Each note was played just perfectly. I mean, it could be nostalgia, but I honestly think Gary was as good at the age of 16 as he was later on. He was just unbelievable. And with Bernard Cheevers leaving Skid Row, the timing was totally perfect.'

Stunned but ecstatic, Scully and Murray charged back to Club 72 to tell Brush Shiels his prayers might have been answered. Within minutes, all three were back in Club A Go Go, where Skid Row's leader had his

on the Cork guitarist's debut solo album of 1971 and the seminal *Live In Europe* a year later. Sadly, a fear of flying scuppered his ability to tour and Campbell left Gallagher's employ in 1972.

own epiphany. 'Frank says "You've got to see this guy . . ." So, I went to have a look,' Shiels later told Stuart Bailie. 'I couldn't believe it. Gary was playing Clapton straight off the *Blues Breakers* LP. He had the sound and he looked terrific. So, we waited until he stopped, told him we were looking for a guitar player and it went from there.'

Actually, it nearly didn't go anywhere at all. Though Moore was flattered by Shiels' offer, when it became apparent that Skid Row were not a blues band, but closer to 'American West Coast stuff', his interest rapidly faltered. Like Clapton before him, the thought of joining a group not dedicated to preaching the gospel of Freddie King, Howlin' Wolf and Muddy Waters was somehow just distasteful. Yet, the ever-resourceful Shiels persuaded Moore to come and see Skid Row at Club 72 and then make up his mind.

Smart move. Walking into the room for the band's late-night set, Moore was confronted with the sight of 'A big black guy singing . . . and making all these incredible sound effects with an echo unit. I'd never seen anything like it.' Between Philip Lynott's way with an echoplex, the band's bizarre light show and a truly unique take on The Beatles' 'Strawberry Fields' ('It was even wackier than the original . . .'), Gary was sufficiently intrigued to reconsider Shiels' pitch. When wages of £15 a week and a place to stay in Dublin were also mentioned, his resolve cracked and Moore was in. '£15 a week?' he later grumbled. 'I'm still waiting for it . . .'

Though Moore was now a member of 'Ireland's biggest band', there were still principles to be adhered to. Having given his word to The Method, he saw out his remaining gigs with the group before a fully recovered Dave Lewis returned to the fold in late 1968.[4] Moore also spoke with Platform Three manager Bill Allen to tie up any loose ends there. More a gesture than much else given the trio hadn't gigged in

---

4   Always a dab hand at getting gigs, The Method continued to tour throughout the UK following Moore's departure in September 1968. A year later, the band changed their name to Andwella's Dream and relocated to London, where a record deal was secured. The group's debut album *Love and Poetry* was released in mid-1969. Two more LPs under the slightly less psychedelic name 'Andwella' followed, but when both failed to chart the band broke up in 1972, allowing singer Dave Lewis to forge an extremely colourful and varied solo career, the details of which can be found at: davelewismusic.com.

several months, Allen still appreciated Moore squaring the circle with him. All that was left to attend to now was Bobby.

In truth, Bobby Moore was never likely to stop Gary leaving Belfast for the lights of Dublin, despite the fact his son was only 16 years old. Having invested his emotions, time and money in aiding Gary's musical cause, Bobby knew that joining Skid Row represented a real opportunity for the teenager, and one that wouldn't hang around long. Equally, he and his wife Winnie needed the space. Since Gary was born in 1952 the couple had four further children, Margaret (or 'Maggie'), Patricia (or 'Pat'), Michelle and Cliff, making Castleview Road quite full at the best of times. With their eldest now on the move, at least one of the Moore clan would be able to stretch their elbows a bit.

Still, despite such practicalities, Bobby still wanted things done right. Brush Shiels was dispatched north to placate his concerns and make sure Gary would be well looked after while in Dublin. 'Gary said to me "OK, meet us at the gates of Stormont",' Shiels told the BBC. 'So, I went up to Belfast . . . met him and his pal and went around to his [dad's] house. Bobby was 36 at the time. His dad says, 'He wants to go down and play with you. Will you look after him for me?' And I said, 'Yes, of course.' Hah! I couldn't even look after myself, but what else could I say? So, yes, that was it, and Gary came down [to Dublin].' As for Moore himself, the move was inevitable. 'I was a bit apprehensive, but I joined Skid Row anyway,' he later told author Graeme Thomson. 'It was good for me to get away from home [as] I was having a lot of trouble with my father at the time. So . . .'

With assurances sought and provided, no matter how nebulous or fanciful, Gary Moore was on the move and back in Dublin with Skid Row by October 1968. His new environment took some getting used to. 'When I first met Gary, he wasn't cocky at all,' said Paul Scully. 'In fact, he was very shy. He was happiest when he had a guitar in his hands, hiding behind the hair. But then, it's easy to forget he was only a kid when he arrived in the city.' Indeed, but a kid who still needed somewhere to sleep and a bite to eat. Thankfully, Philip Lynott stepped up to provide not only accommodation, but several life lessons too.

40

Despite a near three-year age gap (huge when you're a teenager), Moore and Lynott seemed to bond almost immediately, with Philip marking the beginning of their friendship by introducing Gary to his first Chinese meal at The Peking Duck restaurant on Dublin's busy Grafton Street. The experience proved enlightening. 'I absolutely hated it,' Moore later said, 'so Philip happily finished [my food] off with a big grin on his face. That taught me everything I needed to know about him in five minutes.' Lynott was obviously forgiven, because he and Gary were soon discussing their favourite bands over several pints at the Flamingo before heading off to get a bed sorted out for the young guitarist. Their destination was a roomy house in Sandymount, the picturesque Dublin suburb known for its long, if sometimes gusty beach. Nicknamed the 'Second Orphanage', the impressive dwelling Lynott and Moore were heading for was inextricably linked to a folk trio named Dr Strangely Strange.

Once described by a fan as 'Psychedelic superheroes', Dr Strangely Strange featured the talents of twenty-something fine art graduates Tim Goulding, Tim Booth and honorary 'Englishman abroad' Ivan Pawle. Formed in early 1967, The Strangelies were a curiously beguiling proposition. Reminiscent of fellow odd men out The Incredible String Band, but with a whimsy and otherness all their own, The Strangelies' brought a striking new angle to Dublin's expanding folk scene.[5] 'Well, Goulding and myself were painters,' said Tim Booth in 2020, 'and [Dr Strangely Strange] was a part of what we did. We liked the avant garde, the idea of being different. So, when the whole hippie thing came in, it kind of subsumed us. We grew our hair, started wearing ridiculous clothes, [became] "counterculture". That's the word you need, counterculture.'

This pursuit of 'Progression, not convention' was not only reflected in the group's music. In typically welcoming fashion, Tim Goulding and his then girlfriend Patricia 'Orphan Annie' Mohan had opened the door

---

5   Though Booth, Goulding and Pawle remained the group's engine room, several other gifted musicians passed through the ranks of Dr Strangely Strange, including guitarist Humphrey Weightman, singer Caroline 'Lucas' Greville, drummer Neil Hopwood, Brian Trench, Joe Thomas and gifted musical couple Gay and (future Pogue) Terry Woods.

of her rented house on 55 Lower Mount Street, near Dublin's imposing Merrion Square to near anyone who chose to visit. 'Yes, the Orphanage,' said Tim. 'That's what we called it, and I suppose that's what it was.' And that's what it became, the house's huge fireplace providing a space to gather at all hours of the day and night for any number of artists, poets and other colourful characters. 'There was something in the air and we were at the centre of it, I suppose,' said Ivan Pawle. 'And, of course, grass was just starting to come in from New York, which definitely added a certain . . . flavour to everything. But you know, I didn't like the word "hippie", and I'm not sure we were, really. I felt we were being categorised unfairly. We thought,' chuckled Pawle, 'we were much more like "Beatniks", man.'

By October 1968, things had moved on again, and The Strangelies' Tim Booth had taken up the mantle of housemaster at the 'Second Orphanage' in Sandymount. With a new house came a new cast of characters, but also some more familiar faces, including Lynott. 'Well, we were always aware of Philip,' said Booth. 'He was "friends of friends", so to speak, [and] after a while started popping into our gigs, so we ended up playing music together.' Soon enough, Lynott was a regular visitor to the first Orphanage, where he conducted a short, but touching affair with another, older house guest, Annie Christmas. 'He and Annie had a lovely thing, you know, very . . . yin and yang,' said Ivan.

When Lynott turned up this time, however, it wasn't for romantic reasons. '[We'd left] the first Orphanage because it was being redeveloped and had ended up over at Sandymount,' confirmed Booth. 'Anyway, Philip arrived at the door and said, "We've got this new kid joining us in Skid Row and he's coming down from Belfast. Would you be able to look after him for a few days – put him up, you know?" So, I said, "Where is he?" One hastily arranged meeting at The Bailey later, and 'In comes this skinny kid – spotty, with lank, dirty hair – wearing this really tight corduroy jacket with big, highwayman lapels. He was very, very shy. But you know, we got talking, and . . . well, I just liked him. So, I said to Philip, "Yeah, we can put him up for a while." So, he came and stayed with us at Sandymount where Ivan was also staying at the time. Of course, the kid was Gary.'

Improbably for a 16-year-old on his first real adventure outside Belfast, Moore proved himself a model housemate. Though late to rise (a lifelong habit), Moore was neither lazy nor particularly untidy. 'Well, Gary didn't cook, but he did other things to help,' said Booth. 'He'd keep his space tidy and he'd wash up too.' And when the washing up was done, there was music. 'There were always lots of instruments to draw on at the Orphanage,' Booth continued. 'Aside from guitars, there was a mandolin, even [Tim Goulding's] harmonium, and Gary would work out chords on that for various songs and then show us. He could really play any kind of music. For instance, the new Fugs album had just come out at the time, *It Crawled Into My Hand, Honest*, and Gary just learned all the songs in no time and played them back to us. If I put Appalachian music on the stereo, again, no bother to him at all. He'd just pick up the mandolin and start playing along. Same with Spirit. We had both Spirit albums and Gary would play all of Randy California's solos. He was a brilliant mimic with a fantastic ear.'

Tim Booth's fellow Strangelies agreed, with Ivan Pawle even giving Gary's gifts a regional spin. 'You know, the music went straight through Gary. Big hands. The way he held a note, that vibrato. Maybe it's a Belfast thing. Listen to [the flautist] James Galway and then listen to Gary. The sound they can get out of an instrument.' For Goulding, Gary might well have been from the moon. 'Honestly, he was one of the most gifted and brilliant musicians I'd met in my life,' he said. 'I remember him in the room there, playing along to the radio, and whatever song that came on, he'd pick up an instrument, usually the guitar – though it could have been any household utensil, really – and just play along with it. All the chords. All the changes. All in time. I don't think I've met another musician like that, before or since. Michelangelo sculpted 'David' when he was 21. Mozart had written some pretty good symphonies at about the same age and I think Gary was one of those. I really do believe that.'

In a matter of weeks, Gary Moore had been kidnapped by The Method, courted by Skid Row and was now a member of Ireland's 'biggest band'. During the same period, he had flown the family nest, befriended one of Dublin's greatest charmers and moved into a 'psychedelic monolith' where exotic aromas emanated from every room. Yet, despite the physical wrenches, emotional uncertainties and general sense of discombobulation that must have accompanied them, Moore's belief in both his talent and decision to leave Belfast remained steadfast. 'If I didn't think I had something,' he later said, 'I wouldn't have been doing it.' Now all he had to do was prove it.

CHAPTER FOUR

New Boy In Town

Gary Moore's tenure with Skid Row would go by in a haze of hard gigging, quicksilver solos and some of the strangest time signatures known to man or drummer. Band members were sacked or temporarily disappeared. Heroes were met and not found wanting. Managers changed, then changed again, while deals were signed and planes boarded. Drink was drunk and tablets taken. And among all this delicious lunacy, Gary met a girl and fell in love. 'Skid Row,' said Melody Maker: 'Mad melodies played by mad men.' All things considered, they were probably right. In later years, Moore would refer to the period from October 1968 to December 1971 as 'one of the happiest times of my life'. It was also character-forming, emotionally instructive, physically and psychically demanding, and filled with more notes than stars in the sky. For those reasons, and many more besides, it's probably worth examining it in some detail.

As with most fledgling relationships, things began with a honeymoon period, as the band's line-up coalesced around Brush Shiels, Noel Bridgeman, Philip Lynott and new boy Moore. Following a brace of live dates in the late autumn of 1968 where departing guitarist/aspiring electrician Ben Cheevers handed over riffs and solos to Gary on stage,

Skid Row again shrank back to a quartet. Keen to mark this changing of the guard, a demo had already been cut of one of Shiels' songs; the seldom heard 'Photograph Man', at Irish TV host Eamonn Andrews' studios[1] on Dublin's Harcourt Street.

Essentially a huge space filled with separation boards, electrical cables and power points placed at curious angles, the 'Television Club' (as it was known) was the city's only real recording facility of note, and became a regular stop-off for the band. It also had its own Cinderella-like curfew. Come what may, at 7 p.m. groups were ordered to down tools and vacate the premises so it could be turned into a dancehall for use later that night. 'Odd, but very Irish,' this draconian measure at least ensured Skid Row worked to the studio clock rather the bell tolling last orders at the local pub.

The band's manager, Ted Carroll, travelled to London to hawk 'Photograph Man' to the record labels, but no one bit. Meanwhile, back in Ireland, Shiels was reviewing Skid Row's touring options. Soon enough, his review led to Carroll departing again for England for a much longer stay. 'While I had Dublin sown up for contacts and places to play, I didn't have many contacts elsewhere in Ireland, and Brush by that point wanted to cast the net wider,' Carroll confirmed. 'So, he decided – as I was also booking other bands for my company Galaxy Productions – that he could dispense with me and get someone else in who could put them on the [bigger] ballroom circuit.'

As new manager Roy Esmonde took ownership of getting Skid Row into larger regional venues, Carroll took a temporary diversion of his own into public transport. In what can only be described as a lateral move, Carroll upped sticks to Bournemouth, where he settled by the sea and worked as a bus conductor. 'Well, the money wasn't bad,' he later quipped. Suffice to say, Carroll would return.

As Brush Shiels had correctly deduced, until Skid Row secured a

---

1 Lantern-jawed, cordial, but also handy in a fight – he won Ireland's junior middle-weight title in 1944 – Eamonn Andrews was a ubiquitous presence in both Irish and UK broadcasting from the mid-fifties until his death in 1987. Sports commentator, panel show presenter and chat show host among other things, Andrews remains best known for fronting weekly biography programme *This Is Your Life*.

record deal, they remained dependent on Ireland's live circuit for their income. Thankfully, gigs were now there in abundance, both in Dublin and further afield. Ever the showmen, the band had sought even bolder ways to engage their existing audience while bringing in new converts too. In addition to the liquid light shows that had become a Skid Row trademark, smoke bombs were now employed to provide even more thrills, though one concert in Cork reportedly came close to prematurely ending when the dancehall vanished in a fluffy white mass.

The successes outweighed the failures. Inspired by Sidney Poitier and Tony Curtis's performance as fist-fighting chained convicts in prison escape drama *The Defiant Ones*, Shiels and Lynott handcuffed themselves together while staging a mock punch-up as Moore and Bridgeman played on.[2] Though the duo were no doubt making some form of extended social comment on themes of brotherhood within the film, the punters simply thought the fisticuffs were real and took to cheering them on. The segment was quickly dropped. 'Little Mick' Flanagan's 8mm films, however, continued to beguile. No longer content to just project footage of Pope Pius XII saying mass, or JFK's assassination as a theatrical back-drop, Flanagan was now filming Skid Row at one venue, only to air the results behind the group at their next gig. Circles within circles. Wheels within wheels. As ever, when it came to doing 'weird', Skid Row remained well ahead of the curve.

Musically, too, the band were growing at an impressive rate. Only six months before, the majority of the set was heavily reliant on cover versions of Byrds and Beatles tunes, albeit in radically altered form. 'They did a gig at Trinity College and performed an astounding version of 'I Am The Walrus',' recalled Tim Booth. 'I remember thinking, "How did they do that?" I had no idea how to even attempt such a thing.' Yet, with the introduction of Gary Moore, Skid Row had moved past where they had left off with Bernard Cheevers and become a full-on jam machine.

---

2 Or it could well have been Moore and Robbie Brennan doing the watching, as Noel Bridgeman disappeared for several gigs around this time to tour Europe with singer Colm Wilkinson. Brennan – who later worked with Christy Moore, Paul Brady and Clannad, among others – deputised in Bridgeman's absence.

Geed on by the dexterity of their new recruit and Shiels and Bridgeman's growing admiration for the likes of Cream and Jimi Hendrix, shows now took on an even wilder dimension, as Skid's rhythm section followed Moore down a series of ever-stranger musical rabbit holes.

Unfortunately, these sustained flights of instrumental fancy meant Lynott had become increasingly reliant on his echoplex unit to keep up, with whistles and repeats replacing vocals for minutes at a time. 'The original Skid Row were a really melodic band influenced by all sorts of stuff,' said road man Paul Scully. 'But then, the music started to change. "How many notes can you get to the bar?" became the new thing.' For Lynott, those frantic note clusters began resembling something akin to writing on the wall.

All was still well enough, however, in the spring of 1969, when Skid Row went back to Eamonn Andrews' Television Club studios to cut their first single with Dublin-based label Song. A local enterprise whose previous releases included 45s by the likes of The McTaggarts and Tramcarr 88 (a folk duo produced by Shiels), Song were no Atlantic, EMI or Decca Records. But the company were willing to dip into their pockets and fund Skid's debut, which represented major progress for the band. In turn, the quartet tried hard to make a return on their investment, handing over a lovely little tune in the form of 'New Places, Old Faces'.

Written by Shiels before the group's newfound obsession with staging musical dogfights took hold, 'New Faces' harkened back to the bassist's love of American West Coast stylings, with a dash or two of Donovan-style hippie folk thrown in for good measure. All gently plucked acoustic guitars and plaintive tin-whistle – courtesy of Johnny Moynihan from Irish traditional supergroup Sweeney's Men – Shiels' lyric was brim-full of artistic promise. Delicately outlining a family coming to terms with having to leave their home in the face of a compulsory purchase order, Shiels had drawn on his own clan's experiences of a similar dilemma several years before. One couldn't really knock Lynott's vocals either (though doing so would become something of a blood sport in coming months), his silken delivery light years away from the 'none more macho' baritone he would call his own in subsequent years.

As far as Gary Moore's contribution to 'New Places, Old Faces', again, there could be few complaints. Spryly picking away at the song's melody lines, Moore seemed intent on keeping his fingers interested in spite of its unhurried pace. That said, he was even more energised on the single's B-side, 'Misdemeanour Dream Felicity'. Composed by Moore himself (his first songwriting credit), 'Felicity' was a bluesy, off-kilter shuffle in 5/4 time, with Moore's fizzing, folky lead lines recalling Pentangle's Bert Jansch and John Renbourn, two players he had recently come to admire.

Unusually for a guitarist so in love with ear-splitting volume, neither 'New Places' nor 'Felicity' featured any real electric guitar, as Moore turned to six- and twelve-string acoustics. Even a year before, that would have been anathema to him. 'When I was 15, I knew about Robert Johnson (and the acoustic bluesmen), but I didn't like it,' he later told *Guitarist*. 'It was too deep and I couldn't handle it. To be honest, if there was no electric guitar, I couldn't be bothered with it.'

Indeed, Moore was not ready to abandon the power of electricity anytime soon. As well as the much-coveted 50-watt Marshall amp and homemade, slanted 4x12 inch speaker cabinet he inherited from Bernard Cheevers when he joined Skid Row – 'It was covered in Formica . . . very nice! But it sounded great' – Moore had also upped his guitar arsenal. Finally placing his Olympic white Telecaster to one side, Gary's purchase of a 1967/8 Gibson SG Special got him one tantalising step closer to the thick, creamy tone used by Eric Clapton. Within months, he would trade up yet again, buying a modified and very powerful 1952 Gibson Goldtop (with hot-wired P90 pick-ups) that once belonged to Procol Harum's boxer-faced lead guitarist Robin Trower.

A pleasant enough calling card, if a little too 'eau de hippie' for some, 'New Places, Old Faces' didn't trouble the charts too much in Ireland, let alone anywhere else. But its relative failure wasn't going to stop Skid Row. In June 1969, the quartet redoubled their efforts and pulled off quite the coup when booked to appear on RTE's weekly live TV music show *Like Now!* As important to Irish teens as *Ready Steady Go!* was to UK audiences in its heyday, this was a potentially career-defining moment. On the night, however, Skid Row's take on The Beatles' 'Strawberry Fields' was severely hampered by a sub-par performance from Lynott, his voice spinning off pitch again and again. With friends in the studio smiling through gritted teeth and family watching it all unravel at home, the failed television spot was a hammer blow to the band and its collective ego.

It wasn't the first time Lynott's voice had let him down. Noel Bridgeman remarked on the variable quality of the onstage vocals on several occasions, while Shiels had also heard duff notes flying around that couldn't just be attributed to Lynott's way with an echo unit. Therefore, when Shiels investigated the singer's throat and found a golf ball sized tonsil staring back at him, long-standing suspicions were confirmed. Scooped up by his mother Philomena, an ailing Lynott was on a plane to England and under the surgeon's knife within the week. Back in Dublin, however, Shiels, Bridgeman and Gary Moore were busy jamming themselves into a frenzy. 'We thought we sounded easily as good as Cream,' Brush later said. They also discovered that both Shiels and Moore could carry a tune, even while playing at Mach speed. It didn't take a rocket scientist to figure out where this one was headed . . .

In January 1969, 'Philo' had acted as best man to Shiels when he married his fiancée, Mar. God knows, he even tagged along with the couple when they honeymooned at the guest house Philomena Lynott ran in Manchester's Whalley Range. Now, having just returned from surgery, Brush was giving him his walking papers from the band. 'Yep, Brush sacked Philip. That's the simple, honest answer,' confirmed Paul Scully. 'They'd done the TV show . . . and Philip, who I think had a sore throat at that time, kind of cocked it up a bit. He just wasn't hitting the notes. After that, he was gone, gone, gone.' Perhaps understandably, Lynott wasn't leaping through hoops at the news. 'He took it very bad. It was fucking brutal, actually,' Shiels later told author Graeme Thomson. 'Couldn't have been worse. Like a death in the family.' So that Lynott wasn't completely crushed, Shiels offered to teach him bass guitar, even gifting him a Fender Jazz Model that had recently come his way. As parting gifts go, it was marginally better than a kick in the teeth. 'He was my best mate, Phil,' Shiels later said of the whole ordeal. 'Still, [it] had to be done.'

With hindsight, Lynott's sacking from Skid Row was all but inevitable the moment Moore joined the band. Though Lynott would harden up musically in later years, at the time he was a devout melody man in pursuit of 'West Coast stuff, memorable tunes, ones that would last'. However,

Shiels, Bridgeman and Moore had struck out in another direction from which there was no going back. Beguiled by the improvisational dynamics of Cream and Hendrix as well as new kids on the progressive block such as Spirit and King Crimson, the trio were committed to following a similar path. More than that, with Gary, they had the instrumental firepower to get there. Bug-eyed time signatures. Bizarre chord progressions. A million notes per second, then one more for luck. All this and more lay in Skid Row's future. Sadly, Lynott wasn't allowed to tag along. 'I really think Philip wanted to do his own thing [at that time], and [it] helped him fly,' Bridgeman later said. 'He gave him a guitar, showed him a few things and then set him free.' Though no one knew it quite yet, Shiels had actually done Philip Lynott the biggest favour of his young life.

Back in the summer of '69, there was little emotional fall-out between the remaining members of Skid Row and Lynott following his enforced departure. He and Shiels remained close, with Brush delivering on his promise of bass guitar lessons. He had little choice, really. Lynott turned up on his doorstep every morning ready to go. Bridgeman too, was eager to help out when he learned of Lynott's plans for putting his own group together. But it was Gary Moore that gained the most from no longer having Lynott as his bandmate. 'It was actually easier for us to get along when we weren't working together,' he later told author Mark Putterford. 'There was no pressure on us anymore. We could just be friends.' Friends and flatmates too, as it soon turned out.

In the meantime, the newly slimmed-down Skid Row pressed on with more gigs, while also releasing their second single for Song Records, 'Saturday Morning Man'. Heavily in thrall to rock/folk/blues quartet Traffic, from Shiels' Steve Winwood-esque vocal to Bridgeman's shuffling homages to drummer Jim Capaldi, it was a nice enough tune. But even a clever tempo mid-section change dragging Skid Row perilously close to Faces-style cheeky-chappie territory couldn't lift the track above the ordinary. Marginally better was the 'Saturday Morning Man' B-side, the curiously titled 'Mervyn Aldridge'. With a swaying bossa nova beat, jazzy chord changes and Gary's surprisingly bell-like lead vocal (again, another recorded first for Moore), this was more 'Girl From Ipanema' than Mayall's Blues Breakers. Yet, precisely because of the tune's inherent oddness and a despondent lyrical theme completely at odds with the swaying melody that accompanied it, 'Mervyn Aldridge' was the more compelling listen.

While the eponymous protagonist might have wished for death every waking hour, neither the dark/light 'Mervyn Aldridge' nor jauntier 'Saturday Morning Man' particularly reflected the direction Skid Row had recently committed to. Indeed, aside from a fiery burst of Clapton-like soloing on 'Saturday Morning Man' and the fluttering of a gypsy acoustic at the beginning of 'Mervyn Aldridge', both tunes bore little or no resemblance to progressive rock at all. If the idea behind 'Saturday Morning Man' had been to deliberately write a hit, that hadn't worked either. Though the track picked up its fair share of airplay across Ireland, it quickly fell by the wayside, ending Skid Row's brief association with Song Records.

Still, with albums now outselling singles for the first time and bands such as the newly formed Jeff Beck Group and Frank Zappa & The Mothers of Invention all scaling new heights of improvisational dexterity, the idea of becoming cast as a mere 'pop group' probably wasn't particularly inviting anyway. 'We loved other trios, like Cream and Hendrix,' Moore later told *Vintage Guitar*. 'But we also liked King Crimson and other technical-type bands. [Brush] was one of those guys who liked to show off a lot, so he was trying to make the band impressive by writing lots of difficult riffs. Lots of fast, syncopated stuff where we were playing in unison with [Noel].'

Though Gary Moore was clearly intent on scorching eyebrows in the concert hall with Skid Row, when not performing with the band, one might well have mistaken him for something of a folkie. Indeed, given the amount of time he spent either watching or playing alongside Dr Strangely Strange at clubs like Slattery's on Dublin's Capel Street, it was the only logical conclusion. 'Slattery's was a tiny basement club run by a lovely guitarist/ singer called Mick Colvin,' said The Strangelies' Tim Booth. 'There was an upstairs bar too with some music, but we'd usually play downstairs on a Sunday night. We'd go there, manoeuvring [Tim Goulding's] harmonium down the stairs – no easy task, let me tell you – and play as an acoustic trio. Myself, Tim and Ivan. We'd get a couple of quid each, which was quite a lot of money at the time, and that might keep us going for the week. And Gary, of course, would sometimes come down and sit in with us.'

As Booth confirmed, Moore would come and sit in whenever he could, and not just at Slattery's. Whether jamming at The Pembroke – 'God, watching Blueshouse's Ed Deane[3] and Gary playing guitars at The Pembroke. One of the best nights of music I've ever seen,' said The Strangelies' Ivan Pawle – drinking at The Bailey or eyeing up local legends Ronnie Drew or Luke Kelly[4] at O'Donaghue's Moore established himself as a regular presence at Dublin's music venues. The quiet teenager who hiding behind his fringe when he arrived at the Second Orphanage in late 1968 had not only come out of his shell, but was demonstrating an extremely quirky sense of humour too. 'Oh, Gary had a fantastic sense of humour, probably as good as almost any person on the planet,' said Booth. 'One particular evening, I'd taken a tab of acid, probably because we weren't meant to be playing Slattery's that day, and Gary was grooving around with me. Now, I think he was straight . . . yes, I don't think he'd taken anything – actually, maybe we'd smoked some dope – oh, I don't know. Anyway, he thought we should go down to Slattery's and just play. So, we did. Ivan joined us and we did a set with Gary [playing] some beautiful guitar on our songs, and it went down really well.'

It was at night's end, however, that Moore played his comedic hand. 'As we were leaving, Gary said to me, "Why don't we take the lift upstairs?" I said "What lift?" He said, "There's a new lift." Now, you must remember I was peaking from the acid at that point. So, he opened a door among all these beauty boards, turned on a light and we stepped into this tiny space. It was actually a broom cupboard. Then, he starts doing this whole skit, you know, "Going up. First floor, second floor, ladies' lingerie." Then he announces, "We're going back

---

3   An Irish guitarist of note, Dublin-born Deane and his band Blueshouse were a regular draw on the city scene during the late sixties, specialising in the Mississippi Delta stylings of performers like Robert Johnson and Son House. A true journeyman, Deane left Dublin for London in 1971, going on to tour/record with Graham Parker, Frankie Miller, Mike Figgis, Dana Gillespie, Van Morrison and Donovan, among others.

4   Two of the most influential folk musicians of the modern era, singers Drew and Kelly were the foundation stones of The Dubliners, arguably still the city's most beloved group. Scoring their first hit with 'Seven Drunken Nights' in 1967, The Dubliners' rough and ready approach to Irish folk subsequently popularised the form throughout the world, with the band remaining a strong draw on record and in concert until their retirement in 2012.

down again . . . basement it is," and off we went. Anyway, after several minutes of this, we finally "arrive" at our destination – the ground floor. And I'm believing all this, by the way. So, the door opens in the basement, out we come and I look at him and say, "Jesus, Gary, are we really here? Have they redone the ground floor?" He just fell about laughing.'

In addition to Moore's role as resident comedian, he was opening up in other ways. As made clear by his actions at Slattery's, though Moore wasn't known as a big drinker at the time, he had nonetheless found several alternative routes to relaxation. Alongside an occasional fondness for the dope and hash that pervaded Dublin's counterculture, Moore had also experimented with LSD since arriving in the city. Perhaps the drug most readily associated with the psychedelic movement, 'acid' – like grass – was to be easily found in certain circles, and certainly the ones Moore now found himself inhabiting. 'LSD could be characterised as one of the sacraments of the sixties revolution,' The Strangelies' Tim Goulding once explained, 'and was often a precursor of further exploration using meditation.'

Yet, when Moore stepped away from acid and weed and began dabbling with amphetamines, the good doctors stepped right back in. 'There was obviously a lot of dope around, but Gary was also using a bit of speed at the time and we didn't like that,' said Booth. 'So, we told him not to use the speed, but gave him dope and the occasional tab of acid to kind of straighten him out. And you know, he respected us [for that]. Gary liked us. We were like elder brothers to him.' Indeed, given that Moore was now so nimble-fingered that sonic booms followed in the wake of his guitar solos, it was hard to think of anyone less likely to require amphetamines.

Quibbles with speed aside, Gary Moore was obviously at home in Dublin, his youth and foibles melding amiably with the city's new cast of emerging artists, poets, musicians and madmen. But Moore's choices weren't for everyone, including some of his own bandmates. 'Gary was much more sympathetic, much more in touch with the counterculture than many at the time,' reasoned Paul Scully. 'He was good friends with The Strangelies, for instance, while Brush Shiels on the other hand, was very much 'anti' all that stuff. Brush was quite conservative in his ways, really. But you know, there are a lot of people in and out of the rock business who are conservative in their ways, so it's not that unusual.' Scully's point was well made. While Gary Moore may have been open to new ways and new possibilities, he was also inhabiting a country that, until recently at least, remained solidly in thrall to its past.

'Ireland had been a very dull, very priest-ridden society,' said Skid Row's Noel Bridgeman. 'Then The Beatles and the Stones came along with their long hair and this incredible music, and it seemed there might be another way of living.' Ted Carroll readily agreed. 'Well, in the sixties, Dublin began resembling London in many ways. Boutiques and clubs were opening up. People were becoming more flamboyant. Skirts were getting shorter, hair ever so slightly longer. And these changes in fashion, culture and music were also helping to draw the classes together. Even though Ireland had always been very class conscious, kids from all backgrounds were joining together to [experience] what was happening.'

Still, for each challenge made to the existing status quo, there was an equally tall hurdle to negotiate, with these moral snags laid down by Ireland's oldest and most powerful institution. 'Oh yeah,' continued Carroll, 'I mean, the Catholic Church had the power to shut down the bloody pubs and clubs during Lent. That's how it was.' Yet, it was precisely amid this clash of new moralities and old religious strictures that an important development in Moore's young life was now blossoming. 'Ah yes,' laughed Ivan Pawle. 'You mean Gary and Sylvia . . .'

Truth be told, Gary Moore was not known for his success with girls while living in Belfast. No harm there: after all, he was only 16 when he left. But while The Beat Boys' Bill Downey and The Barons' 'Handsome' Pete McClelland had enjoyed steady relationships, and fans screaming their name at gigs, Moore's world appeared quieter. There were a few dates, but nothing serious. Still, he did all the things teenage boys were meant to do. Attended dances. Wore fashionable clothes. Talked the talk. Further, the lack of confidence that threatened to dog his early adolescence had long been vanquished by the waves of applause at many a concert. Yet, despite all this, no one was left nursing a broken heart when Gary left Belfast.

In stark contrast, Moore was in Dublin only a matter of weeks when he began dating Sylvia Keogh. Though a resident of the city, Keogh originally hailed from Nenagh, an old, Norman-built market town that crowns the northern tip of county Tipperary. Working as a civil servant at the time (quite the job to have in sixties Dublin), the story goes that Sylvia first spotted Gary when he was playing with The Method, a band she had previously seen when fronted by Dave Lewis. But it was when their paths crossed at a late-night burger bar that sparks really flew, and the two started dating in the late autumn of 1968. By that Christmas, they were officially a couple, with Keogh spotted among the crowd at Limerick's Savoy Theatre for Skid Row's New Year's Eve celebration concert. 'Well, Gary was only 16 [while] Sylvia was a little older, at 17 or 18, I think, and working as a secretary in the civil service,' said Ivan Pawle. 'But yes, they quickly became an item . . .'

If not quite *Romeo and Juliet*, there was nonetheless a *West Side Story* flavour to Moore and Keogh's pairing. In addition to their slight age difference and the city boy/small(er) town girl vibe, Sylvia's steady government job was also a long way philosophically from Gary's position as a trainee rock god. However, these were minor issues compared with their respective religious backgrounds and the heat such things were beginning to generate in 1969. On a slow burning fuse for hundreds of years, the emergence in the USA of the civil rights movement had spurred Northern Irish Catholics to reassess both their socio-economic and political position within the province, and find them wanting. Tensions between Catholic and Protestant communities began to rise, with marches and demonstrations on both sides now carrying with them the threat of real danger. By August British troops had been deployed to 'keep the peace' in Belfast and Derry, and a new phrase to describe the situation was about to enter common parlance: 'the Troubles'.

With impeccable timing, Gary Moore had exited his hometown just before these tensions arose. 'Although there were loads of troubles in our house, I left Belfast just before the Troubles started,' he later quipped. In fact, Moore had never been (nor would be) one for flying the flag on such issues, preferring to maintain a resolutely apolitical stance on matters of sectarianism, religion and the like. However, he was Belfast born, Protestant by birth and now in a relationship with Sylvia Keogh, an Irish Catholic. Though neither he nor Keogh probably gave it much thought, their burgeoning romance carried its own share of risks and sensitivities on both sides of the border, such was the time and place they now found themselves living in.

In the end, Moore and Keogh's social circle precluded them from falling prey to any such unpleasantness. Indeed, it was hard to imagine a group of friends for whom one's religious persuasion might be less of an issue. As much as the faces, the places Gary and co. inhabited in Dublin were equally free of difficulty. Communing upstairs at Slattery's on a Sunday afternoon for a blues session, only to come back later that evening to watch The Strangelies do their thing. Putting on a tie to gain entrance to the TV club, where the ever-charming Philip Lynott could be found enthusing about his new band Orphanage, named for the good doctors' original 'place de jour' in nearby Bagotstown. Laughing at the mods on their scooters ('Two haircuts on one head!'). Eating at The Peking Duck, now that Moore had warmed slightly to the pleasures of Chinese food. Wherever Gary, Sylvia Keogh or 'the gang' found themselves, there was fun to be had. It wouldn't stay that way, of course. But it was great sport while it lasted.

Yet, away from the restaurants, the blues bars and the folk clubs, there was a job to be done. As ever, Brush Shiels was keen to push Skid Row onto great things, Noel Bridgeman was right behind him like a bushy-haired lieutenant and Moore, equally ambitious, equally driven, probably wanted it more than both of them put together. To secure the dream, the trio now had to break away from small thinking and aim high. This meant scoring an album deal with an international label, touring the world rather than countrywide and above all, putting the fear of God into their contemporaries. For Moore, this was one of the smaller jobs he had to attend to. 'At the age of 17, 18, you're deadly serious about life and just want to kill everybody and blow everything up. That affects the whole attitude to your playing,' he later told *International Musician*. 'It seemed to me [at that age] there were so many overrated people and I was better than most any of them. And I was.' And he was.

Things moved quickly now.

CHAPTER FIVE

Faster, Faster, Faster, Faster

Gary Moore's new life in Dublin continued its pinball-like trajectory throughout 1969, the only real constants being his live performances with Skid Row or the packing of bags for yet another house move. Having laid his hat at the Second Orphanage when he arrived in the city in October 1968, Moore's romance with Sylvia Keogh had seen him move out of Sandymount early the next year to be with his new girl-friend. No easy task, as it turned out. Still practising Victorian-style morals via the cleansing fires of Catholicism, once a landlady spotted Gary in Sylvia's room, he, she or both of them risked being shown out the door as quickly as they had walked through it. 'Yes, [at that time] Dublin was still a fairly repressive place because of the church and the state,' The Stranglies' Tim Booth reiterated. 'It was a place of rich and poor . . . of contrasts and transitions. A very . . . Catholic place.'

With Keogh in danger of losing her lodgings if Moore were caught staying beyond 'permissible hours', Gary was often forced to play hide and seek with the landlady or simply find other accommodation. Thus began a cycle of itinerant living, with the young guitarist either crashing on the sofa back at the Orphanage, or where there was no alternative, a hard, wooden floor anywhere else that would have him.

Though this bout of sofa-surfing sounded horrendous and sometimes put a strain on his relationship with Keogh, Moore seemed to find it tolerable. As long as there was a record player, that is. 'I was actually living with Gary for while [around then], and we had this one particular record called *The Rock Machine Turns You On*[1],' said Paul Scully. 'It was a compilation, just an amazing record, and we wore it out. Then there was Spirit with Randy California on guitar, and Gary listened and listened to that. He was hugely influenced by Randy at that time, you know. Frank Zappa, too. There was always music on. Always music . . .'

One of the longer stop-offs during Moore's wilderness period came when he moved in with his old pal Philip Lynott and new friend Johnny Duhan at the latter's flat in Dublin's Ballsbridge district. As was his style, Lynott had been just ahead of Moore on the guest list. 'It was strange that Brush Shiels actually pointed Philip in my direction [as a roommate], having sacked him,' confirmed Duhan in 2020. 'But I think the reason Brush originally let Philip go was that three-piece rock bands were beginning to take off in England at the time, and he [might have been] following that.'

While the slightly older Duhan and Lynott came from different head-spaces, they proved surprisingly well-suited when it came to sharing a flat, even if the trainee bassist's room was sometimes a little crowded. 'Well, I think it's fair to say Philip was a real ladies' man,' laughed Duhan of Lynott's string of frequent visitors. 'But don't get me wrong. Living with him was an absolute pleasure. He and I weren't the type . . . who'd stay in our beds all day. In fact, he could actually tell the time by the angle of the morning sun in his bedroom.'

When it came to matters of musical experience at least, Johnny Duhan had the start on Philip Lynott. Lead singer, songwriter (and exceptionally fine

---

1   Released in 1968, CBS's *The Rock Machine Turns You On* was the first budget compilation or 'sampler' LP from a major label. Priced at half the cost of a regular album, it made number eighteen in the UK charts, and featured a mix of established and more 'underground' performers such as Bob Dylan, The Zombies, The Peanut Butter Conspiracy and Taj Mahal.

lyricist) with The Intentions, Duhan and his band of Limerick soul men had gone to London seeking stardom in the mid-sixties. For a moment or two, they nearly found it. Taking on a psychedelic hue and changing their name to the groovier 'Granny's Intentions', the group signed to Deram Records and released three fine singles, including future psych-beat gem 'The Story of David'. However, though Granny's garnered interest from musical high flyers such as Jimi Hendrix and gigged at the likes of The Marquee and Speakeasy, it didn't quite happen. After a line-up reshuffle, Duhan and the newly reconstituted Granny's were back in Dublin by 1969 to rethink their strategy and mount another campaign. 'When we drifted back to Dublin from London . . . that's when I met Gary and Philip,' Johnny confirmed. 'They had all the energy I had at the very beginning when I started out.'

Gary arrived on Duhan's doorstep only a matter of weeks after Philip Lynott moved in, his urgent need for shelter apparently driven by an argument with Sylvia Keogh, or as likely, an incident involving a particularly vigilant landlady. 'Yes, it was a big break-up and lasted for a good while,' said Duhan. However, unlike Lynott, who Johnny nicknamed 'Mother' in honour of his domestic prowess, Moore proved less useful around the house. His standards evidently slipped since he moved into the second Orphanage some months before.

'Well, Gary was different,' laughed Duhan, 'and he was very scruffy. When he first arrived, [Philip and I had the beds] and he was sleeping on the floor. [But] he would still sleep late if he had the chance. Then, when he woke up, he'd soon gravitate towards the guitar and that was it. He was gone, completely immersed in it. Philip and I, well, we took care of business, the business of cooking and cleaning. So, I don't remember Gary being very . . . domesticated.' That said, as with The Strangelies, Moore soon built up a rapport with Duhan, leading to a strong and enduring bond between them. 'Gary and I lived together for months, [so] I got to know and like him,' said Duhan. 'And to be honest, I got on a lot better with Gary than I did with Philip. Gary was incredibly loyal and we just hit it off, like childhood friends or brothers, even.'

★

61

With Moore ensconced in Skid Row, Lynott now gigging with his new band Orphanage (they didn't last too long) and Duhan busily working up fresh Granny's Intentions material, the basement flat in Ballsbridge was a hive of musical activity. 'All three of us were constantly either writing songs, listening to music or playing together,' said Duhan. 'Gary didn't so much "practise" guitar as just play it all the time. He'd sit there for hours on end, shooting up and down the fretboard. Philip was different. He was beginning to take the notion of becoming a songwriter more seriously and exploring a more elliptical area. I remember him saying to me, "You don't need too much [to write a lyric], just [use] colourful imagery like Bob Dylan".' Still, when Granny's Intentions ran into potentially choppy waters, it was Moore that Duhan turned to.

Having parted company with Deram, the seemingly reconstituted Granny's Intentions weren't free agents for long. By the autumn of 1969, the band were picked up by Decca Records and began recording the debut album they had threatened to make a year earlier at the label's swish studio complex in London's West Hampstead. Yet, with less than half the LP completed, Granny's guitarist John Hockedy chose to leave for pastures new. To no one's great surprise, Duhan and the group called in Gary Moore. What did surprise them, however, was how easily Moore slotted into Granny's Intentions. 'Gary arrived on incredibly short notice,' said Johnny. 'Of course, at that time he was playing with Skid Row, and you know the type of music they played. But to come in and join us, with me (and the band) having become much more influenced by folk and even country music, and just pick things up, play that type of music immediately, it was truly amazing.'

Though Moore's day job found him testing the boundaries of what could be done with six strings and two hands, his contribution to Granny's LP *Honest Injun* was a model of economy, and restraint. Whether developing sympathetic counter melodies on the likes of 'With Salty Eyes, Dirty Lies', or gently weaving between flutes and vocal harmonies on the queasily titled 'Fourthskin Blues', Gary was obviously as adept at R&B, folk and country as he was at progressive rock and blues.

★

Unfortunately, while Moore's efforts made parts of *Honest Injun* a delight to listen to, the record failed to find an audience when released in the spring of 1970.[2] Perhaps moving from soul to psych to country in under four years had been a step too far for Granny's existing fanbase. Whatever the truth of it, Duhan now deep-dived further into folk, 'I was beginning to lose interest in rock'n'roll at that point'. His bandmates rejected the new direction and it was all over bar the shouting by 1972.[3] However, Moore and Duhan's work together on *Honest Injun* only consolidated their growing friendship while also allowing for future collaborations. 'Everything for me was in the words,' said Duhan, 'and everything for Gary was in the notes.'

One particular set of notes on *Honest Injun* offered real clues as to Gary Moore's musical past, present and future. Found midway through the feisty, Beatles-like 'Susan of the Country', Moore's contribution at first sounded underplayed, perhaps even underdressed. But on closer inspection, each phrase had been specifically chosen to enhance the song's principal melody line while also creating a little tune all its own. Rattling with vibrato, crisp of tone and steeped in the blues, this was a solo from a guitarist more than passing familiar with the work of Peter Green. 'Jeff Beck. Jimi Hendrix. Eric Clapton and Peter Green, those were the four,' Moore once said. 'There were others, but those guys, for me, they were the four.'

As with Clapton, Beck and Hendrix, Moore had been obsessed by Peter Green from the moment he heard Green performing with John Mayall's Blues Breakers. Having taken over the lead guitar spot in Mayall's troupe following serial absconder Eric Clapton's defection to Cream in mid-1966, the east London-born, 21-year-old faced a tough task. With 'EC' having unofficially traded under the name 'God' while with Blues Breakers,

---

2 Aside from Johnny Duhan and departing guitarist John Hockedy, Granny's Intentions'
   line-up at the time also included Pete Cummins on bass, whistles & flutes and John
   Ryan on harpsichord, piano and organ. Pat Nash was the band's regular drummer,
   though it's worth noting Skid Row's Noel Bridgeman also contributed to the album.
3 Well, not quite. After a decade of inactivity, Granny's reunited for several Irish gigs in
   1983 before disappearing again until 1990, when a John Hockedy-led version of the band
   performed a one-off show at The Speakeasy. Aside from the odd CD re-release and a
   film documentary (2004's *The Story of David*), they've been more or less silent since then.

audiences would now only settle for a combination of Zeus, Buddha and Jesus as his replacement. Yet, as Green proved on the 1967 album *A Hard Road*, he too had obviously just stepped down from the clouds.

A remarkable achievement in a year jam-packed with them, Green's work with Mayall and co. on 'It's Over', 'Hit the Highway' and 'Someday After a While' was as good as his predecessor, and on Green's own 'The Supernatural', some might say on a different plane altogether. A shimmering blues instrumental bathed in reverb and feedback, the soaring string bends and eerie grace notes on 'The Supernatural' perfectly announced Green's talent to the world. From now on, there would be few dissenting voices in the audience or talk of other deities. 'Peter had the sweetest tone I'd ever heard,' B.B. King famously said. 'He was the only one who gave me the cold sweats . . .'

Moore had watched some of the Peter Green saga play out when John Mayall's Blues Breakers came to Belfast to promote *A Hard Road* in the spring of 1967. Standing in the crowd at Club Rado, avid Clapton fan Moore wasn't quite sure what to expect of Mayall's new boy. 'Everyone was there, arms folded, like, "OK, let's see what this guy can do",' he later said. But when Green struck up the opening line of Otis Rush's 'All Your Love' Moore and his fellow punters were 'Absolutely transfixed. There he was playing a Gibson Les Paul through an old rented, piece of shit Selmer amp and I'd never heard a guitar sound like it. I mean, the floor was actually shaking.' Indeed, when Peter returned to Rado six months later with his new band, Moore was again rooted to the spot by the power of the Cockney bluesman. 'I mean, it was almost like he had a bloody halo around him.' As Gary found out, he could sing like a 'cockney angel' too.

Peter Green's new group were called Fleetwood Mac. Like Eric Clapton before him, Green had become quickly dissatisfied with his position in Blues Breakers, and by August 1967 pulled together what would become a band of musical 'world beaters'. Featuring fellow Blues Breaker escapees drummer Mick Fleetwood and bassist John McVie[4], co-lead guitarist/occasional vocalist

---

4 Though Peter Green often referred to Mick Fleetwood and John McVie as 'my favourite rhythm section' (indeed, he named his band in their honour), McVie was actually late joining the party. On a good wage with Blues Breakers, he initially stalled

Jeremy Spencer and Peter on guitar/vox, the quartet's ascent to stardom was almost immediate. Come 1968, and Fleetwood Mac's debut LP was nestling comfortably in the UK charts, where it would stay for 37 weeks.

A year later and things were even better, as their follow-up album, *Mr Wonderful*, and a slew of hit singles – 'Black Magic Woman', 'Man of the World' and the magnificent 'Albatross' – helped define the sound of British blues for a generation. Add another gifted guitarist in the form of Danny Kirwan to swell the ranks of an already talented band, and as Gary Moore later said: 'Fleetwood Mac were just brilliant.'

As is often the case in the music industry, Moore and Peter Green's personal roads finally converged in February 1970 when Skid Row supported Fleetwood Mac at Dublin's prestigious RDS Stadium. The position both bands found themselves in could not have been more different. The Mac, on one hand, were continuing on their ever-upward trajectory, with album number three, the heavily experimental *Then Play On*, again having reached the UK Top 10, while the single 'Oh Well (Parts 1 and 2)' just missed out on the number one spot.

Skid Row, on the other hand, were still frantically trying to find the next foothold on the ladder to stardom. Having been one of Ireland's biggest concert draws for more than 18 months, the band's reputation was sealed in sweat across 26 counties. Indeed, the trio had just won 'Top Group' in the Irish *Evening Herald*'s annual pop poll. But without a proper record deal to help translate their live prowess into a best-selling album, the band remained curiously static. That said, lack of confidence was not an issue. 'I honestly believed when we became a three-piece, we were as good as Cream or The Jimi Hendrix Experience,' Brush Shiels later told author Stuart Bailie. 'I honestly believed that at the time and the boys believed it too.'

★

---

when offered the gig by Green, only to change his mind soon after. As a result, Fleetwood Mac's original line-up featured Bob Brunning on bass guitar before McVie took up his spot stage right. After leaving the group, Brunning went on to play with Savoy Brown, teach music and write several rather fine books on the British blues scene.

Skid Row turned out to be almost as good as they thought they were at the RDS Stadium. Feeding off the adrenaline that came from appearing in front of a home crowd, the band were at their frenzied best for over 45 minutes, with Gary Moore earning the lion's share of plaudits. 'You know, Cream were a trio of equally qualified musicians, but Eric Clapton soon became the star,' said Paul Scully. 'And I think, after a time it's true that Gary became the main focus in Skid Row.'

Peter Green shared Scully's viewpoint. Watching admiringly from the side of the stage, he asked local DJ/event compare Pat Egan to invite Gary and the band back to Fleetwood Mac's dressing room for a beer. For Moore, the prospect of meeting his idol was as thrilling as it was terrifying. 'I was so nervous meeting him, you have no idea . . .' He needn't have worried. The pair got on so well that they went back to Green's hotel for a jam after Mac's set, trading riffs and chords until early morning. 'I mean, he was my hero,' Moore said. 'So when he told me he liked my playing, I was so excited and flattered.' When it was all over, Green suggested that Moore and his fellow Skids meet Mac's manager Clifford Davis, saying 'Maybe he could do something for you.'

Beginning his career as an assistant to The Beatles' manager Brian Epstein, Davis had been headhunted by brothers Johnny and Rik Gunnell in 1967 to help them run one of the music business's more established management/booking agencies. In this new role, Davis had met Peter Green, whose own band Fleetwood Mac were overseen by the Gunnells.[5] Green, however, was unhappy with the job they were doing in promoting the Mac's latest single, 'Black Magic Woman', and turned up at the brothers' Soho office to complain. Loudly. Davis tried to smooth over any cracks by going to see the band live, and promptly fell in love. 'They were just astounding,' he later told the BBC.

Sensing in fellow East Ender Peter a man he could do business with, Davis offered to directly manage Fleetwood Mac. Three years and count-less record sales later, Green was now introducing Davis to Skid Row.

---

5 Industry legends, in their time the Gunnell brothers also managed John Mayall, Slade, Long John Baldry and for a brief time, Rod Stewart. The duo was also responsible for running The Flamingo Club, one of Soho's more lively R&B venues from 1959 to its mid–sixties Mod–friendly heyday.

'Yes, Skid played two shows supporting Mac and that brought a major change,' said Paul Scully. 'Clifford [was asked to] sign them up at Peter's request. Now, let's not forget Clifford Davis was a real power broker at that time, and even lived in the stock broker belt if I recall correctly.'

At any other time, these business machinations might have been a bit sticky. Following Ray Esmonde's brief tenure in charge of Skid Row, long established Dublin agents Brian Tuite and Pete Bardon had taken hold of the group's reins, pushing them on to be an even bigger concert draw in Ireland, if not quite securing that elusive album contract. Yet, with Tuite and Bardon now overseeing Philip Lynott's new post-Orphanage enterprise, a trio named 'Thin Lizzy', deals could be done and chess pieces moved into place.

Progress was reassuringly swift. Within weeks of appearing alongside Fleetwood Mac in Dublin, Skid Row had signed on the dotted line with Clifford Davis, secured an upcoming European and US tour and were due to deliver their debut LP to industry giant CBS Records by autumn. On paper, it really couldn't have got any better. Or maybe it could. 'It was the worst [record] deal of all time,' Noel Bridgeman laughed some 40 years later to *Brushfire*. 'Half a percent between the three of us. But we were young, and you know, we were doing it for the right reasons.'

Having rehearsed the opportunity in their heads for so long, Skid Row were quick out of the traps when it came to starting work on their first album. By the early spring of 1970, producer Mike Smith had been dispatched to Dublin by CBS to capture the group in their natural environment at Eamonn Andrews' Studios / TV Club on Harcourt Street. For his part, Smith had real form, scoring six number one UK singles across the sixties for the likes of Georgie Fame, The Tremeloes and Marmalade. Yet, while his production skills worked a treat on jazz and pop, they seemed to hit a wall with Skid Row's more progressive inclinations. As a result, the demo sessions were abandoned with only a handful of songs on tape. That said, the double A-sided single 'Sandie's Gone (Parts 1 & 2)', eerily presaging a kind of Ziggy-period David Bowie had he flirted with country music and hired Eric Clapton on guitar, did manage to escape in late April. Despite being picked up by Radio Luxembourg as a 'Power Play', it failed to chart.

No matter. Skid Row were so busy they had little time to lick their wounds. Scooping up the best of the material recorded with Mike Smith, they were no sooner out of the recording studio than on their way to pastures new, their passage assured by now ex-bus conductor Ted Carroll. 'I came back to Dublin in [the early spring of] 1970,' said Carroll. 'I had a Triumph Spitfire, and had just parked up at St Stephens' Green. There, heading up the road towards me was The Brush. So, we talked.'

Shiels was full of news and job offers. 'It transpired they'd got a deal with CBS and were soon touring Europe and the States. So, he said, 'We need a tour manager. Someone to take care of the band, the tickets, the travel, the money. What do you think?' After nearly two years on the buses, I was just at the [right point] for a change. But it was the prospect of America that really did it. In 1970, the idea of getting to America was a dream wrapped in gold. All that great music! So, I said "Yeah, OK. I'll do it."'

America would have to wait, however. Carroll's opening brief was to get the band across the Irish sea so they could begin gigging throughout the UK, while also taking a second stab at recording that debut LP. Their first destination was London's East End. 'They moved to London in June 1970,' he said. 'I organised a place for them to stay. That turned out to be 55 Planchette Grove, which had been previously rented to some friends I'd worked on the buses with. It had five bedrooms for £10 a week.' With just £1 each to spend on cigarettes, drink and other 'items of relaxation' after household costs were tallied up, the group were hardly in the lap of luxury. 'No, it was the tough end of town, near West Ham football ground in Upton Park,' Moore later said. 'We didn't even like going out [because] the place was full of skinheads. Tough area. No money, Skid Row. Appropriately named, eh?'

With little in the way of funds and some potentially unfriendly neighbours keeping an eye on the length of their hair, hitting the concert trail was now a must for the band. To that end, a tranche of gigs was arranged, with returning road hogs Frank Murray and Paul Scully now aiding Ted Carroll in his task of getting Skid Row there in one piece. 'Well, Frank and I had both decided to get away from it all and gone to London to get jobs,' said Scully in 2020. 'Then Skid Row arrived and asked if we'd work with them. So, we moved over to Planchette Grove, and off we went again up and down the M1 every night. No regrets, though. We had a great time.'

During the early summer of 1970, Skid Row kept themselves busy with concerts as far apart as Glasgow and Devon. That said, one highlight was played out a little closer to their new East End home, when Skid appeared alongside Dr Strangely Strange at Camden Town's ever-reliable Roundhouse. With Gary's mob on the up and The Strangelies now basking in excellent reviews for their own debut LP, the sublime *Kip of the Serenes*, it was memorable night for all.

'Actually, Gary played the Roundhouse with us a couple of times,' confirmed Tim Booth. 'It was always lovely to play music with him because he'd keep you on your toes. We'd all play better if he joined us [on stage]. His timing was immaculate. He'd do loads of unexpected cross-tempo things that were delightful – so we'd follow him. He'd just lead you through it.' However, Moore hadn't given up frying the eyebrows off the front rows. 'Yes, he was a spotty, long-haired scruffy youth,' laughed Ted Carroll, who had seen Gary and Skid Row tear it up at Dublin's RDS, 'but God, the guitar playing. He had such a melodic, expressive style, [and was] obviously a talent. Now, you had Brush who was the showman, throwing all these shapes while dressed in a long suede girls' coat, huge hat, baggy checked trousers and Donald Duck shoes. Pure flamboyance, was Brush. And then there was Noel, this fine drummer giving it all that behind the double kit. But you couldn't not see Gary, the 'new boy' playing this fantastic guitar, with all those flying histrionics. It just all worked [together]. I was impressed. Well, we were all impressed.'

There was little doubt in anyone's mind that Moore and Skid Row had earned a reputation as a formidable live act. But harnessing that energy in the recording studio remained a lingering problem. Having failed at the first attempt in Dublin with Mike Smith, plans were hatched for Fleetwood Mac's Peter Green to take up the mantle of producer. Yet, for reasons that would soon become apparent, Green turned down the opportunity, leaving the band in a temporary vacuum. Keen just to get on with it, and still in ownership of some halfway decent material from

White Knuckles

their previous sessions[6], the decision was made for Clifford Davis to act as overseer. Moore summed up what happened next better than most. 'Well, we re-did [the album with Clifford] and managed to make it worse than the first time [with Mike Smith].'

Housed in an outlandish sleeve featuring what appeared to be an artistic cojoining of an ancient crow and a circus clown (actually the work of abstract British painter Terence Ibbott), the band's debut disc, *Skid*, finally arrived in shops in late September 1970. The album's contents were as perplexing as the artwork. Essentially a composite of five tunes first recorded with Smith several months earlier and four new songs hastily written by Shiels before recording, *Skid* was wildly inventive, musically challenging and easy to admire. Yet, it was also dense, disorientating and difficult to love. 'Well,' said Carroll, 'just listen to the first album and you'll get the picture. Fast and complex, messy and trite.'

On the upside, when *Skid* was good, it was very, very good. Opening track 'Mad Dog Woman', for instance, was wholly indicative of the band's rambunctious concert appearances, its start-stop time signatures, scattershot vocals and flailing guitars conspiring to provide listeners with a nervy, if thrilling ride. Another Shiels creation, 'Virgo's Daughter', also motored along nicely, recalling Cream at their contrary best, while the country-jazz of 'Heading Home Again' (Shiels again) was carried along by a pleasant enough tune. A group composition, 'Unco-Op Showband Blues', found Skid Row intent on re-inventing the 12-bar structure, adding so many percussive and chordal variations one critic referred to the song as 'Blues from outer space.'

Elsewhere, however, things were less impressive, with 'Awful Lot of Woman' and 'For Those Who Do' guiltily highlighting a band sometimes too clever for their own good. Often sacrificing melody in favour of endless unison riffing, both tracks were little more than a barrage of notes chasing around an ever-decreasing rhythmic circle. The same could be said of 'The Man Who Never Was', as several potentially tuneful ideas

---

6 For those wishing to hear the nine songs Skid Row recorded with Mike Smith, they were first released in 1983 by CBS Japan under the title *Dublin Gas Cooker Comy. & Meter Factory*, then again as a CD in 2000 by Castle Communications. Five of these tracks were subsequently reworked for the band's debut album.

70

again became lost in blasts of dissonance. This fault was nowhere more apparent than with Moore's own 'Felicity', which seemed deliberately constructed to impress rather than enchant. Opening breezily with some pleasing jazz chords and clever percussive inversions, 'Felicity' soon deteriorated into yet another excuse to head off into the musical ether, this time for 11 rather long minutes. Perhaps in the hands of a more experienced producer, such excesses might have been reined in. Unfortunately, while Clifford Davis might have been a fine manager, he was not an experienced producer, a fact underlined by the general sense of muddiness pervading almost every track on *Skid*.

Of course, one could argue that what Moore, Shiels and Bridgeman were doing, however disappointingly captured, was a breath of fresh air when compared with the work of other, less evolved rock bands. The trio's mastery of their instruments and collective will to produce something genuinely progressive was both laudable and refreshing. But one couldn't help but feel that there was also a strong degree of showboating behind these extremities of sound. 'Brush's plan, I think, was [to create] a cross between Cream and King Crimson – this very complex sound, with shifting musical patterns and odd time changes,' said Ted Carroll. 'He'd deliberately write tunes in 11/13, for instance, with the idea of impressing other musicians. Not a bad idea, perhaps. But honestly, sometimes I didn't think the material was very good.'

Carroll's viewpoint was echoed down the years by several others. '[Skid Row] seem[ed] unconcerned with melody,' wrote author Mark Prendergast, '[and] disorientation and blackness is what one feels after listening to the record.' Moore later acknowledged that he was aware of such criticisms and his part in enabling them. 'I don't know how I played with those guys, to be honest,' he told *Q*'s Mat Snow some 20 years after the fact. 'The spotlight was on me, this 16, 17-year-old guitarist. People were looking for a new guitar hero, I suppose.'

Clever, if dark. Self-indulgent, but worthy. In the end, it was down to each individual to make up their own mind about Skid Row. But in October 1970 the collective at least, seemed behind them as the band's debut LP landed at number thirty in the UK charts. Further, they had picked up a champion in the form of influential BBC Radio 1 DJ John

Peel, who seemed more than willing to shout the trio's praises from both rooftop and radio microphone.[7] 'Skid Row,' Peel opined at the time, 'are one of the best groups I have heard anywhere . . . a better group than Ten Years After or Jethro Tull.' Maybe so. But both Alvin Lee's blues rock tearaways and Ian Anderson's folk-rock terrorists had already achieved considerable success in the USA. If, as Peel suggested, Skid Row were the better proposition, then they had better get cracking in the same territory.

Thankfully, Clifford Davis was now back at his managerial desk and cannily using Fleetwood Mac's US profile to leverage some dates there for the trio soon after their album's release. The band's mode of travel was nothing if not novel. 'Well, we got See America tickets for $299,' laughed Ted Carroll. 'We got them from a great little agency called Acton Travel. The way they worked was we flew to Los Angeles, and then could use the tickets for as many flights as we liked, as long as we were going eastwards.'

Following a brief sojourn to Scandinavia, where delightfully, rock fans had been among the first to take Moore and the band to their hearts, Skid Row's assault on the States began in earnest at Los Angeles airport in late October 1970. As beginnings went, it wasn't ideal. Reportedly mistaken for a criminal with the same name by local law enforcement officers, Brush Shiels found himself answering question after question in a small room as band, manager and road crew sat waiting outside. After an hour or so, he was released to a slow hand clap.

Mercifully, things improved for both Shiels and Skid Row. 'We started off at the Whisky a Go Go for three nights with a band called Pollution supporting us,' said Carroll. 'They had two lead singers. One was Dobie Gray, the other Táta Vega, who went on to have albums released by Motown's Tamla label. After that – and in keeping with the ever eastwards theme – off we went to San Francisco for four nights at the Fillmore supporting Boz Scaggs and Frank Zappa & The Mothers of Invention.' For Gary Moore, the notion of appearing on the same bill as Zappa at the legendary venue was a scintillating prospect. 'I mean, Gary loved Frank Zappa. Loved him,' said Paul Scully. 'He and Philip Lynott were always

---

7 Putting his critical heft behind the group, Peel presented two concert programmes featuring Skid Row, in June 1970 and January 1971. The trio also did a session for his radio show in July 1970, which he repeated four months later.

listening to him back in Dublin, and they loved Zappa's music and guitar playing. So, yeah, supporting Frank, that was a big moment for Gary.'

There were other moments to savour. As the tour trundled ever-eastward across the USA, Skid Row shared bills with the great and the good, including a memorable night in Motor City with one of the best groups America had to offer. 'Yeah, The Allman Brothers,' laughed Scully. 'To be honest, before we supported The Allman Brothers, we'd never even heard of them. That should give you an idea how much of an eye-opener that tour was! I mean, Ted was [running the road], Brush had the venues written down in a book and we just drove to the gigs with the guitars in the back. But all of a sudden, you'd realise what you were actually doing. That night, when we rolled into Detroit, there it was, written in big, stencilled letters above the venue: "The Allman Brothers, The Stooges and Skid Row".'

While Iggy Pop and his fellow Stooges were certainly 'eye-opening' in their intensity, it was The Allmans that caught the air in Scully and Moore's lungs. 'I mean, we walked into the hall and there were The Allmans soundchecking with those fantastic twin harmony guitars. I looked at Gary. Gary looked at me. And at the same time, both our jaws dropped. From that moment, we knew who they were, all right.' As was the case in mid-sixties Belfast, Moore was quick to introduce himself to guitarists Duane Allman and Dickey Betts, his enquiries concerning string gauges, amps and harmony lines met with southern hospitality and no little humour. 'Gary loved them both,' said Scully. As time came to show, Moore was taking extremely detailed notes of the conversation.

With each new city came a new set of adventures. In Cleveland, Skid Row provided support to Jethro Tull, whom John Peel had recently announced were musically inferior to them. Unfortunately, Tull's latest album, *Benefit*, had just reached number eleven in the States, a chart placing Moore and co. could as yet only dream of. Days later, at the Boston Tea Party, Skid came face to face with another power trio in the shape of Mountain, though this time there was no potential embarrassment to negotiate.

Driven along by the relentless thrust of bassist/singer/producer Felix Pappalardi, hulking guitar star Leslie West and drummer Corky Laing, Mountain actually had several things in common with their visitors from overseas. For one, each band took major inspiration from Cream, with Pappalardi even producing Clapton, Baker and Bruce's second album, *Disraeli Gears*. But it was the all-out in-concert attack that both Mountain and Skid Row specialised in that made them musical blood brothers, their melding of instrumental prowess, involved arrangements and shattering volume leaving audiences sonically bruised, but happily so. What's more, thanks to Leslie West's deft playing[8], Moore spotted what a Les Paul Junior could sound like in the right hands.

While Skid Row and Mountain bonded over a shared love of Cream, things had the potential to be considerably less cordial later in the tour when Moore's path crossed with that of guitarist Alvin Lee and his blues rocking quartet, Ten Years After. Like Jethro Tull before them, Ten Years After had suffered from John Peel's unfavourable comparisons with Skid Row, and like Tull, proved their mettle with another strong US Top 20 chart placing for their latest album, *Cricklewood Green*. But it was more likely a stray remark from Moore in a well-known British music paper than a DJ's spirited championing of his favourite new band that was likely to cause offence.

Thanks to a fleet-fingered performance at 1969's era-defining Woodstock festival, Lee had recently acquired the title 'Fastest Guitar in the West,' his blazing pentatonic scales on the likes of 'I'm Going Home' marking him out as the Hermes of six-stringers. 'They used to call me "Captain Speedy Fingers",' he later laughed, 'But I didn't take it all that seriously.' However, since Lee's coronation another, perhaps even speedier young player from Belfast had surfaced. 'A precocious talent, Gary Moore . . . [is] a major rival for Alvin Lee's "Fastest Guitar in the West" title,' wrote *NME*'s Nick Logan shortly before Moore and Skid Row departed for their first American tour. No great harm there, one might have thought. But then Moore threw his tuppence worth in. 'I'm just very lucky that I can play like that but although it's fast it's still got taste,' the Ulsterman told *NME*. 'Whereas people like Alvin Lee can play fast but it's just completely tasteless . . .' Oh dear. 'Ah, that "fastest guitar"

8   A class act with one of rock guitar's more recognisable and influential tones, Leslie West sadly passed away on 23 December 2020.

thing!' laughed Paul Scully. 'Well, at the time, I really think Brush was pushing Gary to be the fastest "gunslinger" of them all.'

Indeed, when Moore had started out on the Belfast concert circuit with The Beat Boys and The Barons, he was by all accounts a particularly lyrical player, with an emphasis on melody no doubt enhanced by constantly listening to the likes of George Harrison and Hank Marvin. Yet as the music around him became more progressive, demand grew for a nimbler approach. Moore was more than ready to take up the challenge. By leaving behind the heavy gauge strings and prohibitive actions of those early Framus and Rosetti guitars in favour of the buttery neck and lighter wires of his 1966 Fender Telecaster, Moore had already discovered that he could play fast. Frighteningly fast, actually.[9] 'His speed on guitar,' continued Paul Scully. 'It really was astounding.'

As the age of the guitar hero began to properly coalesce around Clapton, Beck, and Hendrix, Moore found those flying fingers of his were ready to be put to good use by the right band. Or, in this case, band leader. 'When I [joined] Skid Row, [Brush] wanted me to be the fastest guitar player in the world,' Moore later told *Guitar*. 'And I didn't realise how fast I was playing. People think I concentrated on speed but I really didn't know what I was doing. Then,' he added, 'I just couldn't slow down. That was a problem.' In the scheme of things there were worse problems to have, and despite his protestations, compelling evidence to suggest Moore actually revelled in his reputation. 'Oh God, yes!' said a close friend at the time. 'Gary knew he was fast then and he practised playing fast to get even faster! He knew all about Alvin Lee. Of course, he did. He loved all that 'fastest gun' stuff! He was a guitarist, for God's sake!'

---

9 The secret of Gary Moore's speed on guitar has been a matter of some debate for years, with theories ranging from the likely (lots of practise) and plausible (being left-handed gave him more finger strength/dexterity on a right-handed instrument) to the downright fanciful (devils, crossroads, things of that nature). However, one idea does resonate more than others: Moore was unusual in that he often used his middle and index fingers together when playing fast solos/passages, especially on the A, D and G strings. In this respect, he was similar to another lightning fingered player, the gypsy jazz great Django Reinhardt. That said, while Reinhardt employed the technique out of necessity (his fingers were damaged in a fire), Moore just seemed happy to play that way.

Luckily, Alvin Lee appeared not to have read Moore's withering assessment of his speed or how he used it in *NME* when Skid Row came to support Ten Years After at Chicago's Coliseum Syndrome in November 1970. In fact, if reports are to be believed, he and Gary got on rather well, the older musician probably recognising a kindred spirit, or at least someone with similar burn marks on the tips of his fingers.[10] By watching Moore on stage, Lee may have had a small glimpse as to where the future of rock guitar was headed. Like Lee, Moore used many tropes of the classic blues player – the hammer-ons and pull-offs, the scorching vibrato and wild overbends. But Moore's choice of notes and solo lines were not exclusively reliant on standard pentatonic scales, his ideas being drawn as much from jazz, classical, Celtic and even Indian forms as they were from the Mississippi Delta or southside Chicago.

In this respect, Moore's playing was now growing more in line with the decade ahead than the sixties' blues rock sounds that originally inspired him. Spiky, supercharged and capable of displays of astounding technical prowess, Moore's approach presaged a new brand of electric guitar hero intent on driving the instrument into realms of hitherto unexplored complexity. Of course, like Alvin Lee before him, he would get used to having his position regularly challenged by another set of young guns intent on staking their own claim to his crown. And occasionally, it would hurt. But in late 1970 at least, there were few rock guitarists capable of touching Moore in terms of speed, skill or craft. 'For me,' he later said, 'it was always about playing the most exciting guitar I could. That was it. That was all I ever wanted to do.' Faster, faster, faster, faster, indeed.

---

10 Though Moore appeared to pillory Alvin Lee in September 1970's *NME*, some youthful playing to the gallery might well have been involved. In fact, Gary was initially quite the fan of Alvin, first seeing the guitarist in Belfast during the late autumn of 1967 when he reportedly appeared 'on a school roof,' and once again in May 1969 when Skid Row shared a bill with Ten Years After in Dublin. Indeed, during later years, Moore and Lee became good pals, namechecking each other in various interviews and even jamming together at parties. 'He's a very fine, technically gifted musician who can play practically anything,' Alvin told *Guitarist*. In short, no gunfights to be found here.

CHAPTER SIX

The Rocky Road
Out Of Dublin

Gary Moore and Skid Row's introduction to the joys of the American touring life came to an abrupt halt soon after supporting Alvin Lee and Ten Years After, when a proposed date at New York's Fillmore East was cancelled, leaving the band stranded at Boston airport with nowhere to go but home. For road manager Ted Carroll, it seemed as good a time as any to hand in his notice. '[The US tour] was all 35, 40-minute sets, fantastic bills and very lively. [But,] to be honest, though the band were good, technically brilliant, in fact, I didn't really like the tunes. In fact, generally speaking, I hated them. I was also a bit annoyed that Brush was forcing Gary to play this incredibly complex music. I mean, "Don't play three notes when you can play 16. Or better still, 17!" So . . .' Suffice to say, when group and crew arrived back at Heathrow, Carroll went in search of new adventures. In due course, others would follow.

Upon their return, Skid Row had twelve British dates lined up to take them to Christmas, and their first real break in months, before it all started again in 1971. For Moore, this should have been a grand time. With a UK Top 30 placing for the group's debut LP and an Irish tour ready to come in January, things were surely looking up. Further, proving conclusively that he did more than just play guitar 24 hours a day, Moore was going to be a father. Having overcome their difficulties earlier in the year, Sylvia Keogh was now living with Moore in London and five months pregnant. All in all, a time for celebration. Yet when Moore returned home to Belfast for the Christmas holidays, he was greeted with the news that his mother Winnie had left the family home and was staying with her sister Ellen in Somerset. She had also taken Moore's brothers and sisters with her, leaving his dad Bobby alone in the house.

Of course, Gary knew that at times his parents' marriage wasn't perfect. In later life, he would intimate as much and more in one of his most autobiographical songs, the emotionally raw 'Business As Usual'. Yet back in December 1970, the suddenness of the split and the lack of warning around it seemed to genuinely unnerve him. In fact, according to his friends, Moore was affected deeply by the events, subsequently becoming less trusting and more jealous in his own romantic relationships as a result. Though such a reaction might seem extreme, it is worth remembering Gary was still only a teenager when the break-up happened. In the face of any sudden emotional upheaval, all things become possible.

Moore's close friend Johnny Duhan was one of the first to see how he chose to cope with the break-up of his parents' marriage. 'Gary took me to his home in Belfast for an overnight trip to show me where he came from. It was a real eye-opener. I remember going into the house and feeling that things weren't quite right. I think his parents had just broken up. It felt very dismal and dark and it was probably because of the tensions in the house.'

'Now,' Duhan continued, 'when I was growing up, my mother was bi-polar and would sometimes [be greatly affected by her condition], so I understood [such tensions in a house].' But the thing that really struck me about Gary was that the first thing he did when he got home was not introduce me to [anyone at the house]. Instead, he took me around the corner to his neighbour's house and introduced me to the mother of his friend. I remember this woman was mad about him, almost like he was her own son. I think he did that to show me that there was some kind of stability, some kind of normality in his life and that people respected him.'

Though Moore's version of 'normal' had been substantially re-written by recent events, his sense of humour did not fail him. Keen to keep an eye on his father, Moore returned to Belfast when he could, and he often brought friends. 'Oh, Philip Lynott loved Belfast,' he later told the BBC. 'He'd come and stay at my dad's house. The girl next door even fell in love with him when he stayed there.'

However, if Lynott thought his sojourns to Castleview Road might lead to a little northern romance, he had another thing coming. Knowing that Bobby Moore liked nothing better than to have a chat when he returned from the Queen's Ballroom on a Saturday night, Gary would make sure he and Philip were there to greet him, only to bail on Lynott within minutes. 'Philip used to say to me "[Promise you] won't leave me with your fucking father, Gary!"' he chuckled to author Stuart Bailie. 'But the second my dad came in I'd go up to my old bedroom and leave them to it.'

The events of Christmas 1970 would impact on Gary Moore's life for years to come. Yet, come early 1971, and he was back at the coalface for an Irish tour with Skid Row that at the time must have felt like merciful release. The majority of Moore's days and nights were to be kept busy until at least early summer. In addition to a stack of concert dates, he and the band were on the move again to a new home in north London. Again found by Ted Carroll, who after leaving the employ of Skid Row was busy putting together plans for a record-selling business, the house was located in leafy Belsize Park.

'Myself, Frank Murray and Paul Scully moved to 31 Belsize Avenue around the end of February 1971,' confirmed Carroll. 'And at that stage, Gary and his pregnant girlfriend Sylvia turned up, and they moved in too. Most of Granny's Intentions were there before us. It was a huge house with over 20 rooms, individually as "bedsitters", and really, [we took] it over.' By May, there was one more resident at number thirty-one, after Sylvia gave birth to Moore's daughter, Saoirse – her name meaning 'freedom' in Gaelic. Moore, who doted on the child, had no doubts about asking Johnny Duhan to be godfather. 'Yes, I stood for Gary's child Saoirse, though I wasn't actually there [at the baptism],' Duhan confirmed in 2020. 'Someone stood in for me. I felt sorry about that, because had I been there, I'd have kept up connections better.'

Keeping up a solid connection with Gary Moore at the time was no easy task. In addition to his duties as a new father, by mid-1971 Moore, Brush Shiels and Noel Bridgeman were busy cutting their second album, for which they had been granted a whopping 34 hours of recording time. 'Well, we ended up calling the LP *34 Hours*,' quipped Shiels, 'because that's how long we had to record it.' Though Clifford Davis was back in the producer's chair, he had at least the good sense to bring a top-class assistant along for the ride.

Beginning his engineering career with the one/two punch of Jeff Beck's *Beck-Ola* and Fleetwood Mac's *Then Play On*, 21-year-old Martin Birch had consolidated an excellent start by working the faders on both Deep Purple's ambitious classical/rock crossover *Concerto for Group and Orchestra* and its follow-up *In Rock*.

Already on the way to a notable four decades as a producer of near unrivalled distinction[1], Birch would at least make a real stab at capturing Skid Row's peculiar chutzpah on eight-track tape.

Regrettably, while *34 Hours* sounded clearer than the band's muddy-sounding debut, the album was blessed with all the same strengths and plagued by all the same weaknesses as its predecessor, making for another wildly uneven experience. As before, things opened with a bang on 'Night of the Warm Witch'. A moody exercise in fusing long, King Crimson-style instrumental passages and Hendrix-like chord progressions, the song's twists and turns were genuinely exciting to behold. More, Gary's spooky wah and volume pedal-assisted interludes were a pleasure all their own, though the decision to release such an uncommercial track as the LP's first single remained truly baffling. Still, 'Go, I'm Never Gonna

---

1 Over the course of 40 years, Martin Birch engineered or produced some of rock music's finest LPs, including releases by Deep Purple (*Machine Head* and *Made In Japan*), Wishbone Ash (*Argus*), Rainbow (*Rising*) and Black Sabbath (*Heaven and Hell*). He was also at the helm for nine Iron Maiden albums, from 1981's *Killers* to 1992's *Fear of the Dark*. A genuine talent, Birch died aged 71 in August 2020.

Let You (Parts 1 & 2)' also presented its fair share of musical thrills, with the trio demonstrating all those nights on the road had created a 'beautiful madness' to their rhythmic interplay.

It was that same sense of righteous bedlam that once again threatened to undermine Skid Row's progress, as sections of *34 Hours* again fell prey to endless instrumental gymnastics. 'First Thing in the Morning' was a case in point. Offering little more than a collection of riffs played at breakneck speed, it sounded as if the trio were being paid by the note. 'Love Story (Parts 1-4)' also ploughed a distressingly familiar furrow. All elbows, knees and odd angles, it was more akin to a fever dream than a musical composition. But then, that was the thing with Skid Row. So wrapped up were the band in their own adventures, it sometimes sounded as if they didn't care if anyone out there was actually listening.

Or perhaps not. For where *34 Hours* had the edge on Skid Row's debut LP was in the band's occasional compromise in the direction of melody. Whereas for some critics, *Skid* had been one long riff, the presence of 'Lonesome Still' and 'Mar' on *34 Hours* conclusively proved that when they allowed themselves, Shiels and the group could write as tuneful a song as anyone else. Leaning towards country rock and reminiscent of Shiels' beloved Byrds and Flying Burrito Brothers, 'Lonesome Still' found Moore again turning on the style with some mock pedal steel guitars (actually a bottle slide and volume pedal used in combination), while Shiels channelled his inner Hank Williams with a gentle, knowing vocal.

If, however, one had the sneaking suspicion an element of pastiche had been allowed to creep into 'Lonesome Still' – at one point, Brush nearly starts yodelling – 'Mar', on the other hand, was played straight down the line. A touching love song from Shiels to his wife Margaret, 'Mar' featured Shiels on rhythm guitar and road warrior Paul Scully filling in on bass, both in the studio and later in concert. "Mar'? Well, I was thrown completely in the bloody deep end,' Scully laughed in 2020. 'They'd just finished recording *34 Hours* and Brush wanted to do 'Mar' live. Now, it had an acoustic guitar part that he wanted to play, so he threw the bass at me, and said "Paul, you're playing that!" So, my debut gig – in fact, my only time on stage – was . . . at the National Stadium playing 'Mar' in front of 2,500 people. Oh man, I was shitting myself.'

With its cover sleeve featuring a rickety photograph taken at the group's appearance on German music TV series *Beat Club*, and some chatty sleeve notes confirming they were all still very much 'the best of friends,' Skid Row's *34 Hours* hit the stores in the late summer of 1971. Unfortunately, unlike *Skid* before it, the LP did not chart in the UK, causing some consternation among the trio. Any disappointment felt by Moore, Shiels and Bridgeman was subsumed by another heavy round of touring, including a return to the States, where the trio were now promoted by Premier Talent Management. Run by Frank Barsalona and his assistant Barbara Skydel, Premier Talent was the gold standard for promoting US rock acts and having them behind the group was a real boon. 'We were told, "The next time you go to America, you're going to be huge,"' Shiels later confirmed to writer Colin Harper, 'and there was a very good chance we would be.' In a parallel dimension, that might well have happened. Sadly, in the one Skid Row inhabited, the facts proved somewhat different. On their first trip to the USA, enthusiasm for the group's live shows had been high, at least among more serious rock fans. But for whatever reason, CBS Records had been reluctant to get behind the band in the States. Often dodging requests for money, the label had let Skid Row run largely on their own steam throughout the trio's first US tour, and despite new interest from Premier Talent, seemed unsure of backing them to the hilt on this occasion too. As a consequence, Skid shuffled across Canada for a gig here and there, before picking up some club dates, support slots and festivals in America. For every date supporting the tub-thumping Cactus or Caribbean rockers Osibisa in Los Angeles or Cincinnati, there was the galling prospect of facing half-empty rooms in Salt Lake City and San Diego.

The reality of Skid Row's tenuous position Stateside was brought home on 5 August 1971, when the trio performed a set at LA's Whisky a Go Go. Some time after Moore's solo rendition of Robert Johnson's 'Ramblin' On My Mind', which found him not only singing and playing guitar, but banging out a rhythm on Noel's bass drum too, a shout reportedly went up from the audience requesting 'Paddy McGinty's Goat'.

The cry for this old novelty tune about an irritable Irish buck came from a table comprised of various members of Led Zeppelin, then arguably the biggest rock band in the world and surely in no need of an introduction here. Yet, rather than start a fight over insults to their perceived 'Irishness', Shiels et al. invited Zep's singer Robert Plant and drummer John Bonham on stage for a jam. Obviously 'pissed as rats,' Plant supposedly headed for the drum kit while Bonham grabbed the microphone. The result was a truly horrendous rendition of the quartet's then best-known tune 'Whole Lotta Love'[2], with a little bit of Muddy Waters' 'Got My Mojo Working' thrown in for good measure.

Events took a surreal turn afterwards, when the Zep camp learned that no accommodation had been arranged for Skid Row or their road crew while in the City of Angels. Stomping up the cash for them all to stay with him at the Hyatt Hotel[3], 'Bonzo' spent the rest of the night talking drums with Bridgeman while yet more drink was taken. It's a great story. One for the grandchildren, certainly. But it also underlined the harsh truth that outside Ireland, Skid Row were still classified as 'a muso's band' rather than a genuine commercial proposition. Treated with apparent indifference by their record company, sometimes reliant on the kindness of relative strangers for their sleeping arrangements and propping themselves up with booze and industrial strength coffee as a result, Skid Row's situation was far from ideal. It was a fact not lost on Gary Moore. '[At that time] we'd got to a point of doing 20-minute versions of 'Johnny Be Goode', getting drunk and playing as fast as we could.' This was not fighting talk.

After a further spate of cancelled dates and more financial uncertainty, Moore, Shiels and Bridgeman returned to London in September 1971 to lick their wounds and contemplate their future. Despite all the recent disappointments, Bridgeman still missed the States. 'They had real orange

---

2 For those brave souls wishing to hear 'Skid Zeppelin' in action at the Whisky, a bootleg recording can be found on YouTube. Brace yourselves.

3 Officially titled the 'Hyatt Continental' – but nicknamed the 'Riot House' because of what often went on there – Hyatt House was Led Zeppelin's hotel of choice when staying in Los Angeles.

juice in America,' he later quipped. 'I cried when we had to leave.' Unfortunately, there were more tears in the recording studio during early December, when, after having laid down half a dozen songs for their third LP[4], sessions were abandoned following Moore's decision to leave the group. Tellingly, it was Bridgeman rather than Shiels that Gary broke the news to. 'Well, Brush was always a very dominant, very powerful character,' confirmed Paul Scully. 'But you know, someone had to be in charge, get the gigs, organise the songs, get things done. [Maybe] Gary fell under his wing a little too much [in the early days], I think. Just my opinion, but.' But no more, it seemed. After a half-hearted attempt by Bridgeman and then Shiels to change his mind, Moore was gone.

When asked what drove the decision to leave, Gary Moore was his usual blunt self – his answers telling and straight to the point. 'I left Skid Row because I wasn't happy with the music anymore and because I felt it was time to do something new,' he said. 'I think a lot of the hassle was that Skid Row was playing too fast and you can't very well get a good sound when there is too much speed going on.' Evidently, this was a man with no real axe to grind with his bandmates, but more the music they played: a dark, sometimes impenetrable music, and one that would be a hard sell in any era.

For a while at least, it looked like Skid Row might survive Moore's departure. After a guitar player or two tried their luck deputising for him, a promising replacement was found in 19-year-old, Cardiff-born Paul Chapman. Nimble-fingered, hard-drinking and a quite brilliant soloist when a tune truly interested him, Chapman had the goods to fit right in and play right out. Yet, despite overdubbing an 'LP's worth' of Moore's original parts at London's De Lane Lea studios, the young guitarist was soon unemployed again[5], when after battling a variety of

---

4   Songs recorded at this time included 'Morning Star Avenue', 'Girl Called Winter' and 'Crystal Ball'. A CD containing these tunes and several more besides was released by Essential Music in 1990, under the title *Gary Moore/Brush Shiels/Noel Bridgeman*. Ironically, it contains some of the better music Skid Row recorded.
5   Chapman was too good to stay unemployed for long. Following his short tenure with Skid Row for which he received 'a couple of thousand quid,' 'Tonka' – so named for his seeming indestructability in the face of alcohol and anything else thrown his way – linked up with cult Welsh quintet Lone Star before joining wayward, if wonderful, hard rockers UFO in late 1978 for series of fine albums. A great guitarist who could 'bend a note to the moon and back,' Chapman passed away in June 2020.

continuing money problems Skid Row were forced to throw in the towel. Though there were to be several minor returns for the band in later years, back in July 1972 it looked like last orders at the bar.

'When Gary left, we couldn't really replace him,' Shiels later confirmed. 'Paul Chapman was a great guitar player, but . . . we'd run out of money and energy. It was impossible and there was really nothing we could do.' In truth, it was a real shame. Just three or so years earlier, Skid Row were odds-on to be the group to finally put Ireland, both North and South, on the international map. Instead, in their own contrary way, they had laid the foundations for much that was to follow. Still, Shiels could see the funny side. 'What do I miss most about Skid Row?' he once laughed. 'My hair . . .'

A noble failure, Skid Row had nonetheless given Gary Moore, Brush Shiels and Noel Bridgeman much to be thankful for. For one, few their age had travelled so far or so fast, even if they were seeing the world 'from the back of a bloody Avis box van'. Yet, more seriously, they had been granted something only the most privileged of musicians could claim as their own: the chance to play without fear. Thanks to the 'strange, telepathic understanding' the trio enjoyed, Skid Row had indulged themselves on an almost comical level, safe in the knowledge that whenever one of them looked about to stumble, the other two were there to pick them up again. And even if he had grown tired of the instrumental pyrotechnics, Gary would seldom play with such utter freedom or sheer abandon again.

Of course, by leaving the band behind, Moore's real work was only just beginning. Part of a gang for over two years, Moore could always rely on Shiels to do much of the heavy lifting, from writing lunatic riffs to sorting out what was for dinner. However, he had recently seen what might be achieved beyond the confines of the group. Although he'd been drummed out for his sub-standard singing voice, Philip Lynott's new trio, Thin Lizzy, were threatening to go further and faster than Skid Row ever did. With such things in play, perhaps the ever-ambitious Moore could take on the mantle of a leader too.

'Gary's connection to Philip Lynott was always very strong and Thin Lizzy were by then beginning their rise,' reasoned Paul Scully. 'So, I think Gary might have, at least in his subconscious, been exploring the possibility of fronting his own band for a while [before leaving Skid Row]. You see, like Philip, Gary always had his eye on the international stage. And to be honest, it'd be no surprise to anyone [back then] if it were those two who ended up as stars.' Suffice to say, like Lynott, Moore was up for the challenge.

A Postscript of Sorts

If one were looking to capture the sense of camaraderie and creativity of Gary Moore's adventures as a young man in Dublin, then popping into Eamonn Andrews' recording studio during the spring of 1970 was a good place to start. After securing an album deal via Island Records and releasing one of the era's finer folk LPs with 1969's glorious *Kip of the Serenes*, Dr Strangely Strange were threatening to become genuinely popular, their fanbase now extending beyond the basement of Slattery's to larger folk clubs and concert halls both in Ireland and the UK. The only trouble was, the bigger the rooms got, the harder it was to be heard.

'Well, we'd been playing slightly bigger venues and even done a gig at The Lyceum, where the line-up was Santana, Elton John and us, all on a revolving stage,' laughed Tim Goulding. 'I mean, a harmonium and a few acoustic guitars aren't quite the match for Santana and his three drummers sounding like a locomotive coming down the track. We didn't quite cut the mustard and we knew it. So, it was time to get some electric bass and drums.' To help them get some of that electricity on vinyl for their second LP, The Strangelies called on Gary Moore.

As was often the case with recording albums in the early seventies, time was money and money was short. As a consequence, Dr Strangely Strange had only two days – 31 March/1 April – to use Gary wisely and well. Thankfully, Island Records had provided the trio with venerable producer Joe Boyd[6] and another rising star in the form of Fairport Convention

---

6 A Harvard graduate who numbered Muddy Waters, Coleman Hawkins and Sister Rosetta Tharpe among his friends, Joe Boyd not only opened London's most famous underground music club UFO in 1966, but also went on to produce Pink Floyd, Fairport Convention, The Incredible String Band, Nick Drake, John Martyn and REM. Quite the CV.

drummer Dave Mattacks. It turned out Mattacks' skills stretched far beyond the kit in the corner. 'Dave Mattacks was amazing,' said Tim Booth. 'Goulding's electric piano was set up . . . and Mattacks said "If you give me the chord charts, I'll just run through it on the piano." Well, we looked at each other and said "That can't be right, can it? Drummers don't play pianos, do they?" Well, indeed he could . . .' Mattacks was equally impressed with The Strangelies. 'After hearing their music, I thought they had something so good and different going on . . . plus they were such a super bunch of blokes.'

The resulting sessions produced *Heavy Petting*, an LP of real distinction and warmth, the likes of 'I Will Lift Up Mine Eyes', 'When Adam Delved' and 'Jove Was at Home' summing up the appeal of The Strangelies and why they still remain such a cult band. Yet, it does them no disservice to say that Gary Moore's contribution elevates the album to a different level. Indeed, Tim Booth, Tim Goulding and Ivan Pawle would be quick to agree.

'We were very happy with *Heavy Petting*,' said Booth. 'It had a new sense of "electric folk", and I still think that was some of the best playing Gary did at that time. It was both melodic and thoughtful, with plenty of space between the notes. No speeding up or showing off, just decorating our ideas with the most sympathetic hand. I loved him for that. Any time Gary played with us, that's what he did.' To Dave Mattacks, Moore's ability to bend his playing so easily in in the direction of The Strangelies' willowy folk was a delightful surprise. 'Though it was apparent Gary was . . . a fine player, I had a few doubts about the aesthetics of his style melding with the band's music. But everyone just made it work.'

Whether strumming around the beat on 'Mary Malone of Moscow' or cleverly embellishing the melody of 'Summer Breeze', Moore was obviously enjoying the company of friends, even if there was some good-natured ribbing going on too. 'Gary put this incredible energy into that album,' said Goulding. 'I mean, Booth says it all on 'I Gave My Love an Apple' when he shouts out "Step along, Garibaldi Moorhen!" To be honest, Gary didn't like being called "Garibaldi Moorhen". But he let us off.'

There was one song that stood out. All wistful chords and yearning lyricism, 'Sign on My Mind' might have been written by Ivan Pawle, but it was made for Gary Moore. 'Gary's solo on 'Sign of my Mind' was just so spontaneous,' said Tim Goulding. 'It was like someone speaking . . .

a train of thought developing as it went along. I genuinely think that's one of the great guitar solos.' Pawle agreed. 'Ah, Gary. His playing on 'Sign on My Mind' was just perfect.' Or damn close, anyway.

Inevitably, the day job came calling. 'The last number we recorded for *Heavy Petting* was 'I Gave My Love an Apple', you know, "Garibaldi Moorhen!"' said Tim Booth. 'Anyway, I was going to play the bass on it and we were doing a run-through for Dave Mattacks when Brush and Noel turned up. They were in a hurry to get to a gig miles away, so Brush says "Come on Garro, we have to go!" Gary says, "We're just running this song through," at which point Brush asks me, "Have you got the bass part down?" I say "We're nearly there." Brush looks at me, says "How does it go?", I play a bit, Brush grabs the bass, says "C'mon Gary", and they just played it there and then. They had it down perfectly by the second take.' In keeping with Shiels' faster, faster, faster mantra, a matter of hours later, Skid Row were on stage and Moore was once again busy trying to a rip a hole in the fabric of time.

Though he doubtless had a romantic streak, Gary Moore was seldom given to reverie or nostalgia, preferring to talk about the here and now rather than risk becoming lost in the past. However, that attitude softened when it came to his adventures in Dublin, with the musician more than happy to wax lyrical about Skid Row, The Strangelies, Philip Lynott and the other abiding friendships he made. Perhaps it was the excitement of being a young man in a new city. Or maybe the feeling that everything was in front of him. Endless possibilities, wide-open spaces. A time when music wasn't yet a business, nor falling in love quite so complex. No real troubles and everything to play for, then.

It would seldom be this easy again.

PART TWO:

1972 – 1979: Muso, Rock Star, Gone

'Of course, I wanted success. But not at any price . . .'
                                            Gary Moore

CHAPTER SEVEN

Every Warrior
Needs A Sword

When music first came calling for Gary Moore back in early sixties Belfast, he had been spoilt for choice. From The Shadows and The Beatles to The Stones, The Kinks and The Who, good music was everywhere and it just kept on coming. By the middle of the decade things had progressed again, as pop transformed itself into ever more strange and beautiful shapes, and the twisting of old blues tunes offered eager young musicians escape routes into new worlds of improvisation. By now, Moore was also part of the story, his prowess on guitar seeing him clamber from club to club and band to band in an effort to get noticed.

His moment finally came in Dublin during the autumn of 1968 when he was spotted on stage by someone who could harness his talent and place it in the right setting. From learning 'Wonderful Land' to joining 'Ireland's biggest band' in six breathless years. But it was now 1972, The Beatles were gone, Hendrix was dead and Eric Clapton was busy chasing dragons around the Surrey countryside. More, Gary had recently parted ways with Skid Row, Dublin was a fading, if delightful memory, and the guitarist was facing an uncertain future in a musical landscape once again undergoing seismic change. According to Dr Strangely Strange's Tim Goulding, '1971, 1972 was a turning point, generationally and musically . . . The velvet curtains that had been turned into flares were gone, and people were now wearing leather jackets. Velvet turned to leather. That's what happened, really. People and things became harder and darker.'

As the world around him prepared itself for a rollercoaster ride of miners' strikes, crashing shares and skyrocketing unemployment, Gary Moore got on with the business of forming a new band. In this he was aided by a £15,000 advance, brokered by manager Clifford Davis from CBS Records, who were backing his latest endeavour. Moore's first recruit to the cause was Chuck Carpenter, a solid rhythm/lead guitarist he had met in the States while on tour with Skid Row in the autumn of 1971 and subsequently brought home with him. With hindsight, engaging Carpenter was an interesting choice. First, it hinted that Moore was exploring the idea of leaving Skid Row months before the deed was actually done.[1] As importantly, acquiring a second guitar underlined the impact seeing The Allman Brothers had made on him two years before.

To flesh out the remaining vacancies, Moore and Carpenter headed back to Dublin in early February 1972, where they reportedly spent several days drinking, eating and fighting their way across the city before finally getting on with the job at hand. That said, when Moore did engage, progress was swift and fairly sure. Over the coming weeks, they recruited moustachioed ex-Freak Show and Ironhorse drummer Pearse Kelly on drums and former Creatures/Mellow Candle Frank Boylan on bass guitar. At this point, all those involved apparently decamped to a farmhouse procured by Clifford Davis in rural Mayo to begin work on being a group. With few distractions – there was only a pub, petrol station and post office for supplies within a mile of their temporary home – Moore and his crew were free to work on a combination of new songs and a few radically revised blues standards.

By the time the newly christened 'Gary Moore Band' made their nationwide debut supporting classical-folk-jazz rockers Curved Air on

---

1 Some have it that Moore actually made the decision to leave Skid Row following a post-gig argument between Paul Scully and Brush Shiels in Salt Lake City towards the end of the 1971 American tour. Whatever the case, Scully left the employ of the band soon after, with recent road crew recruit Pete Cummins taking over his duties.

their spring UK tour, the quartet had swelled to a quintet with the introduction of keyboardist Jan Schelhaas. A likeable, down-to-earth Liverpudlian, Schelhaas had started his own recording career in 1968 as a bassist with cult Merseybeat soulsters Bernie & The Buzz Band. When that group folded, he switched to organ and formed the National Head Band instead. Cutting an album, 1971's *Albert One*, with Yes producer Eddie Offord, the critics were encouraging but the LP didn't connect with a wide audience, leaving Jan potentially unemployed.

Not for long. Schelhaas was part of Clifford Davis's managerial stable, and Schelhaas soon found himself called up for a spot with Gary Moore. He didn't have to wear a suit and tie to get the job. 'Well, there was no "formal" audition,' Jan laughed. 'Clifford said to me, "Gary needs a keyboard player. Why don't you go down and see him?" So, I popped along to an impromptu gig he was doing (with Chuck Carpenter), and it was great. Very raw, very energetic two guitar stuff. And I thought "I like this," but, I mean, what do you say? "Hi Gary, I'm your new keyboard player." Or "Hi Gary, Clifford Davis sent me. He told me to tell you I'm a genius!" Thankfully, there was no need for any of that. Gary turned out to be a nice guy, we got on well and took it from there.'

In fact, Schelhaas got on with the guitarist so well that when Moore and Sylvia Keogh had another falling out, this time resulting in her and daughter Saoirse leaving for several months, it was Jan that moved into their flat in Belsize Park. 'Yes, after Gary split up with Sylvia, he ended up sharing the flat with me,' Schelhaas confirmed. 'That house was officially supposed to be like a bed and breakfast, or hotel. But the manager got around [that] by putting a bowl of cornflakes and some milk in our basement. In reality, it was a block of flats masquerading as a guest house, and half the band were there.' Half of Moore's new band, and another, unwanted visitor too. 'Ah, the rat,' laughed Jan. 'Well, it might have been a rat. We could hear this rustling on the paper, but you didn't really want to get up and have a look to find out what was making the noise.'

For the most part, however, everyone seemed to be in love with 31 Belsize Avenue. 'We were young, energetic, the world was our oyster and it was an amazing house in an amazing area,' said one-time resident

Paul Scully. 'In the thirties, all kinds of famous writers and artists had lived in and around Belsize Park, and there was still a real atmosphere to it. Of course, it helped that we were all exploring mind-expanding substances at the time, too. We'd head up to Hampstead Heath or Parliament Hill and just walk through the wilderness and woods. There was a sense of spirituality, if that's the right word, to it all.' And with The Strangelies' Ivan Pawle temporarily joining the cast at No 31 in mid-1972, a sense of humour too. 'Yeah,' laughed Scully, 'Ivan would be throwing sticks and consulting the I Ching as to what he was going to do that day!'

Following the opening spot with Curved Air that saw The Gary Moore Band appearing in locations as varied as Aberdeen, Chatham, Plymouth and Brighton throughout April and early May 1972, the group at last got a chance to strike out on their own. Unfortunately, the journeys were seldom glamourous. 'Standard thing, really,' Jan Schelhaas recalled, 'travelling around in an old van, the band in the back with the sleeping bags and all the gear. Very odd mix of gigs, though. We did a few little gigs [in the UK], then off to Germany for a few more before heading back again to London and The Marquee.' It was at the capital's most famous sweat pit and another concert at the nearby Lyceum in mid-July that London punters finally got 'up close and personal' with Moore's latest project.

As expected, he had lost none of his gift for exploring diverse musical settings, with the band's predominantly blues-rock-driven set also including passages of jazz, hard rock and even country. Nor had Moore dialled down the instrumental virtuosity, though his forays into hyper-speed were now neatly grounded by the less busy rhythm section of Boylan and Kelly. Further, with Schelhaas and Carpenter, Moore had found two potential foils who could bring both colour and shade to those knuckle-grinding riffs, these new harmonies a pleasant addition after the dark melodic mists that typified Skid Row.

And if the band's few original compositions such as 'Time to Heal' and 'Boogie My Way Back Home' were heavily bolstered by covers, at least they were good ones. From a mean and moody version of John Lee Hooker's 1966 tear-jerking 'Serve You Right to Suffer' to a Chicago-style mauling of Big Bill Broonzy's classic 'Key to the Highway',[2] it was good to hear Gary revisiting the blues with such vim and vigour. All in all, promising stuff. Along with Messrs Carpenter, Schelhaas, Boylan and Kelly, there was another addition to Gary Moore's band in the summer of 1972: its provenance distinguished, its quality impeccable, its sound perhaps unrivalled. 'The Greeny,' Moore later said, 'is the best guitar I ever played.' Unfortunately, how it arrived in Gary's hands was a story involving one of the sadder abdications in rock music.

On 20 May 1970, only a matter of months after introducing Moore and Skid Row to his manager Clifford Davis, Peter Green left Fleetwood Mac. It had been coming. Though Green's talent as a songwriter and musician was a key driver in pushing the group towards stardom, none of the Mac's subsequent success seemed to make him particularly happy. In fact, as the band grew, so Green's lyrics grew darker, with the sad-eyed introspection of 1969's 'Man of the World' being the first real hint at some as-yet unspoken psychic disturbance.

By the end of that year matters had progressed well beyond the lyric sheet. Allegedly using both LSD and mescaline, Green had also taken to wearing Jesus-like white robes both on and off stage. As worryingly, at least for his fellow band members, he appeared to feel guilty about Fleetwood Mac's growing riches and began talking up giving away the group's earnings. 'I had conversations with Peter around that time and he was obsessive about us not making money, wanting us to give it all away,' Mick Fleetwood later confirmed to the BBC. 'And I'd say, "Well you can do it, I don't want to do that, and that doesn't make me a bad person . . ."'

While his behaviours remained occasionally perplexing, Peter Green's mental well-being was not deemed a serious issue until he hit what bandmate John McVie called 'a fork in the road' at a party outside Munich in March 1970. Swept up by a group of 'German aristo-commune types,' Green was given an unknown substance (possibly an extremely strong variant of lysergic acid) and 'really wasn't the same afterwards'.

---

2   It's likely that Moore became familiar with 'Key to the Highway' after hearing Eric Clapton cover it on Derek & The Dominos' 1970's *Layla and Other Assorted Love Songs*, an album recorded just before EC withdrew from the music scene and into a protracted period of heroin addiction.

Though Green appeared initially to rally following the incident, his decision to leave Fleetwood Mac was made within days and enacted within weeks. According to Gary Moore, he was one of the first to know of Green's choice and subsequent decision to also pull out of producing Skid Row's second LP. 'One day I went round his house and he said, "Oh, let's go for a drive",' Moore told *Guitarist*'s Dave Mead. 'We were driving along and he said, "I'm leaving the band. I've had enough." I was amazed that he was telling me, because no one knew at the time.'

What happened next was equally surprising. Out one night at The Marquee, Moore again bumped into Green, though this time, the discussion turned to guitars. Or more specifically, one guitar. 'Well, after Peter left the Mac . . . he went through a very strange period, you know, getting rid of all his material possessions,' Moore later told *The Georgia Straight*'s Steve Newton. 'Anyway, the guitar that he had always used . . . was this '59 Gibson Les Paul. He'd used it with John Mayall – I mean, it [went] way back – and I'd seen him play it when I was 14 [at Club Rado]. I just thought, "Oh, if I could ever have a guitar like that." And he said, "Do you want to want to borrow that guitar of mine for a few days?"'

The guitar that had caught Gary Moore's eye and ear all those years ago was indeed a 1959 cherry burst Gibson Les Paul, and a rather special one at that. Bought by Green second-hand at Selmer's[3] some time in 1965/6 for £110, the guitar had a unique tone, likely due to the neck pick-up being fitted the wrong way around.[4] Because of this peculiarity, when both the rhythm (neck) and treble (bridge) pick-ups were engaged in the middle position, the Les Paul produced a haunting out-of-phase sound more akin to a Fender Stratocaster.[5]

---

3 Located on London's Charing Cross Road, Selmer's provided instruments for just about every aspiring guitar god throughout the sixties and early seventies. The Kinks' Dave Davies even worked there for a time.

4 A guitar pick-up is a transducer that senses mechanical vibrations produced by the string. It then converts them to an electrical signal which in turn can be amplified through a loudspeaker.

5 As with all such stories, there are competing theories as how exactly the Greeny's famous sound came about. One explanation puts it down to a simple factory defect, while another has it that when Peter took the Gibson into Selmer's for repair, the neck pick-up was incorrectly rewound, thus reversing its polarity. According to Peter himself, in an effort to make his guitar sound more like Eric Clapton's 'Blues Breaking' Les Paul, he removed

In Green's hands, this mutant tone was soon put to good use, first on Mayall's *A Hard Road* and then many Fleetwood Mac classics thereafter. 'It's the same guitar that Peter used when he wrote 'Albatross', 'Oh Well' and all those other hit songs,' Moore told *Guitar World* in 1987. Back in 1971, however, it was simply a guitar that Peter Green seemed happy to part with. 'Well, I went down and I picked it up [from his parents' house], and then a couple of days later he called me up and said, "You can have it if you want, if you want to buy it . . ."'

As extraordinarily tempting as Peter's offer was, Gary thought the cost for such a wondrous guitar would be too high for him, and said so. Green provided an intriguing solution. 'He said, "Sell your main guitar",' Moore remembered, 'and whatever you get for it, give that to me.' At the time, Moore's 'axe' was a late sixties SG – a serviceable enough instrument for sure, but not in the same league as the fine-boned Les Paul.

Yet Green persisted. In the end, Moore sold the SG for £160, but even then 'Peter only wanted . . . what he originally paid for it, which about £110, £120,' Gary later confirmed to *Vintage Guitar*. And that was what Peter Green ended up taking for the Gibson. 'It was ridiculous,' Moore later told *Guitar World*, 'because apart from the collectible value, it was a 1959 Les Paul. I mean, it was also *Peter Green's guitar*, just a fabulous instrument. But Peter had this thing. He wanted it to be as if we had swapped guitars.'

Having just done Gary Moore a planet-sized favour, Green now stepped out of the young guitarist's life for a while, following a road that would eventually lead to troubled times and some genuinely dark places. However, in 1972, no one knew of any such coming storms. In fact, all Moore was concerned about was how to protect his prized asset in the same way a warrior guards his sword. 'Well, when I got that guitar,' he told journalist Willie Moseley, 'my place didn't even have a lock on the door, so I used to sleep with it under my bed. God, I'd even take it to the movies.' While Jan Schelhaas did not recall any visits to the cinema with Moore and his Gibson, he was well aware of his flatmate's obsession

---

the pick-up and put it back in the wrong way around. However, that doesn't quite deal with the sticky wicket of reversed polarity. Probably best filed under 'Divine Mystery'.

with the guitar and where it came to rest. 'Oh yeah,' he said, 'Gary absolutely loved that guitar. Yes, he'd try others now and again, but he'd always come back to it and that 50-watt Marshall of his. [As far as] sleeping with the guitar under the bed . . . well, he might well have done. But there might have been a few other people under the bed too at the time! I mean, there wasn't even room for the rat.'

A charmed guitar with many stories yet to tell[6], 'the Greeny' accompanied Moore not only to bed, but also across the UK and Europe, as he and his group racked up the tour miles throughout 1972 and well into the following year. It was also during this period that Chuck Carpenter became the first casualty of the band, albeit in bizarre circumstances. 'Well, [it started when] we were going through customs in Germany at the border,' Jan Schelhaas confirmed, 'and we managed to drive a bit too close to a Portacabin. In fact, we knocked it off its [mount] with all the guards inside.' However, it wasn't poor driving or irked officials that did for Carpenter, just good, old-fashioned British bureaucracy. 'When we got back to Dover, the [border] guys wouldn't let Chuck in.' Though papers were offered and excuses made, the officials weren't budging and Carpenter was soon out of the picture permanently.[7] 'Yep,' laughed Schelhaas, 'so that was Chuck gone.'

Carpenter's replacement was Philip Donnelly, aka 'the Clontarf Cowboy'. As his nickname suggested, Donnelly was another one of those colourful characters that only Dublin seemed capable of producing. 'A great storyteller,' natty dresser and 'pretty nifty on guitar, too,' Philip had

---

6 According to Moore, even the Greeny's guitar case came with a story. 'Peter told me that Eric Clapton gave it to him after [EC's] Les Paul had been stolen, so I think I've got the case from the guitar . . . on *Blues Breakers*, and the guitar that was on *A Hard Road*. Scary!' Jan Schelhaas agreed. 'That guitar was strange, though. It's like that film about the cat, with all the different owners it had and how it changed their lives.' Though it's a longshot, Schelhaas might have been referring to the cult 1963 Disney movie *The Three Lives of Thomasina*.

7 Chuck Carpenter appeared to drop off the map following his time with Gary Moore, though he did resurface again in the early nineties due to his involvement with 'Tric Pic'. 'The world's first illuminating guitar pick,' the Tric Pic was battery run, touch sensitive, and by the looks of those advertising images, could be seen from the moon via its inbuilt LED light. Sadly, the company – and Chuck Carpenter with it – seemed to disappear again in 2014.

toured the world with hippie poet Donovan in 1969, before coming home to Ireland to take up arms with cartoon-referencing riff rockers Elmer Fudd (later just 'Fudd'). When that didn't work out, Donnelly returned to Donovan's backing band before the vacancy with Gary Moore presented itself. Capable of fusing 'Celtic, blues, country and cosmic,' on just six strings, Donnelly sounded quite the catch. 'Oh yeah, Phil was a lovely bloke and a lovely player,' said Schelhaas. 'He was also quite brave to take on guitar duties in a band with Gary!'

In the end, the Clontarf Cowboy had precious little time to worry about what he might be taking on. Within weeks of joining up, he, Moore and co. were ensconced in the studio recording the band's first (and as it turned out, last) album, *Grinding Stone*. At the helm was Martin Birch, mercifully promoted to the role of producer in the absence of an otherwise occupied Clifford Davis, while Moore acted as sole song-writer, providing his group with six tunes to chew on. 'We all put in an effort,' said Schelhaas. 'We were working with what I think was Gary's musical journey up to that point. The sum of his parts, or what he called his "work in progress". From the early blues days up to The Allman Brothers, it was all there.' Which might just have been the problem. For while the contents of *Grinding Stone* were diverse, musically varied and occasionally enjoyable, they also lacked cohesion and an overall theme. In short, the album, like its writer, seemed intent on proving that when you could play anything, the temptation to play everything was all pervasive.

Still, one could not accuse Gary Moore of aiming small. Over the course of *Grinding Stone,* he and his band found themselves negotiating hard rock, R&B, progressive whimsy and roadhouse blues with some flair and no little purpose. Within the title track alone, the group managed to meld King Crimson-like power riffing and Zappa-style vamps to a Santana-approved Latin groove, no doubt inspired by Gary's brief stint supporting the Mexican guitarist with Skid Row in 1970.

Live favourite 'Time to Heal' also doffed its cap to another act Moore had opened for some years before, the track's rich, opening harmony lines with Phil Donnelly clearly a tribute to The Allman Brothers. However, it wasn't long before Moore dispensed with those southern flavours for a more raucous approach, as 'Time to Heal' turned into a mid-tempo riff rocker, replete with howling vocals from Moore himself. 'Sail Across the Mountain', on the other hand, offered gentle jazz chords over a looser, sedentary rhythm, Moore's voice now more smooth soul singer than chest-beating Viking raider.

Of *Grinding Stone*'s three remaining tunes, 'The Energy Dance'[8] and the striking (if very long) 'Spirit' again flirted with jazz-rock and Latin ideas, the latter's samba beat, acoustic flourishes and drifting keyboards clearly in thrall to Carlos Santana's 1972 disc *Caravanserai*. 'Well, luckily I didn't have any troubles mixing acoustic and electronic textures, which helped the sound, I hope,' said Jan Schelhaas. 'But then, I'd been listening to Santana a lot at the time. I thought, "Well, if Gary can nick a few riffs from The Allman Brothers, I can get something from Santana!"'

Yet it was on *Grinding Stone*'s final song, 'Boogie My Way Back Home', that The Gary Moore Band actually sounded like they were having real fun. Opening with cod-thirties bottleneck guitar and a bluesy vocal from Moore, things quickly took off in the direction of proper seventies pub-rock, as pianos tinkled, basses walked and Moore slipped and slid his way around the neck of his Greeny. Not the most dazzling instrumental display, perhaps. But as was proven at The Lyceum in July 1972, 'Boogie My Way Back Home' certainly worked as a set closer in any bar or club, from Neasden to Nebraska.

Immaculately performed, pleasingly melodic in places and featuring some bravura work from Moore (his 'bob and weave' wah solos on the title track and 'Spirit' were worth the price of the LP alone), *Grinding Stone* was certainly a step in the right direction. Regrettably, it was a step in several other directions too, as the LP floundered for lack of clear musical focus. In later years, Moore admitted as much. 'I'd written a couple of songs in Skid Row,' he told *Guitar*, 'but *Grinding Stone* was the first time I had to write all the tunes myself. Hard work. They were all right I suppose, but nothing special.' As he was now finding out, being

8 The Moog synthesiser passages on 'Energy Dance' were actually played by Gary Moore.

band leader, sole composer, lead guitarist and singer in a group bearing your name was not for the faint-hearted.

Housed in a 'phallus-centric' (or just plain ropey) cover sleeve featuring two scantily clad cartoon females posing before what appeared to be a row of giant egg cups, *Grinding Stone* was released to stores with little fanfare in July 1973. It did not sell well, though according to Jan Schelhaas, decisions around the band's finances and future were already in train before *Grinding Stone*'s poor commercial performance. 'The sackings? Well, really it was a case of [his management saying] "The band aren't making enough money, Gary. So, we are going to have to change things. [You can have] . . . a bass player and a drummer. The rest of you, you're all sacked." Chop! And he had to go along with it. Which explains why there are [two] bubbles on the album cover without heads in them.'

The 'bubbles' Schelhaas referred to were on the back sleeve of *Grinding Stone*, each of these spaces reserved for a band member's photograph. However, as the design confirmed, there were only three portraits on display, with Schelhaas' and Donnelly's faces now absent from view. The Gary Moore Band had been shrunk from a quintet to a trio with the flick of an accountant's pen.

The fall-out wasn't that bad, really. Exceptionally talented musicians, neither Donnelly nor Schelhaas had much trouble finding work. In the case of the Clontarf Cowboy, it really was a case of 'Have guitar, will travel', as Donnelly returned to backing Donovan in 1974 before setting off to the USA for a decade or so to work alongside country-rock legends such as John Prine, Emmylou Harris and Johnny Cash, among many, many others.

Schelhaas too, was no slacker. Following a short stint providing organ and keyboards for Thin Lizzy (more of that later), Jan joined post-psychedelic Canterbury progressive rockers Caravan. Then there was a none-too-brief affair with similarly themed proggers Camel before finding his way back into the welcoming arms of Caravan once again.[9] Like

---

9 For those seeking confirmation of what a fine keyboardist and songwriter Jan Schelhaas really is, look no further than Caravan and Camel's back catalogue or his 2008 solo album *Dark Ships*. Lovely stuff.

Donnelly, Schelhaas remained on good terms with his former employer. 'Oh yeah, Gary and I occasionally ran into each other over the years on tour and it was always good to see him and have a catch-up,' he said fondly. 'He was wonderfully single-minded, you know. Gary had that approach to life. "I'm going to do this and nothing's going to stop me," you know. And the guitar playing! Yeah, that was Gary. He was quite good, wasn't he?'

Single-minded or not, keeping his band on an even keel following the (enforced) departures of Jan Schelhaas and Phil Donnelly remained a challenge for Gary Moore. Shortly after making his contribution to *Grinding Stone*, Frank Boylan also left the band, the bassist joining Irish pop rock act Chips, where he found himself working alongside Moore's former colleague from The Beat Boys, drummer Robin Lavery. Boylan's replacement was John Curtis, whose most recent job had been providing four-string support to ex-Manfred Mann drummer/now keyboardist/singer Mike Hugg. Though arriving too late to actually play on the LP, Curtis did at least receive a credit on the sleeve of *Grinding Stone* to mark his ascension to the group.

Unfortunately, said group was now falling prey to the law of diminishing returns. For while Moore and whatever iteration of musicians he chose to surround himself with could still 'pack the faithful in' at London's Marquee Club, his appeal remained far more selective elsewhere across the UK and Europe. Hence, after their successes in the capital, Moore, John Curtis and remarkably enduring drummer Pearse Kelly found themselves winding their way through a maze of bars, small theatres and what once might have been called 'juke joints' from Birmingham to Frankfurt for £60 or £70 a show.

There was the odd highlight. A well-received slot supporting heavy, but humble Uriah Heep at Alexandra Palace as part of the 'London Music Festival'. A hastily arranged, if enjoyable jaunt across the centre and north-west of England in the autumn of 1973. Yet by the time the trio made their way back to the ever-loyal Marquee for a post-Christmas knees-up on 30 December, the general feeling was The Gary Moore Band was on its last legs. 'Well, Clifford Davis had agreed to manage the band,' said Moore's old friend from Dublin, Ted Carroll, soon about to make a timely reappearance, 'but he was off [fighting fires with Fleetwood Mac], so poor old Gary ended up dealing with a lot of the hassle himself.'

After spending the best part of two years trying to establish a group in his own name, Gary Moore had found that even with the best of intentions, the fastest of fingers and the finest of players gathered around him, success was not guaranteed. Indeed, Moore's ability to play whatever he wanted in whatever style he chose may have even have been an impediment to progress – that diverse musical spirit of his bewildering a wider rock audience used to more straightforward thrills. Of equal concern was that he found the experience of running his own show 'bloody exhausting', with decisions about this, that and the other thing draining his energy precisely when he needed it to perform. What he really needed was a holiday. What he got was the next best thing. 'At 19, I nearly had a nervous breakdown,' he later told Q. 'So, when I had the opportunity to just join a band and have the pressure taken off me, I jumped at the chance.'

That band was Thin Lizzy.

CHAPTER EIGHT

Guitarist Without Portfolio

I f you had to back a band capable of planting flags for Irish rock music
across the world in the late sixties, there really were only two contenders:
Skid Row and Taste, featuring Rory Gallagher. That said, woe betide
anyone foolish enough to mention them both in the same breath to
Brush Shiels. 'Don't compare us with Taste,' he cautioned when *Spotlight*
magazine raised commonalities between Gallagher's trio and his own
band of brothers back in 1969. 'The only similarity is we've both got
drums and two guitars. Oh, and Gary's hair is about the same length as
Rory's. That's as far as it goes.'

By January 1974, however, the comparisons were moot. Gallagher had
ended Taste three years before in favour of pursuing a successful career
as a solo artist, while Shiels' latest attempt to resurrect Skid Row with
the single 'Dublin City Girls' had met a tepid response from audiences,
despite being really rather good. If one was looking for an Irish group
to do some proper world-conquering then, Philip Lynott's Thin Lizzy
were better placed than most to give it a go. Unfortunately, Lynott was
having his fair share of troubles too.

Lynott had not rolled himself up in a little ball following his sacking
from Skid Row in early 1969. Far from it. A tenacious sort, and as time

would tell, tough as old boots when the situation demanded it, Lynott had instead begun the process of pulling together a band of his own. 'I knew what I wanted to do,' he later said. 'I just had to find the right people to do it with.'

The first person he turned to was Crumlin-born drummer Brian Downey, with whom he went to school and also shared a stage in The Black Eagles during the mid-sixties. 'When I auditioned for The Eagles in '65, we just sort of hit it off,' said Downey in 2020. 'Philip said, "I think I know you from school." I said, "Well, I know you," even though I'd never spoken to him before. Anyway, it went from there. He smiled and said, "Do you like The Kinks?" Now we're talking! The next thing I know I'm on stage at St Paul's Hall playing 'You Really Got Me' with Crumlin's famous Black Eagles.'

Following his spell with The Eagles, Downey again struck gold with Sugar Shack, a progressive blues outfit whose woozy cover of Tim Hardin's 'Morning Dew' saw them into the Irish Top 20 in 1968. 'I wanted to play blues like Clapton and . . . B.B. Albert and Freddie King,' he said. 'For me, any band I joined had to be into that . . . so my luck was in. Sugar Shack were great players and knew all the blues tunes. I mean, of course they did. We were all obsessed!' When Sugar Shack couldn't quite monopolise on their early success, Lynott swooped, and alongside guitarist Joe Staunton, bassist Pat Quigley and 'floating member' Terry Woods on additional guitar (formerly of Sweeney's Men), Downey found himself playing Jeff Beck, Bob Dylan and Free covers with Lynott in a new band called Orphanage.

Orphanage weren't around long[1], but crucially long enough to be seen at Dublin's Countdown Club in December 1969 by visiting Belfast lead guitarist Eric Bell and organist Eric Wrixon. Gifted journeymen whose previous, individual credits included showbands, blues acts and

---

1 Joe Staunton and Pat Quigley returned to their former band following the break-up of Lynott's quintet in early 1970. However, the pair revived Orphanage three years later with entirely new members. This version didn't last too long either. Fellow Orphanage man Terry Woods went on to play with both Dr Strangely Strange and Steeleye Span after the original demise of the group, before settling into a new folk-rock act alongside his wife Gay. As per a previous footnote, Woods eventually found his way into the ranks of The Pogues, with whom he continues to perform.

the final iteration of Them with Van Morrison, the pair had bonded over a wish to form a proper rock group. On the night, Bell liked Downey's playing. In turn, Lynott and Downey liked Bell, who they knew by musical reputation. Numbers were exchanged and following a quick trawl through children's comic *The Dandy* for a suitable band name[2], Thin Lizzy were born. 'Philip's songs were so good,' said Bell, 'I knew I could put my style around them.'

By February 1970, and with Lynott switching to both vocals and bass guitar (those lessons with The Brush had paid off), the quartet were gigging. From the off, the auguries were with them. Press reviews were good, punters delighted, and as a result, record companies interested. Wrixon left four months later, though his departure couldn't stop the new group's momentum. Thin Lizzy became a trio and released their first single, 'The Farmer', on EMI Records. 'Quick work if you can get it,' laughed Brian Downey.

The greyhound-like speed with which Lizzy found a record company willing to back them was impressive, but unfortunately not sustainable. 'The Farmer' sold just 283 copies, EMI lost interest and the band soon moved into a cycle of 'two steps forward, one step back' that would define their fortunes over the coming years. By the spring of 1971, for instance, a new deal had been brokered with Decca and the band's self-titled debut LP was in the shops. By then, Lynott and co. had moved to London, landing right next door to Skid Row in Belsize Park. 'A proper little Irish enclave, that was!' laughed The Strangelies' Ivan Pawle. However, despite the album's pleasing mix of Celtic, soul and blues rock, and Lynott's winning way with a lyric (the wordplay on both 'Éire' and 'Look What the Wind Blew In'), *Thin Lizzy* sold only sparingly. Worse, the group's sophomore effort, 1972's *Shades of a Blue Orphanage*, followed a similar sales pattern, its contents arguably inferior to the previous disc.

Then the sun broke from the clouds, with a late-1972 UK tour

---

2 In a bind as to what to call their new group, Eric Bell flicked through the pages of *The Dandy*, his eye chancing on the comic's long-running robot character, 'Tin Lizzie'. Chuckling at the fact that the Dublin pronunciation of 'Tin' and 'Thin' were essentially the same, he suggested 'Thin Lizzy' as a band name to Lynott and Downey. 'No one really liked it,' he later said. "But for some reason, we used it.'

supporting glam rock titans Slade teaching Philip Lynott many a valuable lesson in showmanship. Particularly taken with headliner Noddy Holder's reflecting hat, Lynott hit upon the idea of hanging a budgie mirror from his bass to catch the stage lights with. Once appropriately captured, he would redirect the beam at female members of the audience. The prop worked, on stage and backstage too. What also worked was releasing a cover of the old Irish folk standard 'Whiskey in the Jar' as a single. While neither Lynott, Downey nor Bell felt 'Whiskey in the Jar' to be emblematic of the harder-edged, Celtic psych-rock now beginning to define their sound, they really couldn't argue with the sales figures. Topping the charts in their native Ireland, it reached number six in the UK, resulting in Philip's trademark sly smile beaming itself into British homes on *Top of the Pops* for the first time in February 1973.

In typical Lizzy fashion, however, no sooner had the clouds parted than the sun went down again. A brilliant follow-up 45, 'Randolph's Tango' tanked everywhere outside the Republic of Ireland. Then the band's third LP, *Vagabonds of the Western World*, featuring an impressive guest appearance from Jan Schelhaas on 'Mama Nature' and the wonderful 'Hero and the Madman', again sold only moderately, despite critical raves. 'Up, down, and all around.'

Things worsened yet again on New Year's Eve 1973 at Queen's University, Belfast, during Thin Lizzy's latest round of touring, when Eric Bell uncharacteristically walked off stage only minutes into the band's set. In truth, Bell's actions were a long time coming, his growing belief that Philip Lynott was pursuing 'stardom' over music coupled with recent health and relationship problems leading to the guitarist's dramatic, if inevitable exit. According to Brian Downey, drink might also have been involved. 'We'd been living in London, and Eric's come home after some time away,' he said in 2020. 'That morning, he says, "I'm off to see my aunt." The soundcheck was about four, but he turned up a little late . . . [and] we'd noticed he'd been drinking. He said, "Yeah, I've had a couple of drinks, but I'll get some coffees and I'll be all right." But he wasn't. By the time of the gig, Eric seemed more drunk than he was when he came back [from his aunt's]'.

For a moment or two, it looked like all might not be lost. But in typical Lizzy style, the moment soon passed. 'Well, for the first couple of numbers Eric sort of handled it,' said Downey, 'but then the shit started to hit the fan. He ended up crouching beside his amp. It looked like he was melting.' After several minutes of indecision, Bell finally left the stage, came back for a moment, only to leave again after throwing his guitar in the air. 'Thankfully,' laughed Downey, 'it was New Year's Eve and the audience were nearly all pissed. So, no one really noticed.'

Apart from Philip Lynott that is. 'Christ, Philip was really upset,' continued Downey, 'I mean, fuming. We had to finish the set with just bass and drums. One hour of just bass and drums.[3] Again, thank God it was New Year's Eve. Otherwise, we'd have been lynched. Anyway, Philip said, "That's it for Eric." I said, "Well yeah, but he'd had a drink . . ." Philip looked at me and said, "No. He's not playing tomorrow night. I've made my decision. Did you like playing as a two-piece? No? Well, there you go. No. I've already had Chris Morrison cancel tomorrow's gig and contact Gary Moore."'

According to Moore, he was in bed at his new flat in Cricklewood recovering from a night out when the knock came. Greeting the news from Thin Lizzy's manager Chris Morrison that Bell had exited the group and a space needed filling, he recalled saying only two things. 'Saw that coming' and 'When's the flight?' Of course, it wasn't quite that easy. Moore had known Eric Bell for almost a decade. In fact, the pair first met when Bell's band The Deltones played at Bobby Moore's dancehall in Holywood around 1966, with young Gary making admiring noises about a treble booster the slightly older Bell was using to overdrive his Vox AC30 amp. A firm friendship developed as a result.[4]

Flash forward to the spring of 1971 and the guitarists were even living next door to each other in Belsize Park, their respective partners both heavily pregnant at the same time. To ward off a potentially awkward

3 According to Eric Bell, he did return to the stage, albeit reluctantly, to help finish the set. 'I got pushed back out on stage [by a roadie],' he told author Mark Putterford. 'We must have sounded awful.' That said, Brian Downey believes it was just he and Philip Lynott that finished the show.
4 In addition to many a jam between the two, Moore also spent time playing with The Deltones and Bell's subsequent group Shades of Blue, though the extent of Gary's involvement with either band remains uncertain.

situation, Moore obviously wanted to make sure Bell was OK before taking the gig. By the sounds of it, Eric was beyond caring. 'I had to leave,' he later told *Guitar Magazine*'s Richard Mann. 'It was exhaustion. On one side, I had my health problems. On the other, I had a chance to make a lot of money, a lot of fame and everything else that came with it, for which I'd worked for all my life. I chose my health, which was more important.'[5]

The set-up Gary Moore found himself entering was one in considerable flux. In addition to Bell's departure, Thin Lizzy were coming to the end of their contract with Decca Records, a company that had apparently failed to monopolise on the success generated by 'Whiskey in the Jar'. The band's business affairs had also been something of a merry-go-round. By 1973, manager (and former Skid Row associate) Brian Tuite began running down his involvement with the trio, handing over responsibility to a promising young Scot named Chris Morrison. Until then a business partner at well-respected booking agents Acorn, who handled the affairs of Manfred Mann and Status Quo, among others, Morrison loved Thin Lizzy with a passion and wanted to make them a major act. 'I thought they were fantastic,' he told author Graeme Thomson, 'but their finances were a nightmare.'

Helping him dig the band out of this financial pit was Chris O'Donnell, to whom Morrison had turned when running double-duties as both agent and overseer proved impractical. 'I'd already been working with Chris, and he said he was finding it difficult being their agent and their manager, so he asked if I could come on board,' O'Donnell later told *Hot Press*'s Colm O'Hare. 'They were just bringing out *Vagabonds* when I became their agent. On the New Year's Eve after Eric left . . . I became their manager.'

Also in the mix at this point was former Skid Row road manager Ted Carroll, whose long-standing friendship with Brian Tuite was deci-

---

5   The nature of Eric Bell's departure from Thin Lizzy has been written about many times over the years. However, despite Philip Lynott's anger concerning his performance and Gary Moore being brought into the band, Bell is adamant he resigned following Thin Lizzy's infamous Belfast gig. 'It was Thin Lizzy or me,' he said in 1993, 'and I chose me.'

sive in his coming on board the Thin Lizzy express two years before. 'I'd gone back to Dublin and while there, I'd seen Brian Tuite,' Carroll confirmed. 'Anyway, Brian said that he and Peter Bardon[6] – another old friend of mine – were managing Thin Lizzy. They played me the band's debut album, and I was impressed with the melodies, the songs, Eric's guitar playing, and of course, Philip and Brian. Then, Tuite said, 'Do you want to get involved?' At that point, I was planning to drive buses in London, save a load of money, then open a record shop in a north London back street. But they invited me in as a partner [to look after several other bands too]. So, that's how I got involved with Thin Lizzy.'

Once an important part of Skid Row's set-up, Carroll had kept tabs on Gary Moore over the years, the two even remaining in touch when the guitarist left leafy Belsize Park for the slighter grittier climes of Cricklewood. 'Well, Chris Morrison called Gary and got him in, and that was fantastic for Gary. Before then, he was in a stressful situation with his own band, having to book gigs and sort out vans and trucks himself. Then, suddenly, he's parachuted into Lizzy, who at the time, were . . . playing to packed houses in Ireland and being taken around in a chauffeur-driven limousine. So, of course, he took the gig and the money, and really enjoyed it from day one.' Of that, there was no doubt. 'All I had to do was play guitar on stage for two hours,' laughed Moore. 'Easy.'

Putting his own band on hold – bassist John Curtis and drummer Pearse Kelly[7] were understanding sorts – Gary Moore was on the plane, then in rehearsals with Thin Lizzy within a matter of hours. Already passing familiar with several songs in the band's set, it didn't take Moore long to learn the rest. 'He was like a super-sub in a football team,' laughed Frank Murray, now on the road with Lynott's group following his time with Skid Row.

For Brian Downey, Moore's arrival allowed him to finally work alongside a guitarist he had known and admired for years. 'In 1967, 1968, our

---

6 A long-time associate of Brian Tuite, Bardon had surrendered his interests in Thin Lizzy some time before the management reshuffle of 1973/74.

7 Pearse Kelly helped out Thin Lizzy for several dates earlier in the tour, when a blister on Brian Downey's finger turned septic and he had trouble doing drum fills.

group Sugar Shack had a few gigs in Northern Ireland,' he recalled. 'Unusual for the time, but great anyway. [The big one] was at Sammy Houston's Jazz Club in the heart of Belfast. We'd just had a hit single in Ireland, so it was going well for us. We also knew we had a support band called Platform Three, but to be honest, it didn't ring any bells. Then they started their rehearsal, and we were just struck by the guitarist, who looked about 14, maybe 15 years old. Not so much the playing, but *the sound*. It was really raw. I mean, he just had the Clapton, Mayall, Blues Breakers sound so right. Anyway, our mouths are hanging open, and our guitarist Dermot comes up and says, "Is it me or is that guitar player incredibly good for his age?" I just looked at him and said, "Fucking right he is!" He was absolutely incredible.'

After two spirited sets from Sugar Shack and Platform Three, Downey found himself talking to the young Belfast hotshot. 'It was a great night and both bands held their own. Mutual respect, really. So, after the gig, we all had a drink and a chat. That's when I first met Gary Moore. I found him really friendly, just a modest, humble, nice guy with no side. We had the same interest in blues, that Mayall-Clapton thing, and I remember us talking about *Melody Maker*, which was our bible back then. We were talking about these clubs like The Marquee, The Flamingo and Blazes, and how fantastic it would be to get to England and play them. Little did we know.'

There were to be no long-winded emotional catch-ups. With two gigs already cancelled on the Irish leg of the tour because of Eric Bell's unfortunate exit and a dent in the band's finances as a result, Thin Lizzy had to be 'back at the races double quick.' Hence, Gary Moore found himself on stage at Red Island in Skerries, just outside Dublin, on 4 January 1974, with only a new pair of platform boots and a 1959 Gibson Les Paul to protect him from a hall's worth of expectant punters (and any of Eric's old fans angrily pining for their hero). 'No worries,' smiled Brian Downey. 'Gary picked things up super quick, so the bits he didn't know, he just winged. By night two [in Waterford], he'd fucking nailed it.'

As Downey confirmed, Moore's stint with Thin Lizzy over the remaining dates of the band's Irish tour was a triumph. Performing a heady cocktail of established crowd pleasers and newer material, Lizzy went from quiet and floaty ('Little Girl in Bloom') to quiet, then funky ('Showdown') to not very quiet at all ('The Rocker', 'It's Only Money') over the course of 90 minutes. In between the tunes they had written, there were also some inspired covers to relish, including a rollicking take on The J. Geils Band's 'Hard Drivin' Man'. Keen to show off their new boy, Moore was given his own numbers to sing: John Lee Hooker's vampish blues 'Crawling'[8] and Stevie Wonder's life-affirming 'I Love Every Little Thing About You', plus another, finger-numbing instrumental nick-named 'Gary's Jig'.

Opening with some tasty jazz chords and light flamenco flourishes, it wasn't long before Moore was skidding around the neck of his Greeny in pursuit of old Irish reels and gentle airs, such as 'Limerick Lamentation'. Eventually these Celtic flavours coalesced into Thin Lizzy's latest tune, 'Sitamoia'. The track was based on an old Gaelic jig called 'Sí Do Mhaimeo Í' (or 'The Wealthy Widow') and represented bold new territory for the band. 'Sitamoia' also allowed Moore another opportunity to let fly with those lightning fingers, the guitarist adding a blast or two of the frenetic traditional jig 'The Mason's Apron' to the song's middle section. However, he would soon remove the snippet, putting it in storage for another five years until the time was right to present it in 'the perfect musical setting'.

From Omagh, Belfast and Dromore in the north to Dublin, Waterford and Killarney in the south, Thin Lizzy's Irish jaunt had gone like a dream, proving the group could function perfectly well without Eric Bell, and perhaps even better than before. 'They came on stage and just exploded,' Chris O'Donnell later told author Graeme Thomson. 'I said to Chris Morrison and Ted Carroll, "We could take on the world with a band like this".' Both Morrison and Carroll were having similar thoughts. 'Behind the scenes,' said Carroll, 'Philip, Chris Morrison and I were plotting to offer Gary the gig full-time . . . at the optimum moment at the end of the Irish tour in January 1974.' Yet there were still doubts that Moore would take the bait. 'If truth be told, I think Gary looked down slightly on Thin Lizzy as being sort of a regular rock band,' Carroll

---

8 Moore's version of John Lee Hooker's 'Crawling' wasn't exactly new. In fact, he had been performing it on and off for several years with both Skid Row and more recently in his own band.

continued. 'I think his own ambition was to create something musically more sophisticated.'

There were other reasons that Moore might not be entirely serious about taking the gig with Thin Lizzy, should it be offered. Temporarily freed from the responsibilities of running his own band, the 22-year-old was treating the tour as an opportunity to catch up on everything he had missed out on in the previous 24 months. 'For me, joining Lizzy [at that time] was like one big holiday after all the shit I'd been through,' he later said. 'I hadn't had a proper drink for about two years as I'd had to pull myself together to deal with all the responsibility I'd had. So, with Lizzy, I could go right off the rails, get pissed every night and go wild.'

Having been driven to distraction by his previous experiences of managing The Gary Moore Band, one could easily understand his attitude. But as road manager Frank Murray confirmed, Moore was taking no prisoners in the early spring of 1974. 'Gary was in a bad way with the drink and pills [at that time],' he said. 'We'd carry him from the dressing room to the car . . . drive him home and literally dump him on his doorstep. I don't think he sobered up all the time he was with the band.'

Yet, if Gary Moore's nights were a blur of drink and whatever else, he always managed to keep himself in some sort of shape for the concert stage. This was confirmed when Thin Lizzy arrived in England for part two of the tour. Fulfilling their teenage ambitions by headlining The Marquee together on 5 February, Moore, Brian Downey and an ever-watchful Philip Lynott continued to garner excellent reviews, with Moore's performance singled out for particular praise. 'Moore,' said an enthused *Melody Maker*, '[should] be retained as a permanent member' of the group. The reviews were even better when Lizzy topped the bill for an afternoon event at Camden Town's Roundhouse, featuring solid support from pub rockers Ducks Deluxe and new rockers Heavy Metal Kids. 'They really rose to the occasion that day,' confirmed manager Chris O'Donnell. Moore heartily agreed. 'The highlight of that whole time was the gig at the Roundhouse,' he said. 'I remember thinking we'd finally made it.'

As well as the steady procession of gigs across England and Scotland in February and early March, Thin Lizzy managed to find time to visit the studio, where the band made what turned out to be their final recordings for Decca. At the helm was producer Nick Tauber, an honest, unpretentious man who cut his musical teeth playing in R&B combo Shy during the mid-sixties before accepting a job at the A&R department of Decca. From there, it was a straight line through to studio engineering before he was given the chance in 1971 by Philip Lynott to produce Thin Lizzy's self-titled debut LP.

For that honour, Tauber remains ever grateful. 'A fucking amazing man was Philip,' he said in 2020. 'From the melodies and lyrics to that mirror scratch plate on his bass. I mean, take his connection with the people at the label, the people at the plant, straight through to the press. Even if he was knackered, he'd get up off his arse and make the effort to connect with those people. Consequently, when a Lizzy record came out, people worked their balls off to help it along because they liked him and how he'd treated them. Sure, he could be tough and he knew what he wanted, but inside him was a warm, good man. Remember, he gave me a proper break. Before Lizzy, I had no track record. I had nothing, but Philip still gave me a shot. I'll never forget that.' Neither did Lynott. So impressed was Lynott with Tauber's efforts, he called him back to co-produce the band's third LP, *Vagabonds of the Western World*, featuring one of Lizzy's best loved tracks, 'The Rocker'. 'Ah, 'The Rocker',' said Tauber. 'Well, it was done live, just one take, you know. Live vocals, live drums, live guitar solo. That's why it just flies off the vinyl.'

The two tracks Tauber was tasked to record at Decca's Tollington Park studios were 'Sitamoia' and another new tune earmarked as a single, 'Little Darling'. Having already formed a strong bond with Eric Bell, one might have assumed it would take time for Tauber to do the same with Gary Moore. Not so. In fact, Tauber was immediately impressed by the guitarist, even if he did almost deafen one of his helpers.

'Gary brought in two Fender Twin Reverb amps and two echoplexes, and put his guitar through a dual outlet to get his tone. The sound was brilliant. It was loud, though. He nearly blew the head off the assistant engineer, Alan. He'd put his head near the speaker and Gary didn't see him. Wallop! It was so fucking loud!' Yet, as the session progressed, Tauber began to see it wasn't all about volume. 'God, no. Gary was polite, calm and very good to work with. He knew what he wanted all right, but why the fuck not? He was a stunning guitarist. His technique, his intonation, his timing were all amazing.'

Producing 'Little Darling' while also going to see the band in concert allowed Tauber a clear insight into Moore's working relationship with Thin Lizzy's fearless leader, Philip Lynott. For him, it was complementary. Mostly. 'Big egos, those two, but also big respect for each other. Gary could play the most amazing guitar solos and have you in tears, but Philip could walk down to the crowd and they'd just adore him. He did it better than any rock star I've ever seen. The charm, the look, the sheer elegance that Philip brought to the band. And you know, Gary respected that. He respected Philip's natural connection with the audience. When he joined up with Lizzy, he knew he was joining a band, being part of a band and their fans, and he played that game perfectly. You had to admire Gary for that.'

The result of Tauber and Thin Lizzy's studio endeavours was impressive. In 'Sitamoia', the band had turned corner in terms of innovation, with Downey's sweeping rhythmic patterns and Lynott's exuberant vocal glossolalia creating both a high-energy 'party of a song,'[9] and new musical direction, should they wish to pursue it. That said, it was post-glam-rock firecracker 'Little Darling' that more accurately predicted the band's future. Coming in on a wave of subterranean horn rumbles and roaring, multi-tracked guitars, 'Little Darling' was full of braggadocio and swagger, with Philip Lynott showering the object of his lyrical affections with every pick-up line he could muster.

Moore's guitar solo was the proverbial cherry on top, his lemon-squeezing tone and bluesy overbends a perfect accompaniment to Lynott's salty come-ons. 'Gary's playing [on 'Little Darling'] was more modern, more aggressive, more technical,' said Tauber[10], 'but it retained a commer-

---

9 Sadly, 'Sitamoia' would languish unreleased for a while yet, eventually turning up on the Thin Lizzy compilation LP, *Remembering – Part One* in August 1976.

10 1974's 'Little Darling' marked the end of Nick Tauber's recorded association with Thin Lizzy, though remained friends with the band. A fine, versatile producer, he has since overseen countless other projects including albums/singles by Def Leppard, Toyah, Marillion, UFO, Slaughter & The Dogs, The Brink and the much-missed Bernie Tormé.

cial edge.' But not quite commercial enough for the pop crowd. Released as a single in April 1974, 'Little Darling' bopped agreeably around the UK airwaves for a while, but again failed to chart. With over a year since Thin Lizzy's last chart hit, something had to be done, and sharpish.

Fortunately, the band's management team were all over it. 'At that stage, we were coming to the end of the three-year Decca contract,' said Ted Carroll, 'and Chris, myself and the guys didn't really want to sign with them again as we didn't think they were committed enough to the band, or would do enough promotion for a new album.' That said, a short extension with Decca was agreed, gifting the band £10,000 to record 'Little Darling', while also helping them tread water on any long-term decision while alternatives were sought. 'Yes, we were talking to other record companies at that time,' Ted continued. 'Island, for one, were very keen, but that didn't work out. Polydor, CBS and several others also turned us down.' Then things took a potentially drastic turn. 'Well, Decca withdrew their offer because they probably heard we'd being talking to other labels! So, off we all went to Pebble Beach Studios in Worthing to cut some demos for a new album – ones we could use to drum up more interest for a potential record deal.'

Indeed, Thin Lizzy's visit to Pebble Beach Studios in early April 1974 turned out to be exactly the new beginning they were hoping for, even if it took a while to see the results. In fact, their streak of good luck began with the man who greeted them at the studio door. Overseeing the sessions was chief engineer Tony Platt, whose previous credits included assisting on landmark releases such as Led Zeppelin's 'Stairway to Heaven', The Who's *Live at Leeds* and Bob Marley's *Catch a Fire*. 'I'd also done sessions with Free, Mott The Hoople and John Martyn, so yes, I guess you could say I was quite well versed in rock music,' he laughed. Then temporarily down by the seaside to manage his friend's studio, Platt was both surprised and pleased by the variety of musical traffic coming his way. 'My friend had bought the place and I guess I was working as chief engineer,' he said, 'We were getting all sorts of acts, including Ducks Deluxe and [a pre-punk] Stranglers. But then Thin Lizzy came in with Gary on guitar.'

The song the band worked on at Pebble Beach was a smouldering late-night ballad, lyrically full of regret and musically full of soul. Entitled 'Still in Love With You', it was subsequently credited to Philip Lynott, who had written it in honour of (ex-)girlfriend Gail Barber. Yet, to this day there remains some issue as to whether he was the sole author. 'Well, I wrote part of 'Still in Love With You',' Gary Moore later told writer Mark Putterford, 'but I never got credited for it, as usual!' According to Moore, both he and Lynott arrived in Worthing with two tunes bearing more or less identical chord sequences and similar titles. 'Mine was called 'I'll Help You See It Through',' said Gary, 'his was called 'Still in Love With You'.' To save time, a decision was made to fuse them together. However, the track would soon bear Lynott's name alone. 'I'm not moaning about it though,' Moore later grumbled. 'It's just the way it is. Back then, the stakes weren't so high.'

Though 'Still in Love With You' would cause Gary to occasionally smart in later years, at the time he and everyone else gathered at Pebble Beach knew they were onto something potentially timeless. "Still in Love With You' was one of those tracks that even when it was [being recorded], you knew it was going to be very special,' said Tony Platt. 'And when Gary played that solo, well, it was one of the best around.'

A majestic effort that found Moore plucking every ounce of emotion out of the Greeny over the course of one breathless minute, Gary's soaring solo on 'Still in Love With You' was so good it left his colleagues in a bit of a quandary. 'Gary's solo was so spectacular [on the demo] that we just had to keep it,' said Brian Downey. 'So, [that meant] we eventually had to re-record all the drums and bass with a new vocal from Phil [for the new record].' Another keeper from the original Worthing session was a gloriously brandy-soaked vocal from Glaswegian singer-songwriter Frankie Miller[11], who had accompanied Lizzy to the seaside and ended up duetting on the track with Lynott. Then a big drinker, Miller was so refreshed during the take that he fell off his chair. 'Yeah,' said Downey, 'You can actually hear the microphone being hit when Frankie falls down.'

---

11 A 'musical triple threat, who could as easily write a hard rock opera as a country ballad,' Miller released several strong albums over the years before suffering a brain haemorrhage in 1994, which sadly left him unable to perform. Still, his back catalogue and a 2016 LP featuring previously unreleased vocals are well worth seeking out.

Though Thin Lizzy's latest tour had been well attended, well-received and extremely well-reviewed, it was the demo of 'Still in Love With You' that finally landed the band a new record deal. 'Nigel Grainge had just got a job with A&R at Phonogram, and he popped over to my record stall on Golborne Road,' said Ted Carroll. 'We were chatting away, and as he's about to go, he says, "Well, if there are any good bands you think I should take a look at, let me know." The penny didn't drop for a moment . . . but then I thought, "Ah." So, I said, "Richard, actually Thin Lizzy are looking for a deal . . ." Manna from heaven, really.'

Lizzy manager Chris O'Donnell took up the story. 'By that time, Island, EMI and RCA had all passed on the band,' he said. 'But then Phonogram's Nigel Grainge heard a demo of 'Still in Love With You' and loved it.' A three-album deal 'with options' was soon being discussed. For the man who produced the song, none of this was at all surprising. 'Gary was just astonishing and Thin Lizzy were an amazing band with Gary,' confirmed Tony Platt. 'I'd always been a fan of the classic "power rock trio" and they were the perfect embodiment of that.'

Yet, while Philip Lynott and Brian Downey were more than happy to put their signature to a new record contract with Phonogram, they would do so without Gary Moore. 'Gary came to me at the end of March 1974 and said, "I think I should leave,"' confirmed Ted Carroll. 'He said, "I know you guys are looking for a new deal and you'll sign one shortly. I'll be expected to sign that deal too. But I don't want to sign it, because I don't want to have any ties. I want to do my own band. So I think it'd be better if I left at this stage. Otherwise, it'll create problems for you guys getting a deal." And you know, that made sense to me.'

In fact, Moore's logic appeared downright infectious. 'Well, I thought, "Then, that's me gone too,"' said Carroll. 'Eric Bell had left three months earlier. Now Gary was going, and I'm thinking, "It's Philip's band. There's always going to be problems with lead guitarists and that's going to hamper their long-term career. So, I'm going to get out."' But before he could, there was an endgame to be played. 'Well, leaving might have made sense for Gary,' laughed Carroll, 'but it left Thin Lizzy in some deep shit.'

On the cusp of a potential deal on the back of their latest recordings with the now departing Moore, Thin Lizzy had not only just lost their new talisman, but were also a man down in the face of an upcoming European tour. However, Philip Lynott's steely pragmatism once again came into play. Aware that the band would always be vulnerable with just one guitarist in their ranks, Lynott switched his strategy and got two in instead. Temporarily recruiting former Atomic Rooster man John Du Cann and young German hopeful Andy Gee, Thin Lizzy managed to discharge the majority of their concert obligations without major incident.

Unfortunately, neither Du Cann nor Gee proved suitable and a disheartened Downey almost left the group as a result. Thankfully, the next two candidates did work out, leading to a new contract with Phonogram in July 1974, and the slow severing of ties with the more whimsical elements of Thin Lizzy's musical past. In its place would be a markedly different band: harder-hitting, certainly harder rocking, and with the acquisition of 'feisty Glaswegian wunderkind' Brian Robertson and 'laid back Californian heartthrob' Scott Gorham, an enduring opportunity for Gary Moore to boast: 'It took Lynott two bloody guitarists to replace me!'

Of course, in subsequent years Moore's decision not to take up arms with Thin Lizzy has led to various theories, from Moore being jealous of Lynott's way with a crowd to his supposed view that the band were no more than a Celt-rock bagatelle: pleasant enough to listen to for a moment or two perhaps, but lacking any real heft or substance. However, while there may be a grain of truth here and there, such ideas tend to wilt in the face of testimony from those involved at the time. 'No, Gary was never asked to join permanently,' said Brian Downey. 'I think the arrangement was that he had gigs to go back to with his own band, and that was made plain from the start. We knew it wasn't going to be a permanent thing. In fact, [following the last show] as we were all living in London, we got in the same car and Gary headed straight back to his own group afterwards.'

Moore also confirmed that joining Thin Lizzy was never really on the agenda. 'Look, Lizzy was successful, the pressure was off me and I was having fun,' he told *Mojo*. 'But after four or five months, I really was doing myself in, drinking and getting high on the whole thing. I was really committed to Lizzy [but also spending] half my time on stage on my back, going crazy and playing as flash as I could. I needed discipline and a direction that would get me out of the rut of the typical rock guitarist's self-destructive streak I [was in] at the time.' From Moore's point of view, that discipline was most likely to come from once again leading his own band. If only it were that easy.

CHAPTER NINE

Life Lessons

If Gary Moore hadn't wanted to join Thin Lizzy in the spring of 1974, it was fair to say the experience of hooking up with Philip Lynott and Brian Downey did him little harm either. Across the space of four action-packed months, Moore had what he later described as a 'paid holiday' with the band, his gallivanting around the UK and Europe a nightly procession of clubs, pubs and God knows what else, punctuated by 90-odd minutes on stage. The partying didn't get in the way of the performances, though. Reviews of Gary's time with Lizzy were little short of ecstatic, and his fiery guitar style re-activated interest in the group precisely when they needed it to land a new record deal.

Moore's contributions in the studio were impressive too, with 'Little Darling', 'Sitamoia' and the gorgeous 'Still in Love With You' proving conclusively he was a natural fit for the Dublin band. 'Phil was so impressed with Gary's solo on 'Still in Love With You',' said Downey, 'that every guitarist we had afterwards had to play it literally note for note.' Still, it wasn't to be. Moore wanted to lead from the front again, and by hook or crook, he was going to do it. 'I was killing myself [with Thin Lizzy],' Moore later said, 'So, it was time to install some discipline back into my life and music.'

Regrettably, if Gary was going to take on the world, he would have to do a fair amount of the legwork himself. Having returned to the coalface that was his solo career in May 1974, Moore found that manager Clifford Davis was still heavily embroiled with the fortunes of Fleetwood Mac, though this time, the two camps were butting heads over a series of recently cancelled US dates, among other things. In short, no joy there. Had circumstances been different, Moore might have turned to Ted Carroll to aid his cause. But though technically a free agent following his departure from Thin Lizzy's managerial team, Carroll's acquisition of a new second-hand record stall in London's Chinatown meant he was a busy man, and about to get much busier. Within a year, Carroll would open his flagship store Rock On in Camden Town, creating a little oasis of high-quality vinyl smack in the middle of north London.

Despite the lack of managerial cover, Moore was still keen to press ahead with pulling his band back together. However, he would now do so without the help of bassist John Curtis, who had set off for less precarious climes earlier in the year. Still, Moore and ever loyal drummer Pearse Kelly quickly found a potential replacement for Curtis in the form of the talented four-stringer Steve York.

A Jack Bruce/Graham Bond fanatic with a proper grounding in jazz, York met Gary when he played bass in blues-rocking hopefuls Vinegar Joe. 'When I was working with Vinegar Joe,' York said in 2019, 'we did quite a few double bills with [Gary's solo band] around 1972, and he and I kind of formed a mutual admiration society. We'd have a beer and chat, and just got on well.' Therefore, when Vinegar Joe began their slow disintegration two years later – 'I thought we might really go somewhere, but didn't know that [Island Records boss] Chris Blackwell was grooming [vocalist] Robert Palmer for a solo career' – the idea of hooking up with Moore seemed eminently logical.[1]

Thanks to a mutual friend, they were on stage together within literally minutes. 'An old mate, Alan Reeves, was working for a London publishing

---

1 Formed in 1971 from the ashes of soul rock combo Dada, Vinegar Joe were for a little while at least tipped for stardom. However, it wasn't in the stars and the band are perhaps now best known for launching the solo careers of singers Robert 'Addicted to Love' Palmer and Elkie 'Pearl's a Singer' Brooks.

company and got wind that Vinegar Joe . . . were folding. Anyway, I was coming back from a concert in Norway, and Alan had arranged an impromptu gig for Gary and I opening for someone at The Marquee.' According to York, despite a lack of preparation, the bones of a great band were there for all to see. 'Well, we went in unrehearsed, but it was still magical,' he said. 'We played for 45 minutes and the chemistry was there. Straight blues rock standards, but at a very high level. Gary on guitar and vocals, me on bass and Pearse Kelly on drums. It just worked.'

Given the quality of York's bass playing and Moore and Kelly's well-honed musical sympatico, this had all the makings of a fine little band. However, it was when the trio recruited ex-Skip Bifferty/Arc frontman Graham Bell that things went a little haywire. An undoubted talent, Bell's pure-toned vocals and soulful delivery certainly gave the fledgling group real commercial gloss. Unfortunately, he and Moore also seemed to bring out the worst in each other. 'Over time, we cobbled together some songs,' confirmed York. 'But here's the basic problem. Every time we got together [to work], we'd end up going out and Gary and Graham would get into bar fights.'

Despite his wish to exert some self-discipline after his spell of riot with Thin Lizzy, Moore was obviously in no mood to leave the party behind just yet. In Graham Bell, he had also found an ally more than willing to indulge his continuing adventures. Sadly, the pair's buccaneering approach to the art of pub craft was doing them and everyone else no favours at all. 'Pearse and I really wanted to get this band going,' said York. 'So, we called a meeting with Gary and Graham . . . in the Portobello Hotel. Now, we met at the bar.' Big mistake. 'Anyway, Pearse and I said, "Look, we want to carry on with this, but it's one thing to go partying, but we've also got to have sober rehearsal and writing sessions. And if we're gigging around the clubs and you guys [keep] getting in bar fights, well, we're done. So, it's got to stop."' No prizes for guessing what happened next. 'Ten minutes later – ten bloody minutes – and guess what? Gary and Graham got in a bar fight. Pearse and I left them to it, and that was the end of that.'

Several tales from this period in Gary Moore's life seem to point in a similar direction, with the guitarist serious about pulling together a killer band, but at the same time, going out on the tiles whenever and wherever he could. Though there was no doubting Gary's continued dedication to the musical cause, his new, more hedonistic lifestyle may have been the result of recent upheavals in his personal life.

Already shaken by the dissolution of his parents' marriage, his relationship with Sylvia Keogh had also continued to deteriorate. Having separated for a while in 1972, there were reconciliations now and then, but by the autumn of the next year, she had thrown him out of their flat for good. Breaking point was apparently reached when Keogh discovered Moore had been seeing Goldsmiths' College fine art student and dancer Jeannie Campbell behind her back for some time, Gary's affair officially rubberstamping the fact that after four or so turbulent years, things were finally over.

Of course, as with Keogh before her, Moore had become totally smitten with Jeannie Campbell since the pair met at a gig at the University of Exeter earlier that year, and once their romance became 'public', it wasn't long before they were sharing a place in London. To drive home his apparent ardour, The Gary Moore Band were even performing a song called 'Jeannie' as part of their set during the summer 1973 tour, a clear indication that Campbell was by then the guitarist's primary muse. Yet, despite Moore's onstage overtures and willingness to sacrifice his relationship with Keogh for Campbell, the affair eventually floundered. After a brief period of discord in December 1973, he broke things off, and in almost soap-opera like fashion, took up with Jeannie's sister, Donna, instead. One can only imagine what Christmas was like that year . . .

Twenty-year-old Donna Campbell first encountered Gary Moore some four years before, when after hearing a Skid Row session on John Peel's radio show, she hitchhiked 145 miles to London from her native Somerset to see the band. 'I even got backstage and met Gary,' Donna later told *Bridgwater Mercury*. Then working as a nanny, but 'absolutely mad about music', Campbell took the plunge and moved to the capital, soon becoming a mainstay on the rock scene alongside sisters Cathy and Jeannie, who was already on a romantic collision course with Moore. When that relationship stalled, Donna found herself taking up the mantle of Gary's girlfriend, a position she would retain for the next five years.

Their union was officially sealed when Campbell posed for the publicity photos accompanying the release of Thin Lizzy's single 'Little Darling'. With her trademark Cleopatra fringe, schoolgirl uniform and cocked straw boater, Donna provided a saucy contrast to Moore, Lynott and Downey's hackneyed tough guy poses alongside her. 'Benny Hill meets The Three Bloody Amigos,' quipped one wag. According to most every source, Donna Campbell was also in attendance at one of the more grisly and unfortunate events of Gary Moore's young life. Though details vary as to when (probably the early summer of 1974) and exactly where the incident happened, the results were unpleasant and permanent. While on a night out at the Kensington Park Hotel in London's Ladbroke Grove – others have mentioned Dingwalls in Camden Town, but that's unlikely – Moore got into an altercation with a fellow drinker. In at least one version of the story, said drinker was an old flame of Campbell's and paying her unwanted attention.

'It feels like a dream, seems like a dream,' said bassist Steve York. 'I think it was a pub or hotel near Holland Park. Pearse Kelly, Graham Bell, Gary and I were there, though I honestly don't remember if the girls, Donna and her sisters were.' (As above, Donna was surely present.) 'Anyway,' York continued, 'Gary went to the bar to buy a round and the next thing I see is that some guy hit him in the mouth with a beer glass.' Again, there is some dispute here as to the exact truth of what happened. What appears likely is that Moore took exception to the behaviour of another customer (presumably the one known to Donna) and poured a drink over his head, causing the man to allegedly strike out with a glass. But in yet another version of the story, the glassing was accidental, as a shard from a pint pot broken against a wall in anger flew off and hit Gary on the upper chin. If so, it hit him pretty hard and pretty accurately. 'There was blood all over the place,' remembered York.

What no one disputes is that Moore was badly injured and rushed to hospital. However, after receiving stitches, it appears he asked to go home, rebuffing any more efforts to help with the wound, even though he

risked permanent disfigurement as a result. While this refusal of assistance
sounds far-fetched, even in later years, Gary sought no further treatment
for the resulting scar, reportedly turning down the chance of plastic
surgery when it was offered.

Something he would remain conscious of for the rest of his life but
curiously chose not to tend, few thought Moore's scar was just physical.
'It did change him,' Gary's friend Eric Bell later told author Mick Wall.
'A lot of pent-up anger and emotion would come out in his playing,
and in other ways too. It must be a hard thing to come back from
something like that.'

However troubling and traumatic, the Kensington Park incident of
1974 provided Gary Moore with the first real warning-shot that his then
current lifestyle might need a major overhaul. And while it would take
time for him to properly heed the signs, some emotional and artistic
stocktaking did take place. After several months of trying to re-launch
his solo career, Moore finally threw down his sword and cut professional
ties with the remaining members of the band.

It wasn't too hard. Steve York was already well on his way to working
with the former Vinegar Joe singer Elkie Brooks and troubled chanteuse
Marianne Faithful, while the ever-loyal Pearse Kelly finally moved back
to Ireland to try his luck there. With only singer Graham Bell now left
to drown his sorrows alongside, Gary had little choice but to again
return to the drawing board. Mercifully, there were some fairly detailed
plans already scrawled there, thanks to a new association with Jon
Hiseman.

One of the UK's better drummers, Hiseman first come to attention
in the mid-sixties when he replaced fellow percussion giant Ginger Baker
in The Graham Bond Organisation. When that didn't quite work out,
Hiseman moved on to R&B scenesters Georgie Fame & The Blue Flames
before taking a sideways turn into progressive blues with John Mayall in
1968. The resulting album *Bare Wires*, featuring future Rolling Stone
Mick Taylor on guitar, remains a classic to this day.

That said, Mayall's band was always going to be a stop gap for Hiseman.
Musically restless, he dreamed of creating a jazz-rock-blues-progressive
hybrid, where tunes could grow in unexpected melodic or rhythmic

directions. By early 1969, he, like several other similarly pioneering types of the time, had a group trying to do just that.[2] Featuring old friend/ organist Dave Greenslade and saxophonist/fellow Graham Bond Organisation escapee Dick Heckstall-Smith, among others, Hiseman called the group Colosseum. Their debut album, the ancient gladiator-referencing *Those Who Are About to Die Salute You* (or *Morituri Te Salutant*, if you prefer Latin) reached a respectable number eighteen in the UK charts.

Four more LPs and a similar number of line-up changes followed, but by October 1971, Jon Hiseman had brought Colosseum to an unexpected close. Still, his logic for doing so was mercifully free of the usual nonsense that ends such collaborations. 'I think that bands are living things and that at the end of the day they have a kind of natural life,' he later said. 'We'd done the live album (1971's *Colosseum Live*) . . . it had been incredibly successful and I just felt that we wouldn't do anything as good.'

As good as his word, Jon's next move was to form Tempest with keyboardist/singer Paul Williams, bassist Mark Clarke and Allan Holdsworth, a guitarist as exceptionally gifted as he was occasionally stubborn. When fellow six-stringer Ollie Halsall joined Tempest alongside Holdsworth in 1973, the first 'jazz-rock guitar dream team' appeared on the cards. Then Holdsworth decided such dreams weren't jazzy enough for him, and the band were back to being a quartet. By the spring of 1974, they had broken up. Two years, two reasonably reviewed albums (*Tempest* and *Living in Fear*) but this time, no chart appearances. As ever, Hiseman was philosophical. 'In a strange way, when I first formed Tempest, I felt that we might be too late, running out of our time,' he said of the

---

2 In the same way blues was commandeered by a new generation of experimentally inclined young musicians in the mid-sixties, so jazz found itself reshaped by a similar wave of players. In 1966, guitarist Larry Coryell's band Free Spirits were among the first to marry the electricity of rock to the jazz stylings of giants such as Miles Davis and John Coltrane. 'We loved Miles,' Coryell later said, 'but we also loved The Rolling Stones.' Never knowingly late to a party, Davis himself was soon experimenting in the same musical playpen, with landmark fusion releases *Bitches Brew* and *In a Silent Way* the result. In quick succession, many of those who helped Miles release the jazz-rock genie from the bottle now formed groups of their own, including guitar giant John McLaughlin's Mahavishnu Orchestra and keyboard magus Chick Corea's Return to Forever, featuring Gary Moore's beloved Bill Connors. A plethora of like-minded bands followed.

group's lack of commercial success. 'In [the] way the original Colosseum was a moment in time . . . Tempest was *almost* a moment in time.'

As with many guitarists drawn to the luminescent solos of Allan Holdsworth and Ollie Halsall, Gary Moore was already a fan of Tempest, having a real fondness for the band's sparky rendition of The Beatles' 'Paperback Writer'. Moore was also there at the group's last London gig in the spring of 1974, making himself known backstage and even suggesting to Hiseman that they might work together in the near future. 'Gary said, "I'd like to form a band. Could we do it together?"' Hiseman later told *Let it Rock*. Yet, it was Hiseman and Moore's involvement in updating one of Russian composer Sergei Prokofiev's more famous compositions that shunted Moore's suggestion ever closer to reality.

The brainchild of former Blodwyn Pig multi-instrumentalist Jack Lancaster and jazz fusion keyboardist Robin Lumley, the conceit behind *The Rock Peter and the Wolf* was fairly straightforward. Take Prokofiev's 1936 'symphonic fairy tale for children' and reboot it for a modern audience with 'distinct instruments' voicing the various characters. Obviously spotting an opportunity to get paid as well as have 'a bit of a laugh', musicians from all over the rock and jazz world queued up to join the party, with the likes of Genesis's Phil Collins, Manfred Mann, singer Julie 'Wheels on Fire' Driscoll and even Hot Club legend Stéphane Grappelli all coming on board. 'A great pleasure . . . was working with one of my personal childhood heroes, Stéphane Grappelli,' said Jack Lancaster. 'He played 'The Cat' with great panache.' Unfortunately, unlike violinist Grappelli or Roxy Music's Brian Eno, who made 'a wonderful wolf', Gary Moore was not given the coolest of characters to portray. That said, he made the best of what he got. 'Ha! Gary was a superb wah-wah duck!' laughed Lancaster.[3]

John Hiseman obviously thought so, too. In fact, so impressed was the drummer with Moore's performance that he saw forming a group with him as 'almost inevitable'. Moore held a similar view. 'Jon played everything

---

3   Gary joined Jack Lancaster, Robin Lumley, bassist Percy Jones, drummer Bill Bruford and guitarist John Goodsall in the studio for a one-off project named The Soul Searchers. A subsequent single, 'Scaramouche/Head Stand', was later released by EMI. It was not a success.

I ever heard in my head,' he later told *Sounds*. 'He played everything I thought a drummer should play.' The only problem the two now faced was expanding their mutual appreciation society into a working band.

Various permutations of old friends, acquaintances and former band members were brought in to resolve the issue, with Uriah Heep all-rounder Ken Hensley and ex-Tempest bassist Mark Clarke among the first to try out. Neither worked. Nor did future Cockney Rebel pianist Duncan McKay. Andy Pyle – Jack Lancaster's bass playing pal from Blodwyn Pig – was next in and was impressive enough to be asked to stick around for a while. However, when a stable line-up failed to gel, Pyle moved on too. The same was true of Moore's drinking buddy Graham Bell, who lent his voice to a few rehearsals only to leave again, this time for good.[4] Weeks stretched to months. Hiseman re-mortgaged his house to raise capital and pay Moore a small wage for his time. Progress remained hellishly slow. 'It was taking bloody ages,' Moore later said.

Things began to finally gel in the late autumn of 1974, when Hiseman's wife Barbara Thompson (and renowned saxophonist in her own right) happened upon vocalist Mike Starrs. Then signed to Marquee Productions as a solo artist, Edinburgh-born Starrs already had 'a couple of singles and one album' under his belt, as well as a weekly residency at the delightfully named Three Rabbits pub on east London's Romford Road. 'Jon and Gary came to hear me [there],' Starrs later told journalist Kevin J. Julie. 'We then had a few rehearsals, and then I was their singer.'

The last pieces of the puzzle arrived like buses: two at a time. First to draw up was Don Airey. A Sunderland-born, classically trained pianist with a degree in music from the University of Nottingham, Airey had broken into the rock scene playing keyboards for drummer/general force of nature Cozy Powell's band Hammer. 'Cozy was an amazing musician, especially in a recording studio,' Airey later said. 'He was multi-talented

---

4 A fine singer who once graced the cover of *Sounds* under the headline banner 'The Man Most Likely To', Graham Bell kept threatening to carve out a career in show business. But a combination of bad timing (too rock for punk) and musical choices (too soulful for rock) meant permanent success eluded him. Bell died of cancer in 2008, shortly after his 60th birthday.

as well. I mean, Cozy could have made a career as a racing driver, or at show jumping – (he was) an incredible horseman apparently.' However, the real fun for Don came not from Powell's way with horses, but his knack of scoring hit singles. 'We were always on *Top of the Pops* or flying off to Europe to do television,' he told the BBC, 'On the back of three hits, there were three or four gigs a week for a year or so, mainly to an audience of delectable young ladies!'

When Powell decided to quit drums for motor racing (albeit temporarily) in the spring of 1975, Airey suddenly found himself auditioning for jobs. As a result, Moore and Hiseman got themselves a first-class keyboard player, though he seemed quite impressed with them too. 'Jon Hiseman was one of the greatest professionals I ever met,' Airey later told writer Jeb Wright, 'and of course, there was the youthful genius of Gary Moore.'

With Airey came another immensely promising talent in the shape of Neil Murray. Edinburgh-born, 24-year-old Murray began his musical life taking lessons in trombone and piano as a child before gravitating to drums after hearing The Shadows. But it was when 'somebody at school converted a guitar into a bass' that he had a revelation. 'I just felt comfortable with the instrument and immediately took to it.'

By then, Murray was already in thrall to the British blues rock boom of the late-sixties, using his nights off studying typographical design at the London College of Printing to see the likes of Led Zeppelin and The Jeff Beck Group. By 1972, he was on stage himself, playing bass with part-time jazz fusioneers Gilgamesh before scoring his first professional gig with funk/blues-rocking singer Junior Hanson. Two years later, and Murray moved on again, hooking up with Don Airey and guitarist Bernie Marsden in Cozy Powell's Hammer for one last hurrah before the drummer shut down his band.

As it turned out, Neil Murray had already auditioned for Jon Hiseman some months before joining Powell, though he hadn't made the strongest of impressions. 'Well, I'd borrowed a bass [and] didn't do so well on the first audition,' he said in 2020. However, Murray now had friends in high places exerting a little influence. 'Yes,' he laughed. 'By then, Don Airey had his audition and got the job. So, he persuaded them to give me another go, by which time I'd got a much better bass.' Having secured the gig, Murray now found himself in the company of some seriously fine players, including the fleet-fingered Moore. 'From the first rehearsals, I was struck by Gary's abilities, passion and energy as a musician,' he confirmed. 'He was a very likeable guy too, and we had a lot of the same musical interests. To be honest, he wasn't interested in much else!'

With the line-up complete and several tracks already at a demo stage, it was time to find a record deal. But as Jon Hiseman already knew, despite his previous success with Colosseum, companies weren't exactly queuing up to sign his and Gary Moore's bold new venture. 'It was very difficult,' he told Hit Channel's Από Thodoris. '[We'd tried] for nine months or so to get a deal and nobody would give us one. They didn't think the music was commercial.'

One could see the record companies' point. After all, what Hiseman, Moore and co. were attempting was among the trickiest of all musical propositions: an experimentally inclined, instrumentally-driven, difficult to pigeonhole group with a lead singer sitting awkwardly on top and no obvious hit singles to speak of. 'We wanted to do something that no one else was doing,' Moore told *NME* in 1975, 'a hot instrumental band with strong vocals.' Unfortunately, doing something no one else had previously tried usually meant only two things to most music business types. Either it really was an original proposition, and therefore financially risky to invest in. Or even worse, no one had tried it before because it was a simply terrible idea.

Thankfully, there was someone out there willing to give the band a go. Having financially backed Jon Hiseman's last group, Tempest, Gerry Bron at Bronze Records again stepped forward with an offer. However, there was one important caveat. 'Just call it "Colosseum something",' Bron said, 'and I'll give you a record deal.' For Hiseman, this was potentially a step too far. Proud of what he had done with Colosseum, and not wanting to trade on past glories, the idea of resurrecting his old band's name just felt wrong.

That said, he was thousands of pounds in debt with a re-mortgaged house hanging around his neck and no great interest from anyone in a band he had invested so much time, effort and cash into. 'We wanted to call the band "Ghost",' he told Hit Channel. 'We thought Ghost was a good name.' 'Bottomless Money Pit' was probably more apt. After talking to his fellow musicians about his financial plight and Bron's stipulation around the group's name, a unanimous decision was made. 'Ghost' was no more. Instead, the quintet was to be called 'Colosseum II'. By August 1975, Colosseum II were signed to Bronze, Jon Hiseman could again return his bank manager's calls and Gary Moore had bought a brand-new green leather jacket to mark the occasion.

Having spent the best part of a year stabilising their line-up (and almost bankrupting Hiseman), Colosseum II were eager to get moving as soon as they could. But while the band started playing concerts almost before their signatures on the Bronze contract had dried, recording their first LP moved at a significantly more leisurely pace. 'Well, recording was quite . . . indulgent,' confirmed Neil Murray. 'It started in August 1975 at Roundhouse Studios in London, but actually went on through September, October and even November, with quite a few gigs in between. We didn't actually finish mixing [the album] until the following January. A long period, on and off, and it must have been quite expensive. But then we were using Bronze's own studios at The Roundhouse, so . . .'

There were advantages to Colosseum II's unhurried approach to recording. By regularly gigging between spells in the studio, each player was getting to know the others' instrumental idiosyncrasies in a high-wire environment, thus creating a shared, if often fiery musical shorthand between them. This forging of trust was also taking place in the songwriting department, where Moore and Hiseman were tasked with producing the lion's share of compositions. With Moore surrounded by some 'almost jazz level readers', there were bound to be disagreements, especially when the university-trained ear of Don Airey took exception to Gary's occasional disregard for accepted harmonic theory.

Still, Airey was often more melodic enabler than academic stick-in-the-mud. 'People . . . like Gary, they [could be] very uncertain of themselves, [in that] they don't know how they do what they do,' he later told *Antihero*. 'Whereas when you're a keyboard player, you know exactly what it is that you do. So that's really how you can help. That's the main role for a keyboard player: you just give them a background that makes them feel comfortable and makes them feel that their music is worth playing. Because I'm not ever sure that they think it is.'

After months of on/off recording peppered throughout by mini-tours and one-off gigs, Colosseum II's debut album, *Strange New Flesh*, arrived in record stores on 19 April 1976. A creditable effort, if not quite completely free of the influences that helped shape it . . . *Flesh* was nonetheless one of the better attempts by a British band to close the gap on existing jazz-rock pioneers such as Mahavishnu Orchestra, Return to Forever and Billy Cobham. Thanks to the presence of Moore and Neil Murray, the album also carried rockier overtones than the average 'fusion' release, with their long-standing love of progressive blues adding both grit and fire to Colosseum II's overall sound.

'The musicians I'd worked with around that time had all originally been influenced by the British blues boom, especially guitar players [like Gary],' said Murray. 'They all loved Clapton, Beck and Peter Green. And while I suppose the next wave of interest came with fusion and jazz rock – groups like Weather Report or Mahavishnu Orchestra – it's worth remembering that neither Mike Starrs, Gary nor I were jazz players, though Don perhaps more so. We were [still] rockers at heart, so it was more a case of people trying to play at the top of their ability, similar to how jazz musicians approached things, but with a much harder edge.'

This added thump was obvious from the get go, with opening track 'Dark Side of the Moog' rattling along like an angry skateboarder. With its title very much a pun on Pink Floyd's 1973 monster hit album *Dark Side of the Moon*, albeit with added synthesiser references[5], 'Dark Side of the Moog' found Moore and Don Airey jousting brilliantly over an odd, but engaging rhythm courtesy of drummer/producer Jon Hiseman. 'It's in 13/8 time,' he once helpfully explained. 'Well, 13/4 if you count hard enough.'

The track also illustrated an engaging new influence on Moore: that

---

5 The 'Moog' of the song title refers to the first commercial analogue synthesiser, first developed in 1964 by Robert Moog. Cheap, relatively easy to use and full of wonderful sounds, for a time no keyboard player worth his salt was without one, including Don Airey.

of Return to Forever's brilliant, if artistically restive Bill Connors. Like Moore, Connors could be bluesy and melodic, but lightning fingered too, his fluidity on the instrument marking him out alongside Mahavishnu Orchestra's John McLaughlin as one of jazz-rock guitar's leading lights, and one Moore was keen to acknowledge, if not slavishly copy. 'It's nice to see musicians [like Bill] display a bit of honesty and [pursue] what they're really about instead of trying to do something just for the sake of selling records,' Gary later told *Guitar Presents*.

After the eccentric note choices and rapid-fire soloing of 'Dark Side of the Moog', the LP's second tune, a cover of Joni Mitchell's 'Down to You', was akin to a warm bath after a punishing workout. All drifting chords and elastic vocals from an impressive Mike Starrs, Mitchell's emotionally charged lyric to 'Down to You' also provided Colosseum II with their album title, with one of its more barbed phrases picked up by a lynx-eared Neil Murray. 'Well, the album title *Strange New Flesh* is just a quote from 'Down to You',' he laughed. 'No genius there, really. More "Where can I steal something from?"' A favourite of Moore's, who loved the work of Joni Mitchell with a passion and celebrated it with a fine, whammy bar-assisted solo played on his new [possibly borrowed] Fender Stratocaster[6], 'Down to You' was one of *Strange New Flesh*'s more engaging moments.

Revving up the engines once more, 'Gemini and Leo' found Colosseum II and Gary Moore in particular referencing the funkier aspects of Jeff Beck's recent move from blues rock to jazz rock with 1975's *Blow By Blow*. One of the first instrumental albums to sell more than one million copies, and one that also made Beck an arena-sized draw in the USA, *Blow By Blow* was essential listening for Moore throughout 1975, and his twisting lead lines on 'Gemini and Leo' were proof of it. 'The only guitarist who can be flash and emotional is Jeff Beck,' Moore later said. 'He can be dead subtle as well. He's just beautiful.'

Followed up by *Strange New Flesh*'s most straightforward track in 'Secret Places' (complete with another soulful vocal from Starrs), it was left to

---

6 Though Moore was still in love with the odd tonalities offered by his Greeny, he had also begun using a Fender Stratocaster in Colosseum II as a way of creating a more distinct mid-range voice while playing alongside Don Airey.

the elegiac 'Second Thoughts' to slowly draw listeners towards the end of the album and its closing track, the Mahavishnu-like 'Winds'. Featuring Hiseman and Murray's polyrhythmic prowess, Airey providing all manner of orchestral magic and Moore blazing away with some tasty bottleneck slide – a device he professed to hate, but always put to good use – it was a wonder that Mike Starrs could fit in the song's title, let alone three verses of lyrics before everything went quiet again.

Six tracks in all and five of them bearing Moore's name, *Strange New Flesh* was the most technically accomplished album Moore had yet put his name to. It also represented an eye-catching calling card from a new and musically audacious group. '*Strange New Flesh*,' reasoned early Colosseum II supporter Chris Welch at *Melody Maker*, 'is both exuberant and imaginative.' Unfortunately, though only just released, the LP was also at risk of being well past its sell-by date. 'Hmm,' said Neil Murray, 'if Jon Hiseman hadn't actually got a pre-existing connection with Gerry Bron and Bronze Records, we might not have even got a deal. You see, the market for very complicated, "intellectual" music was actually starting to fade away by 1976.' For Gary Moore and Colosseum II, that was going to be a bit of a problem.

CHAPTER TEN

A Change In The Weather

Back in 1966, the progressive blues boom that so thrilled Gary Moore had felt incredibly fresh and exciting, the songs produced by the likes of The Yardbirds, Cream, Jimi Hendrix and Fleetwood Mac full of possibility and wonder. Yet, as the movement expanded over time, so did its musical waistline, with extended jamming and rampant displays of instrumental virtuosity beginning to sound suspiciously like over-indulgence. By the mid-seventies, a second tier of groups inspired by 'blues rock' and its offshoots only consolidated this growing sense of corpulence, as solos stretched from minutes to hours and tunes began to take up entire sides of albums. Some called it artful experimentation. Others artistic intemperance. Gary probably called it two years served with Skid Row. But the big bang of fifties rock'n'roll and all it had set in motion now seemed very far away indeed.

Of course, it would be unfair to tar Moore's new band Colosseum II or their jazz-rock loving forbears with the same brush then basting the worst of these progressively inclined acts. After all, fusion, like bebop before it, had its roots in extended improvisation and individual prowess. Yet, by 1976, all such things were developing an unfortunate taint to them, and the critical buzzards were starting to circle. Tired of ever more

136

sybaritic displays of instrumental peacocking and the pompous behaviours being exhibited by certain bands, parts of the British rock press were becoming openly hostile to what they saw as a 'bloated rock aristocracy', labelling them 'dinosaurs' and 'enemies of change'. If nothing else, it sold papers.

Still, this air of dissatisfaction was being mirrored by younger music fans, who also appeared to be tiring of bands presenting themselves as satin-caped wizards or self-appointed monarchs of the realm. For instance, lean, mean R&B quartet Dr Feelgood were well on their way to their first number one UK album (*Stupidity*), with the solos of madcap six-string guitarist Wilko Johnson more resembling short, sharp shocks than the 15-minute mini-symphonies of certain other rock guitar gods. Soon enough, the shocks would become even sharper, as the first wave of a new musical movement called 'punk' began to make itself known in the clubs of London, Manchester and elsewhere.

As bassist Neil Murray already confirmed, Colosseum II were patently aware that the band had launched itself at precisely the time pop and rock music's tectonic plates were again beginning to shift. In fact, their leader was probably resigned to it. 'When [we] formed Colosseum II,' Jon Hiseman later confessed to Hit Channel, 'even as we went on the road, I knew [the band's] time was over . . . over before it even started, commercially. The world had moved on, but we were still playing music from 10 years before.' Yet, having fought so long and so hard to pull together the group, he and co-founder Gary Moore were in no mood to fall on their swords before they had even reached the battlefield. '[In rehearsals] we'd get there at ten in the morning and go on through till five. There's no mucking about in this band,' Moore told Pete Makowski of *Sounds*. 'I know we're going to have a hard time when we start gigging. I know we're going to get a hammering from the press or maybe go over people's heads, but we're not going to change for anybody.'

Deeply unfashionable then, but with nothing to lose because of it, it was unsurprising Colosseum II were determined to prove their mettle on stage as well as on record. Having already put in some serious road-work before the release of *Strange New Flesh*, the band now wasted no time in picking things up where they left off. After a hop around Europe in mid-May 1976, which included stop-offs in Denmark, Belgium and Switzerland, the quintet returned to Moore's old stomping ground of London's Marquee club on 16 June for a sell-out show before taping a BBC radio *In Concert* appearance 10 days later.

Now a reliable set opener, the opaque charms of 'Dark Side of the Moog' led the way for all that was to follow, namely an hour or so of frenzied solos, unearthly rhythms and the occasional tune impeccably sung by Mike Starrs. Indeed, whether furiously swapping lead lines on 'The Dark Side of the Moog', searching for grace notes on 'Down To You' or chasing after every derivation of the minor pentatonic scale on 'Gemini and Leo', Colosseum II made for an intense live experience. 'We never quite captured it on record,' Don Airey later confirmed, 'but live the band was absolutely explosive, maniacal even.'

The group was also short-lived, at least in that form. First to go was vocalist Mike Starrs, whose 'extravagant onstage persona' reportedly rankled the powers that be at Bronze Records so much they instructed Jon Hiseman to move him on, and pronto. Having already spent huge pockets of time waiting to sing while the rest of Colosseum II soloed themselves into infinity, Mike took the sacking in his stride. 'You win some, you lose some,' he later told *Universal Wheels*. 'All water under the bridge.'

Within days of Starrs' exit, Neil Murray was the next member of Colosseum II to find himself unexpectedly looking for work. According to the bassist, while Jon Hiseman had already expressed his preference for a more 'in the pocket' playing style than Murray's upfront approach, the exact reason for his sacking remains unknown. 'Well, it's very hard to know [what happened],' Murray said in 2020. 'At that point, the band had done a very long and tiring European tour . . . with very few days off and I was pretty exhausted. So, when someone from Bronze Germany came along to the second last show and asked me how was it going, I was pretty negative. Looking back on it after the fact, after the firing, I wonder what exactly prompted that. And I [think the rep] may have gone back to Gerry Bron or even Jon and said, "Neil's really negative. He's not into it." Well, that wasn't true. I was just completely knackered! Whatever the case, the reason [I was let go] was never put across to me, though my later understanding was that it came from Bronze Records who, for whatever reason, felt Mike and I didn't fit in.'

With Starrs now on his way to German hard rockers Lucifer's Friend and Neil Murray heading in the direction of jazz-progressive outfit National Health, Colosseum II's remaining members had some quick decisions to make. Solving the first issue by deciding that Moore should take over on lead vocals as and when required, the trio then recruited East Londoner John Mole after spotting the bassist playing in a pub.

A polite sort with a wry sense of humour, Mole certainly fulfilled Jon Hiseman's desire for a more in-the-pocket player, though he was also nimble-fingered enough to deal with Moore's often stretching compositional requirements. 'I'm one of these people who, when I write on the guitar . . . tend to forget people's capabilities,' Moore told *NME* at the time. 'And the next thing you know is that you've written this amazing collage of notes that people can't really reach unless they've got a really wide range.'

Line-up stabilised and then blooded with an impressive, if sweaty performance supporting Moore's old mate Rory Gallagher at a scorching hot Reading Festival on 29 August 1976[1], Colosseum II now appeared ready to move past recent difficulties and get on with the business of making music. It was at exactly that point Bronze Records decided to let them go. 'So, the band dispense with a lead vocalist, bring John Mole in on bass and then Bronze Records drop them!' said a mildly irked Neil Murray. 'I mean, why did Mike and I have to leave if you're going to bloody drop them?' The answer, it seemed, lay with the poor sales of *Strange New Flesh*, which while surprisingly well reviewed by an ever more hostile rock press, had hardly set cash registers ringing across the UK. Having only been in the band a matter of weeks, Mole must have wondered what he had got himself into.

Salvation was mercifully swift. Hearing of Colosseum II's dilemma, established business manager, co-founder of Morgan Records/Studios and long-time jazz fan Maurice 'Monty' Babson stepped forward with a

---

1 As anyone there at the time will confirm, the summer of 1976 was volcanically hot and still holds the record as the 'second hottest average summer temperature in the UK since records began.' *Scorchio*.

rescue package for the group. The deal he brokered with MCA Records wasn't perfect, with various contractual clauses around future rights and recordings. But it did get the band back on an even keel, and as importantly, back into the recording studio.

Hence, upon returning home from yet another European trek, Colosseum II found themselves in now chilly north-west London during mid-December 1976 to begin work on their second album at Morgan Studios. Located on the corner of Maybury Gardens and Willesden High Road, Morgan had sprung to life some ten years before as a single recording space, before Monty Babson and business partner Barry Morgan added to the brickwork and created a second studio and control area upstairs.

By the time Colosseum II rolled up, there were four rooms in all, so no matter what hour of day or night, a space could always be found for the group to commit ideas to tape. That said, much of the hard work had already been done, with the majority of compositions having taken shape either on the road or at Moore's flat in Cricklewood. As a result, after a week of further rehearsals, Colosseum II were in a position to cut their album live on the studio floor with a minimum of overdubs.

Released six months after the Morgan sessions concluded, Colosseum II's *Electric Savage* arrived in stores on 12 June 1977. Again produced by Jon Hiseman, the album was a considerable leap forward for the band, not only consolidating the early promise of *Strange New Flesh*, but also making the very best of their recently restructured line-up. In fact, more than 40 years later, Hiseman was still keen to sing the record's praises. 'Yes,' he confirmed in 2008, 'I think *Electric Savage* was one of the better records I was involved in.' At the heart of it all was a powerhouse performance from Gary Moore.

Moore made his presence felt on *Electric Savage* from the get go, with album opener 'Put it this Way'. A frenetic instrumental that employed a spiralling melodic ascent at its compositional centre, Moore's solo was 'sweet, sour and sticky,' alternating between passages of ultra-high-speed picking and light touch vibrato. 'I got into the picking thing much more [with Colosseum II], instead of just playing with one hand,' he later confirmed. 'Up until then, I'd been playing a very orthodox sort of rock guitar. But I got more into the John McLaughlin, Mahavishnu thing and . . . really had to strengthen my picking technique. To be honest, I couldn't have coped with the lines [we were playing] if I hadn't been able to have got that picking down a bit better.' This radically improved, jazz-infused technique was also gainfully employed on the classical-leaning 'The Scorch', which fused Don Airey's best 'Keith Emerson does Carl Orff' impression to Moore's tachyon-scaring solo excursions.

Of course, it wasn't just all about Gary Moore. Jon Hiseman practically owned entire sections of the album, his much admired, much-copied dual bass drum pedal technique put to good use on the funky-leaning 'All Skin and Bone', while the cymbal work displayed on the contemplative 'Am I' was in a class of its own. Bassist John Mole also clarified in some style why he had been chosen to join the band. Whether underpinning Moore's high-flying runs on 'Put it this Way', or providing a few flamenco-like flourishes of his own on the menacing 'Desperado', Mole was a lively presence throughout *Electric Savage*.

There were a few potholes in the road. Gary's love song to girlfriend Donna Campbell, the well-intentioned, if somewhat underwhelming 'Rivers', exposed what Colosseum II had lost by sacking Mike Starrs. Though Moore was a capable singer and getting better with each passing year, 'Rivers'' complex melody and high-rising chords often stretched his voice to breaking point, letting the song down as a result. In fact, two more tracks Colosseum II performed live when Starrs was still a member of the group, 'Siren' and 'The Awakening', were reportedly dropped from the album when Gary found himself unable to carry them off vocally.

Elsewhere, the Celtic-themed air 'Lament' was also something of a mixed blessing, its uneasy conjoining of faux Christmas bells and busy percussion jarring with Moore's slow-moving, almost weightless lead lines. First demoed for *Strange New Flesh* and always a bit hit or miss live, the tune, though memorable enough, was more missed opportunity than bullseye. The same couldn't be said, however, for *Electric Savage*'s final hurrah, Don Airey's turbo-driven 'Intergalactic Strut'. Originally called 'Interplanetary Slut' until someone had the good sense to change the title, 'Intergalactic Strut' summed up all that was exciting about Colosseum II in just under six minutes. Beginning with an inspired drum intro from Hiseman before Airey's itchy keyboard line took hold, Moore and Mole soon arrived to give the tune a proper hard rock workout, before the mood changed yet again and the listener was gently lowered into more jazzy waters. Inevitably, this honeyed interval didn't last too long, with Moore once again picking up the pace and Airey giving frantic chase before the whole thing came to a juddering halt in a blaze of paradiddles.

Containing shades of prog, jazz, hard rock, blues and even snippets of Irish folk, one couldn't accuse *Electric Savage* of lacking in variety. Yet in the six months the album had taken to make the leap from recording studio to record shop, Britain's musical landscape had shifted even further away from Colosseum II. By the summer of 1977, the UK punk rock scene had broken cover and reared its gloriously spiky head for all to see, as Sex Pistols, The Damned and The Clash led the charge towards national infamy on the back of some gloriously anarchic singles, politically barbed albums and riveting live performances.

In line with the new chaos, songs were becoming shorter, lyrics more acerbic and jeans tighter around the ankle. Unfortunately, the average member of Colosseum II was still sporting shoulder length curls, kimono-like tops, thick moustaches and bell-bottom flares. 'The band,' said *Melody Maker*, 'have all the energy of a punk show, but without the spitting.' Perhaps they did. But to the average punk rocker, Colosseum II still looked suspiciously like the enemy.

With *Electric Savage* heading swiftly for the bargain bins, punk in the commercial ascendant and drawbridges being hastily pulled up at the castle of many a rock star as a result, things appeared dicey for Moore and his cohorts. 'We were still gigging, but always seemed to be bloody broke,' he later complained. 'Records-wise, it just wasn't amounting to anything.' Thanks to the keen ear of a future Lord, however, Moore and his fellow band members were saved the prospect of financial penury. 'I told the boys, "It's Andrew Lloyd Webber,"' John Hiseman later laughed, '"and he's going to pay us real money!"'

Though not yet 30 years old, composer Andrew Lloyd Webber was still one the most recognisable faces on the UK theatre scene, thanks to an uncanny knack for writing hit musicals such as *Joseph and the Amazing Technicolor Dreamcoat* and *Jesus Christ Superstar*. However, when he lost a bet concerning the fate of his beloved Leyton Orient FC to equally football mad younger brother Julian, Lloyd Webber found himself returning to the classical music that informed his youth – or at least, a variation of it. 'I bet we'd get the draw we needed to [avoid relegation] and he didn't,' Julian recalled on *The South Bank Show*. 'Anyway, we drew 1-1 with Hull City and I won the bet. So, the forfeit was that Andrew had to write the cello piece he'd been promising [me]. *Variations* was born.'

For several years, Andrew Lloyd Webber had been promising to write a piece for his esteemed cello-playing brother. Yet, time, tide and the not insignificant soundtrack album he had been working on for his latest musical, the soon to be hugely successful *Evita*, all got in the way. Thanks to Leyton Orient, not any more. Struck by the idea of expanding the eighteenth-century classical violin virtuoso Niccolò Paganini's[2] glorious 24th caprice into 23 further variations, Lloyd Webber was keen to align his sibling's renowned bowing skills with the sound of a live rock band.

'I wanted to write something that six or seven musicians could actually perform without having to use tapes,' he later said. For brother Julian, while the project was surely enticing, it was also potentially career-ending. 'I'd been playing professionally for about five years and a lot of people in the classical world said, "You just can't do that, you just can't make a recording with a hard rock band, you'll ruin your career."' Thankfully, the cellist's agent – the legendary Emmie Tillett, or 'the Duchess of Wigmore Street' as she was known – offered some novel advice. 'Emmie said, "You should do it and see what happens. If it goes wrong, you can always say you had to do it because your brother wrote it."'

---

2 Born in Genoa, Italy on 27 October 1782, Niccolò Paganini was the pre-eminent violinist of his age. Displaying an astounding mastery of techniques such as pizzicato, octave skipping and the creation of artificial harmonics, some believed he had sold his soul to the devil in exchange for his musical gifts. Yep, that one again. Such rumours, appeared to do Paganini little commercial harm. In fact, his intense stage presence, canny showmanship and unrivalled command of the violin made him a huge concert draw throughout Europe at the time, and something of an early model for the modern rock star. Justly celebrated for his composition '24 Caprices for Solo Violin Op. 1', Paganini's work remains popular to this day and has been covered by some of our finer rock guitarists, including Steve Vai, Jason Becker, Yngwie Malmsteen and Uli Jon Roth.

With a clever idea in play and potential failure ably deflected if it all went wrong for at least one brother, the next stage for Andrew Lloyd Webber was finding a cast of strong supporting musicians for the project. They literally fell into his lap while visiting the offices of his record company MCA in the late spring of 1977, when the composer heard a test pressing of Colosseum II's *Electric Savage*. Immediately struck by the quality of the band, Lloyd Webber contacted Jon Hiseman, who in turn visited Lloyd Webber at home to hear the material he had been working on. Within weeks, both Lloyd Webbers, all of Colosseum II and Jon's wife Barbara Thompson were in Morgan Studios hard at work on what would become *Variations*.

With Andrew Lloyd Webber there to oversee the sessions, the responsibility for manning the desk fell to engineer/studio manager Martin Levan, a man whose innate likeability surely played a part when securing a job at Morgan six years before. 'Well, I walked off the street and into Morgan Studios in 1971,' he laughed. 'I met the studio manager and she said, "Have you come about the job?" I said, "Which job's that?" She said, "The tape operator's job." I said, "That's the one" and I started the next morning.' The son of a jazz violinist and theatrical dancer, a guitarist in his own right – 'Nothing major, though!' – and with over a half a decade's experience at Morgan to rely on, Levan was a perfect fit for the forthcoming project. 'I came in very late just before the sessions started on *Variations*,' he said. 'But I approached it as I always did. I listened to the music, twiddled the knobs and made it work.'

Recorded over the course of two weeks in the summer of 1977, *Variations* might not have been the first project to attempt fusing classical instrumentation to a rock/jazz background. But for those involved, there was still something of a learning curve to negotiate. 'Yes, but we didn't try and compartmentalise the material or treat the acoustic or electric instruments that differently from each other,' said Levan. '*Variations* wasn't recorded in the "classical" sense, but more as a rock/pop album. So, Julian's cello was close-miked as you would a rock instrument, [though] his approach was quite studious, as you might expect.' That said, so was the approach of the musicians surrounding him. 'Colosseum II were

144

obviously a rock band, but Jon Hiseman [also] had some real attachments to jazz,' Levan continued. 'Don Airey, on the other hand, [could do] straight ahead rock, but you know, again, he was into other things. Musically, they were a varied bunch, but they were there to work.'

To enable the musicians to deliver their optimum performance in the quickest possible time, Andrew Lloyd Webber provided sheet music for each of the variations. While this made the lives of the majority of players a good deal easier[3], these reams of careful notation were of no real use to Gary Moore. 'They looked like crows on a bloody telegraph line!' Having ducked out of learning any real musical theory as a child and in no great hurry to return to it despite the technical demands of Colosseum II, Moore could have been in trouble. Yet again, the guitarist's proven ear for melody was on hand to save his bacon.

'Gary had a very quick musical brain,' said Levan. 'He could learn melodies almost instantly. In fact, [in a way] it was fantastic working with Gary on *Variations* as [the music] really was outside his rock and blues comfort zone. There was a lot of complex, written out stuff that obviously wasn't his thing. But I always [believed] that his greatest [performance] was on that album because his ability . . . to tackle [any kind of music] so quickly and successfully proved for me that he really was the complete player.'

Drawing on inspirations as disparate as Rachmaninoff, cool jazz, vintage British music hall and even Moore's childhood heroes The Shadows, *Variations* was as diverse a record as one might come across. It was also another confirmed hit for Andrew Lloyd Webber, with the album reaching number two on the UK charts when released in January 1978. 'I think *Variations* arrived at exactly the right time,' said Martin Levan. 'Andrew was an up-and-coming force in the musical world, it was a great album

---

3 In addition to the Lloyd Webber brothers and Colosseum II, several other musicians also contributed to the recording of *Variations*, including songwriter (and former Zombie) Rod Argent, Genesis's ubiquitous Phil Collins and session bass ace Herbie Flowers. 'Rod Argent was around for quite a bit of it, while Phil and Herbie were only on 'Variation One', I believe,' said Martin Levan. 'We'd tried to record that a few times with Colosseum II, but on the day, it hadn't really worked out and Andrew wasn't happy with it. So, we booked a session [to redo it] with Phil and Herbie.' Rod Argent was so impressed with Gary Moore, he invited him to play on his own debut solo LP, 1978's *Moving Home*.

with a clever cover[4] and the mechanism to promote it properly was also there. So, I wasn't too surprised when it did well. Of course, [one of the variations] also ended up being used as the title music for *The South Bank Show*, which didn't hurt either.'

Indeed, the pinched harmonic Moore let fly from the neck of his Greeny as part of *Variations'* opening 'Theme' would ring out at the beginning of ITV's flagship arts programme for another four decades.[5] 'Gary Moore was simply one of the greatest, most underestimated rock guitarists ever,' the (now) Lord Lloyd-Webber[6] said in his 2019 autobiography, *Unmasked*. '[His] DNA screamed heavy metal, yet he was also the most lyrical guitarist I have worked with.' Handsomely paid for their 10-day stint on the album, and with an additional concert or two subsequently performed in support of the project during the summer of 1977[7], Colosseum II's contribution to *Variations* was to be the band's most commercially successful hour yet. Unfortunately, no matter how sterling their input, the LP was not their own. More worryingly, by hoisting their flag alongside that of 'a writer of West End musicals', the quartet were driving an even bigger wedge between them and a punk scene sizzling away across the UK. At the time, Gary Moore appeared outwardly nonchalant about such unfashionable associations. 'Frankly,' he opined, 'I don't care about any of that stuff.' Privately however, like many of his age and musical persuasion, it was likely another matter.

---

4 A novel update of Philippe Mercier's 1733 painting *Frederick, Prince of Wales, and his Sisters, Variations'* cover subverted Mercier's original illustration of the Georgian-era Prince playing cello alongside his musical siblings by placing some very modern images of speakers, microphones, headphones and electric guitars in the background.

5 Part of the 'Theme' from *Variations*, actually variation number three, was used as the title music for *The South Bank Show* until 2010, when the programme ended its 32-year run on the ITV network. However, the show was resurrected by Sky Arts two years later where it continues to be aired this day (2022). In short, Gary's famous squealing harmonic rides again.

6 In 1997, Andrew Lloyd Webber was made a life peer. His proper title is styled as Baron Lloyd-Webber.

7 *Variations* was first performed at 1977's Sydmonton summer arts festival on the grounds of Andrew Lloyd Webber's Hampshire country estate. The festival has since become an annual event.

In the end, Moore and Colosseum II's answer to the problem posed by the shifting sands of British pop and rock was to complete another album, the majority of which was actually recorded live before their involvement with *Variations*. Again, Martin Levan had been present, though on this occasion, he sat in the co-producer's chair alongside Jon Hiseman. However, despite all the anarchy, spitting and questions in Parliament going on outside the studio walls of Morgan, there would be no volte-face in artistic direction for Colosseum II. 'No,' laughed Martin, 'I actually remember Jon mentioning Chick Corea's albums a couple of times from a sound standpoint.'

Released in late November 1977, just a month or so before *Variations* splashed down to ecstatic reviews and high chart placings, Colosseum II's third disc, *War Dance*, popped into shops with little or no fanfare, and as a result, even fewer sales. A pity, because despite its flaws, the LP presented a band brave [or stubborn] enough to explore its own muse, no matter how contrary or at what cost. From Jon Hiseman's bad-tempered title track and the grumbling menace of 'The Inquisition' to the countless mood shifts of the 'Star Maiden/Mysterioso/Quasar' suite, Colosseum II were not writing pretty tunes for radio stations here. Instead, these were intricate, challenging compositions full of sudden rhythmic shunts, finger-tangling scales and odd little tonalities designed as much to confound the ear as bring it delight. This was particularly marked on the ballad 'Castles', where Moore's vocal seemed to linger dangerously on the precipice of discord, before the song's chorus presented him with a melodic escape route. 'It was demanding, complex music,' he later said, displaying a comedian's gift for understatement.

Yet, however testing Colosseum II's voyages to the outer limits of melody might have been, it was impossible to deny the technical skills of those involved. Weird and wondrous beats. Sonorous basslines. Sky-surfing keyboards. *War Dance* really was a player's paradise. 'Absolutely,' said Martin Levan. 'Colosseum II were all-round, incredibly accomplished musicians who could have crossed over to pretty much any musical format – and they did! The band did some extraordinary work on *War Dance*.'

And though it might sound churlish to highlight any one member of the band, Gary Moore's contributions to the LP really were superlative.

147

From the voice-mimicking slide solos and intervallic leaps of 'Major Keys' to the alternative picking of 'Fighting Talk' and 'Last Exit', Moore could no longer be judged as just a fleet-fingered blues rock player with one foot left in the sixties and a mimic's gift for jazz. Instead, he was on nodding terms with some of the better progressive/fusion guitarists of the time, the likes of Return to Forever's Bill Connors, Focus's Jan Akkerman and the marvellous Ray Gomez[8] now closer to equals than distant exemplars. 'There are only a handful of players who when they pick up a guitar it actually becomes part of their body and Gary was one of those players,' said Martin Levan. 'Believe me, listening to him, my jaw dropped, not once, but many, many times.'

Unfortunately, even with Moore's ever-evolving gift for dropping jaws, the commercial failure of *War Dance* proved a critical portent in the fate of Colosseum II. Despite some valuable tie-in publicity around their contribution to *Variations* and another BBC-backed *Sight and Sound* TV concert appearance at London's Victoria Hall in January 1978, the band's continued inability to sell albums meant any remaining goodwill at MCA Records was diminishing fast. Having battled valiantly for so long without any great reward, Jon Hiseman knew the band's time was up. 'We made some great music,' he said in 2015. 'But commercially, there was never a chance.'

In the end, it took the best part of a year for Colosseum II to properly disperse and step into their various futures. At the wheel as a band leader for the best part of a decade, John Hiseman was the first to switch seats, joining his wife Barbara Thompson on the passenger side of her new jazz project, Paraphernalia. The couple also continued their association with Andrew Lloyd Webber, helping the composer out on yet another of his musicals, Cats[9], among other enterprises. John Mole was

---

8   For those looking to discover one of jazz-rock's finest, but criminally unsung players, look no further than Ray Gomez. Whether tearing it up with bass supremo Stanley Clarke on 'School Days' or redefining the perimeters of fusion guitar on his own compositions such as 'West Side Boogie' and 'Make Your Move', Gomez's work is little short of breath-taking.

9   Moore was also on hand to help Andrew Lloyd Webber when he was putting together the musical *Cats*, with the guitarist providing a 'gorgeously lyrical' solo on an early recording of the show's key tune, 'Memory'.

not to be left out either, becoming Lloyd Webber's go-to bassist for several years and many a soundtrack album. As for *War Dance*'s talented co-producer, the sky was the limit, with Martin Levan providing award-winning sound design for several ALW future shows including *Phantom of the Opera*, *Cats*, *Kiss of the Spider Woman*, *Starlight Express* and *Sunset Boulevard*.[10] 'Andrew's is a family approach,' confirmed Levan. 'It doesn't always last very long, but while it lasts, it really is like a family.'

Don Airey, however, sought a different kind of thrill. Having duelled his way across the musical skies with Gary Moore for so long, Airey was in no great hurry to stop now. By December 1978, the keyboardist had accepted an invitation to join former Deep Purple guitar magus Ritchie Blackmore for yet more instrumental thrills and spills in the 'man in black's' latest outfit, Rainbow. That said, Airey was taking his memories of all those jazz-rock dogfights with him. 'Colosseum II were a great band,' he later said, 'and Gary really was at the top of his game during that period.' Their flight paths would cross again.

As for Gary Moore, the end of Colosseum II was no doubt a bitter-sweet time. Committing wholeheartedly to the idea of a 'hot instrumental outfit with a great singer', he and co-founder Jon Hiseman had seen the band through three rewarding, if enormously difficult years, only to have their efforts finally fall away to commercial and critical indifference. With hundreds rather than thousands choosing to bear witness to the group's in-concert gifts, and jazz rock now well and truly in the descendant, the jig really was up. '[We] didn't sell much,' Moore later said. 'No matter. It was what I was into at the time and I'm glad I did it.'

If Moore's concise assessment captured the bones of his tenure with Colosseum II, it also masked some of the discomforts he had experienced being part of such a high performing band. 'We were clever dicks, showing off on our instruments and seeing how incredibly complicated we could make our music,' he told *Q*'s Mat Snow in 1994. However, delivering at

10 In addition to his innovative theatre sound design work, Martin Levan also produced/engineered cast albums for many ALW-related productions. The Broadway cast recording of *Cats* – which he co-produced with the composer – won a Grammy Award for 'Best Cast Show Album'. Levan now owns and operates Red Kite Studios, a fine recording studio sitting neatly 'on the border of the Brecon Beacons.'

such a level came with a price. 'Every guitarist at that time was listening to John McLaughlin and playing in weird time signatures,' he continued, '[but] the people doing it properly, Mahavishnu, Weather Report, Chick Corea, were from a jazz background. I came from a rock background and was trying to emulate those guys. I didn't have the theoretical or harmonic knowledge to quite pull it off, so sometimes I'd be so drained after a gig, I'd have to lie down for an hour.'

Yet, despite the pressure, Moore had persisted. Indeed, even when an old friend came knocking in early 1977 with a not-so-covert offer to join his band, and as we shall soon see, a rather successful band at that, Moore would only commit to helping out for a short tour before again returning to Colosseum II. A promise had been made to Hiseman and co., and as one of Moore's friends confirmed, 'Gary had his faults, but [lack of] loyalty usually wasn't one of them.'

Of course, loyalty could carry Moore only so far, and with Colosseum II now slipping into history, Moore faced yet another search for where best to place his talents. At 26 years old, he was also no longer the 'teen virtuoso' or 'hot young gunslinger' who scorched Alvin Lee's ears way back in 1970. A seasoned professional with well over a decade on the musical clock, if Moore was to come good on all that early promise, making the right moves was crucial. As was ever the case, it boiled down to two distinct choices: strike out on his own or join another band. He solved the issue by doing both.

CHAPTER ELEVEN

A Short Detour Concerning The Deserved Success Of Thin Lizzy And How Gary Moore Finally Came To Join The Band

All things considered, Thin Lizzy had done quite well for themselves while Gary Moore was jazzing it up in Colosseum II. Given what was ahead for both parties, however, it's probably worth rewinding the clock to see exactly how they did it . . .

The road had been bumpy at first. Following Moore's short spell with the group in early 1974, several replacements came and went. Drummer Brian Downey grew so exasperated with it all he almost followed them. But when new guitarists Scott Gorham and Brian Robertson took up their marks stage left and right respectively, band leader Philip Lynott at last had a line-up that might well take on the world. 'Maybe so, but there was no great secret to it,' laughed Gorham in 2020. 'The chemistry was just there. It was a combination of people who were very different to each other, but when they all played together, something cohesive happened. A shared language, you might say, that led to a [mutual] trust and a confidence. When I first started playing with the others, I thought "I want to be part of this." We all did.'

Again, it didn't happen immediately. The quartet's first LP for their new record label Phonogram was a disappointment. Released in November 1974, *Nightlife* had the makings of a good album, but its disparate musical styles and anaemic production values (courtesy of the otherwise reliable Ron Nevison) meant the disc lacked for both cohesion and teeth. 'I called it the cocktail album,' quipped Gorham, 'because parts of it sounded like lounge music.' Yet within just 18 months, they hit the bullseye. After 1975's presciently named *Fighting* signposted the band's growing penchant for tougher, rock'n'roll-based sounds and inventive use of twin guitar harmonies, 1976's *Jailbreak* finally delivered the knock-out commercial blow Philip Lynott had been promising since Brush Shiels fired him from Skid Row nearly a decade before.

Full of classic tunes from the rumbling swagger of the title track to the rodeo-riding, lonesome bronco-buster of the immortal 'Cowboy Song', *Jailbreak* was pure entertainment from start to finish. That said, the album was defined by two towering compositions capturing the very essence of the band. In the case of 'Emerald', Lynott had transmuted his long-standing obsession with Ireland's rich mythology and its history of long, bloody conflicts into musical gold – the song's tale of grizzled glen-dwellers vanquishing their rulers driven ever forward by a distinctly Celtic-sounding riff.

Where 'Emerald' was all broadswords, bones and blood, 'The Boys Are Back in Town' made those listening simply glad to be alive. Properly introducing the record-buying public to the lilting guitar harmonies Brian Robertson and Scott Gorham had been working hard on since *Fighting*, Lynott again plugged into another of his primary lyrical fixations: turning the lives, loves, fisticuffs and fumbles of the Average Joe into something altogether more romantic, buccaneering and worthy of celebration.

152

A Short Detour Concerning The Deserved Success Of Thin Lizzy

Oozing wit, guile and some genuinely spellbinding songs, *Jailbreak* put Thin Lizzy into the UK Top 10, earned the band a gold disc and even gave them a hit album/single in the USA, where the LP and 'The Boys Are Back in Town' peaked at number eighteen and number twelve on the *Billboard* charts. This being Lizzy, however, any hope of a sustained breakthrough there faltered when Philip Lynott fell ill with hepatitis following the first leg of the band's American tour. Still, once Lynott was given time to recover if he would actually allow himself to), they would be back on the plane and back in the game. 'We had the bit between our teeth [for cracking the USA] by then,' said Brian Downey.

A new disc entitled *Johnny the Fox* arrived in shops by the autumn of 1976. Written mainly by Lynott while recuperating from his illness, the album – though impressive in places – was not as focused or memorable as *Jailbreak*, a fact no doubt exacerbated by Lynott's grim health over the previous months. Its recording was also a deeply unpleasant experience for all concerned, with Lynott and Brian Robertson clashing over choice of material[1], and as detailed in the next chapter, songwriting credits.

This clattering of egos between the two was a marker of things to come. Unlike Scott Gorham, whose gregarious nature and West Coast charm made him a perfect foil for Philip's alpha-male ways, Robertson's spells of emotional volatility, sometimes drink-related, and Glaswegian bluntness caused him to verbally clash with Lynott. Again and again and again. Worse, Robertson's keenly honed musical ear and quite brilliant guitar playing made everyone forget that only 12 months before, they had been dealing with a teenager. 'Maybe so, [but] Robbo's father was a professional jazz saxophonist. He was in the Art Blakey band, for God's sake,' said Gorham. 'His mother was a piano teacher. So, Brian knew music, all the scales, all the majors and all the minors. He was young, yes, but he knew all of that. Me, I knew none of it.'

---

1   This wasn't the first time Lynott and Robertson had butted heads in the studio over songs. During sessions for *Jailbreak*, the two had fallen out over the tune 'Running Back'. Robbo thought it was 'too Little Feat', and wanted to 'do it like a blues'. Philip did not. After words were exchanged, the Scotsman left for the pub and Lynott, Gorham and Downey finished the track without him.

153

The beginning of the end came on Tuesday, 23 November 1976, the day before Thin Lizzy were due to travel to the States and pick up their touring campaign where they had left it dangling several months before. While Lynott, Downey and Gorham hunkered down for the night in advance of the next morning's flight, Robertson chose instead to visit long-time rock'n'roll watering hole The Speakeasy in London's Marylebone. 'I shouldn't have,' he later told *Classic Rock*'s Johnny Black, 'but I was sitting in my flat, there was nothing to eat, so I went out for a meal.'

After finishing his dinner (pepper steak and Champagne, for those interested in such things), Robbo was invited to join guesting R&B band Gonzalez on stage for a few tunes. Exactly what happened next remains something of a mystery. But it appears when a somewhat refreshed Frankie 'Still in Love With You' Miller decided to sing along too, things rapidly turned sour. Words were allegedly exchanged between certain members of Gonzalez and Miller backstage, a bottle was smashed and according to Robertson, it was headed 'straight for Frankie's face'. Sticking out his hand to protect his friend, Robertson was caught instead. 'The glass went straight through my fingers, then sliced down and cut the tendons and nerves,' he said. 'It cut my artery as well. There was blood all over the stage.' Within an hour, Robbo was in surgery at St Mary's Hospital, Paddington. 'They told me I'd never play guitar again.' The ramifications of Robertson's actions were potentially as serious as his injuries. 'The road crew were already in the States preparing for the tour . . . and I had to call and tell them it was off,' said Thin Lizzy's manager, Chris O'Donnell. As for the band themselves, this was as close to professional suicide as it came. 'The night before our flight to the USA,' said Brian Downey in 2020. 'I mean, Jesus. We really thought we'd blown it. The end of Lizzy in America.' Scott Gorham was howling from the same rooftop. 'The timing couldn't have been fucking worse! I mean, you can't make that shit up. The fucking night before the tour. What are we going to do? Who are we gonna call?' There was only one man for the job. 'Philip says, "I know this guy . . ."' Scott continued. 'I said, "What? This guy's going learn the set in one night?" He said, "Yeah. He can do things like that." I said, "Who is he?" Philip says, "Gary. Gary Moore."'

As with the first time he saved Thin Lizzy's blushes back in 1974, Gary Moore was again mercifully free to help out when the call came in from Philip Lynott. Though he had recently been busy recording Colosseum II's second LP *Electric Savage*, a break in the band's schedule now meant Moore could take up arms alongside Thin Lizzy in the States. Reading between the lines, he might have been expecting it. 'I think Phil had been having problems with Robbo for a while,' Moore later told author Mark Putterford, 'and really, he wanted me back in Lizzy. In fact, we were going to discuss [it] when the band returned from the States, but then fate accelerated the situation.'

Lynott had never really stopped hoping Gary Moore would rejoin his band. Fan, friend and flatmate of the guitarist since their days together back in Dublin, Lynott had not forgotten his brief but electrifying turn with Thin Lizzy following Eric Bell's departure from the group. Indeed, he was still insisting that Brian Robertson replicate Moore's solo note for note on 'Still in Love With You' each night on stage. 'You can imagine how well that went over,' quipped Gorham. If rumours are correct, Lynott had even immortalised Moore in song, his coded reference to 'good looks' and 'scars' on *Jailbreak*'s 'Romeo and the Lonely Girl'[2] a sly nod to Moore's unfortunate glassing two or so years before. Now that Moore was back in the ranks, he might have the opportunity to play on his own tribute tune.

With Brian Robertson out of the picture, and very possibly out of the band too, Gary Moore rolled up his sleeves in January 1977 to join Thin Lizzy for their hastily rescheduled tour of North America. That said, while Lynott and Downey were more than familiar with Moore – 'When Phil said, "Well, why don't we ask Gary back?", I thought, "bloody great idea!"' laughed Brian – Scott Gorham had not had the pleasure of making his acquaintance. 'The first time I actually met Gary was on the plane to the States heading for pre-tour rehearsals,' said the guitarist. 'Then there we are at the rehearsal studios in New York. For

---

2   Though Philip Lynott never publicly acknowledged it, it's a fair bet that 'Romeo and the Lonely Girl' is indeed a tribute to Gary Moore. There are three excellent reasons to believe so. First is the 'scar' reference in the song's second verse. Second, 'Romeo' is an anagram of 'Moore'. Last but not least, Gary once said it was about him. So . . .

me, it was like, "Fuck. This guy can play. I'm going to have to up my game here!" But I also thought this is going be great for Lizzy.'

Potentially, it was. Though the group had recently lost ground in the States to Lynott's hepatitis and Robertson's skewed, if honourable antics at The Speakeasy, Thin Lizzy now had the chance to make amends with a high-profile jaunt supporting the mighty Queen. Described by ever-present road manager Frank Murray as an opportunity 'to really play with the big boys,' Freddie Mercury's quartet were then in their pomp and Lizzy were genuinely fortunate in securing the opening slot for 42 shows. 'Big responsibility,' continued Gorham. 'I mean, Queen were huge at that point and these were some big dates. But you know, we had some pulling power of our own by then. Not major perhaps, but enough. So, all in all, we had to have our shit together. And you know what? We did.'

As was the case in early 1974, Moore's arrival in Thin Lizzy triggered a renewed wave of energy within the band. Though they only had 40 minutes of stage time each night to call their own, Lizzy used it well, leaning on the more recent commercial earworms in their repertoire to create maximum impact with audiences. Arenas across the USA found themselves reverberating to 'Jailbreak', 'Massacre', 'Emerald', and in a rare blast from the past, Moore's original guitar showcase 'Still in Love With You', the song's solo section now returned to its rightful owner. 'After two or three gigs,' confirmed Gorham, 'we were flying.'

In fact, Thin Lizzy were doing so well at times that one member of Queen felt his group's trademark 'thunder and lightning' was being pilfered right from beneath their regal eyes. 'Apparently Freddie Mercury was very intimidated by Lizzy,' Moore later told author Mark Putterford. 'People would tell us he was stomping up and down in the dressing room while we were on stage saying, "Listen to that applause! Get that band off now!"' Brian Downey doesn't quite remember it that way. 'No,' confirmed the drummer in 2020, 'Queen's guitarist, Brian May, was a big Lizzy fan, so he and the band made it really easy for us.' Scott Gorham concurred. 'Nobody in America had really seen us and being on stage was our main stomping ground,' he said. 'So, Queen gave us a chance to do that, to show America . . . what Thin Lizzy was all about and what we could do. We all became great friends, too. We loved touring with them, [and] I'll always be in debt to Freddie, Brian, Roger and John for helping us out.'

Marked by occasionally atrocious weather, 'a couple of shows were cancelled due to severe blizzard conditions,' said Moore, and a curiously lacklustre turn from the band at New York's Madison Square Garden ('We didn't even get an encore,' said Scott), Thin Lizzy's Stateside adventure was still deemed a triumph. 'For me at least,' continued Moore, 'It was better than my first stint in the band, and it was the best thing Lizzy ever did in terms of raising their profile in the USA.' Philip Lynott felt the same way. 'Oh yeah, Philip wanted Gary to join at that point,' said Gorham. 'Let's be honest. He was particularly pissed off at Brian. Robbo had ruined everything by going out the night before we were meant to start this massive tour. So, I guess Philip thought, "We don't need to get Robbo back. Let's get Gary in and keep on going."'

Yet loyalty can be a funny thing. Though Colosseum II could hardly fill out a small church hall and had only a fraction of Thin Lizzy's record sales at the time, Moore again turned down Lynott's offer to join the group. 'Well, they wanted me to stay . . . after that,' he later told *The Georgia Straight*'s Steve Newton. '[But] the thing was I was still with Colosseum II and we'd just made a record. I didn't want to just walk out of the situation. So, yes, I went back to Colosseum II.' For Moore, when it came to Jon Hiseman and co. at least, it really was all about 'semper fidelis'. 'I had a lot of loyalty to those guys, and I didn't want to walk out and leave them in the shit.' Not every group Gary subsequently joined would inspire quite the same fealty.

After Moore's surprise exit, Thin Lizzy pressed on to some effect. Buoyed by their recent American experiences, the group entered Toronto's Sound Studios in May 1977 as a trio to record their next album, the rather wonderful *Bad Reputation*. With no Moore or Brian Robertson to aid him, Scott Gorham did much of the heavy guitar lifting, and a fine job he did of it. Whether soloing out of his skin on the title track or harmonising with himself on 'Southbound' and 'Soldier of Fortune', Gorham's impressive performance almost raised the question as to whether Thin Lizzy really needed another guitarist. Almost. 'Even when we were recording *Bad Reputation*, creating all those harmonies and guitar lines on my own, I still wanted Robbo to come back,' said Scott. 'He was the guy we started this thing with, and he was the guy we needed to keep the continuity going. I'd never been in a situation where you changed horses mid-stream. In fact, I deliberately didn't play any solos on two or three songs because I was still arguing with Philip over Robbo.' At first, Lynott was having none of it. 'He just looked at me and said, "No fucking way."' But by sheer force of logic, Gorham got Thin Lizzy's leader to reconsider his position. 'I said, "Hey, you know when the album's finished, we'll be back on the road, and who's going to play the harmony guitars? We can't do it as a trio, Phil." Eventually, he cracks and says, "OK, we'll get him back in. But when – not if – when he fucks up, it's on you." "Fair enough," I say.'

Against medical odds, Brian Robertson had made a full recovery following The Speakeasy incident of November 1976, a fact stunningly confirmed on the solos he provided for *Bad Reputation*. Dropping his black 1960 Gibson Les Paul Custom into the spaces left for him by Scott Gorham on 'Opium Trail' and 'Killer Without a Cause', Robbo's snake-mean, wah-pedal assisted runs proved once and for all that when he was in the zone there really was no guitarist better suited to Thin Lizzy. With Philip Lynott now in reluctant agreement, Robertson was first allowed back into the band as a 'special guest', before once again joining Lizzy on tour. 'Yep,' said Scott. 'But you know what happened next.'

In commercial terms at least, what happened next was the release of 1978's *Live and Dangerous*. Probably the finest concert album ever, though fans of The Who, Deep Purple, Johnny Cash or UFO[3] might beg to differ, *Live and Dangerous* was essentially a composite of two 'greatest hits' shows recorded at London's Hammersmith Odeon and Toronto's Seneca College Fieldhouse in 1976 and 1977, respectively.[4] Featuring just a smidgeon under

---

3   Those who do not believe Thin Lizzy's *Live and Dangerous* to be the best live album ever may point instead to The Who's seminal *Live at Leeds*, Deep Purple's *Made in Japan*, Johnny Cash's *At Folsom Prison* or UFO's masterful *Strangers in the Night*. Truth be told, there are scores of other worthy contenders, but *Live and Dangerous* takes some beating.

4   It later came to light that two shows at Philadelphia's Tower Theater on 20/21 October 1977 had also been recorded and possibly used for the LP. The smart money, however, is on the Hammersmith Odeon gig of 14 November 1976 providing the majority of tracks featured on the album.

70 minutes of Robertson, Gorham, Downey and Lynott on a planet of their own making, *NME* called the double LP 'the best live album we ever heard', thereby rubberstamping what record shop retailers and the band themselves already knew. Thin Lizzy were on their way to becoming superstars.

'*Live and Dangerous*? Great album. Went to number two in the UK!' chuckled Gorham. 'The only group keeping us off the top were the fucking Bee Gees. And I love The Bee Gees! I mean, we were selling 60,000 copies of the album a week, it was the train that just kept rolling. Five, six nights at Hammersmith Odeon. Big all over Europe. Even now, I look back and think, "Fuck, did that really happen?"'

Rest assured, it did. But even the runaway success of *Live and Dangerous* and the 'mega tour' that followed in its wake couldn't stop the rot between Philip Lynott and Brian Robertson. By his own admission 'totally out of control . . . [on] a lot of whiskey and . . . a lot of speed', Robbo's already fiery personality was now entering uncharted territories. Unfortunately, Lynott – increasingly irritated by the guitarist's behaviour, and as we shall soon see, now not without problems of his own – had also reached the end of his rope.

'Philip was just unhappy with Robbo,' said Brian Downey. 'He was always in the wars. The drinking. The clubs. The Speakeasy. I mean, Philip never forgot that. He was like a fucking elephant. He just never forgave him. I know Robbo was trying to help Frankie Miller that night, but . . . it was too late. No one had an excuse for Brian Robertson. Philip said to me "I've been thinking about this for a quite a while. I don't think I can work with him anymore." It was a long goodbye. But it was goodbye, nonetheless.' Following a fierce post-gig argument between the two in Ibiza on 6 July 1978, a meeting was called at the band's offices in Soho. Brian Robertson left Thin Lizzy soon after.[5] 'I started off by

---

5 Following his exit from Thin Lizzy, Brian Robertson formed melodic rockers Wild Horses with fellow Scot and ex-Rainbow bassist Jimmy Bain. After cutting two fine, if commercially unsuccessful albums for EMI, the band folded and Robertson surprised many by joining gnarly genius Lemmy in Motörhead. The union lasted for one LP (1983's *Another Perfect Day*) before both parties went their separate ways. Since then, Robbo has guested with various acts and even released a solo disc – 2011's *Diamonds and Dirt*. For many, he remains the best guitarist Thin Lizzy ever had. He'd probably agree.

thinking "I'll form a band where everybody is equal, and we can all do what we want, right?"' Lynott once said of his issues with the Scottish guitarist. 'And that's OK if everybody is playing to the rules. But if somebody's using a different set of rules, well . . .' Well, indeed. 'In the end,' concluded Downey, 'Philip just wasn't listening to Robbo [anymore].'

In all likelihood, Philip Lynott had heard all he wanted to when news of Colosseum II's impending demise reached those finely tuned ears four or so months before. Tired of warring with Robbo and still sure that Gary Moore was key to the perfect Thin Lizzy, Lynott had probably already made up his mind as to where to take the band next, and with whom. 'When Robbo left, Philip said, "It's got to be Gary" and I said, "Fucking A,"' Gorham confirmed. 'There was no one else in the frame. There was the old friendship. The Irish connection. He'd proved himself once and everyone knew what he could do, and how it could be done. Gary,' said Scott, 'was the obvious choice, so Philip asked him to join.'

Back in early 1977 when Philip Lynott had last asked the question, Moore's response had been gracious, but empathetic. 'No, I'm going to stick with Colosseum II,' he had said, 'give it another year, see what happens.' Yet, after 12 more months of traipsing around small venues, only to be rewarded by even smaller record sales, things were very different. 'Colosseum II? Well, we had a go,' he later told *International Musician*. '[But] I don't think that kind of music will occupy a large place in the history of rock.' Wounded by punk. Killed by new wave. Whichever way you spun the bottle, the result was the same. Pragmatism as much as loyalty was now a major consideration for Moore.

After all, the facts were plain to see. Thin Lizzy were heading towards 600,000 units sold for *Live and Dangerous*, a number then unheard of in the UK for a two-disc concert set from a 'hard rock' band, no matter how mellifluous or lyrically inventive. As importantly, Lizzy could now fill venues as cavernous as The Empire Pool, Wembley, twice in a row. With almost 9,000 punters through the turnstiles each night, that was quite the gate. Hit singles. Best-selling albums. Adoring fans. It was all there for the taking.

Moore took it. By late July 1978, a deal was struck. Ostensibly, he became an 'employee' of Thin Lizzy, his fortunes tied to forthcoming record releases and concert receipts rather than songwriting royalties earned by previous line-ups. There would be hiccups later about exactly what this meant. But for the time being at least, everyone appeared happy. At last, Gary Moore was in the band. The media were informed. Given Moore and Lizzy's shared history, no one was that surprised.

'I was absolutely delighted when Gary signed up, because we had a definite plan of action,' said Brian Downey. 'Gary was a good friend of the band, as well as an amazing musician. We'd known him for years, from Belfast to Dublin, then London. He'd helped us out in the past, knew what we wanted to do and he was dependable. At the time, I just felt relief.' For Scott Gorham, relief was subsumed by happiness. 'Well, yeah,' he said. 'Philo had always said that I had to be 100 per cent happy with the decision about Gary joining. After all, I was the guy who was going to be playing guitar with him. But I mean, how could you not be happy playing alongside Gary Moore, for God's sake? . . . But then,' Gorham continued, 'Phil said, "Don't trust him. Ever." Wait a fucking minute. We just got this guy in the band and you're saying, "Don't trust him." What are you fucking talking about? Phil just repeats it, but won't really go any further than that. So, now I've got a question mark hanging over the whole thing, though I don't really know why or what he means. Well,' Scott concluded, 'I soon did.' It was all about to get very complicated.

CHAPTER TWELVE

It Started Off So Well . . .

By joining Thin Lizzy in July 1978, Gary Moore finally surrendered his old nickname 'Super Sub' to become the band's new star striker. That wasn't quite the end of it, however. In addition to his succession to Lizzy's front bench, Moore had already signed a record deal with MCA for a solo album, while also forming a punk/rock supergroup to keep him in readies for the pub. Surprisingly, this hectic arrangement would work out rather well for him, until unforeseen circumstances put an abrupt end to some, if not all of these activities. Still, in the summer of 1978 at least, it was all going roughly to plan as Moore juggled his time and commitments in an effort to keep both himself and everyone else happy.

Helping keep all the balls in the air was Thin Lizzy frontman Philip Lynott, who appeared content to support and even indulge Moore's various commitments. In fact, despite the apparent and thus far, seemingly groundless reservations he had privately expressed to Scott Gorham about the guitarist's trustworthiness, Lynott sounded publicly delighted to have someone of Moore's calibre back on board. 'Gary has only the highest aims as a musician and instrumentalist,' he said, before adding with a trademark wink, 'I mean, he's into jazz rock, and all that . . .

technical stuff.' Yet, beyond the sly asides, Lynott knew exactly why he had asked Moore to join his band. 'Phil wanted to work hand in glove [with Gary],' said Brian Downey, 'and to make sure that work really paid off.'

Whatever the professional ambitions Philip Lynott had in mind with, or for, Moore, Thin Lizzy's leader also seemed determined to ensure the guitarist fitted the band stylistically, as well as musically. Just as he had in Dublin 10 years before when 16-year-old Moore first arrived in town, Lynott was now hell-bent on introducing Moore to London's hipper clothing shops in an effort to sharpen up his jazz-rock wardrobe. Long used to wearing the 'flowing blouson, flares and leather boots combination' so beloved of serious musicians in the early seventies, Moore was urgently in need of a fashion upgrade, and Lynott knew it.

Hence, Moore was bundled into the back of Lynott's blue Mercedes and chauffeur-driven towards London's King's Road, where he found himself rummaging through the racks at ace rockers' clothing shops like Johnson's. Already a firm favourite with Lynott, outfitters like Johnson's and several other stalls in nearby Kensington market would provide Moore with a new look comprised of ultra-skinny jeans, leopard print shirts, studded belts and a variety of biker, drape and silver lamé jackets. To cap it all off, he also invested in a fine pair of white leather brothel creepers, which Moore wore at most every opportunity. Originally modelled by English teddy boys in the fifties, but recently commandeered by the punk movement as their footwear of choice, these crepe-rubber-soled wonders would complete Moore's transformation from dated hippie fusioneer to sharp-cut, new wave-style rocker, albeit one still sporting shoulder length hair. As it turned out, Moore's radically revised threads blended in perfectly with the new friends he made at Lynott's house in Cricklewood some months before.

Unlike many of his contemporaries, Lynott had neither scorned punk, nor hid indoors waiting for the revolution to pass. Instead, he invited the key players around for tea and biscuits. 'Well, Philip was always a great catalyst for what was going on [musically],' Moore later told *Norwich Evening News*' Rob Garratt. 'In fact, if you felt uncomfortable about what was going on around you . . . he would just trivialise it. I mean, I was really worried about [the impact of] punk and he said "That's just rock with safety pins.'"

Lynott was perfectly correct. When punk first came screeching around the corner in 1976, some rock star types were privately terrified of what it meant for their futures, Gary Moore included. Yet, when one placed aside all the faux Situationism and ill-defined threats of anarchy, punk conformed to the standard model of most youth-driven cults. In short: a gang of talented working-class kids trying to escape their circumstances by making a lot of noise in return for a lot of money. An old Crumlin warhorse like Philip Lynott had no trouble understanding that, or how to make it work for him and his band. 'Philip was paranoid he might get left behind,' Moore said in 1993. 'So, when punk came along, he'd befriended the likes of Sex Pistols' Steve Jones and Paul Cook to stay in touch. Also, I think Thin Lizzy were accepted by the punk community because [unlike some other bands], we weren't so much older than them, really.'

With Pistols guitarist Steve Jones and drummer Paul Cook already on side[1], it wasn't long before other punk stars were knocking at the door of Lynott's home on Cricklewood's Anson Road. As well as Jones, Cook and The Clash's Joe Strummer, Lynott found himself playing host to The Boomtown Rats singer/fellow Dubliner Bob Geldof and his girlfriend Paula Yates, while also entertaining 'Mr Ferocious' himself, the none-more-punk Sid Vicious. Yet, unlike his terrifying public image, Sid and American partner Nancy Spungen seemed neither ferocious nor particularly vicious, the doomed pair apparently more content to play old Elvis films on Lynott's brand-new video recorder than wreak any lasting havoc.[2] According to Lynott's close friend, then-housemate and

---

1 By all accounts, Lynott became friendly with Jones and Cook when all three guested on 1978's *So Alone*, the debut solo LP from former New York Dolls/then current Heartbreaker Johnny Thunders.

2 On 12 October 1978, Sid Vicious awoke in his room at New York's Chelsea Hotel to find girlfriend Nancy Spungen dead on the bathroom floor, a stab wound to her abdomen. Vicious was later charged with her murder. While out on bail, he succumbed to a heroin overdose, dying on 1 February 1979. He was only 21 years old; Nancy was 20. 'Their end was tragic beyond words,' Chalkie Davies later said, 'but it fitted the legend that they had already carved out for themselves.'

still much esteemed rock photographer Chalkie Davies, 'Chez Lynott' was never really modelled on the last days of the Roman Empire anyway. 'People think it must have been non-stop partying,' Davies told author Graeme Thomson, '[but] no. We slept. I don't ever remember having a party. Life off the road was quiet, because you were exhausted.'

It was while relaxing in this atmosphere of punks, rockers and other temporary house guests like Heavy Metal Kids vocalist Gary Holton (more of him later) that Gary Moore happened upon on one of his more novel ideas. 'Well, Gary was the one who came up with the idea for The Greedy Bastards,' Davies confirmed in 2020. 'Sort of, anyway. There was a few of us at Anson Road one night – Philip, Steve Jones, Paul Cook, Gary, Me and Scott Gorham – and Gary was laughing away, going on about the fact he didn't have a manager and just wanted to just get paid in cash. And this evolved into doing gigs for cash. Now, Frank Murray had just found the Electric Ballroom in Camden Town, it hadn't been used for years, and the idea arose that this [new band] would debut there.' For Moore, who was no longer with Colosseum II, but not quite yet an official member of Thin Lizzy at the time of his brainstorm, this was glorious news. 'No managers, no guest lists,' he later laughed, 'just play the gig, get paid, then good night!' All that was needed was a name. 'Phil came up with it,' said Moore. 'He said, call it "The Greedy Bastards".' The Greedy Bastards it was.[3]

According to rumour, when word got out that various members of Thin Lizzy and Sex Pistols were lining up a concert, just about everyone wanted to be part of it, including some very unlikely names. 'Yeah,' Moore later told author Mark Putterford, 'even Elton John wanted to do it!' But he didn't. That said, the line-up that stepped on stage at Camden's Electric Ballroom, ironically, once a dancehall catering for Irish immigrants, on 29 July 1978 was still impressive. Joining Moore (by now officially a paid-up member of Thin Lizzy) and Lynott were Scott Gorham, Brian Downey, Steve Jones, Paul Cook, session guitar supremo,

---

3 Another story has it that The Greedies' wonderful nom de plume was actually coined by the Electric Ballroom's manager, Bill Fuller. When booking the band, he asked how much they wanted, and was told '75 per cent of the door.' 'What a crowd of greedy bastards,' said Fuller. The name supposedly stuck. Even if it isn't true, it should be.

occasional solo artist 'and all-round good bloke' Chris Spedding and Rainbow/Wild Horses' Jimmy Bain.

Perhaps unsurprisingly, the set was heavy on Lizzy tunes, with 'Jailbreak' kicking things off, before 'Don't Believe a Word' and 'The Boys Are Back in Town' followed in rapid succession, Moore already putting his unique stamp on each. It wasn't just the 'Phil and Garro show,' though. Before long, Jones stepped up to the microphone to lead those assembled through his own group's 'Black Leather' and 'No One Is Innocent', after which Chris Spedding delighted the crowd with a lusty version of his recent hit 'Motorbikin''. From there, it was a race to the finish, the octet chancing their collective arm with a cover of the vintage sixties surf instrumental 'Wipe Out', before handing in a chaotic rendition of the Pistols' 'Pretty Vacant', christened 'Pretty Greedy' especially for the occasion. 'That night was insane,' Lynott said after the event. 'We had a set list, which everybody threw something into, and it didn't really matter whether anyone knew the words, or even the song. It was like, "Here we are. This is what we want to play, and if you think we fucked up, you can fuck off."'

After the controlled chaos of the Electric Ballroom, there would be other Greedies shows. One took place six months later on 16 December at the same venue, this time featuring Bob Geldof storming the stage for a raw take on The Boomtown Rats' 'Lookin' After No 1'. Another two gigs followed within four days, this time at Dublin's cosy Stardust club. Here, Gary's old mates Brush Shiels and Noel Bridgeman joined in the fun, while post-punk cherubs U2 offered mild-mannered support to the sweary headliners. (Their time would come soon enough.) A single, though not involving Moore, would also make its way into the world, with 'A Merry Jingle' landing at number twenty-eight in the UK charts almost 18 months after Gary first thought up the joke. 'It'd probably all worn a bit thin by then, though,' Lynott grimaced, with later events neatly underlining his point.

Still, in July 1978, Moore's scheme had served a valuable (if probably quite unintended) purpose, allowing a wily cowboy like Lynott to tie his horse to a passing stagecoach called punk, and in so doing, keep Thin Lizzy 'cool, fashionable and current'. As importantly, at least in Moore's eyes, The Greedies had also gifted Gary the opportunity to purchase a rather attractive 1955 sunburst Gibson Les Paul Junior from The Pistols' Steve Jones, himself no slouch when it came to the art of guitar mangling. 'Yeah, I got it from Steve,' Moore later told *International Musician*, 'so [it's got] a pretty good pedigree.' A simple but deadly weapon he had first seen wielded by Mountain's Leslie West nearly eight years before, Moore would soon take the 'Melody Maker' for a quite stunning test drive across Australia with Thin Lizzy. However, before that happened, there was the not insignificant task of promoting his recently recorded LP.

At the start of what was rapidly becoming an eventful year, Gary Moore had dealt with the impending dissolution of Colosseum II by activating a pre-existing clause with MCA Records to cut a solo album. Looking through the rear-view mirror decades on, the move was a consolidation of Moore's standing at the time. Increasingly the band's star player, it was Gary who sang the songs and often spoke to the crowds in concert, his position centre stage also underlining that, while Jon Hiseman's name had secured Colosseum II their album deal, Moore was now unofficially fronting the show. 'Jon was very much the leader,' said former Colosseum II bassist Neil Murray, 'and he . . . really wanted a band where everyone was as good as each other – [not one] that operated as a platform for guitar solos. It was more, "Here's some very interesting and complicated material, vocally, instrumentally, you name it." But it has to be said Gary [became] a standout performer.'

With Thin Lizzy still several months away from making him an official offer, Moore had begun recording the bulk of material for his first official album as a solo artist (lest we forget, 1973's *Grinding Stone* was credited to The Gary Moore Band) in the early spring of 1978.[4] His choice of producer for the project was a brave one. Instead of seeking out a 'name' or 'hitmaker', he chose instead to go with Chris Tsangarides, the promising, but still largely unproven engineer with whom he had worked on Colosseum II's last two albums.

For Tsangarides, this was a vertiginous promotion, but not an unwelcome one. 'Gary said to me, "Well, you might as well produce it with

---

4 According to some reports, Moore may have even begun recording material for the LP in the summer of 1977, though this is hard to verify.

me,"' he later told writer Malcolm Dome. 'I never thought he actually meant it, but of course, he did. I suppose our relationship was very much that I was the studio technician and Gary was the artist. It was a case of, "You play it son, and I'll record it."' Though a surprising choice, Tsangarides turned out to be a perfect foil for Moore, with the two becoming firm friends over the course of making the LP. 'Gary had never really done a "solo" album before,' he said. 'So there was no precedent. Anything was possible. And,' he concluded, 'I was cheap!'

At first, Moore seemed keen not to stray too far from his recent forays into jazz rock for the album's musical content, a fact underlined by the original tranche of musicians invited in to help him out. Further, with both John Mole and Don Airey returning to their former roles as bassist and keyboardist, respectively, the LP's formative recording sessions were already looking suspiciously like a reunion of sorts. One name, however, didn't appear to be on the guest list. 'Why wasn't Jon Hiseman involved?' Airey later said. 'Well, that would have made it just another Colosseum II record . . . wouldn't it?' With Hiseman committed to other projects and seemingly happy to let his former colleagues get on without him, a replacement drummer was required. Finding one as good as Hiseman would be problematic, but, as it turned out, not impossible. 'John Mole on bass, Don Airey on keyboards, Gary Moore on guitar. Three quarters of Colosseum II right there. So, ladies and gentlemen, the part of John Hiseman will be played tonight by me, Simon Phillips!'

Only just into his twenties, but already a hugely in-demand session man, Simon Phillips' first gig of note had been working alongside former Roxy Music luminaries Brian Eno and Phil Manzanera in 1976's promising, if short-lived supergroup 801. After that, it was a short walk toward metal gods Judas Priest to play drums on their 1977 LP *Sin After Sin* before those session dates really began to pile up, including several at Morgan Studios where Gary's record was being cut. Already a fan of Phillips, Tsangarides suggested that Moore give him a try. 'I first met Gary . . . at Morgan Studio One, the upstairs studio with 16 tracks,' Phillips remembered. 'I'd actually been playing with Jack Bruce at that time and Gary was a huge fan of Jack's. So, in a way, he was a bit like a kid, asking all these questions about Jack, you know, really interested.'

That interest led in turn to a jam, and then a firm offer to play on Moore's album. 'Up until that point, I hadn't done a lot of "jazz" records,' Phillips confirmed. 'It had all been rock'n'roll or pop sessions. So, it was going to be really interesting to play some jazz, some real fusion.'

With players in place, 'They really should have called it Colosseum III,' someone quipped, Morgan Studio One became Moore's place of business, with everything set up just the way he liked it. 'John Mole was on the right, Don was near the control room and Gary was on my left behind a couple of those old BBC-type sound screens that did fuck all, basically,' laughed Phillips. 'He had four Marshall 4x12s, two WEM Copicat echo units and two Marshall heads, which I'm guessing were 50 watts. Gary's 50-watt Marshall was a very sweet-sounding amp. AC/DC's Angus and Malcolm Young and UFO's Michael Schenker were all using them [at the time] because the 100-watt heads were just too powerful and loud. Remember, there's a limit to the amount of volume [you can use] in a studio.' That said, when Moore plugged in 'the Greeny', the earth moved. 'Ha!' laughed Phillips. 'Yep, when Gary started playing, my snares would start buzzing away.'

Between them, Moore, Phillips, Airey and Mole recorded seven tracks in all, with four of those destined for the final running order of the LP.[5] As had been the way with Colosseum II, the songs were recorded more or less live, with Tsangarides overseeing levels from the control room while simultaneously cracking jokes to keep the atmosphere smooth and trouble-free. 'Oh, Chris was a laugh a minute,' Don Airey told journalist Malcolm Dome, 'and that rubbed off on everyone else.'

There is little doubting both the joy and energy present at the Morgan sessions, as the quartet tucked into a menu of prime fusion-influenced cuts all written by Gary, each with their particular flavour. Evidently, 'Flight of the Snow Moose' found Moore in search of some-

5 Three compositions recorded for the album, 'Road to Pain', 'Track Nine' and 'Track Ten', were omitted from the final running order. In the case of power ballad 'Road to Pain', Moore seemed to be channelling both Cream and Hendrix, his solo taking particular inspiration from Jimi's own tour de force 'Machine Gun'. The moody 'Track Nine' and 'Track Ten', however, could easily have been Colosseum II outtakes. As of 2020, only 'Track Nine' has been released (on a 2013 reissue of the LP), though both 'Road to Pain' and 'Track Ten' can be tracked down via the usual sources.

thing a little exotic to chew on, the tune's opening acoustic guitar flourishes and high-pitched keyboard lines[6] recalling Maurice Jarre's wintry soundtrack to the 1965 movie *Doctor Zhivago*. This being Gary Moore and Don Airey, however, it wasn't long before the starting gun sounded and both musicians began running rings around each other in a heady blaze of notes, riffs and power chords. 'Hurricane' took on a similar approach, with Moore this time allowing Phillips off the lead, the drummer's speed around the kit rivalling Moore's own liquid runs on the fretboard. 'Song for Donna', on the other hand, gave Mole his chance to shine. Another of Moore's occasional odes to girlfriend Donna Campbell, Mole's lilting bassline provided this Stevie Wonder-like tune with some real heart as well as thump, as Moore simultaneously poured out his romantic hopes, and woes over a pleasingly melodic three minutes.

After the dreamy interlude that was 'Song for Donna, 'What Would You Rather Bee or a Wasp' marked a significant change of mood and pace. A funk-leaning, free-falling instrumental almost as clever as its title suggested, 'Would You Rather Bee or a Wasp' might have owed an idea or two to the peerless Jeff Beck's then-recent album *Wired*, but at least they were good ideas. Content at first to rumble along on the back of a clipped rhythm guitar figure and Mole's stop-start bass, when the pace finally picked up, so did Moore. All bluesy pentatonic scales, modal inversions and passages of super-fast picking, his solo was as frightening in its intensity as it was deft in its execution. 'At that time,' Don Airey reiterated, 'he was a genius, really . . .'

As good, and certainly harder rocking, than anything Moore had put his name to with Colosseum II, the Morgan sessions of early 1978 represented an auspicious start for the LP. That said, while the material he had recorded with Don Airey, John Mole and Simon Phillips[7] would

---

6 'Flight Of The Snow Moose' found Don Airey using a brand-new Yamaha CS-80 synth to fine effect. The analogue synthesiser was one of the few instruments at the time capable of approximating an orchestral string section.

7 Moore and Phillips again worked together at Morgan Studios on former Brian Auger & The Trinity/Isotope guitarist Gary Boyle's 1978 Latin-fusion LP *Electric Glide*, with Moore guesting on the track 'Hayabusa'. For those seeking another fine, fleet-fingered player for the collection, then Boyle's your man.

no doubt please fans of his former band, it was also unlikely to set cash registers ringing. As history had come to show, demand for Colosseum II's particular brand of jazz rock was selective at best. If Moore wanted sales, then he had to write a hit, or at least work with someone who could. Following his new business strategy, he chose to do both, on this occasion turning to Philip Lynott to help him over the line with a tune or two he had sitting on the back-burner.

In fact, only weeks before Moore began the task of putting together the bones of his new LP, he found himself in Battersea's Ramport Studios, where Lynott was doing something very similar. Having first cracked the songwriting code back in Dublin while living with Moore and Johnny Duhan, Thin Lizzy's frontman had more or less been writing tunes for sport ever since, amassing a reservoir of material as a result. 'He never seemed to take time off from music,' Frank Murray later said. 'He just loved it.' So when Lynott's record company, Vertigo, invited him to consider cutting an LP under his own name, he jumped at the chance. Not only did it give him the opportunity to find a home for songs he had written that might be unsuitable for Lizzy, it also allowed for even more musical scrivening. Whether for use on his own forthcoming solo disc or gifted to other artists and friends (for a price, of course), Lynott was free to accumulate tunes and re-direct them wherever he saw fit. 'Philip,' said old friend Paul Scully, 'was like a one-man song factory.'[8]

One of the stray tunes 'from the Lynott conveyor belt' that Moore had been working on at Ramport Studios eventually turned up on his own LP. A crunchy, mid-tempo thing, 'Fanatical Fascists' took its cue both lyrically and tonally from punk, with Lynott plugging into the recent 'Rock Against Racism' movement to warn against the rise of right-wing extremism. Reportedly demoed with an interested Steve Jones and Paul Cook in attendance[9], Gary also had to prise 'Fanatical Fascists'

---

8 According to author Graeme Thomson, of the 500 or so unreleased tracks/snippets recovered from the Thin Lizzy archive, a significant proportion were recorded between 1978-1979, when Lynott was often in the studio, either with the band, or as likely, whoever happened to be around at the time.

9 It's long been rumoured that Moore, Lynott, Jones and Cook cut a track or two together at the Ramport sessions, but thus far, nothing's turned up for release.

away from Heavy Metal Kids singer Gary Holton, who had earmarked the track as a possible single to launch his own solo career. Moore's version prevailed, his snotty vocal and chugging rhythm part perfectly aligning themselves with Lynott's angry bass and Brian Downey's equally bad-tempered snare cracks.

Philip Lynott was again present to provide backing vocals and hand claps when Moore cut the title track of his own LP, this time back at Morgan Studios. Introduced by a high-necked, cycling arpeggio played so fast it still confounds many a guitarist to this day, 'Back on the Streets' was on one level full of sneaky jazz chords and tricky little riffs, these musical sleights of hand no doubt enhanced by the presence of Simon Phillips and Don Airey. But when one peeled away the parlour tricks, it was also a cracking and surprisingly direct rock song, giving Moore a mighty cheer when he performed it as 'a featured piece' alongside Thin Lizzy during their autumn tour of 1978. Inevitably, it was this ever-strengthening connection with Lynott and Lizzy that was also at the heart of *Back on the Streets'* two finest compositions, one a moody, magnificent resurrection of a recently rejected idea, the other destined to become Moore's signature tune and an international hit, to boot.

Back at the *Johnny the Fox* sessions in August 1976, Philip Lynott had presented 'Don't Believe a Word' to his Thin Lizzy colleagues as a slow blues nailed onto some passing soul chords. Brian Robertson memorably deemed the song 'shite' and an irked Lynott left in a huff. In his absence, Robbo and Brian Downey reworked Lynott's idea, and by the time he returned, 'Don't Believe a Word' had a shuffle beat and spunky little guitar riff. Within six months, it went to number twelve in the UK singles chart, albeit with Lynott still credited as the song's sole author. Unsurprisingly, neither Robertson nor Downey were elated at the oversight. Arguments of attribution aside, however, Lynott had always preferred the tune in its original form. So too had Gary Moore. Judging from the performance of 'Don't Believe a Word' that appears on *Back on the Streets*, they had a point.

Again featuring Philip and Brian Downey on bass and drums, with Lynott also trading vocals alongside Moore across the song's verses, this version of 'Don't Believe a Word' was a million miles away from the one that appeared on Thin Lizzy's *Johnny the Fox*. Now more 'The Supernatural' period Peter Green than steely, cynical rocker, by again slowing things down, Moore had re-established the sense of vulnerability Lynott had always intended for the song.

The lyric too, also took on an added emotional resonance due to the drop in tempo. Before, Lynott's tone had sounded cocksure and dismissive, his words as likely to injure as warn off the subject of his 'affections'. Yet, when sung here, he and Moore managed to introduce a genuine note of hesitancy, one might even say self-loathing, to proceedings. Indeed, Lynott's lyrical alter-ego now seemed intent on pushing away anyone stupid enough to fall for him. Replete with a gloriously restrained solo from Moore, and as Brian Downey confirmed, 'Don't Believe a Word' circa 1978 had the all makings of a future classic. 'Gary's solo . . . is just perfect,' said the drummer. 'He could approach things with so much soul and there's so much emotion on that song.' The last tune to appear on what would become the album *Back on the Streets* was 'Parisienne Walkways'. As with all 'monuments to rock guitar,' there are discrepancies about its exact origins and construction, but the essential story behind the song remains more or less the same. By all accounts, Moore had the tune and basic chords in his back pocket for a while, its slow, central descending melody evolving from Colosseum II's 'Biscayne Blues', a piece he used to play with Don Airey[10], and which, in turn, took a smidgeon of inspiration from jazz trumpeter Kenny Dorham's own hard-bopping 'Blue Bossa'. At this point, likely mid-1977, Moore seemed content to keep the piece as an instrumental. Yet, he soon changed his mind after Philip Lynott got an earful of it. 'It was about seven in the evening around Philip's place,' Moore later told Marshall TV. 'I was playing acoustic guitar. He heard the chords and said "That's great. It sounds a bit French. I could write some words for that."'

Leap forward a year, and Moore, Lynott and Brian Downey were ensconced in Morgan Studios recording the results. According to Chris

---

10 Regrettably, Don Airey was not asked to play on 'Parisienne Walkways', the session taking place after his own contributions to the album were recorded. 'I was disappointed not to be asked to play on [the song],' Airey told author Malcolm Dome, 'But years later, Gary did tell me how remorseful he was about it.'

Tsangarides, the trio proved themselves a model of efficiency, with the basic track laid down in 'two, maybe three takes at most'. Predictably, Moore knew what he wanted from the off. 'Oh yeah,' said Downey, 'Gary had very definite ideas about how he wanted the drums to sound, for instance. No sticks, just brushes. I remember the guitar was very loud in the studio during the recording, and I kept thinking "That'll drown out the brushes!" But he was insistent. Just simple brushes, bass and that guitar. And you know, it worked. You can hear the brushes sweeping across the track, creating that simple, soulful feel.'

To ensure the tune also conveyed 'the jazzy, late-night French thing' Moore and Lynott were hoping to capture, a fretless upright bass was put to use, its slim wooden neck marked with chalk so Philip knew where to hit the right notes. In addition to the bass experiment, the pair employed a piano accordion, Lynott pumping the wind instrument's bellows while Moore played the supporting melody on its keyboard. To complete the overall effect, Moore overdubbed a faux-mandolin part, created by aligning an early Solina string synthesiser to a 12-string guitar, on which he played a series of trills.

Of course, there were two more hugely important areas to nail down before the song was done. Both were in good hands. On the lyrical side of things, Lynott excelled himself yet again, using a few choice lines written in previous months to tell a tale of lost love, ageing roués and improbably old Beaujolais wine, all set in the summery sidewalk cafés of France's capital city. Being a clever fellow, Lynott also used the opening line of 'Parisienne Walkways' to embed a coded message of sorts, secretly namechecking his father, Cecil Parris, and the year of his own birth, 1949. Just as with 'Romeo and the Lonely Girl', Lynott never mentioned these hidden meanings to Moore, who only found out in later years from other sources.

With Lynott's romantic reveries now committed to tape, the only thing left to capture was Moore's guitar part. 'But what a fucking guitar part!' laughed Brian Downey. In essence a gentle stroll down the A minor scale punctuated by some emotive string stretches and a touch of warm vibrato, 'Parisienne Walkways" seven note-pattern (eight if you count that passing A♭) was surely among the simpler things Gary Moore had played.

Yet, it was also among the most memorable, with each note torn from the neck of his ever present, seemingly indestructible 'Greeny'[11] dripping with emotion. Furthermore, Moore was so on point when laying down the backing track, he created a perfectly timed space for the tune's famous sustained note to ring out without benefit of a click or count-in. 'Gary left a gap for the big, long note, and then [the band] started up again,' Tsangarides later told *Sound On Sound*. 'I couldn't understand how [later on], he'd know when the band [would] come back in. But he did [it] in one take in perfect time. Unbelievable.'

A smorgasbord of fusion, classic rock, blues and even French *chanson*, all *Back on the Streets* now required was an album sleeve to wrap things nicely within. In yet another Lizzy-related connection, photographer Chalkie Davies was on hand to provide the winning image. Slyly satirising the LP's title, Davies's shot presented Moore leaving London's Wormwood Scrubs prison, guitar case in hand[12], while girlfriend Donna Campbell waits patiently outside in pink hotpants, lime green tights and high heels. 'Well, the shot was actually done early in the morning,' Davies confirmed. 'For some reason, I think you could actually rent the front of Wormwood Scrubs, probably because it was the best-looking prison in London, or possibly because it's got that front gate. Anyway, the gate only lets you into the bit outside the main gate itself. So, there was no real risk of trouble. Basically, the prisoner would have to exit the main gate first, then walk through [the pictured] gate towards his freedom.'

Preceded by the release of its title track as a single, *Back on the Streets* arrived in record stores on 30 September 1978. But there would be no great promotional push for the album, at least for now. Moore was already on the road with Thin Lizzy, the band again criss-crossing the USA, from

---

11 Sometime before the recording of *Back on the Streets*, Moore was involved in a serious car accident near Chiswick Flyover. However, while the car was reduced to scrap, his beloved guitar survived. Just. 'I opened the car boot and although the [Greeny] was in a flight case, its neck was completely broken,' he later said. 'But we got it repaired amazingly well, [with] a steel bolt in the neck. I mean, the car was completely written off, so you can imagine.'

12 According to Moore, the guitar case displayed on the cover of *Back on the Streets* is indeed the same one that housed Eric Clapton's now legendary (and still missing) 'Blues Breaker' Gibson Les Paul.

East Troy in Wisconsin to Utah's Salt Lake City, and sometimes back again. With trainee planet-eaters AC/DC as their support act, or in turn providing support to the likes of Journey, Blue Öyster Cult and Kansas, the onus for Moore and co. was breaking the territory once and for all, one gig at a time.

That said, back in Blighty, despite its musically schizophrenic nature, *Back on the Streets* was garnering reasonable word of mouth and some rather good reviews, resulting in it placing at number seventy on the UK charts. Not quite a platinum seller, then. Yet, with 'Parisienne Walkways' earmarked as a second single and the song already picking up healthy radio play, the signs were there that Moore's latest album might yet have an extended shelf life. 'Not bad, eh?' Moore might have said.

In practical terms, Gary Moore was in for an extremely busy year. Now a paid-up member of Thin Lizzy, there was an upcoming tour of Australia to attend to before returning to the UK for some renewed promotional activity around *Back on the Streets*. After that came perhaps the biggest test of the guitarist's career: cutting a new record with Lizzy – one that finally might break them in the USA, and turn he, Philip Lynott, Scott Gorham and Brian Downey into continent-straddling superstars. Yet, to paraphrase Charles Dickens, the coming months would represent both 'the best of times' and the 'worst of times' for Moore, while being a pretty grim time for just about everyone else.

CHAPTER THIRTEEN

Brushed With Oil, Dusted With Powder

Thin Lizzy touched down in Sydney, Australia, on 18 October 1978. It was Gary Moore's first trip to the country, and one not forgotten in a hurry. After completing the opening US leg of their worldwide *Live and Dangerous* tour, he and the band had arrived at Los Angeles airport, an arduous, 19-hour long-haul flight with stop-overs in Hawaii and New Zealand still ahead of them. But before they could even take their seats on the plane, a bomb scare delayed their departure by another five hours or so. No great shakes, really. It gave everyone enough time to locate the bar and start drinking. When they did eventually climb on board, two of Lizzy's technical crew got into a fight. They were sacked at 38,000 feet, then ejected by the captain upon arrival in Honolulu. 'Thin Lizzy,' Scott Gorham once said, quite correctly, 'were the fighting-est band in rock'n'roll.'

When the plane took off again, Philip Lynott promptly fell asleep and missed his in-flight meal. Upon waking, words were had and snacks were brought. When he returned to snoozing, Moore was photographed dangling chips above the singer's wide-open mouth. Lynott soon saw the Polaroids and made his displeasure clear to all. Loudly. 'Don't ever do that. I'm a fucking star!' he protested. Moore, comically hiding under his blanket as the drama unfolded, tried to stifle a fit of giggles. 'I thought it was hysterical,' he later said. Ten years before in Dublin, Lynott would probably have thought the same thing. Things change. Moore logged it, all the same.

Still, if the somewhat joyless start to Thin Lizzy's Australian odyssey hinted at tired frontmen and expanding egos, there were compensations ahead too, even if the group that arrived in Oz were not quite the same one Moore had joined three months before. In a move that perhaps surprised even himself, Brian Downey had left the band soon after Moore arrived, citing publicly a need to spend more time with his family. Behind the scenes, however, Downey was 'shattered' both physically and mentally, while also privately bored with playing more or less the same set list for over two years. Needing to walk away fast, he informed an irked Lynott of his intentions before disappearing to a small cottage in Cork in search of peace, quiet and 'good fishing'.

Having already lost valuable coverage in America to liver disease and fighting Scotsmen, Lynott was in no mood to dither when it came to Brian Downey's surprise exit. A tour was booked, a replacement drummer was needed, and this time, America would not fall. 'Well, Philip, Gary and I did auditions in LA,' said Gorham. 'The first guy we considered was [former Frank Zappa sticksman] Terry Bozzio, who was just amazing. But he wanted us to fly his girlfriend Dale everywhere [with the band]. At that point, it was strictly no wives and no girlfriends on the road. So, you know, 'Next!' Then Mark Nauseef comes in. He's a great guy, a great drummer and he just nailed it.'

A New Yorker whose CV included recent stints with Ronnie James Dio's Elf and The Ian Gillan Band, Nauseef had both jazz-level chops and a dry sense of humour. Like Gary Moore, he could also learn a set in next to no time, which came in handy for his first performance with Thin Lizzy on stage at Mississippi Coliseum on 8 August 1978. 'We were ready, willing and raring to go!' laughed Gorham. Delivering handsomely on this simple, but effective philosophy across the States throughout the late summer, the band then exported it to Australia, where over the course of 12 days and five gigs, they once again confirmed that, in a live setting at least, there were few who could really touch them.

Opening their in-concert account with a corking performance at Brisbane's Botanical Gardens on 20 October 1978, the group then sauntered down the Gold Coast for a date at Newcastle's cavernous Sports Centre 48 hours later. Here, Moore was simultaneously surprised and delighted to see food being cooked on barbecues at the back of the stadium. 'They were throwing prawns on the bloody barbie!' he howled. From Newcastle, band and crew made their way to Melbourne's Myer Music Bowl where between shows, Philip Lynott found himself judging a beauty contest. It was a task Lynott repeated with apparent relish back in London some weeks later, this time offering his opinion at the somewhat higher profile 1978 Miss World Pageant.[1]

As pleasant and diverting as the beauty contests and barbecues undoubtedly were, the focal point of Thin Lizzy's trip to Australia came on Sunday, 29 October, when the band staged a 90-minute free concert on the steps of Sydney's Opera House. With audience numbers ranging anywhere between 25,000 to 200,000 depending on who you asked, 'I've heard 100,000,' laughed Scott Gorham, 'But you couldn't really tell as the crowd stretched all the way back.' This was still a huge turn-out by anyone's (over)estimation. Filmed by Channel Seven TV, broadcast live on national radio and brilliantly captured in a series of iconic photographs by the ever-present Chalkie Davies[2], the Sydney gig was surely a defining

---

1 The story goes Lynott actually became 'involved' with one of the contestants in a broom cupboard before the pageant was even over. Ribald tale. Sounds like the type of thing Lynott might do. Probably not true, though.

2 'It was taken during the seventh or ninth note of 'Jailbreak',' said Davies of his now classic photograph of Lizzy facing down the crowds at Sydney Opera House. 'I knew their routine better than anyone, really. Rock'n'roll concerts are a bit like American football matches, [with] set pieces within them. So, I knew when the flashes would go off for 'Jailbreak', and it was then just a case of the smoke clearing.' A wonderful image, it's almost as good as Chalkie's most famous pic: the iconic front cover shot of Thin Lizzy's *Live and Dangerous*. 'When Philip came out on his knees [on stage in San Antonio], I got three, possibly four frames,' said Davies. 'He hadn't done [that pose] before, and it was a long time before he did it again. Believe it or not, he was always a bit shy. And you know, Philip really didn't want that photograph to be the cover, because it didn't have all four members in shot. But I showed it to Brian Downey and he said, "I don't mind," so . . .' So, indeed.

moment for Thin Lizzy, their popularity now crossing oceans rather than just seas. It was also a bumper day for Gary Moore, whose scorching solo rendition of Australian's unofficial anthem 'Waltzing Matilda' during Lizzy's final number 'Me and the Boys' raised some of the biggest cheers of the day.

All in all, Sydney seemed to agree with Moore, even igniting his romantic side. The night before Thin Lizzy stormed the steps of the Opera House, Gary and the band were taken out for dinner, during which the guitarist was introduced to Lisa Franklin, a young woman then working for Lizzy's music publishers. 'Yes, I met Gary in Sydney at a dinner date,' Franklin later told Songfacts. '[We] were introduced through a mutual friend.' At the end of the evening, Moore had hoped to invite her to the concert. For a variety of reasons, it didn't happen. But when he called Franklin again, a new date was arranged. This time, things went well, and after the group's business was concluded in Australia, Moore followed Franklin back to her home in Los Angeles.

Upon returning to London, Gary's indiscretion was discovered by girlfriend Donna Campbell who perhaps, unsurprisingly was less than thrilled with her partner's conduct. Words were had, a guitar was smashed, 'though thankfully not the Greeny!' quipped a friend, and, after some five years together, Moore and Campbell parted ways. Within 12 months, she had married actor Gary Holton, now former singer of The Heavy Metal Kids, former housemate of Philip Lynott and the very man Moore had prised the song 'Fanatical Fascists' away from for use on his own solo album. Yet, despite all the shared history, there appeared to be little in the way of emotional detritus for the trio to deal with.[3] As was Moore's way, he had already moved on, immediately focusing his attentions on Franklin, with whom he was besotted. As it turned out, both Franklin and LA would provide practical and psychological refuge for him at a crucial juncture not long up the road.

---

3   Campbell and Holton's union did not last. Within two years the pair had split up, though they remained firm friends and never officially divorced. Sadly, having just found acting fame with ITV series *Auf Wiedersehen Pet*, Holton succumbed to a morphine overdose in 1985. Following his demise, Campbell went on to re-marry and even spend some time in rock management. She now lives happily with her husband in Somerset.

In the meantime, there were concerts to be played and a new Thin Lizzy album to be recorded, albeit not before yet another line-up change. Having gamely filled the vacancy created by Brian Downey, Mark Nauseef must have felt confident of being appointed the group's new drummer. It wasn't to be. Following a heart-to-heart between Downey and his former bandmates, he was asked to come back, leaving rural Cork, the fishing rods and some 20 pounds in body weight behind him. 'I don't think they recognised me when I walked back in,' he laughed. 'Well yeah, Brian re-joined the group,' confirmed Gorham. 'I mean, Mark Nauseef must have thought, "Hey, I'm in Thin Lizzy," so I don't think he was too happy. But you know, it was all about the continuity, even if Phil was still angry about Brian having left in the first place. But I worked on it. "Hey Phil, give me some love here," and finally Downey's back, the team is reunited and we're off again, this time heading towards a new record with Gary.'

With Nauseef on his way (though Moore would keep track of his whereabouts), Thin Lizzy welcomed Downey back just in time for their annual Christmas 'hoolie,' this one staged at London's Hammersmith Odeon on 17 December 1978. Aside from a spray of Greedies gigs popping up here and there, the Hammy concert represented the first occasion the band's London-based fans had to see Gary Moore up close and personal. 'Well, at least the soundcheck went well,' he later quipped.

For those there for the show itself, that was scant consolation. Following Moore's suggestion to freshen things up by swapping 'carved in stone' set opener 'Jailbreak' for 'Are You Ready', everything else seemed to fall into the abyss thereafter. The group's trademark flash-pot entrance proved so explosive that Moore et al. were left cowering behind Downey's kit until the smoke and sparks cleared. After that, the volume cut stage right, leaving half the audience struggling to hear. An embarrassing procession of missed cues and technical gremlins soon followed.

Worse was to come. When a roadie handed Moore a strapless guitar for his solo interlude – 'My moment of glory!' – the instrument predictably fell straight to the floor, leaving him red-faced before an audience of more than 3,000 fans. It was all too much for the Ulsterman. Chasing his prey into the wings, Moore swung a well-aimed boot into the nether regions of the guilty party before returning to the stage to smash up a microphone with his still mercifully uninjured Gibson Melody Maker. By the time the axe's former owner Steve Jones joined Lizzy on stage for a dishevelled rendition of Frank Sinatra's 'My Way', it was all over bar the bad reviews. 'The gig was a fucking disaster from start to finish,' Moore later told author Mark Putterford. 'Gary still managed to hog the stage though,' laughed Brian Downey.

Such was the good will towards Thin Lizzy throughout 1978, the band could weather an occasional kicking in the music press without much fear of lasting damage. Besides, there were now more pressing matters than snippy reviews to attend to. In addition to their Greedies gigs in Dublin and a recent, new addition to the extended Thin Lizzy family (more of that later), the quartet was also busy prepping their latest album at Soho's Good Earth Studios with 'The Brooklyn Boy' himself, Tony Visconti.

Then as now a legend of record production, Visconti had already been behind the faders for some of Marc Bolan and David Bowie's finest LPs, before more recently overseeing two of Lizzy's own landmark releases: *Bad Reputation* and *Live and Dangerous*. 'Tony was great,' said Scott Gorham in 2020. 'He calmed me down for *Bad Reputation* [when I was the only guitarist]. I'd never done the lone ranger thing before, you know, "Here I come to save the day!", so, for me it was a case of "What the fuck is going on?" But Tony and Philip kept encouraging me, bolstering me along.'

Before recording began Philip Lynott and Scott Gorham joined Moore on 9 January 1979 for a two-song appearance on BBC2's somewhat creaky, if still reliable late-night music show *The Old Grey Whistle Test*. There to help re-promote *Back on the Streets*, Lizzy's old guard found themselves in the midst of a jazz-rock supergroup, with Moore, his former Colosseum II colleague Don Airey on keyboards and Airey's new band-mate in Rainbow, Cozy Powell, behind the drums. 'Between us pulling together the Lizzy album,' laughed Gorham, 'Philip was still doing bits of his solo stuff while Gary was promoting his own LP on *Whistle Test*. It was like being in a washing machine – no – a cement mixer of music!'

On the night in question, it was actually more like a visit to the dog track, at least when it came to the opening number, 'Back on the Streets'. Keen to get cracking, Moore's top-draw pick-up band galloped their way through things so fast the song was almost over before it had begun. In contrast to this breathless, but brilliant start, Moore's take on Lynott's 'Don't Believe a Word' was truly sublime, his angelic solo flight[4] and Lynott's soulful vocals a match made in TV heaven, as well as boding extremely well for Lizzy's musical future. Another benefit that came out of the *OGWT* performance was Moore's live introduction to the pneumatic drumming style of Cozy Powell. Sharing a mutual love of speed, precision and power, it came as no surprise when Gary contributed to several of Powell's later solo albums, including *Over the Top*, *Tilt* and *Octopuss*.[5]

Promotional duties temporarily discharged for *Back on the Streets*, though 'Parisienne Walkways' continued to simmer away nicely on the back-burner, Moore was now free to throw his weight behind Thin Lizzy. That meant joining the others on a plane to Paris, were they were to again hook up with Tony Visconti, this time at EMI's celebrated Pathé Marconi Studio, to begin recording what the producer hoped would be their 'grand work'. For Moore, that meant one thing. 'It was an opportunity for me to absolve [myself for not staying with the band before]. I was there to try my very best.' In fairness, so was everyone else, though that ended up meaning different things to different people. 'Ah, Paris,' sighed Scott Gorham. 'Paris was great, but Paris was also where it all started to go tits up.'

Over the years, the phrase 'Thin Lizzy, Paris 1979' has taken on grim connotations, invoking a time and place when some of the band began to lose the run of themselves and fall prey to the worst excesses the city had to offer. In line with Gorham's bleak admission, there is real truth

---

4 Moments before his lead break, Moore broke the Greeny's low-E string. Thankfully, it had little impact.
5 By 1979, Gary Moore's jazz rock days were more or less behind him. However, the tracks he later wrote/cut with Cozy Powell for the drummer's solo LPs – 'Killer' (*Over the Top*, 1979), 'The Blister' and 'Sunset' (*Tilt*, 1981) and 'Dartmoore' (*Octopuss*, 1983) – all retain something of his mad-eyed days with Colosseum II. Not surprising really, as Don Airey frequently guested alongside Moore on Powell's work, even writing some of the tunes.

in that. Yet, one would also be hard pressed to find evidence of such a decline when investigating the group's early schedule at Pathé Marconi. As it turns out, the making of what became Thin Lizzy's ninth studio LP appears to have been a mostly positive and timely experience – at least at the start.

Gary Moore and Scott Gorham, for instance, struck up a strong working partnership from the off, even if by his own admission, the Californian guitarist had his work cut out keeping up with 'the Belfast Express'. 'Oh, the recording side was fine,' Gorham confirmed. 'Gary and I got along great, coming up with some really cool guitar bits together. Still, occasionally he'd play something and I'd be like, "Woah! Slow that down, buddy!" I mean, some of the harmony lines [we did]. He'd say, "It's just a straight run down." Well, yeah, technically it is. But you really have to practise it to get it right. Gary was such a precise player, and I really had to tighten up my act.'

Tony Visconti was on hand to witness this relationship develop, the producer being particularly struck not only by Moore's skill, but his graciousness towards Gorham. 'Gary was an incredible technician,' Visconti later told author Harry Doherty. 'Really, he could have played both guitar parts on [the album]. But I recall him sitting . . . with Scott teaching him the second parts slowly until he could play them perfectly. Gary,' Visconti concluded, 'was a real gentleman.' According to Moore, the feeling was mutual. 'I used to sit with Tony for ages working on the sound. I really admired the guy. At one stage though, he said, "What the fuck are you doing with this band?"' Give it time.

With backing tracks and guitar parts being committed to tape at an impressive rate, the band could now step away from the studio to explore their surroundings. And that was when the fun really began for Philip Lynott and Scott Gorham. 'Oh man,' Scott confirmed in 2020, 'the nightlife in Paris was amazing. The clubs, the wine, the atmosphere. And then there was the drug dealers.' Of course, with the drug dealers came the drugs. 'Well, Paris was where the heroin came into the band,' said Gorham. 'I remember distinctly Philip calling me from his hotel room and saying, "Hey, I've got something here. Do you want to come down and check it out?" Now, I'd done heroin before I'd even come to England.

184

A cherubic, 12-year-old Gary Moore smiles for the camera with his first band, The Beat Boys, in 1964. The teenage quartet performed throughout Belfast for eighteen months before parting ways in mid-1965. (L-R, Bill Downey, Moore, Robert Thompson and Robin Lavery). BILL DOWNEY

Skid Row. Comprised of Gary on guitar/vocals, drummer Noel Bridgeman and bassist/singer Brendan 'Brush' Shiels, Skid Row were often called 'Ireland's answer to Cream', but the band lost momentum when Moore left in late 1971. JORGEN ANGEL/GETTY IMAGES

The Super Sub. Gary Moore first joined Thin Lizzy in January 1974, temporarily filling in on guitar when Eric Bell left the band. Though his time with the group initially proved brief, he returned to help Lizzy out again in 1977, before becoming an official member a year later. (L-R Drummer Brian Downey, Bassist/Singer Philip Lynott and Moore). MICHAEL PUTLAND/GETTY IMAGES

Moore on stage fronting his own band, circa 1973. 'When Gary played,' said his friend Paul Scully, 'your jaw just dropped.' DAVID WARNER ELLIS/GETTY IMAGES

'Friendship is an act of bravery'. Firm friends since Gary came to Dublin from Belfast in the autumn of 1968, Moore and Thin Lizzy's Philip Lynott were also musical soulmates. But their relationship was tested several times, with often explosive results. MARK SULLIVAN/GETTY IMAGES

Doyens of the British jazz rock scene, Colosseum II struggled to find success in the face of punk and new wave. By 1978, the band had folded, leaving Gary free to finally join Thin Lizzy. (L-R Moore, singer Mike Starrs, drummer Jon Hiseman, bassist Neil Murray and keyboardist Don Airey). ERICA ECHENBERG/GETTY IMAGES

Glory days. Thin Lizzy on stage at the Sydney Opera House, 29 October 1978. 'I've heard there were 100,000 [people there],' said Lizzy guitarist Scott Gorham. (L-R, Gorham, Lynott and Moore). CHALKIE DAVIES/GETTY IMAGES

'When I'm playing, I get completely lost in it.' Moore entering another realm while on stage with Thin Lizzy. By July 1979, he had exited the band for the final time. GUS STEWART/GETTY IMAGES

Made up of various members of Thin Lizzy, Sex Pistols and 'whoever else was hanging around at the time,' punk/rock supergroup The Greedy Bastards made a glorious noise. 'No managers and no guest lists,' said Gary in 1978. 'We just play the gig, get paid, then goodnight!'

G-Force. A brave, if doomed, attempt on Gary's part to create a 'new, cutting-edge power soul' sound for the eighties, G-Force broke up after just one album. (L-R vocalist Willy Dee, Moore, drummer Mark Nauseef and bassist Tony Newton).

Gary and Peter Green. A 'huge hero and friend' to Moore, Green's work with Fleetwood Mac in the late sixties inspired Gary to pursue a life in music. Moore would repay his artistic debt to Peter with 1995's *Blues For Greeny*, a tribute album covering some of Green's best-loved songs.
PATRICK FORD/GETTY IMAGES

The Greeny. Sold to Gary 'for a song' by its owner Peter Green in the early seventies, Moore later described the cherry-burst 1959 Gibson Les Paul as 'the best guitar I ever played.'
NIGEL OSBOURNE/GETTY IMAGES

The Belfast Bluesman: Gary Moore blazing under the lights in 2009. 'Gary really was one of the greatest blues players ever,' said his friend Tim Goulding, 'music ran through his veins…' JORDI VIDAL/GETTY IMAGES

Below: In 1990, Gary Moore stepped away from hard rock and returned to the blues. Although a risky move commercially, this change in sound and image resulted in his biggest success yet, the multi-platinum selling album, *Still Got the Blues*.
JOHN STODDART/POPPERFOTO

I knew all about it, and to be honest, moving to England [in the seventies] had saved my life because it had got me away from it. But there we are [in Paris], and Philip's got this brown powder. He says, "Do you know what this is?" And I say, "Yeah." "You ever done it before?" "Yeah." "You want to do some now?" "Yeah . . ." And that was it. We were off running uphill or downhill – whatever the right way is to put that, I suppose.'

Like Gorham, Lynott had always been an enthusiastic imbiber of drink and drugs, even earning the nickname 'Philip Why Not?' for his adventurous nature and cast-iron constitution. In his Dublin days for instance, pot, hash, LSD and booze were all tried and enjoyed, sometimes in rapid succession. The moment fame came calling, Lynott added cocaine to his pharmaceutical kit bag, the drug's restorative qualities staving off tiredness and thus helping him keep up his new schedule as a busy rock star. 'And Philip was one of the great . . . gold-plated, bona fide rock stars,' Boomtown Rat Bob Geldof later said, 'because he completely believed in it.'

Heroin, however, was different: an upping of the stakes. When the drug became prevalent on the London punk scene, Lynott saw its effects on The Ruts' Malcolm Owen, Heartbreaker Johnny Thunders and Sid Vicious first hand, often left aghast at the narcotic haze they would descend into. This point was rammed home in brutal fashion in February 1979, when Vicious died from a heroin overdose. Tragically, Malcolm Owen would follow suit within 18 months. Yet, the glimmer and glint of smack, and the 'wrapping of cotton wool' it provided users, were difficult to escape, even for someone as apparently in control as Philip Lynott. From Charlie Parker and Billie Holiday to Janis Joplin, Keith Richards and a thousand more besides, heroin and stardom went hand in hand. Now, it appeared Lynott and Gorham were intent on finding out why.[6]

Watching with growing disdain the slow, but sure change in his

---

6 There has always been some dispute about exactly when Philip Lynott first tried heroin. In an interview with *The Irish Times*' Michael Hann, Brian Robertson places the date as far back as 1976 when Thin Lizzy's frontman allegedly contracted hepatitis from using a dirty needle. However, others remain adamant that Paris is where Lynott fell into heroin's orbit.

bandmates' behaviour was Gary Moore. Moore had been no saint in his youth, the guitarist enjoying the pleasures of recreational drug use, and sometimes alongside Philip Lynott. As one might imagine, there was many a tall story told. Moore on his 18th birthday, drunk on Lynott's homemade cocktails and howling like a dog out of the bathroom window in Ballsbridge.[7] Moore and Lynott skittering around St Stephen's Green, giggling and laughing at colours only they could see after a hit of some particularly strong acid. There was even a rumour Moore had contracted scurvy after a prolonged spell staying at Lynott's flat near Clontarf Castle. Three fine anecdotes for sure, and who knows, they might all be true but for the fact that scurvy isn't caught from sleeping on a couch . . .

Yet, recent years had seen a marked shift in Gary Moore's attitude to such things. Whether it was the physical demands of his stage work with Colosseum II, the scar he wore as an unpleasant reminder of his drink-fuelled misadventure in a Kensington bar, or simply the ever-growing boredom of 'late nights and early morning hangovers' that changed Moore's mind remains unclear. But by 1979 a line had been firmly drawn in the sand. With his own drug use already long jettisoned, Moore was now mostly drink-free too, the odd can of beer his only real vice. 'I'd been getting out of my brains,' he later said of his mid-seventies binges, '[but then] I wanted to keep away from that type of thing . . . and straighten out as a person and a musician.'

This was to be no easy task the longer Thin Lizzy were ensconced at Pathé Marconi. With 'One [dealer] selling smack, one selling coke and another selling hash,' the studio was rapidly becoming a home away from home for Paris's drug dealing community. 'There they were, beating on the studio doors trying to come in, and we said, "Sure,"' admitted Scott Gorham. 'Then, it just became a regular thing. I'm sure Gary and Tony Visconti were thinking, "What the fuck: do you really need these guys [in here]?"'

Moore's way of dealing with the dealers and the chaos that surrounded them was to stick to the task at hand. 'Gary really was a lone wolf and uninterested in the "extracurricular activities", shall we say,' Scott told

---

7 The story goes Philip Lynott concocted the cocktails in a plastic dustbin, pouring spirits into the mix until it looked 'sort of right'. Given Lynott's methods, both he and Moore were lucky to be alive after drinking the results.

the BBC. 'He just wanted to do the music.' Gorham also offered another intriguing explanation for Moore's conversion to the straight and narrow. 'Yeah, that drink thing with Gary,' he said in 2020. 'Really, I'd only seen him drunk a couple of times and he'd got kind of mean on it. And you know, I think that's why he was staying away from it. Looking back, that was pretty smart of him, really. He knew, "If I've got a problem with this, I'm just going to make an arsehole of myself, so I'll just stay away from it altogether."' It was a viewpoint shared by Moore's close friend Paul Scully. 'Gary recognised fairly early on that whiskey didn't agree with him. He recognised that some people shouldn't drink [a particular spirit], if it didn't suit them, and he addressed that [issue] by stopping.'

Despite the revolving door recently installed at Pathé Marconi and the dealers regularly coming through it, Thin Lizzy wrapped up business in Paris by mid-February 1979, the band even finishing slightly ahead of schedule. A well-drilled unit, which had given several of the new tunes an in-concert test drive before bringing them to the studio, not even the introduction of Class A substances to the mix could slow their pace. For Brian Downey[8], this was largely down to both Moore's professionalism and the still strong bond he shared with Philip Lynott. 'It was Gary who really lifted the band in Paris,' said the drummer. 'He wanted to put his stamp on the album and in the studio his personality really shone through. Gary and Philip really gelled [at Pathé Marconi]. They worked hand in glove on the songs and it really paid off.' It would not always be this way.

Only two months after leaving the Pathé Marconi behind, the band were ready to release the fruits of their labours to the world. Arriving in mid-April 1979 contained in an eye-catching cover sleeve designed by artist Jim Fitzpatrick[9], *Black Rose* lived up to all the potential one

---

8 Like Gary Moore, Brian Downey steered well clear of heroin at Pathé Marconi. However, that's not to say he wasn't familiar with the drug. 'I tried heroin once,' he told author Paul Elliot in 2011, '[but] it wasn't for me.'

9 Fitzpatrick's artwork depicted the black rose of the title with blood on its petals, his idea probably inspired by Irish nationalist poet Joseph Plunkett's 'I See His Blood upon the Rose'. The renowned Irish scribe James Mangan used a similar phrase in his own ode to Irish freedom, 'Dark Rosaleen', which as we'll see, was a major influence on Philip Lynott when writing the title song of Thin Lizzy's LP.

might reasonably expect from the musical union of Thin Lizzy and Gary Moore. An ambitious enterprise, crammed with memorable songs, wily lyricism and one bolt-on, bona-fide 'Celtic classic', the album has been rightly hailed as among the group's finest work, and still sounds fresh as a proverbial daisy some forty years later.

Opening with the pop metal sheen of future UK Top 20 single 'Do Anything You Want To', Moore was immediately in his element, he and Gorham's bubbling guitar harmonies a perfect accompaniment to Lynott's tongue-tying ode to free will and the power of positive thinking. So committed was Moore to the tune, he even had a say in 'Do Anything's' thundering drum sound. 'The kettle drums!' said Brian Downey. 'Well, we'd started off with me playing an 18-inch floor tom, then Gary said, "Sounds pretty good, but we really need a heavier sound." I laughed and said, "Well, you can't get anything heavier than an 18-inch tom." He replied, "You could if you used a timpani drum!" His idea. So, we got one and you know, it really worked. We even ended up double-tracking it to make it sound even louder.'[10]

Moore was also instrumental in the delivery of *Black Rose*'s next track, the aggressively punk-leaning 'Toughest Street in Town'. Driven by a chunky five-note riff written by Moore while in New York – 'Good place to come up with a song like that,' he told writer Martin Popoff – 'Toughest Street in Town' also featured a quite extraordinary outburst from the guitarist. While Moore could approach his solos like a fine artist, planning each brush stroke with meticulous care, on other occasions it sounded like he had plugged his guitar directly into an electrical socket and was riding the results. Such was the case here. Grabbing the tune's mid-section by the scruff of the neck (written incidentally, by Gorham), Gary set off like an unruly mare, his fingers running around in multiple directions before appearing to explode at the end of twenty or so seconds.

---

10 Released as a single in June 1979 (It reached number fourteen in the UK), 'Do Anything You Want To' had a David Mallet-directed promo video which features all four members of Thin Lizzy bashing away on timpani drums, while British dance troupe Hot Gossip – dressed variously as judges, police officers, schoolgirls and traffic wardens – take turns to chastise the band.

A neat trick, and one Moore also gamely employed on the lead break for 'Get Out of Here'. Another snotty little ode, this time co-written by Lynott with glam-pop-punk-futurist-in-waiting Midge Ure, 'Get Out of Here' featured a fretboard ascent so nimble it fair tickled the eardrums.

Elsewhere, Moore appeared content to work on his team player skills, providing chords and riffs while Brian Downey rode the sticks on Lynott's zesty 'S&M', its not-so-veiled lyric celebrating the pleasures to be found in a sado-masochistic relationship. 'A brilliant song,' said Downey. 'Philip just seemed to have these riffs that just came out of the woodwork. That came together really quickly. He said, "Listen, I've got this bass riff . . ." and I responded to it. 'S&M' was like something Sly Stone might do . . . a hard-hitting, funky thing.' Delightful outro solo aside, the bittersweet 'With Love' also found Moore mostly leaning back for the sake of the composition. Probably born over a drink at Anson Road in Cricklewood a year or so before, the track represented Lynott's attempt to write 'a totally honest love song' where solemn 'late-night promises might end up shattered into a million little pieces by morning'. Originally destined for use on his own yet-to-be released solo LP, 'With Love' was probably just a little too good to be left off the track listing of *Black Rose*.

Whether the same could be said of 'Sarah' remains a bone of contention, its inclusion on the album still dividing Thin Lizzy fans to this day. A jazz-inflected butterfly of a song '80 per cent written' by Moore on an acoustic guitar and demoed long before the *Black Rose* sessions began[11], 'Sarah' was again headed in the direction of Lynott's long-gestating solo project until the singer had a change of heart. Having fallen head over heels with 18-year-old PR assistant Caroline Crowther[12] in February 1978 – 'She was the one,' said Chalkie Davies, 'You just knew' – Lynott's whirlwind romance saw him become a father in just over nine months.

---

11 The demo version of 'Sarah' featuring Moore, Lynott, drummer Mark Nauseef and a guesting Huey 'Power of Love' Lewis on harmonica is apparently the version that appears on *Black Rose*, albeit with a new vocal and solo tacked on by Lynott and Moore. Judie 'Stay With Me Till Dawn' Tzuke is also credited with providing backing vocals on the track.

12 The daughter of TV presenter Leslie Crowther, Caroline met Lynott while working for Tony Brainsby, the well-respected PR guru who oversaw publicity for Thin Lizzy at the time.

Born in Dublin on 19 December (courteously between Greedies gigs), his new daughter Sarah Philomena[13] immediately turned Lynott into a 'doting dad,' and one who wanted to capture the moment in song. Bolting a new lyric to Moore's existing demo, 'Sarah' was born again as a Thin Lizzy tune. Deemed 'a little candyfloss' by Scott Gorham, 'though its heart was in the right place,' 'Sarah' reached number twenty-four when released as a single in October 1979.

Much more in line with Thin Lizzy's pre-existing signature sound was the glorious 'Waiting for an Alibi'. An old idea[14] reupholstered at sound-checks on the band's recent US tour before being introduced to Australian audiences to test their reaction, 'Waiting for an Alibi' was Philip Lynott's most persuasive anthem since 'The Boys Are Back in Town'. Telling the tale of Valentino, a care-worn bookie whose own gambling habit threatens to undo his finances, health and love life, 'Waiting for an Alibi's jerky, push–pull rhythmic structure perfectly complemented its lyrical hero's frayed nerves.

The track also featured a set of mid-section harmony lines played so blisteringly fast by Moore that one critic referred to them as 'heavy metal science fiction'. Scott Gorham knew exactly what that meant. 'Oh yeah, I mean those harmonies are just fucking scary!' he laughed. 'But you know, working with Gary really was making me a better player.' This fact was confirmed by Gorham's solo on 'Waiting for an Alibi', its gliding, expressive lines a perfect entrée before Moore set the controls to hyper-speed. 'Well, Scott and I did some really nice things together for the album,' Moore later confirmed. A near perfect 45, 'Waiting for an Alibi' climbed to an impressive number nine on the UK singles chart in late February 1979, its action-packed video also providing documentary proof that Lizzy were primed and ready for the arrival of MTV.

For all the fine work to be found throughout *Black Rose*, like *Jailbreak* before it, the album was defined by two compositions. On 'Got to Give

---

13 Lynott's daughter Sarah Philomena was named for his grandmother and mother accordingly. In fact, Lynott had already used the name as a song title once before, with Lizzy's 1972 track 'Sarah' dedicated to his gran.

14 An early, somewhat slower version of 'Waiting for an Alibi' was reportedly demoed with Brian Robertson on guitar in February 1978, four or so months before he exited the band.

It Up', Philip Lynott finally acknowledged the slippery path he was walking within the confines of a sullen, though hard-hitting rocker, this time written with partner in crime, Scott Gorham. '[The lyric] to 'Got to Give It Up',' Lynott told author Harry Doherty, 'is to do with trying to give up your bad habits when you know you don't really stand a chance. [The song] is relevant to a lot of people, and I try to give these things up . . . with all the sincerity I can.' Using alcohol rather than heroin to inform his wordplay[15], Lynott's message still hit home hard, the Lizzy man's crushing description of a drunk spiralling out of control summoning up the addict's plight in the course of just a few lines.

Yet, for all Lynott's confessional tone, there was also a pulse of bravado running quietly, but firmly in the background, leading one to believe that despite the apparent candour, Philip might have been reticent to take his own advice. "Got to Give It Up'? I think [the lyrics] were more a subliminal thing,' confirmed the song's co-author, Scott Gorham. 'I think Philip could see where it might be going, but he wasn't quite there yet. But then, he also knew that this shit was so good, and getting [addicted] was a real possibility. So 'Got to Give It Up' was probably a warning to himself that he never really heeded.' Given that Lynott reportedly recorded his vocal with a joint in one hand and a brandy in the other, if this really was a cry for help, it was one that came with a nod and several winks.

And so, to the title track itself. 'Black Rose', or to give it its proper Gaelic name 'Róisín Dubh: A Rock Legend'. Inspired by Irish patriot James Mangan's politically charged nineteenth-century poem 'Dark Rosaleen'[16], 'Black Rose' found Philip Lynott attempting to channel the

---

15 While 'Got to Give It Up' doesn't specifically mention heroin or cocaine, Lynott does refer to a certain 'powder' during the song. However, Lizzy's frontman grabs the bull by the horns elsewhere, his reference to 'smack' sung clearly enough for all to hear on 'Toughest Street in Town'.

16 Though on the surface 'Dark Rosaleen' reads like a simple love poem, it is in fact a thinly disguised plea from Mangan to the Spanish government to dispatch a fleet of ships and rescue their fellow Irish Catholics from British rule. Mangan's veil of poetic secrecy was a necessary evil, because at that time (the late 1840s) any declaration of Irish nationalism was banned by British authorities.

191

myth and mystery, spirit and history of the Celts in seven rich minutes of song. With a lyrical cast list that included sullen demigods, dewy-eyed mystics and hard-drinking footballers, Lynott damn near did it too. From Cúchulainn, WB Yeats and the mountains of Mourne to George Best, Oscar Wilde and the long road to Tipperary, 'Black Rose' was as close to an epic as Philip would ever put his name to. 'Well, we'd done 'Emerald', 'Banshee' and several Celtic-themed songs already, but yeah, I'd agree,' said Scott Gorham. 'And you know, I actually think Gary was as keen [to master that style] as Philip, especially on the title track. I mean, the guitar work he did on 'Black Rose'. It's just "What the fuck . . . ?"'

The work Gorham referred to first reared its head two minutes into the track, when 'Black Rose' ceased being a rumbling, mid-tempo rock song enhanced by some erudite wordplay and a grand-sounding Celtic riff. Now taking on an altogether more ambitious musical shape, the tune developed four distinct instrumental strands, principally designed by Moore, with each one based on a familiar folk melody referencing the lineage of Lizzy's band members, past and present. Hence, listeners were treated to 'Danny Boy', its links to Ulster a homage to both Moore and now long-absent Eric Bell, while 'Will You Go Lassie Go''s Scottish connections deliberately put one in mind of the errant Brian Robertson. 'I might have said I liked an [air] or a particular reel,' Lynott said of Moore's intertwining constructions, 'but it was Gary who had the technical ability to put it all together.'

When it came to acknowledging Scott Gorham's roots, the old American traditional 'Shenandoah' was pulled into service by Moore. Given Gorham's exact point of origin, however, he might have been better setting their sights much closer to home. 'Well,' laughed Gorham, 'my mother was full Northern Irish – her ancestry straight out of Enniskillen – and I was born on 17 March, St Patrick's Day. I've also got green eyes. So, yep, I can see where you're going here.'

Thus far, Moore and Gorham had dovetailed on the various melodies running throughout 'Black Rose', these traditional airs a gift to Lizzy's harmony guitar team. But when it came to Moore's interpretation of the old Irish reel 'The Mason's Apron', he really was on his own. 'Well, as you know, 'The Mason's Apron' actually had its roots in the song 'Sitamoia',' confirmed Brian Downey. 'We did that song a lot live in 1974 when Gary depped with the band and he used to play 'The Mason's Apron' as part of 'Sitamoia'. But it's funny. When we came to record 'Sitamoia', he didn't want to put 'The Mason's Apron' in it.' As already evidenced, back in 1974 Moore felt that his take on the eighteenth-century reel required a more ornate setting. Five years on, 'Black Rose' provided it. 'That's right,' continued Downey, 'I asked Gary, "Why are you taking it out of mothballs now?" and he replied, "I was waiting for the right time to use it properly."'

The stunning centrepiece of 'Black Rose', Moore's rendition of 'The Mason's Apron' truly was a 'what the fuck' moment. Indeed, given such complex reels were traditionally performed on smaller necked, 'fifth-tuned' compact instruments like violins and accordions, the fact Gary was playing 'The Mason's Apron' so fast and cleanly on a 22-fret, six-string Gibson guitar was all the more remarkable. 'I mean, nobody else could play 'The Mason's Apron' like that really,' confirmed Brian. 'But you know, he used to play it even faster back in 1974. So, what you're hearing on 'Black Rose' is actually the slowed down version of 'The Mason's Apron'. Gary's playing it slowly. Now, think about that for a minute . . .'

Lovingly produced by Tony Visconti and sympathetically adorned by cover artist Jim Fitzpatrick, *Black Rose* presented itself as the perfect Thin Lizzy album. That said, if one picked beneath that immaculate surface, faults could be found. While 'S&M' and 'Get Out of Here' were canny enough tunes, there was an element of filler to both: one essentially a skinny, three-minute funk sketch, the other a throwaway pop song beefed up by industrial strength guitars.

Elsewhere, Philip Lynott's wordplay towards the end of the title track also rankled some critics. By loading the fadeout with several cheesy puns involving the first and last names of literary giants such as Brendan Behan and Oscar Wilde (among others), Lizzy's frontman was accused of skimming the permissible limits of intellectual 'Paddywhackery'. Not so, said Philip. This was all about acknowledging Ireland's rich literary covenant, cheekily or otherwise. 'What I love about the Irish writers is they all had their own degrees of being unique,' he told *NME*'s Chris

Salewicz. 'They weren't just men with pens, they were living the lives of artists, whether that meant getting drunk and brawling in Dublin pubs like Brendan Behan . . . James Joyce fucking off to Paris and being a bit weird, or even occult dabblers like Yeats. I love them because they're all a bit out there, and for me it's the power of the word that I love.'[17]

In the end, *Black Rose*'s occasional faults, and they really were just occasional, didn't hold the album back on the sales front. Barging into the UK charts at number five on 20 April 1979 before rising three more places a week later, *Black Rose* was only held off the top spot by *The Best of Leo Sayer*, and even then, it was close. 'First The Bee Gees keep *Live and Dangerous* off number one, then Leo Sayer stops *Black Rose*!' laughed Gorham. Of course, for Lynott, Gorham and Brian Downey, this was their second time skirting the summit of Olympus, commercially. But for Gary Moore, the experience was much more novel. Though successful by association via Andrew Lloyd Webber's *Variations* a year or so before, *Black Rose* still marked the first occasion Moore's own songs had featured on a hit record, and as sales topped 100,000 units, a gold disc at that. Some 40 years later, he still sounded proud of the fact. 'You know, I thought it was a really good album,' Gary told author Harry Doherty in 2010, 'and honestly, the guitars on that record were as good as anything [Lizzy ever recorded].'

Consolidation of friendship. Conjoining of talent. Call it what you will. Gary Moore's musical union with Philip Lynott and Thin Lizzy on *Black Rose* had been little short of a triumph. Yet, for all the surface bonhomie and gold-plated sales, Moore's experiences in Paris alongside Lynott also pointed at two men with very different approaches to the

---

17 The charge that by concentrating so earnestly on his country's past in song, Lynott had chosen to ignore Ireland's then-current political and financial troubles was curiously absent from most critiques of *Black Rose* at the time. However, *Hot Press* writer Dermot Stokes did at least raise a flag over the subject, while also answering why Lynott might have been reticent to engage with such potentially thorny subjects. 'The brooding intensity, the love-hate, the fire, the brimstone, the anger so familiar among other émigré Irish artists is absent [on the title track],' Stokes wrote in 1979. 'Instead, [there is] almost a nostalgia, a backward look at a more innocent Heroic Age. [But] I guess . . . modern Ireland isn't much to write home about, much less to make an album about.'

job at hand. One was a serious musician. One was a serious rock star. Thankfully, both were brilliant at what they did and *Black Rose* was the proof. However, while Moore and Lynott's working relationship at Pathé Marconi flourished, their decade-old bond was now to be tested in a very different arena. Here, there would be nowhere to hide foibles or fault lines, nor a chance to press the reset button when something went wrong or someone went too far. After nearly five years of trying, Thin Lizzy were off to finally crack America. As it turned out, America ended up cracking them.

CHAPTER FOURTEEN

Do Not Anchor Here

As part of Thin Lizzy, the spring of 1979 saw Gary Moore come face to face with both the demands and delights of full-blown rock stardom. From tours and TV to press junkets and radio spots, Moore and his distinguished co-workers were here, there and everywhere. Bits of it, like the band's appearance to promote 'Waiting for an Alibi' on ITV's anarchic *Kenny Everett Show* looked like genuine fun, as Moore, Lynott and Gorham mugged to camera while Brian Downey stoically kept the beat behind them. Other duties, such as early morning rounds with journalists who had no great interest in *Black Rose* or the group that made it were to be endured rather than enjoyed. Still, having spent many a night sleeping 'on top of an amp in the back of a van on the way to a gig in the middle of bloody nowhere,' this was surely heaven on a stick for the returning Moore. 'Gary had flawlessly stepped in and we hadn't missed a beat,' Gorham later told author Paul Elliott. 'I don't think he needed much persuading. This time he really wanted to be in the band.'

Moore's commitment certainly didn't seem in question as Thin Lizzy struck out on the road in support of their new LP, first for a short series of US dates during March in support of grizzly Scottish rockers Nazareth before again returning to the UK and Europe as part of their own headlining tour. Drawing on a set from all points of the group's history, Moore found himself re-sharpening vintage gems such as 'Don't Believe a Word', 'Warriors' and 'The Rocker' while also displaying newly cut stones like 'Get Out of Here', 'Got to Give It Up' and 'Waiting for an Alibi'. As ever, some of the biggest cheers of the night were reserved for his solo on 'Still in Love With You', though hearing Moore motor his way through 'The Mason's Apron' as part of 'Black Rose' was now equally responsible for unhinging as many jaws. 'Gary really was lifting the band; he was on fire,' said Downey.

Away from the onstage pyrotechnics, there were darker paths to negotiate. While in New York, Lynott and Gorham had hooked up with streetwise R&B troubadour Willy DeVille, then enjoying moderate success with his latest album *Return to Magenta*. A talented, if unsettled soul, DeVille was also a functioning heroin addict, and one apparently willing to share his stash with some visiting rock star types. What was once restricted to Paris was now becoming an on-the-road habit in the USA, and one that quickly followed the band back to London. At first, both Lynott and Gorham were careful to cover their tracks. But when mistakes started happening on stage because of the duo's escalating drug use, Moore had words, albeit quietly at first. 'Yeah, there was a little bit of strangeness on the UK tour, but not enough to piss Gary off that much,' said Gorham. 'I mean, he might have made a couple of comments [about our drug-taking], but Phil and I were just "OK, we'll get right on that." I mean if Gary wants us to stop, then we'll stop. Yeah, right. Actually though, we probably should have taken his advice.'

A brief respite from these tensions came for Moore when 'Parisienne Walkways' finally broke cover and began climbing the singles charts in early May 1979. Helped on its way by some generous radio support from the BBC, a semi-regular spot in Lizzy's concert set and a 'so bad it's probably good' video promo, 'Parisienne Walkways' ended up at number eight in the UK[1], one place higher than 'Waiting for an Alibi'

---

1 In addition to scoring a Top 10 hit in Blighty, 'Parisienne Walkways' went to number nine in France, proving once and for all that Gary Moore and Philip Lynott could sell coals to Newcastle. Moore was also delighted when his childhood heroes The Shadows covered the tune for their 1979 album *String Of Hits*. That LP went to number one.

had just managed. Though Moore was careful not to laud the victory over his bandmates, after all, he had co-written the song with Lynott, it was validation that if ever required, there was life beyond Lizzy. 'Oh, Gary wanted to be a rock star for sure,' said Chalkie Davies, before sounding a note of caution. '[But] I think the potential trouble was that Gary [also] wanted to be his own frontman.'

As the melody of 'Parisienne Walkways' wafted its way around the UK's airwaves, Moore, Lynott, Downey and Gorham continued their travels in Europe. A small riot marked Lizzy's arrival in Gothenburg, Sweden, on 5 May, when audiences refused to leave the concert hall following the band's set. Wisely, the band hid backstage while the police sorted it out. Five days later, and the group were in Copenhagen. Now a dab hand at such things, Lynott marked the visit by judging yet another beauty contest. Throughout May, there were outings to Stockholm, Munich, Hamburg and Cologne – where Lizzy jammed on stage with Moore's old friend, Rory Gallagher – before things hit a temporary glitch on route to Holland. The official story was that Lynott contracted food poisoning from drinking sour milk, and several gigs were cancelled when he flew home to London to recuperate. Yet, given this wasn't the first time Lynott had taken to his bed in recent months, less courteous rumours pointed at overindulgence of a different kind.[2] The truth probably sat somewhere in the middle.

By early June, Thin Lizzy's frontman was sufficiently recovered to board a plane with Gary Moore, Scott Gorham and several others, their destination Nassau. Originally sold to both guitarists as a welcome break in the 'beautiful capital city of the Bahamas' the trip actually turned out to be a working holiday, with demos recorded at Compass Point Studios for Lynott's slowly evolving solo LP.[3] 'Not so bad, though,' said Scott. 'Philip paid for everything.' This new arrangement also suited Moore, who put

2 While in Paris making *Black Rose*, Lynott was ill for three days, his perilous state of health scaring the bejesus out of Tony Visconti. 'I seriously thought he was going to die,' the producer later told author Harry Doherty. 'When he emerged from his hotel room, we had a good heart to heart about his drug abuse, but he assured me it was under control.'

3 Also making the trip to Nassau were Mark Nauseef and Huey Lewis, who like Moore and Gorham, worked on Lynott's demos while there.

down backing tracks for his follow-up single to 'Parisienne Walkways' while there. Another co-write with Lynott and another song with a distinctly European musical flavour, this time flamenco, 'Spanish Guitar' would unfortunately have to wait a while before being completed, however.

With the majority of tasks behind them and only weeks to go before a major US tour, Moore's bandmates were now in the mood to drink some cocktails, try a few 'local delicacies' and relax by the pool. Moore wasn't. 'I had no interest in what they up to,' he later said of Lynott and Gorham's extracurricular interests. 'In Colosseum II, I was the bad boy. In Thin Lizzy, I was the choirboy. It was all relative.' As Lynott and Gorham kicked off their shoes, enjoyed the sun and whatever else came to hand, Moore kept a distance, 'sitting under an umbrella,' his walking boots firmly on.

And so, to America.

During the spring of 1975, Thin Lizzy had toured the States for the first time. The group worked its way from east to west in support of Bachman-Turner Overdrive and Bob Seger. Philip Lynott even liberated one of Seger's songs, the propulsive 'Rosalie', for Lizzy's own purposes, and swore he and the band would conquer the USA within the space of two years. With 'The Boys are Back in Town' and its parent album *Jailbreak*, they almost did. But momentum was lost and opportunities squandered. Now they were back, and with the addition of Gary Moore to their ranks, Lynott firmly believed his beloved group had the goods to break the States wide open. 'Everybody's talking about Thin Lizzy as a band that's been around a long time,' he confirmed shortly after the release of *Black Rose*, 'whereas I think it's just the start because Gary's in the band now. Gary, for the first time, has given [us] a commitment.' So it appeared.

After the ups and downs of Nassau, Moore, Lynott and Gorham flew together to LA where they were joined by a returning Brian Downey to begin rehearsals for their upcoming tour. This time out, they would be supporting AOR giants Journey, then one of the biggest bands in the USA. In line with their current status, Journey were on a sell-out run of arenas, with average crowds topping 10,000. If they played their cards right, that was 10,000 potential new fans for Thin Lizzy too. Yet, according to Scott Gorham, when the quartet stepped on stage at Long Beach Arena on 30 June 1979 for the first of two nights in LA, quite a few of those gathered were already on their side. 'Yeah, the arenas were packed for our set, which doesn't often happen for a support band,' he confirmed. 'So, there's the evidence right there that we were beginning to crack this American thing open.'

Four days later and audience numbers now swelled to over 50,000, Thin Lizzy again rendezvoused with headliners Journey, The J. Geils Band, UFO and Nazareth in Oakland for a 'Day on the Green'. The brainchild of the redoubtable promoter Bill Graham and something of a West Coast institution, Day on the Green had been running since 1973 and over the years featured landmark sets from Led Zeppelin, Fleetwood Mac and The Who. Though they were only fourth on the bill, this was a chance for Lizzy to shine in the California sunshine, allowing them to engage not only with the gathered crowds, but a nest of influential music business types too.

Unfortunately, the concert did not go as well as hoped, and strong words were exchanged between Gary Moore and Philip Lynott afterwards. But it was only when the band arrived back at their hotel that the severity of the disagreement came to light. 'We started pulling things together for the next show and then the penny dropped,' Gorham confirmed some 40 years later. 'Gary was gone. Just like magic. All of a sudden, it's, "Where the fuck is Gary?"' As it turned out, Moore had just left Thin Lizzy for the third and final time. 'Phil's shouting, "I told you, don't trust this guy!" Too fucking late now.'

With benefit of hindsight, Moore's ignominious exit from the band could have been seen coming from the moon, with small dissatisfactions and minor grievances slowly building over previous months to the unpleasant climax of 4 July 1979. According to Brian Downey, Moore's issues might be traced to Australia almost a year before. 'Oh, there were personal issues between Gary and Philip,' said the drummer, 'and I think they might have gone back to the Australian tour I missed. Gary had said Phil was really overindulging at that time, that his attitude, his whole personality was changing. Apparently, with the drug-taking, Philip had become belligerent, arrogant, even obnoxious, particularly on that plane trip [at the beginning of the tour]. I'll be honest here. I never saw that side of Philip. Christ, he was no angel and he could be difficult, but I really never saw the arrogance or belligerence Gary described. But those were the words he was using. Gary seemed flabbergasted by it.'

Of course, if Moore was already carrying concerns from Australia, they would have been amplified tenfold by the events of Paris, when Lynott and Gorham's experiments with heroin started to take hold. However, despite an obvious discomfort with what was happening at Pathé Marconi, Moore appeared content to silently judge the pair from a safe distance rather than confront them directly. That approach seemed to work for them too. 'Well, it was always me and Philip,' confirmed Scott, 'going out, hanging out, hitting the clubs and Gary was never really included in that. But because of . . . the drug thing, there was a bit of a divide there.'

While creating a safe space between the two parties was possible in the studio, it wasn't going to work on the road where the errant duo's habits were now intensifying right under Moore's nose. Though his criticisms started quietly enough, by the time the group got to Europe, Gary was linking Lynott and Gorham's poor performance to drug use like an Olympic doping inspector in reverse. 'It was like, "If you guys weren't so stoned all the bloody time . . ."' said Scott. 'He absolutely hated it.'

In the end, it was two separate incidents occurring in rapid succession that seemed to tip Moore over the edge. The first came in Los Angeles when during an early break from supporting Journey, he and Philip Lynott hired a studio to complete backing vocals for Moore's forthcoming single 'Spanish Guitar'. Brian Downey, who was adding drums to the track, arrived too late to catch the fireworks, but got the gist of what happened some months later. 'Gary told me he and Philip hadn't been getting on at all at the studio,' the drummer said in 2020. 'I said, "Well, it didn't look that way," and he replied, "Ah, but you were only there for an hour. You didn't see what happened beforehand. We were arguing badly and I didn't like Philip's attitude. There were other things. Lots of little things. But when you arrived, things changed."'[4]

---

4 It transpires one of the reasons Moore might have been angry at Cherokee Studios was the quality of Lynott's vocals, which sounded somewhat thick and 'gummy' – the result, possibly, of a 'big night out' the evening before recording commenced.

Four days later, and with 'a blizzard of coke . . . above the stage' came Day on the Green. Always meticulous about rehearsal and stage performance, even the slightest scuffed note or wayward rhythm could rankle with Moore. Many in the audience, and sometimes even the band, might not notice. But for Gary, such lapses in concentration were a red rag to a bull, and he had been counting them assiduously. 'With Gary,' said Brian Downey, 'every gig had to be perfect.' Therefore, when Philip Lynott reportedly fluffed his lines 'again' on stage in Oakland before angrily kicking over his microphone in front of 50,000 paying punters, something snapped in the guitarist. When Lynott then sang over one of Moore's solos, it broke clean off. 'I looked at Philip,' Moore told *Classic Rock*'s Mick Wall, 'and thought "If that's what being a rock star's all about, I don't want anything to do with it."'

After a heated exchange backstage, Gary Moore left for West Hollywood's Le Parc Suite Hotel where he was staying with his (now) fiancée, Lisa Franklin. Steam still escaping from his ears, the guitarist remained adamant he was leaving the band. There and then. When Moore failed to materialise the next morning, alarms were sounded in the Lizzy camp, and Franklin found herself fending off phone enquiries as to his whereabouts. By then, as Scott Gorham already confirmed, 'Gary was gone. Just like fucking magic.'

Moore's assistant in pulling off his disappearing act was former Deep Purple bassist Glenn Hughes. Making LA his home after the dissolution of Purple back in 1976, Hughes had been in the same studio as Moore and Philip Lynott just days before, and struck up an immediate rapport with the guitarist. In fact, according to Hughes, Moore had asked him to form a band there and then. Now Moore was holed up at Hughes' home in the Northridge Hills some 50 kilometres outside the city trying to figure out his next move. Then the phone rang. 'At three in the morning, I got a call. It was Philip,' Glenn later told *Classic Rock*. 'He said, "If you've got Gary there, I'm going rip your throat out and shove it up your arse." So, there I am living in fear of this crazy Irishman coming around to knock my block off. I had to lie though, and say Gary wasn't there.'

The deception proved temporary. With Thin Lizzy due back on stage supporting Journey in Reno, Nevada on 6 July, time was of the essence and the group's manager, Chris O'Donnell, wasted none of it. Demanding to speak to Moore, a meaningful conversation at last took place. Though no one was taking notes, Scott Gorham remembers it this way. 'Chris O'Donnell finally tracked him down to Glenn Hughes' house. I'm sure Glenn was saying something like, "Hey Gary, you don't need those guys. Join up with me, and we'll start a band!" But seriously, Gary's on the phone telling Chris he gets no respect. Meanwhile Phil's [in the background] saying, 'Bollocks to respect. Are you getting on the plane or what?' The respect thing, it was never going to work in Phil's mind, we all got an equal amount of respect. But I guess Gary just wanted a little bit more. Anyway, I remember Chris saying to him, "Are you getting on the plane?", but Gary wouldn't budge. So, Chris says, "OK. You're fired" and slams the phone down.'

Gary Moore didn't remember it going quite like that. As the Thin Lizzy publicity machine ramped up, citing unreliability as the reason for his 'sacking', Gary took to the airwaves to tell his side of the story. 'I left Thin Lizzy,' an empathic-sounding Moore told BBC Radio One's Richard Skinner days after the event. 'There were a lot of personal problems between Philip and myself, [and] I didn't feel he was performing to the standard the band deserved. Plus, [there were] personal things I don't really want to get into. The reason they're saying I was fired is because they are annoyed I walked out in the middle of a tour. I'm very sorry to the fans,' he concluded, 'but I think people who pay to see a band deserve higher quality music than they were getting.'

Moore's explanation sounded sincere enough, and though he might have dwelled further on the exact nature of his personal problems with Philip Lynott, common sense, and presumably, the last vestiges of friendship, prohibited it. Yet, the elephant in the room still remained. If Moore had not been sacked, then by his own admission he had walked out of the band in the middle of a tour, and in so doing, broken one of the cardinal rules of the music business. More than 40 years later, the anger concerning his actions remains palpable. 'I don't know when or at what point he made the decision to get out,' said Chalkie Davies. 'I don't recall if Gary had a manager at that point, and you know, maybe that was it. Maybe he didn't have anyone to stop him. But you just don't do that. You really fucking don't. No [member of a] group, no matter how much they fucking hate each other, would have done what Gary did.' Scott Gorham echoed the photographer's sentiments in 2007. 'If you're having a bad time, at least make it to the end,' said the Californian. 'To pack a bag and leave everyone else in the shit is just not on.'

The reason for Davies and Gorham's obvious ire was the damage Moore's actions might have caused, not only to Thin Lizzy themselves, but the people relying on them. By then a substantial business enterprise employing managers, road crew and support staff, any injury sustained by the band during a US tour could create potential havoc for all concerned, including concert headliners Journey, who had hired them to provide support. By Moore walking out, Lizzy had been put in 'serious fucking jeopardy' and extreme solutions were required. 'Well, Phil looks at me and says, "Scott, you're up."'

Hence, while a mad scramble went on behind the scenes to find a replacement for Gary Moore, Thin Lizzy became a three-piece for four fairly hairy, if rewarding concerts, with Scott Gorham covering all major parts. 'Journey were brilliant to us,' he said. 'They did not want us off the tour. In fact, their guitarist, Neal Schon, came up to me and said "Whatever you want. I can get two more speakers for you on that side of the stage, two more on your side. PA. Lights. We got you covered." I mean, that's pretty fucking cool. So, yeah, we kept going [as a trio] for four shows. And yep, we got encores, which made me feel pretty bloody good. It was like "Fuck you, Gary!"'

When Moore's replacement was found, he had little time to dwell on the niceties of Thin Lizzy's back catalogue, their contribution to harmonic theory or whether Gary had been shown a metaphorical finger by his former bandmates. Thrown 'guitar in hand' onto Concorde at Heathrow Airport, 'I thought I'd have eight hours to learn the set, but Concorde got to the States in about three', Midge Ure was on the plane, in rehearsal and on stage with the band by 18 July 1979. A good friend of Philip Lynott (and as detailed, the co-writer of 'Get Out of Here') Ure was also a capable player whose pop/rock past with Slik and Rich Kids gave little indication of his impending future fronting new romantic overlords Ultravox. That said, when the 25-year-old Scot stepped out under the lights at New Orleans' Warehouse Theater, his unofficial title might well have been 'Godsend'. 'So, the Scotsman gets on Concorde with three hours to learn a set,' laughed Gorham. 'Poor Midge! A lovely man though, with a great sense of humour who did a great job. Oh, I know our first gigs [with him] were scary as hell. But that was Philip. Philip was not going to give up or give in.'

With Midge Ure's help, Thin Lizzy completed their American tour. Moreover, *Black Rose* even got to number eighty-one in the US charts, though the band could no longer perform its title track – at least in its original iteration. 'Ha!' laughed Brian Downey. 'Well, as I said, when Gary left no one else could play the fucking middle bit!' There were more serious and lasting consequences to deal with following Moore's sudden departure. 'We had some great nights on that tour,' Downey continued. 'And you know, I'm sure we might have been booked again. But when Gary left, well, [the promoters] just seemed to lose interest in Thin Lizzy. It looked like we weren't dependable. Philip had already come down with hepatitis on a tour, we'd had the Robbo thing and now Gary had taken off. I mean, US promoters weren't impressed. Would you be? They also knew getting Midge in, God bless him, was a stop-gap measure and they just felt, "We can't really book you." So, when Gary left, it really was the first nail in the coffin. In America,' he concluded, 'we were dead.'

By leaving Thin Lizzy, Gary Moore had not only caused the band a series of headaches in the USA, but also set off a chain reaction of business-related issues that would drag on long after the events of 4 July 1979. To begin, a flat Moore had bought on Hampstead's busy Fitzjohn's Avenue with money generated by joining the band now became the subject of litigation, with both parties claiming ownership of the property. Moore won that one. However, when Lizzy's US record label allegedly threatened to stop the Stateside release of Moore's album *Back on the Streets* because of Philip Lynott's presence on two tracks, things again soured. To his credit, Lynott reportedly waved such stupidities away, but Moore took Lynott's vocal off the American version of 'Don't Believe a Word' anyway.

By late September 1979, Moore's new single 'Spanish Guitar' arrived in stores. Correctly described by *Kerrang*'s Neil Jefferies as a 'shamelessly contrived and vain attempt to repeat the formula that made 'Parisienne Walkways' a hit,' the tune was at best undistinguished and rightly ignored by record buyers. Still, Lynott's vocals again had to be removed and replaced by Moore's for 'the suits' to be happy.[5] Six months later, and there was a similar kerfuffle when someone spotted Lynott's own forthcoming solo album, *Solo in Soho*[6], featured a ditty called 'Jamaican Rum' with Moore on lead guitar. By then, the storm clouds were beginning to pass and the LP landed in shops with Moore's contribution intact. Unlike all the other contributors to *Solo in Soho*, however, Moore was not thanked for his efforts on the album sleeve. No great surprise, really.

Yet, as managers, lawyers and accountants sought to clean up the mess, the questions still remained as to how and why things had come to this. For two of the managers directly involved, Moore's attitude and ego were clearly to blame. 'Gary had ulterior motives,' said Thin Lizzy's Chris O'Donnell. 'He was always looking to do something more credible.' If O'Donnell believed the jazz-rocking Moore looked down upon the more direct musical charms of Lizzy, Chris Morrison felt the guitarist had simply misunderstood his place in the scheme of things. 'Thin Lizzy was a benign dictatorship [run by Philip Lynott],' Morrison later told journalist James McNair, 'and Gary found it hard to be just a partner.'

Chalkie Davies held a broadly similar view, while again hinting at Moore's possible ambitions for a solo career. 'How could you have a "partnership" within a four piece? No, it could never be a partnership. Really, it was a mutual admiration society, those two,' he said in 2020. 'Philip and Gary genuinely recognised and respected each other's talent. But Gary wanted to be a star and I think he knew he wasn't going to be a star if you're playing second fiddle to a bass player. Maybe he [was]

---

5 Though Lynott's vocals were removed from the single version of 'Spanish Guitar' throughout most of Europe, 1,000 copies did escape the net in Sweden, where the 45 was released with Lynott's distinctive, if gummy tones intact.

6 Some three years after starting the project, *Solo in Soho* was finally released on 18 April 1980. A wildly eclectic effort, it reached number twenty-eight in the UK.

looking towards the centre of the stage watching the audience reaction, and thinking, "I'd much rather do that than just blues solos. And maybe I could."'

Watching from the other side of the stage was Scott Gorham, who offered a few choice theories of his own. 'You know what it is?' he said. 'When Gary first joined Lizzy [in 1974], he wasn't that well known. So, joining up gave him some real publicity, got his brand known. He used the situation to "Up your name, up your game", you might say. And that's fine, no problems there. But [in 1978], things were very different. Gary joined up, but Philip and he weren't best friends [any more]. Friends, sure, but not quite the same, and the dynamics had also changed. I think he and Philip were using each other a bit for mutual gain at that point. I don't know. Maybe I'm wrong, but that's the way it looked to me, at least.'

Perhaps such a change could have been weathered over time. But when heroin entered the equation, it created an insurmountable bridge between Moore and Lynott. 'Philip was very creative, but he wouldn't always be in the right condition to work,' Moore later told *Mojo*'s Dermott Hayes. 'On tour it would be a toss-up whether he could go on. He'd be sitting in the soundcheck with stomach cramps. The band were a shambles and it got to the point where I couldn't face one more gig. So, I left in the middle of the tour.'

That decision would weigh heavily on Gary Moore, its emotional impact considerable and sustained. Back in 1979, he was keen to stress that professionalism and the need for constant improvement were key drivers behind his choice to leave. 'I have a standard,' he told the BBC, 'And anyone who knows my history will know I'm used to working with musicians of a very high standard. But if you fly down from that, then you'll keep going down. And I don't want to go down. I want to go up.' Yet, as the years went by and the ramifications of his actions became clearer, so the doubts began to creep in. 'I was always proud of my professionalism,' he later said, 'but I let myself down by walking out like that.' Former Colosseum II colleague and close friend Don Airey was there to witness Moore wrestle with his choice. 'He felt terrible, subsequently, at what he had done,' Airey told *Classic Rock*. 'But then, he felt he had no choice. I think he thought Phil was a goner.'

Ego, ambition, legitimate anger at Lynott and Gorham's antics or simply a clumsy attempt to save an old friend from himself. All were possible factors in Moore's abrupt departure, either on their own or in parallel. But at the time, it didn't matter a jot. As the phones were slammed down on the morning of 5 July 1979 any second chances for Moore and Thin Lizzy to reconcile were quickly replaced by what Brian Downey called a giant, everlasting 'What If?' 'I do think that if Gary had stayed in the band, we'd have been much more popular, particularly in America,' said the drummer. 'But I think by then Gary felt Philip was becoming a bit of a bollocks. Sometimes though, I have thought that might have been a bit of an excuse on Gary's behalf. But I don't know. I just don't know. I guess we'll never know.'

Some 30 years after the event, when the smoke from burning all those bridges had long cleared, Gary Moore was asked to name his favourite Thin Lizzy album. The answer, quick and honest, said much. 'My favourite Lizzy album? *Jailbreak*. That's a classic album from the classic line-up. But, you know,' he added, 'in terms of quality, *Black Rose* does come a close second.' Sadly, there would be no opportunity to hear Thin Lizzy follow up *Black Rose* with Moore. 'Bad luck,' said Brian Downey. 'Just call it bad luck.'

Right or wrong, it was done. Gary Moore had left Thin Lizzy. Time to move on.

PART THREE:

1980 – 1989: New Decade, New Tricks

'You make a breakthrough and another door just opens. It's like you go into a candy shop and everything's there for the taking.'

Gary Moore

CHAPTER FIFTEEN

Crawling From
The Wreckage

Having just driven over an enormously important crossroads in his life behind the controls of a large tank, Gary Moore was a free agent once again. Though his recent decisions had come at some cost both professionally and personally, the guitarist was now technically able to pursue whichever musical direction he chose. However, that freedom came loaded with potential dilemmas. 'Well, Gary had no clue what to do next [when he left Thin Lizzy],' his friend Don Airey later told author Mick Wall. 'It was just [after] 'Parisienne Walkways' was breaking. So, he had a hit but he really didn't know what to do about it.' Happily for Moore, there were a queue of characters more than content to provide him with valuable advice.

At the front of the line was Jet Records boss Don Arden. A semi-mythical figure in music business circles whose robust methods earned him the nickname 'The Don Corleone of Pop', Arden had actively pursued a career as a singer/comedian during the late forties before leaving the spotlight behind to concentrate on concert promotion. In this he excelled, overseeing UK tours for Little Richard and Jerry Lee

Lewis before trying the management game on for size with rockabilly wild boy Gene Vincent in 1960. When Vincent allegedly pulled a knife on him Arden walked away, but only from Vincent, who was probably lucky he did. Wisely replacing temperamental rock'n'rollers with pop stars, Arden signed up Small Faces and The Nashville Teens, his personal empire growing at the same rate as the number of hair-raising tales circulating around him.[1] In 1974, Arden set up Jet Records. A year later, the mighty ELO delivered the company's first million seller. Move the clock forward four years to 1979 and Arden had extended the reach of Jet's affairs to America, where he opened an office for the label in Los Angeles. Gary Moore now happened to be in the same city.

At this point, the stars started to align and Jet agreed to distribute Moore's latest LP *Back on the Streets* for a US audience. The man reportedly behind the deal was Moore's recently appointed financial manager Colin Newman, who would subsequently become one of the musician's most trusted and long-standing advisers. The arrangement Newman brokered with Jet also proved the precursor to an offer of a proper solo deal for Gary. However, it was Don Arden's daughter Sharon rather than the man himself who would sign and personally oversee Moore's affairs with the company. Then only 25 years old and with little experience of the industry, one might have thought Gary was taking a chance placing his artistic interests in the hands of such a young, untried manager. But as time came to show, Sharon Arden was an extraordinarily fast learner. 'Gary was the first guy I managed and I loved it,' she later told DJ Eddie Trunk.

---

1 Nashville Teens keyboard player John Hawken witnessed the more fearsome side of Don Arden first hand. 'We were owed a load of money by Don,' he said in 2015, 'and after a while we asked for it.' But when Arden handed him a cheque for £20 rather than the agreed £120, Hawken questioned the amount. He soon found himself in potentially dire straits. 'Arden put me over the lower bar of his office window and I'm looking at Carnaby Street down below. He said, "You're going down, John, you're going down." and I really thought he was going to do it. Then he relaxed his hands and brought back into the room. Well, I thought, "£20 is better than nothing." After a fruitless visit to a police station, Hawken decided to put the matter down to experience. 'God, you know, I hate to speak ill of the dead, but in this case, I'll make an exception.'

With a deal signed and a new manager on side, stage two for Gary Moore was pulling together a band. Waiting the call-up was Glenn Hughes. A valuable, if somewhat petrified ally when Moore was making good his escape from Thin Lizzy, Hughes' star might have dimmed somewhat since those halcyon days of playing with Deep Purple. But as the singer/bassist's most recent solo release, 1977's *Play Me Out*, proved, he could still pen a memorable tune and belt it out with the best of them. Further, Hughes' ability to fuse funk, soul and rock flavours intrigued Gary Moore, who was eager to incorporate some of those elements into his own songwriting. By combining their strengths, there might be the makings of a tasty little group here. Hughes obviously thought so. 'For me Gary Moore was the jewel in the crown,' he later told *Rock Candy*. 'To sit next to him on my couch and to see him play with those insane fingers and come up with those insane melodies, well, it was out of this world. I've sat with a lot of guitar players, but this man spoke to me directly.'

There was one more recruit required before Moore and Hughes could properly take up arms. After conversations with Cozy Powell came to naught, Gary turned to drummer Mark Nauseef. Sympathetic to Moore's cause while they were both in Thin Lizzy, Nauseef was a gifted percussionist as well as a loyal friend. Indeed, in addition to recently playing alongside Moore, Nauseef had provided rhythmic support for Glenn Hughes when he recorded *Play Me Out* two years before. In short, the signs were good, and by all accounts so were rehearsals, with the trio pulling together a tentative set list within weeks of forming. Described by Nauseef as 'a kind of "power soul"' (several years before Prince used the phrase on 1987's *Lovesexy*), when demos were cut at LA's Cherokee Studios, Jet were ready to break out the champagne. Unfortunately, when they did, that was the end of Glenn Hughes.

Like Philip Lynott before him, Hughes' ability to meld memorable bass lines with soulful vocals was never in doubt. However, again just like Lynott, that talent came with an addict's appetite, Hughes' particular drugs of choice being cocaine and alcohol. Such was the depth of Hughes'

213

addiction, it had shortened his time with Deep Purple[2] and scuppered many prospective projects thereafter. Of course, he had hoped that this time with Moore, it would be different. But when Hughes got drunk and argued with Sharon Arden at his own 28th birthday celebrations, the pendulum swung back with full force. Waking with little recollection of the night before he called Arden, only to be told that his drunken threat to quit the band had been considered and accepted. 'Basically, I fired myself on my birthday,' he later told *Deep Purple Forever*. 'Sharon Osbourne held a big party for me and I got so drunk that I said "I'm gonna leave the band." And they said "OK, great."' Though the kill shot was fired by his manager, Moore might well have loaded the gun. Already heartily sick of the problems that came with 'the drug life', Moore was in no mood to revisit them with a new band member. Hughes was out. At least for a while.

No time was wasted in replacing Hughes, with Moore and Mark Nauseef holding auditions for his successor at a roomy studio complex nestled high in the Hollywood Hills. Their task wasn't easy. Hughes had held down not only vocals and fretless bass within the trio, but also contributed keyboards and foot pedals too. 'I sung about 60 per cent of the songs,' he later said. What's more, some of the material they had been working on came directly from Hughes' pen and these tunes would now be lost to them. Still, there were many hopefuls interested in filling the former Purple man's shoes, including bassist Doni Harvey from cult prog-rock quartet Automatic Man and Nauseef's old buddy in The Ian Gillan Band, John Gustafson. Both were good. Neither were suitable.

---

2 According to much-missed Deep Purple keyboardist Jon Lord, Glenn Hughes' addiction issues were a strong factor in the band's break-up of 1976. 'At the [Liverpool Empire] show, Glenn said to the audience, "I'm sorry we're not playing very well, but we're very tired and jet-lagged,"' Lord later confirmed. 'I remember spluttering to myself, "Speak for yourself." I was working like a Trojan . . . Paicey was playing like a madman [and] . . . Coverdale was singing his socks off. So, to hear this guy who was extremely high on various substances telling the audience, "I'm sorry, *we* aren't playing well" kind of rankled me a bit. I came off stage, went straight to [the] dressing room, and said, "Ian . . . that's it, isn't it? That's absolutely the end of this band as far as I'm concerned." So, he and I shook hands and said, "It's over. Thank God." About ten minutes later, Coverdale came in and said, "I'm leaving the band!" "David," we said, "there's no band to leave".'

Another round of musical interviews began; this one threw up several further candidates as well as a [patiently untrue] rumour that Rush's Geddy Lee was circling the duo about a job. 'Can you fucking imagine!' laughed one of Moore's friends. No Lee, then. But thankfully on this occasion, two names did stick.

In the case of Tony Newton, Moore and Nauseef had landed squarely on their feet. Born and raised in Detroit, Newton had experimented with 'all the woodwinds' and saxophone while at school before gravitating to electric bass as a teenager in the early sixties. 'Players like James Jamerson and Chuck Rainey [made bass] the foundation of a band,' he later told journalist Ivan Williams. By the end of the decade, Newton had backed legends such as John Lee Hooker and Smokey Robinson before the seventies found him doing the same for The Mamas & The Papas and Aretha Franklin. 'I could read and had studied music theory. So, I considered myself school trained and street trained!'

Yet, it was Newton's work with jazz drummer Tony Williams's New Lifetime and his appearance alongside German pianist Joachim Kühn on 1978's *Sunshower* that alerted Moore and Nauseef to the scope of the bassist's talent. Not only could Williams play extremely complex melodic lines with a jazzer's discipline, but he had a real flair for funk and R&B rhythms too. When one threw in the fact that Newton could sing and was also well used to working with guitar hero types, (*Sunshower* featured both Jan Akkerman and Ray Gomez), there was little doubt the duo had found their man.

Nevertheless, despite Moore and Williams's strong vocal ranges, neither fancied stepping up to the microphone as lead singer with the band. For Moore, this was an old problem in a new form. Since the days of Colosseum II, he had been seeking 'the right vocalist', only to end up reluctantly doing the job himself. With Glenn Hughes out of the picture and Philip Lynott unlikely to help out, the search for 'Robert Plant meets Sam Cooke' was now back on. Strangely, Moore found the answer to his problem was a former drummer.

At 32 years old, Willie Dee had done the rounds with various groups before meeting Moore. Born William Daffern, he spent his formative musical years behind the drum kit with sixties R&B/progressive rock outfits such as Hunger and Truk before joining Captain Beyond in 1976 as lead vocalist for their third, aptly titled LP *Dawn Explosion*. Though the band, comprised of ex-members of Deep Purple and Iron Butterfly, had much to commend them, Daffern's time with Captain Beyond was short. Within a year, the quartet was no more, and Daffern, now trading under the name Willie Dee, moved on to more jazz-rocking pastures. There was a stint with former Vanilla Fudge/Beck, Bogert & Appice bassist Tim Bogert's latest group Pipedream as well as an impressive guest slot on Jan Akkerman's album *3* ('She's So Divine'). But again, it was Dee's appearance alongside the Dutch guitar master on Joachim Kühn's expressive *Sunshower* that really caught Gary Moore's ear. Though Dee sang only two tunes on that album, his soulful delivery and three octave-plus range were enough to secure a job with Moore's new outfit.

From walking out of Thin Lizzy to sealing the deal with Willie Dee had taken Moore the best part of six months. But he was still willing to sacrifice a few more weeks in search of the right producer. Though top tier choices such as Roy Thomas Baker (Queen), Steve Cropper (Jeff Beck Group) and Eddie Kramer (Led Zeppelin) were all considered, none were exactly what Moore had in mind when seeking to realise his 'power soul' sound. Further, Tony Visconti, who might well have been a perfect solution to Moore's problems, was busy in New York helping David Bowie re-invent himself yet again with *Scary Monsters (And Super Creeps)*. Uncertain of exactly how to proceed, the quartet chose to produce themselves, a decision Moore would repent at leisure.

In advance of the LP's release, the final pieces of the puzzle concerning Gary Moore's first post-Thin Lizzy project were sent to journalists by Jet Records. After toying with calling the group 'Red Alert', Moore had settled on 'G-Force', a pleasing, if obvious play on Moore's first name and the presumed musical power of his new outfit. To accompany the press kit confirming G-Force's name was a set of publicity photos, wherein lay the real surprise. Instead of presenting a bunch of hirsute, hard-rocking types, the members of G-Force had undergone a striking, if suspiciously youthful makeover, as tailored leather trousers and skin-tight wind-cheaters with angular button arrangements were modelled without the slightest hint of irony. On top of all these peculiar angles, Moore had

216

cut his hair above the shoulder for the first time in nearly 15 years, Gary's spiky black coiffure now more resembling the bearskin hat of a renegade Grenadier guard than the flowing locks of a jobbing guitar god. One only hoped the sacrifice had been worth it.

Mercifully, Moore's new album was easily good enough to distract from his new wave-styled bouffant. Released on 30 May 1980, *G-Force* turned out to be a surprisingly cohesive blend of pop, soul, R&B and hard rock, with a strong emphasis on melody and musicianship. Moore had also been a generous leader, allowing each band member to contribute songs and ideas to the album. Indeed, some of the best tunes on *G-Force* came directly from the writing partnership of Willie Dee and Tony Newton, the duo responsible for the propulsive 'Because of Your Love'[3] and 'classical soul power' of 'You Kissed Me Sweetly'. Mark Nauseef also proved an able collaborator for Moore, picking up co-writes alongside the guitarist on two of the LP's heavier moments: the none-more-direct thrills of 'Rockin' and Rollin'' and the moody 'She's Got You'. In fact, *G-Force*'s final track 'Dancin'' credited the entire group, the combination of high-octane guitars, roaring vocals, tight-as-tuppence bass and barking mad, sequencer-assisted drum break confirming each's part in its construction.

As one might expect, Moore himself had also written several tunes on his own, with 'You' providing a dramatic opener for the album, its cascading solo, all descending pentatonic scales and twisting harmony lines, recalling the best of his work with Thin Lizzy. 'I Look at You' was another strong composition. Regally serene with some lovely soul-inflected chord work, Moore's gliding lead break was challenged only by the honeyed larynx of Willie Dee.

Moore's 'Hot Gossip', on the other hand, was pure finger-snapping power pop, albeit considerably darkened by a storyline skirting the boundaries of insecurity and obsession. With Moore and Lisa Franklin's relationship reportedly in trouble at the time partly because of his jealous streak, it wasn't hard to see 'Hot Gossip' as closer to autobiography than fiction. This interpretation was only strengthened when the song was

---

3 John Hitchings is also credited as a writer on 'Because of Your Love'.

released as a single, its uncomfortable video promo focusing on a finger-wagging Moore chasing his bored-looking girlfriend around a nightclub.

Away from 'Hot Gossip', it was business as usual, as Moore continued to push his abilities as a guitarist to the absolute limit. In addition to the tight harmonies and spiralling lines of 'You' and 'I Look at You', Moore's leads on 'Because of Your Love', 'Rockin' and Rollin'' and 'Dancin'' were among some of the most dextrous he had yet attempted. There was even a part-unaccompanied solo instrumental to savour in the form of 'White Knuckles'. Clocking in at just over a minute, it provided a lightning-quick distillation of Gary's signature style, full of hyper-speed arpeggios, knotty scale patterns and enough squealing harmonics to scare a field of horses.

Probably performed on a prototype Charvel/Jackson Custom 'Superstrat', hence all that tremolo dive-bombing at the end, 'White Knuckles' was all the more impressive given the industrial strength strings Moore had used when recording it. With the lighter gauge sets that initially liberated those fingers as a teenager now a distant memory, he had again returned to digit-numbingly 'heavy wires', his preference for 0.10-0.52 Dean Markley strings[4] seemingly at odds with all that neck-scampering. Yet, for Moore, it was all part of the challenge. 'Yeah, I like to fight 'em a bit,' he said. 'I grew up playing heavy strings and I need that resistance.' When it came to picks, it was the same story. 'I use Gibson extra heavy picks,' he confirmed. 'A really heavy pick just suits my style better.'

While 'White Knuckles' might have thrown down the gauntlet to other aspiring shredders out there (as we shall see, one in particular had already caught Moore's attention), like the rest of the album, the track did have one rather glaring fault. 'Oh, the famous *G-Force* guitar tone.' In a bold experiment, Moore had dispensed completely with amplification and instead plugged straight into the studio's recording desk to cut his guitar parts. '[The guitar] was direct injected through an overdrive pedal into the studio board,' he later explained to *Ultimate Guitar*. 'I was trying to go for a very fat sound, almost like a synthesiser. But [it ended up]

---

4 If Moore wanted to rest his fingers on tour, he would occasionally swap to a set of lighter Dean Markley .009-0.48 strings.

sounding completely detached from the other tracks.' Far worse was the *sound* of his guitar. 'Well, it sounded good when I did it, but when I heard the actual record, I absolutely hated it,' he later confessed. 'It sounded like a wasp in a bloody honey jar. But you know, it's really hard to get the right tone, really hard.'

Despite the rather embarrassing setback of Moore's waspish guitar tone and a tendency towards overegging the pudding when it came to string arrangements – 'Sometimes it sounded too much like ELO' – *G-Force* remained a strong record, and one the band were keen to tour. Surprisingly, given the LP's commercial sheen, Jet appeared to make no real effort to put G-Force on the road in the States just yet, preferring to point them first in the direction of Great Britain. Hence, Moore found himself returning to London in the summer of 1980 to provide support for former Deep Purple singer David Coverdale's latest success: the reassuringly hairy, blues-rocking Whitesnake.

On paper it didn't look like the happiest of marriages. With their new-wave hair, tailored jackets and studied, three-part vocal harmonies, G-Force were a far cry from the type of act Whitesnake's resolutely denim army were used to cheering on. But G-Force gave it their best shot, with Moore frying the eardrums of those gathered with his (pleasingly restored) wall of Marshall amps. 'Christ, he played loud,' laughed Whitesnake's own resident axe-hero Bernie Marsden, a friend and admirer of Moore's since the early seventies.

In fact, Marsden wasn't the only old chum Moore had in Whitesnake. Following turns in Colosseum II and National Health, bassist Neil Murray had reactivated his original love of progressive blues by taking up an offer to join the band two years before. 'I'd played with National Health, who like Colosseum II, were a very intellectual band musically, and again like Colosseum II, playing very complex, commercially unsuccessful music,' he laughed in 2020. 'So, as a result, I was incredibly broke and if Whitesnake hadn't come along, I might well have given up playing the bass.' Fortunately, Murray now found himself thoroughly enjoying his new position. 'Well, Whitesnake harked back to that blues thing from the sixties and that was a natural fit for all the band members, including me. Also, we weren't seeking to be fashionable. In fact, we were very much not about what was happening musically at that time.'

Having reactivated his friendship with Neil Murray on Whitesnake's latest UK trek, Moore's next step was a headlining show with G-Force at London's small, but perfectly formed Venue on 1 July. As bootlegs confirm, the quartet were probably at their best in such an intimate space. Freed of the antiseptic confines of the studio, songs like 'Because of Your Love' and 'You Kissed Me Sweetly' took on a stronger, more energetic dimension while already harder-edged material such as 'Dancin'' and 'Rockin' and Rollin'' became even more gritty. In fact, when the night ended with a cover of Lizzy's 'Toughest Street in Town', the band's road crew actually threw towels into the sweat-soaked audience.

But one swallow doesn't make a summer, and by the autumn of 1980, G-Force threw in the towel, too. Though the quartet had been in existence just over a year, there were several compelling reasons for their quick demise. For starters, the relationship between Moore and Willie Dee had apparently been found severely wanting, especially when the band hit the road. 'We phone up Willie's [hotel room] saying we're the police and need to see his passport,' Gary laughed to *Sounds*. It didn't end there. 'Once we told him he needed a special visa to get into Scotland. We like pulling tricks on Willie, you see!' Asinine tour japes aside, there were other issues. Moore's habit of sharing vocals on several songs meant that Dee was sometimes underused, which might have rankled with a so clearly gifted singer. If rumours are correct, Moore's perfectionist streak was another factor, while others pointed to Dee's discomfort with the more commercial elements of the group's sound. Whatever the case, Dee and Moore were obviously not destined for the long haul.

On top of his testy relationship with Willie Dee, Moore had been grumbling to journalists about the actual music the band were making. Ever the critic of his own work, he began to find some aspects of G-Force too contrived, and wanted to pursue a 'bigger, bolder, brighter sound'. Unfortunately, that ambition would be thwarted.

For Sharon Arden – who had put in a mighty shift managing Moore and Co. – G-Force's short, if eventful, lifespan provided several useful lessons in the rock management game, some of which she would put to good use in the future. However for now, all that was left to do was cancel the band's upcoming appearances at London's Marquee and Reading Festival, gather up Jet's remaining investment (which, despite G-Force's brief history, must have put a considerable dent in the label's promotions budget) and draw the curtains on the enterprise.

For Gary Moore, the end of G-Force meant heading back to a very familiar-looking drawing board. Still signed to Jet as a solo artist, contracts needed to be honoured and Moore needed a new band to honour them. Now based back in Hampstead, London, he began the process of once again finding musicians to aid his cause, though there was to be no trawling of the capital's music venues in search of fresh, untried virtuosi. Instead, he gravitated towards a cast of proven performers who could deliver at the levels he required.

First in the door was old pal Don Airey, whose near three-year stint with Rainbow was coming to a natural end. Joining the ex-Colosseum II keyboardist was another established talent in former Pat Travers/Black Oak Arkansas drummer Tommy Aldridge. An American 'living in London at the time,' Aldridge had heard stories about how Moore could be 'difficult' but ended up getting on with him like a house on fire. 'Gary and I both had similar work ethics,' Tommy later told *My Global Mind*. 'We liked to get in the rehearsal room . . . [and] spend hour after hour until we got things right. We . . . never had any issues, and he was just a really sweet, honest and funny guy.'

Joining Aldridge as part of Moore's new rhythm section was another old acquaintance, bassist Andy Pyle. Once circling a slot in Colosseum II, Pyle had since worked with the smoking fingers of Alvin Lee and north London's finest The Kinks before again taking up arms with Gary. Last, but surely not least was vocalist Kenny Driscoll, whose tough/sweet tones were most recently put to use fronting Welsh hard rockers Lone Star, a promising quintet later featuring Moore's short-lived replacement in Skid Row, Paul Chapman. Small world, indeed.

It was this line-up plus another familiar face in returning producer Chris Tsangarides[5] that arrived at The Marquee on 5 November 1980 to record a two-night stop-off at London's favourite musical sweat pit. Unofficially billed as 'Fireworks Night with Gary Moore', the band's set drew heavily on recent wins, with G-Force's 'Dancin'', 'She's Got You' and 'You' respectively making their mark. 'Parisienne Walkways' also made an appearance, though Moore chose to perform it as an instrumental rather than have Kenny Driscoll cover Philip Lynott's missing vocals. Perhaps he was worried about stray lawyers gathered in the crowd. Still, with Don Airey opening up the jazzier possibilities of the melody and Gary soaring off into guitar heaven, it worked well enough.

However, the newer material on show did raise a hackle or two. Unlike the sophisticated pop-rock offered by Moore's last band, tunes such as 'Nuclear Attack' and the lyrically risible 'Run to Your Mama' sounded coarse, overly direct and squarely aimed at fans of the then rapidly expanding 'new wave of British heavy metal.'[6] In the past, Moore had been criticised for over-complicating his music. Clearly, recent months had found him re-thinking that strategy to suit the times.

With the tapes of The Marquee performances now in the hands of Jet Records, Moore's next stop of note was Morgan Studios. The site where all three Colosseum II albums and his own LP *Back on the Streets* had been recorded, Moore's return to Morgan in January 1980 was to lay down demos for a new disc's worth of potential songs. It would be done

---

5 On 1985's CD re-release of *G-Force*, Chris Tsangarides is listed as producer. However, he seems to have played no part in the recording of the album.

6 Also known by the abbreviation 'NWOBHM', the new wave of British heavy metal was a label attached to a series of promising young bands taking their musical cue from the likes of Led Zeppelin, Thin Lizzy and UFO, but with a post-punk energy all their own.

with a slightly modified line-up, as bassist Andy Pyle and singer Kenny Driscoll had been replaced by Jimmy Bain and Charlie Huhn, respectively. While Bain had long been an associate of Moore's (and somewhat awkwardly, remained a firm friend of Philip Lynott's), Huhn was something of a surprise, the amiable American having spent the previous two years singing alongside multimillion-selling Gonzo-guitarist Ted Nugent. When one heard the general thrust of Moore's latest batch of tracks, however, Huhn's multi-octave spanning voice came to make perfect sense.

Largely eschewing the poppier elements of G-Force in favour of a much more aggressive approach, songs like 'Bad News', 'Lonely Nights' and 'Really Gonna Rock' were further confirmation that Moore had his sights on the hard rock/metal market. With his amp turned up to 11 and Huhn's impassioned, if nerve-shredding screams filling in any remaining gaps, power rather than subtlety was the aim here.

Among all the chugging chords, squealing whammy bars and unearthly howls, there were some entertaining moments. Anti-war anthems 'Nuclear Attack' and 'Hiroshima' might have been lyrically ham-fisted, but one couldn't deny they also delivered quite the punch. Away from Moore's newfound obsession with atomic conflict, a sprightly cover of Nina Simone/ The Animals' 'Don't Let Me Be Misunderstood' hinted at someone capable of taking an old tune and turning it into a modern hit. Yet, whichever way you cut it, the majority of material recorded at Morgan was ordinary at best, with even Moore's latest solo instrumental 'Dirty Fingers' sounding like a less distinguished version of his recent tour de force 'White Knuckles'. 'The songs were OK,' he later said, his four-word verdict coming across more like a furtive admission than any glowing endorsement.

Ultimately, neither The Marquee tapes nor the unfinished Morgan recordings were given the green light for release by Jet. In fact, the company seemed to have their eye on other things at the time. After a year of fighting various fires on his behalf, Sharon Arden had now stepped away from managing Moore and was concentrating all her efforts on Jet's newest signing: former Black Sabbath vocalist and scourge of bats and doves everywhere, Ozzy Osbourne. This task would take up most of her time for several decades to come. Elsewhere, Don Arden was at the beginning of a series of legal and financial battles that eventually led to havoc for both Jet Records and his own fortune. Faced with several band members leaving to pursue other projects, and a proposal to form a new trio with ex-BBA/Pipedream bassist Tim Bogert and drummer/buddy Cozy Powell falling on deaf ears, Moore made the decision to leave Jet and take his business elsewhere.

While contracts were examined and escape clauses explored, Gary temporarily found himself returning to the world of the hired gun. Always a valuable secondary income stream when the situation demanded it, Moore had been dipping a toe into the session scene since his days with Skid Row, dropping chords and solos on tunes by the likes of Granny's Intentions and Dr Strangely Strange while living in Dublin. That practice had continued in the UK throughout the seventies, as Moore became a squawking 'wah duck' on *The Rock Peter and the Wolf* and a 'whirling dervish of notes' on Gary Boyle's LP *Electric Glide*. Some of these turns, such as on Jonathan Kelly's 1973 LP *Wait Till They Change The Backdrop* or 1975's *The Eddie Howell Gramophone Record* has literally been one or two guitar breaks. Others, such as Moore's recent dalliances with Jack Lancaster on the genre-leaping *Skinningrove Bay* and Cozy Powell's rock/fusion crossover *Over the Top* required somewhat harder graft. Yet, his latest involvement with Greg Lake was to be a far more substantial contribution than most.

Since coming to prominence with Moore's beloved King Crimson in 1969, Greg Lake had gone from strength to strength. Though only part of Robert Fripp's scholarly proggers for a year, Lake's eerily distorted vocals on '21st Century Schizoid Man' and deft bass playing throughout parent debut LP *In the Court of the Crimson King* had marked out his promise for all to hear. One of those listening intently was The Nice's keyboardist, Keith Emerson, who, tiring of his own band, suggested he and Lake put a new project together. Adding ex-Atomic Rooster drummer Carl Palmer, the trio became Emerson, Lake & Palmer (or ELP for short) and a new level of rock star immoderation was born. From three huge haulage trucks bearing each of the band's surnames on their roofs to a road crew so well manned it resembled an invading army, ELP's penchant for the grand gesture became legendary. It also made them a prime target for certain sections of the music press appalled by the group's ostentatious displays of artistic pomp. So, when ELP released their version of Aaron Copland and John Ryan's 'Fanfare for the Common Man' in 1977, journalists hit the trio with everything they had: 'What the fuck do ELP know about the "common man"?' ran one pithy (but perhaps not unreasonable) complaint. The single went to number two in the UK charts anyway.

Yet by the beginning of the eighties, Lake's career was at a crossroads. With ELP silently imploding after the relative commercial failure of 1978's *Love Beach*, and punk/new wave finally making a commercial as well as critical impact on the British music industry, Lake was now a potentially unemployed rock dinosaur. Worse, he was still only 33. 'The problem I had was that I didn't know what to do [or] which direction to go in,' he later said. As America had been commercially kindest to ELP, he first tried finding his way in Los Angeles, mixing amongst the cream of the city's session scene. But when nothing there seemed to click, Lake came home in early 1981 to try his luck at London's legendary Abbey Road. One of his first visitors at the studio was Gary Moore.

Booked by Lake's manager to provide guitar parts for a song Lake had written with Bob Dylan while in LA called 'Love You Too Much', Moore turned up at Abbey Road 30 minutes early. That he had done so at 11.30 in the morning, an ungodly hour for most musicians, immediately impressed Lake. Then Moore played his solo. Within moments, a 'partnership' of sorts was born.[7] 'I liked Gary [not only] because he was such a nice person,' Lake told writer Malcolm Dome in 2010. 'But also, because he was such a great guitarist. At the time, he had a reputation for playing heavy metal, [but] that wasn't really him. This was a player with genuine feeling.' Reconvening at Lake's converted mill house in Stanbridge, Dorset, the pair drew up chairs and guitars and began bolting Moore's ideas to Lake's tunes. The results were then transferred back to

---

7 Moore later confirmed the reason he was at Abbey Road was that another guitar player had blown the session. 'I jumped at [working with Greg], especially since I heard somebody else couldn't do it properly and I wanted to try!' he later told *Kerrang*. 'It was no big deal, though. I got there at 11.30 and was finished by 11.45!'

the studio. 'Gary had me in tears . . . such was his ability,' he said. 'Irish, Elvis, country and western. You name it, he'd play it. Like me, I think Gary was searching for a direction that suited him.'

The resulting album, September 1981's *Greg Lake*, wasn't a bad effort, if a little disjointed, as emotive ballads, fledgling yacht rock and heavy metal chuggers all competed for space on two sides of vinyl. Still, Lake's voice remained impeccable throughout and several tunes including the moody 'It Hurts' and ambitious AOR of 'The Lie' hinted where the former ELP man might head next musically. Sprinkling stardust over every nook and cranny of the LP was Lake's new aide-de-camp Gary Moore. Blues, country, acoustic, even rock'n'roll, Moore covered the lot. In return, Lake offered up space for Moore's own 'Nuclear Attack', dropping the key of the original from G to E to ensure maximum heaviness. 'I liked the song and that's why it's on there . . . that whole scenario about [how] we'd never survive a nuclear attack,' Lake later told Malcolm Dome. 'I also wanted to give Gary the opportunity to really show what he could do.' Moore duly obliged, providing a barrage of power chords, ambulance-mimicking tremolo effects and another in his continuing series of lightning-fast fretboard assaults.[8]

Obviously in no hurry to part company just yet, the Lake/Moore bromance continued a while longer. Bringing together a core group of bassist Tristram Margetts, ex-Sensational Alex Harvey Band drummer Ted McKenna and keyboardist Tommy Eyre, Lake and 'special guest' Moore performed brisk tours of the UK, USA and Canada throughout the late autumn of 1981. In fact, precisely one year after Gary had debuted his own new, if very short-lived outfit at The Marquee, he was now on stage playing 'Nuclear Attack' and 'Parisienne Walkways' to a different, though probably no less appreciative audience at Hammersmith Odeon. There for two nights with Lake, the first gig was broadcast live in the States for *King Biscuit Hour*[9], and later released on CD.

---

8 Though Moore liked Lake's songs, he didn't like the way his guitar sounded on the album. 'No, I didn't really like the guitar sound,' he later told *Ultimate Guitar*. 'Greg used a computer mix thing . . . and it sounded like the fader was going up and down all the time. The guitar is roaring, and all of a sudden, it goes away.'

9 An American syndicated radio show featuring concert performances by rock bands/ artists as varied as Mahavishnu Orchestra and Bruce Springsteen, *King Biscuit Hour* ran from 1973 to 2005.

There were a few other highs along the way. Greg Lake's appearance, for instance, at 1981's Reading Festival went down a storm, with the group getting two encores. Moore too, enjoyed his return trip to America, even if crowds were considerably sparser for Lake as a solo performer than when he was part of ELP. 'Some of those shows were still a joy,' Gary later told *Kerrang*, '. . . it was great for me and I made quite a few friends out there.' Given that Moore was cast as the devil himself the last time he toured the States with Thin Lizzy, this was quite the turnaround.

Another plus point for Moore was the recent acquisition of a gorgeous Gibson ES5 purchased from fellow guitar freak Lake. 'It's a blond 1955 jazz type, semi-acoustic three pick-up model,' he told *International Musician*. 'Absolutely beautiful and not a scratch on it.' Yet, for all its striking looks, the ES5 was not to be hung on a wall and admired for its beauty. As with all of Moore's six-strings, the Gibson was a working instrument, and one that would see plenty of use. 'All my guitars I like and use,' he said. 'I'm not the type of person who goes out and buys a green guitar with yellow spots and a free do-it-yourself blow job kit. The same goes for endorsements,' he continued. 'If anyone gives me something, I'll use it. It's unfair to mislead kids by putting your name on a product . . . if you think it's a piece of shit. A lot of people do that and it's wrong.' Quite so.

Despite their obviously strong friendship, Gary Moore and Greg Lake's association would prove temporary. Drawn together 'like two lost souls' when both musicians hit an impasse career-wise, Lake had received a welcome boost of energy from the Belfast guitarist, while Moore was given a year's employment by a fine musician whose company he also enjoyed. But all good things, etc. 'It was meant to be purely a session thing,' Moore later said, '[but] Greg's a nice guy and I loved working with him.'

To Moore's credit, he didn't leave Lake in the lurch after handing in his notice, writing or contributing to several more tunes for Lake's next solo LP, including 'A Woman Like You', 'Don't Wanna Lose Your Love Tonight' and the (soon-to-be title track) 'Manoeuvres'. Regrettably, like *Greg Lake* before it, *Manoeuvres* failed to find a meaningful audience, thus clearing the decks for Lake to accept an offer from AOR million-sellers Asia to replace their own escaping vocalist/bassist John Wetton. When that union ended in 1985, Greg began slowly, but surely moving towards an inevitable reunion with ELP.[10] Still, he retained fond memories of his time with Moore. 'That was a great group to be with,' Lake later said of his 1981 studio/touring band. 'Great people, great players and Gary was very, very funny.'

But behind all the jokes, Gary Moore's time alongside Greg Lake had its serious side, with the guitarist striving to pull together both his romantic and musical life, while also seeking a new record deal. That process wasn't always easy. After nearly two years, Moore's relationship with Lisa Franklin finally cracked apart, with the couple's move to London from Los Angeles seeming to hasten its end. When things had gone well, they had gone very well. Moore taught Franklin her first guitar chords and showered her with jewellery, including, if reports are correct, an engagement ring. In turn, she covered his tracks during the Thin Lizzy saga and acted as a sympathetic ear while the whole sorry mess played itself out on the American West Coast (indeed, one source has it that Franklin appeared in the original video promo for 'Parisienne Walkways'). But soon the arguments started. Ex-Sex Pistol Steve Jones was reportedly 'on the scene' and Moore was a jealous type. Voices were probably raised and plates possibly smashed. When Moore failed to curb his possessive nature back in London, there were allegedly more arguments, but fewer reconciliations. So it went, until it didn't any more. Gary wrote songs about their time together. Franklin started again.

Mercifully, the professional side of Moore's affairs were in better shape than his love life. Keen to do right by her client before disappearing into the multi-platinum sunset with Ozzy Osbourne, Sharon Arden had introduced Gary to music executive Steve Barnett. It turned out to be a shrewd final gesture on Arden's part and extremely fortuitous for Moore. A former agent at NEMS Enterprises (originally formed by Beatles manager Brian Epstein), Barnett had worked with the likes of Black Sabbath and Elton John throughout the seventies before forming Part Rock at the end of the decade.

An enterprise committed to forward-thinking artist management/

---

10 After leaving Asia in 1984, Greg put together 'Emerson, Lake and Powell' with Gary's old mate Cozy, before drummer Carl Palmer returned to the fold and the original ELP reformed in 1991. The trio played their last concert at London's Victoria Park in 2010. By all accounts a lovely chap, Greg Lake died six years later, aged just 69.

representation, Barnett's partner at Part Rock was Stewart Young. Like Barnett, Young had considerable experience within the music industry. In fact, his own management stable included ELP and Greg Lake, a connection that proved immensely useful for Barnett and Moore when trying to figure out 'Where next?' after the demise of G-Force. Similar in age, outlook and sense of humour, while also sharing a former boss in the shape of Gerry Bron (Barnett had started in the business working for the owner of Bronze Records), the 'firm of Part Rock and Moore' augured well for all future endeavours.

That alliance was soon put into action when Barnett used his contacts to help stimulate interest in Moore's music at British entrepreneur Richard Branson's rapidly expanding Virgin Records. Having already secured a deal with the label's publishing arm, Barnett had Moore cut demos in New York shortly after completing his US tour commitments with Greg Lake in mid-January 1981. The resulting three or so tunes were impressive enough for Virgin to ask for more. When Gary provided almost an album's worth of material recorded at London's AIR Studios a month later, the company bit and Moore found himself lining up alongside Mike Oldfield, Phil Collins, Devo and Human League as the latest signing on Virgin's artistically diverse roster.

With Part Rock now on side, Virgin bankrolling his next album and the recent failures of Thin Lizzy, G-Force and Jet Records fading into the distance, things were once again looking up for Gary Moore. But the decision to effectively re-start his solo career at the grand old age of 29 meant facing up to some familiar challenges. For one, there was assembling another new band that could deliver on the ever-changing sounds Moore heard inside his head. Connecting with the right audience, a matter again linked to Gary's frequent changes in musical direction, was another issue. And as much as he might like to forget it, there was the tricky little problem of finding the right vocalist to sing his songs. According to Sharon Arden, that should never have been an issue. 'Gary Moore didn't need a frontman,' she later told the author Harry Shapiro. 'Gary Moore *was* the frontman.'

CHAPTER SIXTEEN

Building The Brand

Though the observation would have undoubtedly irked him, it is fair to say that at points in his musical life, Gary Moore appeared more like a featured player than the leading man. Onscreen for all the major plot points. Perfectly happy to chew the scenery when required. Deliriously happy, if truth be told. Indeed, as recent events confirmed, Moore even appeared content to play the pantomime villain, though only if the role absolutely demanded it. Yet, despite the frequent scene-stealing and artful dedication to his craft, there remained a nagging feeling he wasn't quite as in control of the narrative as he might have been. By 1982, however, that was about to change.

With his efforts in 1973's The Gary Moore Band resembling an 'all-boys together adventure', and G-Force's sudden demise robbing him of another opportunity to properly lead from the front, Moore was adamant that his next group represent a new start on all counts. This viewpoint was fully supported by his management at Part Rock and Virgin Records, who were both keen to build 'Brand Moore' from the ground up. That meant hard work from all concerned, but mainly Moore. Though he had enjoyed a strong degree of chart recognition via 'Parisienne Walkways' and his (turbulent) time with Thin Lizzy, Moore was still predominantly known as a guitarist: a phenomenal guitarist it has to be said, but a guitarist nonetheless. To become a major player on the eighties rock scene, he would now have to establish himself as a singer, songwriter and leader of a 'world-class band' too. Luckily for Moore, a couple of promising candidates for the last job had just become available, though neither would come cheap.

In the summer of 1980 G-Force had provided support for Whitesnake on their UK tour. While the two bands weren't perhaps a natural fit, Moore's group was shown due respect both by Whitesnake's fans as well as the headliners themselves. In fact, Whitesnake's leonine-haired frontman/leader David Coverdale had even clocked Moore as a potential replacement for then-current guitarists Bernie Marsden or Mick Moody, should either ever lose their charm. Given Moore and Marsden were old mates, and Moore was then fully committed to making G-Force a success, his joining Whitesnake was always an unlikely scenario.

By 1982, David Coverdale had bigger troubles on his plate than poaching guitarists. Plagued by a combination of family-related health issues and management hiccups, the singer had been forced to place Whitesnake in stasis until further notice. That meant Moore's former Colosseum II colleague Neil Murray was now facing an uncertain future. 'At that time, Whitesnake were in effect closing down, trying to get out of the management [deals], the record company, the publishers,' he said. 'So, when the band was put on hold, there was quite a few months of indecision. Also, I wasn't getting any money at the time, with no royalties to fall back on either.' Then fate lent a hand. 'I bumped into Gary at the beginning of February 1982 and he played me some demos. That led to one day of recording at London's AIR Studios [and soon enough], we were in the studio proper recording his new LP.'

Joining Moore and Murray for the ride was Ian Paice. A god among drummers, Paice had been an integral part of Deep Purple since joining the group aged just 18 in 1968. There for all the gigantic moments, when the mighty quintet fell in 1976, Paice formed a new outfit with fellow exiting bandmate/keyboardist extraordinaire Jon Lord. But the resulting trio, Paice, Ashton and Lord, proved a disappointment after the giddy heights of Purple, and Paice soon followed Lord into the ranks of David

231

Coverdale's Whitesnake. Now, of course, that group were kaput (at least temporarily), and like Murray, Paice was seeking other opportunities.

Part Rock, Virgin and Gary Moore almost fell over themselves to land the percussion giant. 'They were all very keen to get Ian in the band and musically he was a very good choice,' said Murray. '[Ian] was also a bridge to audience interest in places like Japan[1], and . . . it fitted the "business calculation" in that having someone as famous as him would be good for Gary's [profile].' Of course, securing Ian Paice's services was expensive. But Moore felt it was a price worth paying. 'It was annoying to know that Ian was getting paid a hell of a lot more than I was when he joined the band,' Murray continued. 'But I couldn't quibble about that. Ian had been in Deep Purple and was a much bigger name.' Despite the escalating wage bill, Moore could see the funny side of it of it all. Just. '[We're calling the group] "Gary Moore and his Expensive Friends",' he quipped to *Kerrang*'s Chris Welch at the time. 'Actually, I came to rehearsals on a bicycle.'

In Ian Paice, Neil Murray and a returning Tommy Eyre on keyboards, Moore had three of rock's better musicians on his payroll. Yet, because aspects of G-Force's studio sound were severely hampered by the group's decision to oversee the album themselves, this time around Moore had no intention of going forward without the right producer. He found his man in Jeff Glixman. Best known for overseeing a series of platinum selling albums by American art rock favourites Kansas, including the stupendous (if unlikely) 1976 hit single, 'Carry On My Wayward Son', Glixman had just scored another hit for talented Brummie prog outfit Magnum, whose third LP *Chase The Dragon* finally saw the band into the UK Top 20. Impressed by his track record and penchant for 'warm, powerful guitar sounds,' Moore invited Glixman to join him and his new band at London's AIR Studios during the summer of 1982, with

---

1 In 1972, Deep Purple toured Japan for the first time, taping several concert shows which were later released as the double album *Made in Japan*. A landmark set and long regarded as one of the best live albums ever . . . *Japan* ratified the band's strong commercial relationship with the country, while also consolidating Ian Paice's profile as a world-class drummer. With Gary Moore also keen to unlock Japan's potentially lucrative music market, the acquisition of Ian Paice for his own group was quite the coup.

additional work to follow at Virgin's own recording complex, The Townhouse.

Despite inspiring the confidence of Virgin Records with his latest demos, the budget allocated for Moore's album was modest, as was the time given to him to record it: 'Twenty-one days', said Neil Murray. In a way, this tight schedule played right into Moore's hands. A stickler for rehearsal, he had already drilled the band at North Kensington's E-zee Studios for two solid weeks during June, while somehow also avoiding fellow E-zee users Thin Lizzy. So when the quartet entered AIR on 8 July, they knew each song, arrangement, accent and key change like old friends. In turn, this meant Glixman could rely on maximising live performance from the floor rather than constructing tunes from endless overdubs.

Another major win for the producer was persuading Moore to place more confidence in his own singing voice. As ever, Moore had hummed and hawed over the question of recording lead vocals for the album, and even considered bringing back Glenn Hughes from the naughty step to do the job for him. Yet, when Glixman heard Moore delivering his own lines while warming up with the band, he urged him to continue. Uncharacteristically, Moore accepted the challenge, eventually providing 90 per cent of the vocals for the LP. 'Jeff Glixman offered great encouragement and pushed me to do things I didn't think I could do, like sing in tune!' he later said. 'Though it's very difficult, I'd really like to be both the guitarist and singer. Then people accept you as a total artist . . . and it helps give you more of an identity.'

The first step in establishing that new identity for Gary Moore was released by Virgin in mid-September 1982. Called *Corridors of Power*, the album's title was apparently suggested by Neil Murray after seeing its sci-fi-leaning cover sleeve featuring Moore standing in a hallway made of giant fretboards, pick-ups and volume controls. 'The title for *Corridors of Power* was my idea,' confirmed the bassist. 'It came from the album photo [design], which we already had. I just looked at it and said "Corridors of Power". It was such an obvious political cliché, but it worked."

The phrase was also an apt descriptor for the contents within. A huge-sounding record built on a series of exceptional performances from

Moore and his bandmates, one could easily make a case for *Corridors of Power* being – *Black Rose* excepted – the most accomplished work of Moore's career. Yet, it was also an album curiously out of time, with one foot stuck firmly in the seventies while the other cautiously poked its toe around the new decade. 'A bit like the musicians who recorded it,' laughed a fan.

Right from the off, *Corridors of Powers* threw down the gauntlet. With 'Don't Take Me for a Loser' and 'Gonna Break My Heart Again', Moore combined the reassuring thump of a rock band with a proper pop tune, thus allowing listeners to whistle each song's chorus while also being bashed about the ears by a series of very aggressive power chords. For those enjoying that sensation, the heads-down no-nonsense boogie of 'Rockin' Every Night' went even further. A frenetically paced successor to G-Force's 'Dancin'' and 'Rockin' and Rollin'', what 'Rockin' Every Night' lacked in subtlety or lyrical invention, it made up for in sheer punch. 'Cold Hearted', on the other hand, was a more sullen animal. Recalling Deep Purple's own slow-burning 'Mistreated' (surely no great surprise given who was behind the drum kit), the track rumbled along moodily before fading out on the back of Moore's spitting, bluesy guitar lines.

So far so classic seventies rock, and that impression was only underscored by Gary's cover of Free's 1972 classic 'Wishing Well'. A long-time favourite of the guitarist, ('I always liked that song,' he told *Sounds)*, 'Wishing Well' had combined soulful R&B and chunky orchestral chording with a masterful performance from singer Paul Rodgers. In short, big boots to fill. Even so, Moore and his band almost managed to improve on the original, with the decision to slow the tune down adding both weight and emotional heft. Moore's vocal was not found wanting either. Sticking closely to Rodger's melody (no mean feat in itself), Moore's heartfelt take on 'Wishing Well' confirmed the faith producer Jeff Glixman had placed in his voice.

If 'Wishing Well' turned the clock back to the seventies, then 'End of the World' paid tribute to the decade before it by allowing Moore to sing alongside one of his true sixties heroes: Cream's Jack Bruce. 'Well, Jack is so talented, and I loved him in his Cream days,' Moore told *Music UK*. 'In fact, he's probably the most talented musician I've ever played with.' Yet, beyond Moore's breathless appraisal lay a more cool, artistic calculation. Like 'Nuclear Attack' and 'Hiroshima', 'End of the World' was another of Moore's apocalyptically-themed anthems, its wordplay this time given to reckless leaders, Cold War tensions and large red doomsday buttons. All themes, incidentally, that Bruce excelled in bringing to life vocally.

'God, yeah,' Moore enthused to *Ultimate Guitar*, "End of the World' was tailor-made for Jack's voice. He has a real way of conveying those doom-laden lyrics.' Behind the opportunity to put Bruce's blood-curdling howls to good use, the fan boy in Moore was also clearly delighted to have the Scotsman sing on his album, even if Bruce was leaving behind his trademark Gibson EB3 bass guitar for the visit. 'It's the first time in Jack's entire career that he's guested as purely a singer,' Moore concluded. 'I was very proud of that.'

Pulled together from the demo Moore had cut for Virgin on 8 February 1982, with Neil Murray on bass and a guesting Bobby Chouinard on drums (more of him later), Moore and Bruce's performance on 'End of the World' lived up to its momentous title, with the pair's voices genuinely sounding under attack from all the 'polished thunder' around them. At last given the chance to work with one of his teenage icons, Moore was also not going to let the occasion go by without providing a suitably earth-shaking guitar break. Hence, we were treated to a whammy bar-assisted barrage of missile strikes, air raid sirens and crashing planes before Gary simply ran out of notes at the very top of the fretboard. From ominous, finger-picked intro to teeth-rattling finale, 'End of the World' might have been designed to be the centrepiece of *Corridors of Power*. But really, it was all about the guitar solo in the middle. 'Ha!' laughed Neil Murray, 'On 'End of the World', when Gary's guitar solo comes in, everything else is turned down to quarter of the volume!'

The guitar Gary had used to unleash havoc on 'End of the World' was a relatively recent acquisition, though it had been around for over 20 years. Purchased a year or so before from much-missed Jon King Sounds in Kingston-upon-Thames, Moore's latest six-string beauty was a 1961 Fiesta Red Fender Stratocaster. Originally the property of fifties entertainer Tommy Steele (the UK's first teen idol), the Strat had originally been offered to Greg Lake. 'I was like, "Please don't buy it. Please don't buy it,"' laughed Moore. But when the bassist spotted a few nicks on the body he went off the idea, leaving Moore to snatch it up. After a quick jumbo re-fret and a bit of tremolo arm tightening, Moore had a monster on his hands. 'It's the best Strat I've ever had,' he gushed. Immensely powerful when plugged into a 100-watt Marshall amp[2], 'It's on the verge of being out of control and I like that. It sounds like the guitar's actually breathing', the Fiesta red would subsequently survive spills, thefts[3] and onstage clatterings to become Gary's second most recognisable axe. 'There was the "red" and the "greeny"', said a friend, 'All he needed was the "amber", and he'd have a set of bloody traffic lights.'

If parts of *Corridors of Power* leaned into the sixties and seventies for inspiration, that didn't mean he was unaware of what was going on around him in the present. 'At that point, Gary had proper management, proper record company support and was very focused on . . . cracking America,' said Neil Murray. 'He – and I – wanted melodic, powerful rock songs with a strong guitar element. So, we were busy listening to bands [of that ilk], such as Journey and Foreigner.' And just like Journey and Foreigner, Moore was committed to writing a huge-sounding, huge-selling power ballad capable of scaling both the US and UK singles charts. In 'Always Gonna Love You' and 'Falling in Love With You', Gary thought he had two. Nor was he ashamed to say so. 'Everyone says I should be ashamed of that, but "heavy metal" singles don't get played on the radio,'

---

2   In addition to the Fiesta Red and 1971 Marshall 100 head, Moore used a Boss distortion, flanger, chorus, octave-divider and Roland 555 chorus echo to create his monumental sound on *Corridors of Power*. With the amp's volume controls set at 10 to get that special 'breathing sound,' Moore recorded all guitar parts in the control room with his speakers safely housed several feet away in another, smaller space. 'I just drove the shit out of my Marshall with the [guitars] and distortion,' he later told *Ultimate Guitar*. 'Jeff Glixman also knew how to record the Strat more than a lot of people would have. He approached it in the right way. I'd compare it to that early Hendrix sound . . . very ambient, very alive.'

3   In 1984, the Fiesta Red was lost in transit during a US tour. Moore believed a customs official stole the guitar before realising who it belonged to. Whatever the case, the instrument was soon found alive and well by Interpol and returned to its rightful owner.

he told *Kerrang*. 'It's good if you have more than one musical side and I have a musical side of me that wants to write ballads.'

The theory was sound, and so were the songs. In fact, 'Always Gonna Love You' and 'Falling in Love With You' were both epically constructed, heart-tugging examples of the type of power ballad that recently managed to charm their way into the pop charts for the likes of Foreigner and REO Speedwagon. Yet, for some unspecifiable reason, neither tune caught the imagination of DJs or the record-buying public when released as singles in September 1982 and February 1983. Not even an attempt by Culture Club producer Steve Levine to sprinkle his studio magic on 'Always Gonna Love You' or the presence of Don Airey and bass session supremo Mo Foster on a remixed 'Falling in Love With You' could change either song's commercial fortunes.[4] "Falling in Love With You' was actually re-recorded with Culture Club's Steve Levine,' said Murray. 'That'll tell you all you need to know about trying to get a hit. I mean, Gary Moore and Culture Club.'

Though Moore might have failed to crack the singles market, he had marginally better luck when it came to album sales: *Corridors of Power* peaked at number thirty in the UK charts. The LP even garnered some much-needed American interest, briefly making an appearance at number 149 on the *Billboard 200*. These weren't huge numbers per se ('It's done about 120,000 copies,' said Moore in 1982), but they were a solid start in the overall masterplan of bringing 'Brand Moore' to the masses. With product already on the shelves, it was now time to take the show on the road.

In fact, Moore had already done a spray of gigs in advance of releasing *Corridors of Power*, including two nights at The Marquee and a late afternoon slot at Reading Festival on 28 August, sandwiched between new

---

4   After the failure of 'Always Gonna Love You' and 'Falling in Love With You' to crack the charts, Moore recorded yet another power ballad entitled 'Love Can Make a Fool Out of You'. However, feeling the moment might have passed, Virgin chose not to issue it at the time. Instead, the tune was gifted to ABBA's Frida Lyngstad for consideration on her first solo LP (she passed), before eventually landing in the arms of Japanese hard rock singer Mari Hamada, who released it as 'Love, Love, Love' in 1985. Moore's version surfaced first in 2002, as part of a re-mastered re-release of *Corridors of Power*, and then again in 2021 on the collection *How Blue Can You Get*.

wave of British heavy metal hopefuls Tygers of Pan Tang and a headlining Iron Maiden. But at the last minute, Moore baulked at handling all the vocals himself and brought back Charlie Huhn to front the band on his behalf. The experiment didn't work. Despite his 'meaty roar' and octave-straddling range, Huhn didn't quite fit the picture for either Moore or Virgin Records. 'The overall impression was that Charlie was a bit too "typical, flashy American frontman" and not down to earth enough in terms of image and maybe even vocal style,' said Neil Murray. 'I'm sure Virgin were also thinking, "Well, we've just done an album where Gary's doing the lead vocals. What's this other bloke doing here?"' Like a growing number of singers before him, Huhn put his time with Moore down to experience, and soon returned to the States where he began writing songs with recent Geffen Records signing and future Yes lynchpin Trevor Rabin.[5]

Having already made a decent enough stab at vocals on *Corridors of Power*, and with yet another frontman proving unsuitable, logic surely dictated that Gary Moore now take the hint and step up to the concert microphone himself. Instead, he turned to Neil Murray for suggestions. 'Gary asked me who I thought might be the better [fit for singer], Graham Bonnet or John Sloman?' explained the bassist. 'Now, Graham had just had his problems in [ex-UFO guitarist] Michael Schenker's[6] band, getting drunk [on stage] and being fired. So, he was seen as too much of a loose cannon. But, of course, having already worked with him, I was biased in favour of John Sloman.'

Like previous Moore vocalist Kenny Driscoll, Sloman had also fronted hard rockers Lone Star during the late seventies. But it was after his short spell with Uriah Heep that the Welshman came to Neil Murray's atten-tion. With Whitesnake on their enforced break and Gary Moore still somewhere in the future, Murray had been impressed by the quality of

---

5 Charlie Huhn would front several bands following his stint with Gary Moore, including German metal troupe Victory, a re-constituted Humble Pie and classic rock supergroup Deadringer before finally settling in with blues-worshipping road hogs Foghat in 2000.

6 One of the few guitarists to truly rival Gary Moore, Michael Schenker's string of albums with UFO during the seventies and as a solo artist in subsequent decades really should be required listening at 'Guitar School'.

Sloman's songs and suggested teaming up. Demos were cut, a group name chosen, 'Badlands' – and alongside former Tygers of Pan Tang guitarist John Sykes, a showcase gig performed at The Marquee for EMI Records. And that's when the delays set in. 'Between EMI taking so long to give John a recording contract [and the problems with Whitesnake], it was all incredibly frustrating,' said Murray. 'So, when Gary said, "I'd like you to be in my group with Ian Paice," well . . . that's what I was going to do.' Now, however, Murray had been given the chance to properly square the circle. Murray played Moore the Badlands demos. Moore liked Sloman's voice. An introduction was made and Sloman was invited to join Moore's band. "It all fell together so naturally,"' enthused Moore.

With the departure of keyboardist Tommy Eyre and an (ever-) returning Don Airey stepping into his shoes, the latest iteration of Moore's group returned to concert duties in the UK during the autumn of 1982. Part of the tour found Moore headlining Hammersmith Odeon under his own steam for the very first time. 'I threw up before I went on [from nerves], but it was really good,' he later told writer Max Bell. 'I'm probably the only guitarist out of Thin Lizzy who could do that, who could go out on his own and fill that place. I knew there were going to be a lot of musicians showing up too, so yeah, I was pretty scared till I got out there.'

The band then headed to Europe before turning left for Japan in December. Here, they found themselves in major demand, partly because of Ian Paice's long-established profile with Deep Purple, but also because of the country's long-standing love affair with all things rock. That now included Gary Moore. 'We played 10 or 11 shows in Tokyo to a total of 12,000 people,' he confirmed to *Kerrang*'s Max Kay, 'which means we could have actually played the Budokan[7] because it holds about the same number. But we decided to play the smaller places first. Next time though,' he concluded, 'we will play the Budokan.'

Keen to monopolise on Moore's popularity, Virgin chose to record two of the group's shows at Tokyo's Kōsei Nenkin Kaikan concert hall

---

7 One of the most iconic venues in the world, Tokyo's Budokan has played host to The Beatles, ABBA, Led Zeppelin and Queen among others since opening its doors to rock music in 1966. The venue has an audience capacity of 14,471.

on 24/25 January 1983 for a Japan-only release later in the year. The resulting album, *Rockin' Every Night: Gary Moore Live in Japan*, only served to highlight the predicament Moore now faced. While the band were tight as tuppence and tunes such as 'Wishing Well' and 'Rockin' Every Night' made an energetic leap from studio to stage[8], with Moore still singing over half the set, John Sloman often seemed underused. Worse, the vocalist's decision to play keyboards while Moore took to the microphone was again compromised by the presence of Don Airey just several feet away. 'Actually, I'd recommended John based on the keyboard parts on his own songs,' Neil Murray said in 2020. 'But it turned out he wasn't so good at learning other people's stuff, at least at the level of skill Gary needed.'

By March 1983, the tour had ended and so too had John Sloman's time with Gary Moore. An amicable parting of the ways – 'What did he do while I was playing a long solo, shake his arse?' Gary later told *Kerrang* – Moore even worked with Sloman to help him secure a deal of his own, guesting on several of his demos, including the impressive 'Hooked on a Dream'.[9] Yet, even if Sloman's tenure with him was brief, it had taught Gary one final lesson about where he wanted to take 'Brand Moore'. While it was sometimes difficult to cover vocal and guitar duties simultaneously, no one was going to sing his songs exactly the way he wanted them sung in concert. So, 'Why don't I just sing them myself?'

Hallelujah.

Having at last made the decision to tackle all onstage vocals, Moore now truly grasped the nettle by agreeing to a series of European outdoor shows in mid-May 1983, including Belgium's Heavy Sound and Holland's renowned Pinkpop, the latter broadcast on Dutch TV. Of course, the

---

8 Perhaps the leap wasn't too far, after all. According to Neil Murray, while the LP was mostly live, there were quite a few touch-ups involved too. '*Live in Japan*? I have to say there are quite a few overdubs on it! Keyboards, guitar, vocals, bass. To be fair, most of the album was live, but certainly not warts and all. Yes, it was tarted up.'

9 Though it took a little while, John Sloman did score a solo deal, his Todd Rundgren-produced debut album *Disappearances Can Be Deceptive* released by FM/Revolver records in 1989. The LP also features an appearance by the late, great fusion guitarist Alan Murphy, whom Sloman and Murray had briefly worked with when putting together their group Badlands back in 1982.

litmus test for Moore's voice at Pinkpop, and most concerts thereafter, was 'I Can't Wait Until Tomorrow'. A slow-burning thriller of a tune building to a roaring climax over the course of eight life-affirming minutes, the song had ended *Corridors of Power* on a real high and justly become a live favourite with fans. Lyrically, it was also a confession of sorts, with Moore offering images of endless searching, thwarted hopes and hollow victories, all no doubt tracking the trials and tribulations he had faced in the previous decade.

'A hard one to sing' at the best of times, until recently Moore had John Sloman to help him reach the octave-splitting summit on 'I Can't Wait Until Tomorrow'. But at Pinkpop, he was on his own. As confirmed by the wonder of YouTube, Moore was mostly up to the task, even if his voice occasionally fell prey to gremlins in the upper registers. As was always the case, he would try to correct the deficit through endless rehearsal. 'From my perspective at least, his singing never quite matched his guitar playing,' said Neil Murray. 'As good as he was, Gary was still a bit of a shouter, and if you've got that imbalance, where someone is so incredibly good on guitar [but] not quite as strong a vocalist, there's [always] a bit of a disconnect in people's minds. But he was still extremely successful, so what do I know?'

Though self-deprecating to a fault, Murray was also correct. Even if Gary practised until his throat bled and his tonsils fell out, he would never be as good a singer as he was a guitarist. But that was OK too. Because in the time it took for Moore to face the future as the singer of his own songs, yet another change had occurred in the shifting sands of the international rock scene. Guitar heroes were back, and if there was one thing Gary Moore knew, it was a how to be a guitar hero.

CHAPTER SEVENTEEN

Have Strings, Will Travel

B ack in the late seventies, punk and new wave looked like ending the age of the guitar hero. In reality, they ended up birthing a few of their own.

Some, like Sex Pistol Steve Jones, Tom Robinson Band's Danny Kustow and The Cars' Elliot Easton seemed to have a modicum of respect for what had come before, their individual styles referencing blues rock, glam and even rockabilly. Others, such as Gang of Four's Andy Gill, Magazine's John McGeoch and Killing Joke's Geordie came from a different place altogether. Pathfinders as much as guitarists, these were angular, sharp-witted players for whom the creation of texture and tension was as rewarding as any elongated solo or clever scale. They weren't the only ones. In Washington, DC, Bad Brains' resident 'action painter' Dr Know was busy helping invent hardcore, while in Dublin, U2's very own guitar scientist The Edge had already begun shaping music's future with the aid of time machines[1]: Television's Tom Verlaine, The Ruts' Paul Fox, The

---

1 Before recording U2's 1980 debut album *Boy*, The Edge discovered Electro Harmonix's Memory Man Deluxe, the effects unit's echo-delay settings allowing him to create novel, huge sounding guitar lines for songs such as 'I Will Follow', 'Stories for Boys' and 'The Electric Co.'.

Police's Andy Summers, The Skids' Stuart Adamson, punks, post-punks, new wavers and reggae rockers. Guitar heroes all, even if they didn't want to be.

Then there was Edward Van Halen, or 'Eddie' to his friends, of which there were soon many. Unlike the mohawk and trench coat brigade, Van Halen didn't come from the lands of punk or new wave. The son of a Dutch jazz clarinettist, his parents had immigrated from Holland to California in 1962, when he was just seven. A musical child, Van Halen's early promise as a classical pianist was compromised only when he started 'noodling around' on his brother Alex's guitar during his early teens. 'Mind blown' after hearing Cream for the first time, Eddie set out to learn 'every lick, chord and note' Eric Clapton had ever played. By 1972, he had his first band: The Broken Combs. Six years later, Eddie, brother Alex (now a drummer), bassist Michael Anthony and vocalist 'Diamond' David Lee Roth were trading under the banner 'Van Halen' and had just released their self-titled debut album. That LP's contents reset the boundaries of rock guitar, moving it beyond the blues scales and double stops that had defined the genre for over a decade towards a new era of virtuosity and adventure. In so doing, that also made Eddie Van Halen arguably the most important guitarist since Jimi Hendrix.

If one were looking for evidence for such a bold claim, then *Van Halen*'s second track, the one minute, 42 second instrumental 'Eruption', provided it. A full-tilt display of whizzing fingers, fizzing harmonics and tree-felling whammy bar abuse, 'Eruption' combined a classical musician's dexterity with a jazzer's disregard for the rulebook. It also showcased Van Halen's revolutionary command of 'tapping'. Executed by using the fingers of the pick hand to 'tap' the strings against the fretboard, the technique produced a stream of arpeggiated notes, not unlike a sonic waterfall. 'It sounded,' said one (unnamed) rocker, 'like fucking Bach playing guitar!' Tapping wasn't exactly new. Some of rock guitar's bigger names, including Led Zeppelin's Jimmy Page, Queen's Brian May and Genesis's Steve Hackett among others[2] had all dabbled with it in previous

---

2 Among the first to experiment with tapping in the late sixties/early seventies was Canned Heat guitarist Harvey Mandel, who believed he might well have inspired Van Halen's use of the technique. 'I was playing at the Whisky [in LA],' he said, 'and

years. But no one had accessed tapping's possibilities to this extent before. In fact, for some, EVH's virtuoso performance on Eruption was akin to a quasi-religious experience. 'All guitarists,' *Classic Rock* later wrote, 'remember the first time they heard 'Eruption'.' And all guitarists wanted to know how Eddie did it, so they could do it too.

Gary Moore probably first came across the joys of 'Eruption' when he saw Van Halen support Black Sabbath on their 1978 UK summer tour. Alerted by rumours of 'a new American kid on the block', Moore dragged Thin Lizzy bandmate Scott Gorham along to Detroit's Cobo Hall on 14 September to see what all the fuss was about. Like the rest of us, their flabber was well and truly gasted. 'When I first heard Eddie, I thought, "There's some stuff I've been doing for a really long time, but in a totally different way",' Gary later told *Guitar Player*'s Tom Mulhern. 'I was impressed because I thought . . . he'd taken it one stage further.'

Having watched Van Halen mesmerise Black Sabbath's audience – 'We were just too stunned to speak,' Ozzy Osbourne said of having to follow their 'support band' on stage every night – Moore spent the next few hours hunched over his guitar trying to figure out exactly what Eddie was up to. Sure enough, there had been players that had raised one or even two of Gary's eyebrows before. Bill Connors, Michael Schenker, Ollie Halsall[3] and Allan Holdsworth, to name a few. But 'for the first time in his life', Don Airey later told *Mulatschag* TV, 'Gary had heard someone that seriously frightened him.'

Come 1979 and Moore had long since processed the shock of hearing Eddie Van Halen. In fact, the two had even become friends, a development driven in part by Moore's temporary move to Los Angeles following the travails of Thin Lizzy, and he and Eddie's shared love of Eric Clapton

---

Eddie came in and saw me do it. The next thing, he's [tapping] on Michael Jackson's 'Beat It'. I wouldn't say I was annoyed, but I wouldn't mind if I got better recognition for doing it first.' According to EVH himself, he had seen Jimmy Page using a simple form of the technique on Led Zep's 'Heartbreaker' at the LA Forum in 1971 and 'just kind of took it and ran with it'.

3 'Ollie Halsall really impressed me,' said Moore of the cult jazz rock guitarist. 'When I first heard these saxophone style phrases on guitar I thought 'What's that?' It was kind of like what I wanted to do myself but hadn't worked it out. He showed me what was possible.'

and Cream. While in LA, Moore also attended several Van Halen shows, and even found himself backstage with EVH at a Rainbow concert. Here, the pair waited patiently for an introduction to Ritchie Blackmore from Don Airey, then playing keyboards with the legendary man in black. But when the big moment came, the temperamental Blackmore was there one minute and gone the next. 'I said, "Ritchie, there's two people I'd like you to meet,"' Airey recalled. '"This is Gary Moore and this is Eddie Van Halen." Well, Ritchie just stormed off. I think he might have thought I was trying to set him up. Then Eddie goes "What did I say?" I just looked at him and said, "Don't worry about it."'

By 1983, avoiding Eddie Van Halen was all but impossible. With a raft of a new players/bands starting to emerge in the wake of 'Eruption' and his trademark 'lickety-split' soloing a prominent feature of Michael Jackson's super-hit 'Beat It', Van Halen had reawakened interest in all things guitar. As a result, record companies, instrument manufacturers and fellow performers were starting to feel the benefit. That included Gary Moore. A long-established axe hero type, and one whose last album, *Corridors of Power*, hinted at greater things to come, Moore was well placed to take advantage of this guitar-happy, crossover-friendly atmosphere. To test the model, manager Steve Barnett organised a US tour for Moore and his band in support of one of hard rock's then biggest (and certainly youngest) acts, Def Leppard.

Once the doyens of 1979's new wave of British heavy metal, Def Leppard quickly shed their provincial origins to concentrate on the holy grail of the music business: achieving success in the States. Though the strategy to so nakedly embrace the USA rankled some at home (the quintet unwisely released a single called 'Hello America'), their eventual accomplishments across the Atlantic were well-earned and long-lasting. In fact, by the time Moore's group hooked up with them at Charleston's cavernous Civic Center on 31 May 1983, the Lepps' third album, *Pyromania*, was well on its way to selling six million copies. Yet, for all their own shiny discs, the band remained in awe of their special guest. 'Gary's one of my favourites players; he's got everything,' said Def Leppard's Phil Collen at the time, while his twin-guitar partner in crime Steve Clark sounded even more committed. 'When Gary was in Colosseum II, I used to buy all their albums just to hear his playing.'

Despite such glowing testimony from the headliners, Moore's jaunt with Def Leppard was a frustrating experience for both him and his group. Placed third on the bill to the Sheffield quintet, the second spot was taken by hardened Swiss road warriors Krokus, Gary had just 30 minutes to capture the attention of those who turned up early enough to see him. 'The Def Leppard tour was where the band was being aimed at that time,' said Neil Murray. 'But in the end, it wasn't particularly useful, being the opening act for just half an hour.' Sadly, alternatives were few. 'Well, we had to do something,' continued Murray. 'If you're just doing a few Scandinavian dates and a small British tour, 10 days or so, before a week in Japan, that's just not enough. You've got to try going to America.'

Even so, the irony of opening for a band who were still in short trousers when Moore and Paice were busy mounting their first touring campaigns was not lost on them. Or Def Leppard, for that matter. 'Gary had Ian Paice from Deep Purple on drums,' Leppard frontman Joe Elliott later told Blabbermouth, 'And I remember our drummer Rick Allen was just . . . beside himself. His drumming hero was third on the bill to us. We were almost apologising for it, you know?'

If there was a degree of frustration (or perhaps even confusion) about their place in the scheme of things while on the road with Def Leppard, things failed to improve when Moore and co. struck out on their own. Without a hit single or album to his name in the US, Moore's success was reliant on support from regional radio and word of mouth among guitarists. Marvellous in itself, and a growing market too. But not one he could bank on for firm ticket sales just yet. 'We did a few American club dates after the Leppard tour and that was a complete waste of time,' Neil Murray said of facing half-empty clubs from Toledo to Battle Creek. 'Very small attendances that weren't getting us anywhere at all. But again, you've got to show willing, [especially] for the American record label.'[4]

---

4   While Moore had signed to Virgin in the UK, the company did not represent him in the USA. '[Part Rock] had gone with Mirage Records in the States,' Neil Murray explained. 'They were a subsidiary of Atlantic, who Whitesnake had also signed with. To be honest, they didn't do much for Whitesnake and didn't seem to do much for Gary either.'

Though Moore's latest US jaunt came with its fair share of disappointments, there was one small victory to savour. When keyboardist Don Airey chose to skip the tour to take care of his pregnant wife, Gary was annoyed (furious actually, if one reads his comments to the press from the time). Yet, without his long-time keyboard partner to rely on, Moore was forced to find a replacement. His choice was inspired. At just 25 years old, classically trained multi-instrumentalist Neil Carter had already pulled together quite the musical CV. Starting his run in the mid-seventies singing with Queen-influenced teen hopefuls Wilder, Carter then spent time in the unlikely setting of Irish singer/songwriter Gilbert O'Sullivan's backing band. One might have thought playing the likes of the poppy 'Clair' or incredibly sad (if really rather wonderful) 'Alone Again (Naturally)' would be draining on any trainee rocker. Instead, Carter was full of compliments for his boss. 'Gilbert was a very nice guy,' Carter later said, 'and encouraged me a lot.'

Encouraged, but obviously missing the sound of loud amplification, Carter's next move was to join Brian Robertson's first post-Thin Lizzy group, Wild Horses. Contributing guitars, keyboards and vocals to the band's 1980 debut album, Carter acquitted himself admirably, but his stay was brief. Having been introduced to UFO by Phil Collen, Carter hooked up with the Springsteen-obsessed hard-rockers just in time for one of their better LPs, 1981's *The Wild, The Willing and the Innocent*. Sadly, things went downhill from there, and UFO decided to call it quits (for the first of several times) in mid-1983. That left Carter free to entertain offers from several potential suitors. 'On the final UFO gig, Gary's representative was on one side of the stage and David Coverdale's on the other,' Carter laughed to *Let It Rock*. 'I don't know if [Whitesnake] were serious or not, but it made me smile!'

Whitesnake never officially clarified their interest in Carter, but Gary Moore certainly did. Still, given that Carter had just spent the best part of three years with two of the hardest-living bands in rock'n'roll – no mean feat, given the competition – Moore was concerned he might be taking on a caner of the highest order. Nothing could be further from the truth. 'Well, [I'm sure] Gary was wary of me given the reputation both bands had,' Carter said. 'UFO were well known for their excesses

247

and Gary was very much against all that. But to be honest, that was a breath of fresh air for me and [his band] were a professional outfit all round.'

Though Carter was by his admission 'no keyboard virtuoso' in the vein of Don Airey, he did have several gifts that set him apart from the pack. Aside from being able to play clarinet (his principal instrument), saxophone, flute, piano and guitar, Carter also had a strong voice that worked well with his new employer's. 'I could sing parts of the lead,' he later told *Heavy Profile*, 'and Gary and I were a good match vocally.' Carter could also write good songs, a skill that would come in extremely handy as his association with Moore grew. 'Well, I came to Gary with other strings to my bow and that's what he needed at the time.'

With Neil Carter successfully incorporated into the ranks of his band, it was time for Gary Moore to turn his attentions to making a new album. Annoyingly, someone had already put out two on his behalf in recent months. In a move one might deem 'opportunistic', Moore's old label Jet Records had licensed his performance at London's Marquee on 5/6 November 1980 and the demos he recorded at Morgan Studios in early 1981 to Sony for release in Japan. Trading under the titles *Gary Moore: Live* and *Dirty Fingers*, both LPs were better left rotting in the vaults, and a furious Moore knew it.

'[*Dirty Fingers*] is a studio album I recorded years ago and Jet chose not to release it at the time,' he growled to *Kerrang*'s Neil Jeffries, 'but because we've had a lot of success in Japan lately . . . they decided to stick it out. I'm really pissed off . . . the production on that album sounds like a joke. It wasn't even finished properly . . . rough vocals, rough guitars, rough mixes on everything. It's a shame they didn't let me finish it . . . but they don't give a shit. They just want to get it out. It won't cost them anything to do that, put a horrible cover on it, watch it sell 30,000, 40,000 copies and make some dough. It doesn't matter to them that it's not going to help my reputation . . . putting out inferior product like that.'[5]

---

5 *Dirty Fingers* arrived in Japanese stores in April 1983 with *Gary Moore: Live* following six months later. *Dirty Fingers* was released in Europe on 4 June 1984.

Determined to keep his reputation intact, Moore put fresh impetus on getting his next LP just right. But it wasn't going to be easy. Originally, he had decided to oversee things himself, yet as was often his wont, Moore changed his mind again close to the start date of recording. Knowing they had worked well together on *Corridors of Power*, a call was put into producer Jeff Glixman, who arrived at London's Sarm West Studios in early October 1983. He wasn't the only arrival. When new owner (and ABC/Frankie Goes to Hollywood producer) Trevor Horn purchased Sarm West a year before from Island Records, he was determined to make it the most up-to-date studio in the UK. That meant a substantial refit so Moore, Glixman and the band found themselves encountering a steady procession of electricians, carpenters and plumbers throughout their near month-long stay.

All this sporadic banging and crashing seemed to have a deleterious effect on the rhythm section. In Ian Paice's case, the issue appeared linked to his internal chronometer, which for reasons unknown, developed a major glitch soon after recording began. A terrifying malady for a drummer to face, Paice struggled to keep tempo for several days before telling Moore it was 'game over'. With Paice only able to contribute to four tracks before withdrawing from the project to sort out his problem (thankfully, it was soon resolved), Moore was forced to bring in another percussionist. On the shortest of notice, Bobby Chouinard once again took up sticks with Gary, the American eventually contributing to a further four songs on the LP.

While Paice's drumming issues proved temporary, Neil Murray's problems were more permanent, and the bassist parted company with Moore soon into recording. According to Murray, the signs might have been there as far back as *Corridors of Power*, when he, Moore and producer Glixman had differed on matters of musical style. 'It was very democratic in Whitesnake,' Murray recalled. 'I could play what I wanted for the most part, whereas with Gary, it was more, "Just play the riff and don't add your own things into it." And that went for the bass sound too, which they wanted to be very generic. Looking back at it now, I guess that was the right thing. But at the time, it really riled me. I just wasn't used to being "the session guy".'

249

These concerns resurfaced at Sarm West, where Murray again found his approach questioned. 'It was pretty much a reoccurrence of what had happened during *Corridors of Power*. Gary basically said, "Play what I tell you to play", and the whole focus from Jeff Glixman was, "This is all about Gary." You can't quibble with it, really. But unlike when I played with Gary live, I didn't feel my work on [the album] was representing me very much, and . . . for the most part, it could have been anyone playing bass. So, I got fired and wiped off [all but one of] the tracks. More fool me.' With Murray now on a circuitous route back to Whitesnake, ('Gary and I did part amicably and remained friends'), Moore was once again forced to play the recruitment game. It would take several attempts, with session ace Mo Foster returning to lend a hand on two tunes, Moore doing the job himself on a further three and Bob Daisley covering a couple more. In the end, it was Daisley that stuck.

Born in Sydney, Australia, in 1950 Bob Daisley first picked up a bass guitar aged 14. By the mid-seventies, he had appeared on albums by Mungo Jerry and Widowmaker before joining Ritchie Blackmore's Rainbow for 1978's cracking *Long Live Rock'n'Roll*. A short, if spectacularly eventful period with Ozzy Osbourne's new band followed, before Daisley got sacked, later filed legal papers over album credits[6] and like everyone else, it seemed, ended up in Uriah Heep. Come early 1983, and he was back with Ozzy again. But after another parting of the ways (and yet more legal scraps on the horizon), Daisley was now on his way to Sarm West to take up where Neil Murray had just left off. 'Gary is very disciplined,' he later told *Fly Guitars*. 'If you're conscientious, professional and good at what you do, then he's fine. Basically, Gary knows what he wants and if you do it, then it's fine.' Daisley would follow this credo more or less to the letter each time he worked with Moore over the next 20 years.

Despite a difficult birthing process, Moore's fourth solo album, *Victims of the Future*, arrived in shops on 10 December 1983, bang on time for the Christmas market. Yet, while the LP hit its marks on the scheduling

---

6 Thankfully not the subject of this book, Bob Daisley's legal issues with Ozzy Osbourne concerning performance and writing credits would rumble on from 1986 for the best part of three decades.

front, the contents were something of a disappointment. Of the eight tracks on show, only four really held one's attention, while the others fell into either the dreaded 're-tread' or 'filler' bin. In later years, Moore called the record 'one of my feeble attempts at heavy rock,' and it was hard to disagree with him.

On the plus side, the album's title track wasn't a bad start. A brooding mini-epic opening with gently plucked acoustic guitars[7] and a tearful string arrangement, 'Victims of the Future' again found Moore returning to his pet topic of incompetent leaders and the inevitability of conflict. As the track got moving, his pessimism only intensified, with each line growled over a lumbering, war-like rhythm. When the solo arrived, it too was typically intense, the normally fastidious Moore even allowing himself the luxury of a fluffed line or two for added emotional impact. 'There's bum notes in there,' he said, 'but I really liked the feel of it.'[8] Sadly, there were a few near misses in the vocals to accompany them. Faced with belting out a robust hard rock anthem at the very top of his range, Moore's voice sometimes sounded tinny and strained, especially at the track's fiery conclusion. While his singing had continued to improve, there were still limits to observe and the avoidance of high A♭ was one of them.

Though 'Victims of the Future' more or less hit the mark, others fell some way short, including the catchy, if hackneyed 'Teenage Idol'. The tale of a youthful rebel escaping scolding teachers and the boredom of factory life to become a rock'n'roll star (no prizes for guessing who this one might be based on), 'Teenage Idol' came on like a rejected Sweet single, and frankly was done much better by Foreigner two years before as 'Juke Box Hero'. 'All I Want' was also disappointing, its Aerosmith-lite riff plodding rather than bouncing along on the back of Bobby Chouinard's drums. That said, Moore's solo was worth a listen, those speedy fretboard ascents still frighteningly present and correct. 'Hold on to Love' held one's attention nicely too. Unafraid to trade on a poppy

---

7 Though Moore favoured electric guitars, he did own two Takamine acoustics, one of which was a 12-string. It was this guitar that was used on 'Victims of the Future'.

8 Moore's 'up, down and all around' solo on 'Victims of the Future' was cut in one take using Steve Jones's 1955 Les Paul Junior.

chorus and featuring some nice keyboard work from Neil Carter, the tune also made the most of Moore's voice. Released as a single in December 1983, it briefly clipped the UK charts at number sixty-five.

The same couldn't be said of the doom-laden trudge-metal of 'Law of the Jungle'. Howled rather than sung by Gary, 'Law of the Jungle' was originally meant to have Ozzy Osbourne guesting on vocals, who would have brought an agreeably banshee-like wail to proceedings. But when scheduling proved difficult, Moore was left to do the wailing himself, with predictable consequences. 'There's a very "dingy" feel about some of the tracks,' he rightly said of the downbeat musical atmosphere in 'Law of the Jungle'. 'And [the lyrics] are supposed to be a comparison between living in a jungle and . . . how dangerous it is to live in a city these days.'

If 'Law of the Jungle' at least tried to break new musical ground, then 'Murder in the Skies' was no more than a crude re-write of *Corridor of Power*'s 'End of the World', albeit one with its heart in the right place. Inspired by the events of 1 September 1983, when a Soviet jet fighter shot down a South Korean passenger plane over the Sea of Japan, killing all 269 people on board, 'Murder in the Skies' was a commendable effort on Moore's part to convey some of the shock and fury that surrounded the incident. Yet, the track's structure and melody remained just too close to 'End of the World' for comfort, with Moore even delving into the same bag of tremolo tricks to emulate the plane's final descent.

'Empty Rooms' was a tremendous improvement. A 'special tune for all concerned,' it had begun life some months earlier when Neil Carter was still part of UFO. Deep in the midst of marital problems, Carter penned the bones of the ballad alone in a Texas hotel room (hence the title), before committing the song to tape. Months later, he presented it to his new boss. Impressed by what he heard, Moore strengthened the melody line and 'tightened a few bolts' here and there. The result was a surprisingly adult meditation on lost love and surely the hit single Moore had been seeking since 1979's 'Parisienne Walkways'.

'Neil and I have written a couple of things together [for the album] which I feel are really strong . . . like 'Empty Rooms',' Moore told writer Neil Jeffries in late 1983. 'It isn't a "sweet-sounding" number like 'Falling in Love With You'. I've managed to stay away from the lovey dovey-type songs this time around, I think.' Despite becoming an immediate in-concert favourite, and featuring one of the most lyrical and restrained solos of Moore's career[9], 'Empty Rooms' stalled at number fifty-one in the UK charts on its release in August 1984. Determined not to take 'no' for an answer from the Great British public, Gary patiently filed the song away before bringing it back in modified form a year later.

One song that Moore had been keen to return to public life for some time was The Yardbirds' stunning 'Shapes of Things'. A huge hit for the band in early 1966, its combination of Eastern-sounding musical flavours and abstract, socio-political lyricism had marked it out as 'the first psyche-delic rock song,' even if no one knew what 'psychedelic' actually meant yet. 'Nothing was "named" back then,' laughed Yardbird Chris Dreja in 2011. 'It wasn't "psychedelic" or "rock", it was just . . . music.'

Of course, a central part of 'Shapes of Things" then unclassifiable appeal was the contribution of Jeff Beck, whose whistling feedback and Indian raga-influenced lead lines had opened a new world of possibilities for guitarists to explore. One of those left agog at Beck's explorations was Gary Moore, whose teenage admiration for the guitarist had only grown stronger in subsequent years. 'Jeff Beck's probably my favourite guitar player,' said Moore in 1983. 'He's the only one who's really got better or really kept going from the sixties.' With another age of axe heroes emerging, the idea of dragging one of rock guitar's original arte-facts into the eighties also appealed to the Ulsterman. 'It's a great song . . . and the lyrics really fit in [with the album] thematically too,' he told *Guitar Player*. 'It's also the kind of song where you have to get in there and do a good version or not bother at all.'

Moore certainly had a go, giving 'Shapes of Things' a thoroughly beefy, hard-rocking makeover. But in dialling up the crunch factor, he also had to sacrifice some of the exoticism of the original. This was underlined by the presence of Slade vocalist Noddy Holder, whose astounding bellow was used to firm up the song's already thundering choruses. 'Noddy's an

---

9 '[The solo] on 'Empty Rooms' was done in one take,' Gary later told *Guitar Player*. 'It wasn't something I really worked out, but I reproduce it live because I like it so much . . . [it's] a great solo that really captures the feel of the song.'

expert on that kind of chanting vocal thing because Slade used it a lot,' Moore told journalist Steve Newton. 'We sort of knew him through mutual acquaintances, so he came in to help us out.'

Where Moore was perhaps unsurprisingly more successful was on 'Shapes of Things' celebrated guitar break. Unafraid to put his own spin on Jeff Beck's extraordinary doodling, Moore had carved the solo section into 'a mini-symphony' of three distinct parts, including a cheeky nod to Beck's slide work on 1966's 'Beck's Bolero'. 'It took a long time to get the three sections just the way I wanted them,' Moore later said. Even so, he still detested employing the dreaded 'bottleneck' as part of the solo. 'I don't use bottleneck slide on stage because it drives me absolutely mad. I hate playing slide, really.' But for the right people, he was willing to make an exception. 'Well, Jeff Beck's heard the song and he really liked it,' Moore told *Guitar Player*, 'So I'm pretty pleased about that.'

With its glistening slide work, endless criss-crossing between major and minor scales and Moore's trademark speed-picking, the solo on 'Shapes of Things' was an encyclopaedia of guitar technique. As such, it inevitably drew the attention of the guitar magazines, all eager to hear Moore's views on the breadth of fresh talent sweeping across the UK and America. Despite his long-established reputation as one the fastest guns in town, Moore sounded a note of caution. 'I think a lot of guys are playing as quickly and as loud as possible . . . [but] . . . they're not reaching people,' he told *Guitar Player*'s Tom Mulhern. 'I think it's a shame . . . because they missed out on the blues side of playing. Eddie Van Halen will tell you. He grew up listening to Eric Clapton, [and] that's what I used to do with Jeff Beck and Peter Green. If you don't have that background . . . then you're missing out on the emotional side of it. If you're doing it . . . just to show everyone how fast you are, then it's rubbish.' Whether Gary Moore had always stuck to his own advice remained a debate for another day.

In possession of a few good tunes and one particularly impressive guitar solo, *Victims of the Future* was still a disappointing work in comparison to *Corridors of Power* or even *G-Force*. Yet, that didn't stop people from buying it. With 'Brand Moore' steadily gaining momentum and

Gary's profile further bolstered by recent bouts of touring, *Victims* . . . saw him enter the UK Top 20 for the first time as a solo artist, the LP making its debut at an admirable number twelve. Icing on the cake came from Scandinavia, where, always keen to embrace a guitar hero when they found one, Moore had been treated like royalty since his days with Skid Row. As *Victims* . . . reached number fifteen in Sweden and an impressive number seven in Finland, Moore took to the rooftops to sing their praises. 'Well, the Irish and Scandinavians really like to go out to enjoy themselves,' he gushed amiably in 1984. 'They have a great passion for living, and a lot of energy and fire within them. So, maybe [we have] something in common there.'

Another territory in which Moore was going from strength to strength was Japan, where after 13 short, but lucrative UK dates, he chose to begin the latest international leg of his tour in support of *Victims* . . . . Predictably, the band that arrived in north-east Asia had undergone another tranche of personnel revisions since recording the LP. With Neil Murray released and Bob Daisley (temporarily) returning to Ozzy Osbourne's group, former Elf/Rainbow bassist Craig Gruber was now recruited to take their place. A jovial chap whose own jazz-rocking instrumental 'Blinder' had served as the B-side to 'Shapes of Things' when released as a single in early 1984[10], Gruber's musical history also included time served with Black Sabbath and criminally unsung cult hard rockers Ozz. To the delight of Japanese fans, Ian Paice was also back in the ranks, having now recovered his original drumming technique after several rather alarming months without it.

Beginning his account at Fukuoka's Sunpalace on 24 February 1984, before heading up country towards Nagoya and Osaka, Moore fulfilled a long-held ambition at the end of the month by headlining Tokyo's monolithic Budokan. According to Gary, such levels of adulation, while undoubtedly flattering, were awkward to embrace. 'It's a bit embarrassing . . . and silly, really,' he told *Sounds* at the time. 'A great guitarist

---

10 Despite a tasty Chris Tsangarides remix and spirited marketing campaign from Virgin featuring a nuclear explosion-themed novelty picture disc (worth a look on Google), 'Shapes Of Things' could only reach number seventy-seven in the UK upon its release in March 1984.

is no better than a great plumber.' Perhaps, but there were few plumbers who could sell out a 14,000+ arena. 'I shouldn't complain,' he conceded. 'It's what we all strive for.'

If selling out the Budokan was a watershed in Moore's professional journey, there was still much to be accomplished in other territories. While *Victims of the Future*'s numbers were extremely healthy across the UK, Europe and north-east Asia (80,000 sales and counting in Japan alone), America had thus far resisted Moore's charms. After his stint supporting Def Leppard had failed to reach the right ears, Gary was keen to try again, this time securing a US support slot with a band whose fans might be more receptive to his approach. Hence, after spending most of March running around Germany, Belgium and Scandinavia, he again ventured across the Atlantic to join the wonderfully uncategorisable Rush on a 40-date trek around the arenas and cowsheds of the United States.

As usual, there were adjustments to make in Moore's backing group before hitting the road. Having regained his mojo in Japan, Paice now bowed out of touring America because his wife was soon due to give birth. So far, so Don Airey. Yet on this occasion, Moore raised no objections. In fact, he even wished the drummer Godspeed when informed that following a humungous cash offer, Paice would be re-joining the classic Deep Purple Mk II line-up for their first album in 11 years. Faced with the prospect of another empty drum stool (but a considerably cheaper wage bill), Moore called Bobby Chouinard. For a moment, it looked uncertain, Chouinard having recently returned to his day job with pop rocker Billy 'The Stroke' Squier. Then due to a serendipitous break in schedules, the percussionist became free at exactly the right moment to hit the road alongside Moore, Craig Gruber and Neil Carter.

As he hoped, the US support slot with Rush proved a better fit all round. Not only were the headlining band 'kind and gracious hosts,' but their audience were also an extremely friendly bunch too. Already appreciative of the premium musicianship provided by guitarist Alex Lifeson, bassist Geddy Lee and 'God's own drummer' Neil Peart, Rush fans immediately warmed to Moore's instrumental prowess, his solos on the likes of 'Cold Hearted' and 'White Knuckles' drawing loud cheers from

256

fellow players in the crowd. This hearty embrace from the guitar community continued backstage. As the tour progressed, Moore was visited by Jeff Beck, Eddie Van Halen and Journey's own axeman extraordinaire Neal Schon, all of whom were keen to see him in action. In fact, Schon was even brave enough to join Moore under the concert lights, jamming along to a spirited version of 'Wishing Well' in Cleveland, Ohio.

. Yet, not even the support of rock's ever-growing guitar community could push *Victims of the Future* to the upper echelons of the US charts, with the album grinding to a halt at a measly number 172. Some blamed Mirage Records for a poorly run marketing campaign. Others pointed at a lack of engagement from America's ever-influential radio networks. Several more criticised the album sleeve.[11] Theories were many. In the States, however, sales remained few. 'Too metal. Not metal enough. Who the fuck knows.'

As Part Rock, Virgin and Mirage tried to decipher exactly why their resident guitar hero continued to miss the mark in America, Moore travelled home to the UK, joining the line-up of the fourth annual Monsters of Rock festival at Castle Donington on 18 August 1984. A sterling effort by promoter Paul Loasby to create a one-day event specifically tailored for the hard rock/heavy metal community, the festival had gone from strength to strength since its launch four years before, when Saxon, Judas Priest and headliners Rainbow put a small dent in the ozone layer above the East Midlands. With expectations set sky high by subsequent line-ups – AC/DC, Status Quo and Whitesnake took top billing from 1981–83 – and approximately 50,000 tickets to be sold, 1984's line-up had to be equally good. Some might argue it was the best yet. In addition to a returning AC/DC, Monsters of Rock '84 also boasted sets from Ozzy Osbourne, hot new ticket Mötley Crüe and tried

---

11 Possibly disappointed by Virgin's subdued choice of sleeve for *Victims of the Future* (jet black cover, Moore's name and album title superimposed in red on two white triangles), Mirage chose to go with another design, this time displaying the LP's details over a painted image of post-nuclear devastation. Subtle, it wasn't, but some fans prefer it. On another note, the US album release of *Victims of the Future* omitted Moore's unaccompanied solo at the beginning of 'Murder in the Skies' while swapping 'All I Want' for the more metal-friendly 'Devil in Her Heart'. 'All I Want' was later reinstated on the American cassette version.

and tested show-stealers Van Halen. Nestled between Mr Osbourne and seasoned American shin-kickers Y&T, Moore would have to be at the very top of his game.

He didn't have the best start. Stepping onto a swelteringly hot stage, Moore immediately ran into sound problems which rendered his guitar signal all but inaudible during classical-themed instrumental opener 'Majestuoso e Virtuoso'. As roadies scrambled to fix the problem, a wag or three in the audience helpfully began chanting 'Why are we waiting?' A well-aimed boot at an offending power line soon set things right, and he and the band were off and running with 'Rockin' Every Night'. Truth to tell, it wasn't Moore's finest gig. 'Cold Hearted' didn't quite click, 'Shapes of Things' dragged on a bit, and the less said about his fire-red boiler suit and huge white trainers the better. Yet, by the time Moore got to 'Victims of the Future', things were definitely on an upward curve, before 'Empty Rooms' and its ambling, airy solo finally put him on course towards a well-deserved encore. 'Just point the spotlight at me,' Moore once laughed, 'and I'll take it from there.'

After the high stakes and hand claps of Castle Donington, Moore and his band continued on the festival circuit throughout the summer of 1984, including two more Monsters of Rock spots in Germany before finally coming off the road in early September. One of the busiest years of his touring life, Virgin chose to mark Moore's progress with an album. Culled from performances over the previous eight or so months, including stop-offs at the Glasgow Apollo, Harpos in Detroit and the landmark gig at the Budokan, the man given the task of pulling it all together on tape was Moore's old associate, Tony Platt.

Since overseeing Thin Lizzy's 'Still in Love With You' at Worthing's Pebble Beach Studios back in 1974, Platt, like Moore, had come a long way. After leaving West Sussex behind, a new association with South African producer Mutt Lange found Platt back in London and engineering two now legendary albums in the shape of AC/DC's 1980 masterpiece *Back in Black* and Foreigner's AOR-defining *4*. 'Everyone in AC/DC knew their role and what was expected of them, and that's why it worked,' Platt said of one of hard rock's biggest selling bands. 'But the turning point is when a band's audience isn't just a bloke in jeans and a black T-shirt listening to their record. It's him and his girl-friend. That's the point where your sales double, and that's what happened to AC/DC.'[12]

After further stints with Acca Dacca (1983's *Flick of the Switch*), Foreigner ('Urgent'), and the terrifying Motörhead (*Another Perfect Day*, featuring Thin Lizzy's second wildest boy, Brian Robertson, on lead guitar[13]), Platt was now back with Moore. 'Well, I'd done some live [album] work before, so I was probably a good fit.' Left largely to his own devices – 'Yes, Gary left me alone. He was pretty good like that' – Platt waded through hours of concert tapes with one thing in mind. 'Dive into what was there and pick out the best performances!' Not so hard, as it turned out. 'Well, Gary had an amazing band, there were some great gigs there such as the Budokan and that made [things] quite special.' With little tidying up to be done – 'No, there really wasn't much overdubbing' – Platt only had to use one magician's trick before the album was completed. 'The main thing I did was to [create] a multi-track audience tape,' he explained. 'I picked out . . . audience [noise] from all of the venues, then . . . used that as a background loop for the album. I don't think it was cheating because it was the actual audience from some the gigs, just not all the audience from all the gigs!'

Debuting at number thirty-two in the UK charts in late October 1984, the resulting double live LP, *We Want Moore*, was a faithful document of the 'Gary Moore concert experience,' capturing all the speed, skill and craft of a typical night out with one of the world's premier rock guitarists. From the apocalypse metal rumble of 'Victims of the Future' and 'End of the World' to the more considered pop rock tunes

---

12 As of February 2022, AC/DC's *Black in Black* had sold a whopping 50 million copies.

13 As alluded to in a previous footnote, when guitarist 'Fast' Eddie Clarke left Motörhead in May 1982, Brian Robertson was the surprise replacement. But the association ended after Motörhead's perma-black-clad frontman Lemmy Kilminster took exception to Robbo wearing tight green satin shorts and espadrilles on stage. 'I thought that he'd carry on looking like he'd done in Thin Lizzy,' Lemmy later told *Classic Rock*. 'Instead, he dressed like a cunt.' When the notoriously stubborn Robertson refused to change his attire, Kilminster said goodbye. 'The thing with Robbo is if you told him not to do something, he'd go and do it four times as badly,' laughed Tony Platt. 'But let's not forget he's still one of the most underrated guitarists in rock.'

of 'Don't Take Me for a Loser' and lonesome 'Empty Rooms'[14], it was all there at the drop of a needle. Yet, *We Want Moore* also served to highlight how far he had come as a frontman, with Gary now finally appearing much more comfortable in his onstage role as singer, guitar player and overall master of ceremonies. 'Well, we had conversations about that,' said Platt. 'When Gary first started singing his own songs, he was scared shitless. But his [recent] experiences on record and in concert . . . helped finally unpin him from that fear. I think Gary was now truly ready to move on, to really become the centre of attention. He had fully adapted into the role of "frontman" and wherever that might lead.'

There was real truth here. With each gig, single and LP, Moore had edged ever closer to the goal he set himself when he signed with Virgin two years before. At that point, the creation of 'Brand Moore' was a tantalising, yet still abstract idea. Now, it was his workaday reality. 'Well, I'm happy now to finally have my own career, and it's the best thing I've ever done for myself,' Moore told *Kerrang* in late 1984. 'I'm in control of it and I'm together enough now to . . . handle it. It's not like a power thing, though. I [just] wouldn't like to think someone . . . less qualified was making decisions for me. Five, ten years ago, I wouldn't have had the confidence to handle the pressure. But I've taken my time, found the right band, the right manager and the right record company. So [now], everything fits together properly.'

Guitar hero, singer–songwriter, successful solo artist. So far, so good. But Moore being Moore, there was were always another mountain to climb. As yet, he hadn't quite cracked the top of the UK album charts in his own name, despite chasing that goal with grim determination. Following two exhausting touring campaigns, America also continued to play coy, the territory respectful of Moore's talent but not willing to reward it with platinum sales. To correct these oversights, Moore still needed to 'cross over', and that meant writing a monster hit single to

---

14 Moore's dreamy instrumental introduction to 'Empty Rooms' on *We Want Moore* – titled 'So Far Away' – was actually written by the bassist Mo Foster and Moore's guitarist friend Ray Russell. Some say the piece might have inspired Jeff Beck's signature guitar miracle, 1989's 'Where Were You'. But then again, some say not.

drum up sales for a monster hit album. Easily said, of course, but as many a rock act will tell you, not so easily done. For the time being, however, the empire building could wait. After more than a decade away, Gary Moore was finally going back to Belfast, and he was bringing Philip Lynott with him.

CHAPTER EIGHTEEN

Crossing The Rubicon

To no one's great surprise, Thin Lizzy had persisted after the departure of Gary Moore in July 1979, even if the band were never quite the same afterwards. Following Moore's exit, the gallant Midge Ure had soldiered on for several months, providing guitar/synth cover for his embattled colleagues. Philip Lynott soon added former Manfred Mann guitarist Dave Flett to the line-up, further bolstering Lizzy's onstage firepower. But by the spring of 1980, Flett and Ure were gone, their places taken by expressive keyboardist Darren Wharton and ex-Pink Floyd session guitarist Snowy White. Keen, fresh-faced and with a real flair for the blues, White seemed on paper to be a fine potential replacement for the errant Moore. But the group he was joining were awash with problems, some of them even musical.

With Philip continuing to work on his solo career and songs being directed 'here, there and bloody everywhere' as a result, no one knew whether they were recording a Thin Lizzy album 'or another Lynott record.' In this increasingly chaotic atmosphere, White managed to complete two LPs with the band: 1980's occasionally inspiring *Chinatown* and the deeply ordinary *Renegade* a year or so later. But by 1982, he too had moved on. 'Snowy was a phenomenal guitar player,' said Chalkie Davies in 2020. 'But there was just too much shit to deal with by then.'

Though *Chinatown* kept Thin Lizzy in the UK Top 10, *Renegade*'s dismal chart showing (a mere number thirty-eight) confirmed them to be in commercial as well as artistic decline. Inside the walls of the band, things were also getting worse. Both Brian Downey and a now heroin-addicted Scott Gorham were forced to take time out, while Lynott's escalating drug use was becoming impossible to disguise. Once pin-sharp and rail thin, Lizzy's frontman now appeared both distracted and puffy-faced, his moods changeable, his temper sometimes short. No longer able to keep things on an even keel and fearful for what the future might bring, the group's co-manager Chris O'Donnell reluctantly stepped away. 'A once-brilliant band,' he said, 'was just turning to crap before my very eyes.'

There was one last hurrah. A born pragmatist despite his woes, Lynott recruited young guitar hotshot John Sykes, formerly of Tygers of Pan Tang, and coincidentally, a huge fan of Gary Moore, thus allowing the Thin men to cut what turned out to be their final studio album, 1983's *Thunder and Lightning*. Heavily reliant on Sykes's aggressive playing style, the LP bruised rather than charmed, but it got Lizzy back into the UK charts at number four, their best showing since *Black Rose*. Sensing an opportunity to go out on a high, a 'farewell' tour was booked and ticket sales proved impressive. So impressive, in fact, that Lynott began having second thoughts at handing in Thin Lizzy's cards. 'We can always put the band back together again,' he told journalist Neil Jeffries. 'I'm the guy who wouldn't mind. Everyone else is going, "We've got to have some integrity". [But] I love the band so much, I'd lie for it. I'd cheat to stay in there.' Scott Gorham had different ideas. Exhausted, addicted and desperate to find a way out of the 'whole bloody mess' before it killed him, the guitarist was adamant. Lizzy was over.

'Honestly, when you're a kid, going on stage seems like a wonderful thing, the best thing ever,' he said in 2020. 'But after so many years, all the work, all the addictions, it felt more like a goddamn nightmare. In my mind, we just shouldn't have been out there doing it any more. We were past our sell-by date . . . and even our [remaining] manager Chris

Morrison had had enough. Maybe if we'd taken a break, stepped back, for a year. Two years, maybe. Fuck it. Coulda, woulda, shoulda. It's all meaningless now. [At the time,] I said to Philip, "Come on, we've got to get out of this before we ruin ourselves".'

To mark their passing, Thin Lizzy erected a tombstone of sorts at Hammersmith Odeon, where over the course of three nights (10–12 March 1983), the band recorded their last London gigs for the double live LP, *Life*. As the album showed, Philip Lynott sounded hoarse, the group (a combustible John Sykes aside) sounded weary and the fact that it was released at all remains questionable.[1] '*Life*? Nope, I still haven't heard that all the way through,' admitted Gorham. Still, the record was successful in capturing the final night's All-Star Thin Lizzy Guitar Jam, with old lags Brian Robertson and Eric Bell joining their former colleagues on stage for rousing takes on 'Emerald' and 'The Rocker'.[2] Somewhat astoundingly, right there among them, 'gurning like a happy fool' and showing everyone how to play 'Black Rose' properly, was Gary Moore.

Realistically, the chance of Lynott and Moore avoiding each other following the malarky surrounding 1979's Day on the Green was doubtful at best. With a limited number of recording studios, nightclubs and private watering holes at their disposal in London, the odds were simply against it. 'London might have been a big city,' said Brian Downey, 'but for musicians, it was a pretty small world.' And so, it proved. First came that near miss at Kensington's E-zee rehearsals in the early summer of 1982. Then there was a party in Cricklewood where Moore walked in one door while Lynott made his exit through another. Still, their luck couldn't

---

1   A so-so epitaph to one of the great bands, *Life* stumbled in the UK charts at number twenty-nine in late October 1983, just weeks after Thin Lizzy played their final concert at Nuremberg's Monsters of Rock festival on 4 September. 'I remember being at the airport in Germany after our very last show,' Gorham remembered, 'and Philip says, "You're going to come to studio to help me mix the concert album, right?" But I said, "No, man. I'm done"'

2   Unlike Robertson, Bell and Moore, Snowy White did not appear with Thin Lizzy at the band's last Hammersmith show. However, his contribution to the group was acknowledged on *Life*, where three tracks featuring White from an earlier gig were included in the running order.

hold out forever. One night in late November, the pair reportedly found themselves inhabiting the same space at reassuringly grimy music industry haunt Dingwalls. Moore was out drinking with his buddy Jeff Beck, Lynott among friends several feet away. Both were secretly eager to draw their tables together, but for reasons of alpha-male dominance, unable to do so. 'I mean, Jesus . . .' laughed a certain Californian guitarist.

Obviously, it couldn't go on, and thankfully it didn't. In January 1983, another chance meeting at Heathrow airport saw the boxing gloves finally come off and the reconciliations begin. 'I think some people thought there was going to be a big fight,' said Moore of he and Lynott's airport tête-à-tête, 'but . . . I was really chuffed we could just speak again.' Within weeks, the pair were back on stage together at Hammersmith Odeon seeing Thin Lizzy off with a bang. 'We were all still there in the bar at five o'clock the next morning,' laughed Brian Downey. 'They couldn't get rid of us.'

Hatchet buried, Moore and Lynott remained on friendly terms over the coming year. But with Gary still trying to make his mark in the States and Philip's new band Grand Slam[3] gigging around the UK and Ireland, opportunities to fraternise were few. Therefore, when Moore was offered the chance of returning to Dublin and Belfast for a series of concerts in the winter of 1984, he invited his old friend along. Offer graciously accepted, Lynott's pre-show publicity campaign confirmed he had lost none of his flair for drumming up business, albeit now for someone else's benefit. 'You can talk about Gary's playing for ages and how good it is,' he said of Moore's upcoming gigs. 'But the best thing is just to go and listen to it.'

Yet, for all Lynott's ebullience, Moore's return to the city that framed his youth could still be seen as something of a dangerous game. For while Moore had kept in touch with relatives and friends[4] in intervening years, it was more than a decade since he had actually played a concert in Belfast. Of course, the Troubles were a major factor in that decision.

---

3 Originally boasting Lizzy's Brain Downey and John Sykes in the ranks before both moved on elsewhere, Philip Lynott's post-Lizzy quintet Grand Slam made their live debut in Waterford, Éire, in April 1984. They would tour the UK and Ireland on and off for the next 12 months.

4 Gary and his former Dublin flatmate Johnny Duhan rekindled their musical friendship around this time, with Moore providing some crisp guitar for Duhan's evocative 1982 release 'Oceans in Motion'.

Flaring up soon after Moore's departure in late 1968, sectarian violence throughout the province had only intensified in intervening years, with almost nightly TV coverage projecting the terrors Northern Ireland had to endure onto an international stage. Given such continuing turbulence, getting US, European or even UK bands to visit Belfast or Derry was difficult, Moore reluctantly included. In the absence of visiting rock deities, Northern Ireland had given birth to a rich, homegrown punk scene, with The Undertones, Rudi and Ruefrex among others[5] all enjoying various degrees of success. As Belfast record shop owner/indie label boss/local hero Terri Hooley said of NI's punk phenomenon: 'New York had the bands, London had the fashion, but Belfast had the reason.'

Now, after several failed attempts, Moore had finally found a way of crossing the great divide. 'In the past, there were certain musicians who had no desire to come to Northern Ireland with me because of the risks involved,' he said, '. . . but there are risks involved in everything. Me and [the band] are now willing to take those risks because I really want to play in Belfast.' It wasn't just Moore and his band venturing north. As well as those taking the stage, some 20-plus staff and 32 tonnes of equipment were also making the journey, with producer Tony Platt and a film crew tagging along to document Moore's every move for the forthcoming video release *Emerald Aisles*. 'Well, the idea behind *Emerald Aisles* was about capturing Gary's whole experience of going back to Ireland,' Platt confirmed. 'So, he had a film crew following him around pretty much all the time.'

On 18 December 1984, Gary Moore stepped on stage at Ulster Hall in front of a crowd of more than 2,000 people. Given his history with both the city and venue, it was always going to be an emotional homecoming. 'Ulster Hall's . . . a big thing for me,' Moore said in advance of the gig. 'I used to watch all the bands there as a kid. It was the place to headline, the home of rock'n'roll in Belfast.' And now Moore was deter-

---

5   While not quite punks, gothic rockers Cruella de Ville surely deserve a mention when talking about the Belfast music scene. The brainchild of twins Colum and Philomena Muinzer, Cruella released a string of wildly inventive singles from 1982-84 before splitting up. Once described as 'Queen meets The Cure', Colum Muinzer was/is a fine guitar player, and worthy of investigation.

mined to make his mark there too, walloping those in attendance with a show that included chase light systems, elevating plinths, billowing dry ice and more guitar solos than you could shake a stick at. In fact, such was the enthusiasm generated by 'one of our own coming home', some fans wanted to get in on the act. 'Well, one of the best moments was when a fan got hold of the bloody microphone,' laughed Platt. 'I'd hung it [from the ceiling] over the crowd to capture the sound and there he was, singing directly into it. We didn't know what the hell was going on until we finally spotted him dangling there.'

The biggest cheer of the night was reserved for the third encore, when a delighted Moore introduced Philip Lynott from the wings to perform a sterling rendition of 'Parisienne Walkways'. 'Yes,' said Tony Platt, 'that link-up with Philip brought the circle around quite nicely.' Come the end of 'Parisienne Walkways', and those gathered were in no mood to let Moore or Lynott leave, causing the guitarist to pull out an old chestnut from his own days watching bands at Ulster Hall. 'Well, we don't know any more songs,' he laughed, 'so here's one we used to play together,' before launching into Peter Green and Fleetwood Mac's old stomper 'Stop Messin' Round'. A triumphant return that left Moore visibly moved, his achievement was perhaps best summed up by the man who first foisted him on a stage some 27 years before and backed his talent ever since. 'I'm very proud of him as a father,' said a visiting Bobby Moore to those filming the event. 'Firstly, as a son, and secondly as a musician. You see,' he concluded, 'Gary did it all without any gimmicks. He did it through his sheer ability.'

With a short break in the schedule, Bobby Moore's prodigal son was able to spend a while with his father and close relatives in East Belfast before again setting off on 20 December for another sort of homecoming, this time at Dublin's SFX hall. In many ways as familiar to Moore as the city he had just left, the opportunity to stroll down memory lane at the likes of Slattery's, The Pembroke or even the gravesite of Club A Go Go, now sadly gone the way of the dodo, was curtailed by press and promotional duties. Come nightfall, however, and it was business as usual with Moore, his band and special guest Lynott rocking Dublin in their traditional fashion. 'He's the best guitarist there is,' said one fan of Moore to the waiting cameras. 'He totally wipes out Van Halen, [Ozzy Osbourne's]

Jake E. Lee, all these guys. Gary's just much better.' Given the hairy rock brigade gathered around him, no one was going to argue.

With Belfast and Dublin again in his back pocket, and a rapprochement with Philip Lynott many thought impossible, Gary Moore should have entered 1985 brimming with energy and confidence. Yet, there was a gnawing feeling that continued to follow him around. 'I feel like I'm still learning,' he said at the time, 'that I haven't reached the peak of my playing and that I've got a long way to go.' Actually, Moore turned out be at least half-right as, with the coming months presenting a series of both personal and professional challenges.

Having come tantalisingly close to a UK Top 10 with *Victims of the Future*, Moore remained adamant that his next album would be 'the one'. To enable that aim, he had already begun reshaping his band in advance of recording, with two musicians leaving before the Belfast/Dublin dates of late 1984. In the case of Bobby Chouinard, the drummer's departure was predominantly driven by a need to return to Billy Squier's group for an upcoming US tour, while Craig Gruber had exited Moore's employ soon after Monsters of Rock to join New York power trio The Rods. The ever-reliable Bob Daisley was quickly drafted in to cover bass duties in Gruber's absence.

If Daisley was a returning soldier, Bobby Chouinard's replacement behind the kit was both a new face and a rather surprising one at that. A vital part of Roxy Music since their formation in 1971, drummer Paul Thompson had worked his way through six albums worth of immaculately performed glam, pop and art rock before a thumb injury saw him leave the group nine years later. Now fully recovered, he was intent on moving beyond the recent smooth surfaces of 'Dance Away' and 'Same Old Scene' for the rockier terrain of 'Murder in the Skies' and 'End of the World'. An ardent devotee of Led Zeppelin's beat monster John Bonham and nicknamed the 'Great Paul Thompson' by Roxy fans in honour of his powerful drumming style, Thompson certainly sounded enthusiastic about joining Moore's hard-rocking band. 'A lot of people play fast stuff and that's all it is, fast stuff,' he said backstage at Ulster Hall in December 1984. 'But Gary, he's very melodic with it.'

Though the addition of Bob Daisley and Paul Thompson could only help his cause, the task Gary Moore set himself when it came to recording his new LP was an imposing one. Not only was Moore intent on delivering both a major creative and commercial breakthrough, he also wanted to do so using the latest tools available. Ever the keen listener, he had been well aware of the revolution in affordable electronic keyboards that helped drive pop movements like new romanticism at the start of the eighties. But thanks to recent and rapid advances in digital studio technology, that revolution in sound was now starting to take the rock world by the scruff of the neck.

From the canny synth/guitar fusions of Billy Idol's *Rebel Yell* to Def Leppard/Mutt Lange's futuristic updating of hard rock on 1983's *Pyromania*, all was change and Moore wanted in on it. 'I acknowledge . . . this sort of technology is not going to go away and I actually love the way [it's] developed,' he told *International Musician* in 1985. 'You now have so many great things that you didn't have 10 years ago. Until this sort of thing came along, I often regarded studios as a pain in the arse . . . a necessary evil. Now I actually enjoy it.'

Another forward-facing album that had greatly impressed Moore was 1982's *Hughes/Thrall*, the work of former Automatic Man/Pat Travers guitarist Pat Thrall[6] and Moore's old mate from his time in the City of Angels, Glenn Hughes. Immaculately produced by former Led Zeppelin/Free/Stones engineer Andy Johns, and built from the same 'power-soul-rock-pop' template Moore and Hughes were toying with back in 1979, *Hughes/Thrall* was a confident, assured debut. Yet, despite extremely positive reviews, the album sank without trace. Some felt the material too sophisticated for a mainstream audience. Hughes himself later confirmed he and Thrall had difficulty getting behind the record's release due to various substance-abuse issues. Neither problem seemed to particularly concern Gary Moore. Convinced he had heard the future, Moore pushed common sense and his record company's concerns aside, and flew Glenn Hughes from Los Angeles to London to get him working on his own LP.

With *Hughes/Thrall* producer Andy Johns presumably unavailable,

---

6 An inventive and exciting player who brought much to his recordings with Automatic Man, Pat Travers and Glenn Hughes, Pat Thrall later contributed to LPs by artists as diverse as Sly & Robbie, Tina Turner, Asia, Jack Bruce and Meat Loaf.

Moore settled on Beau Hill to fill the gap. Then best known for steering Sunset Strip glam metallers Ratt to three million sales and counting for their 1983 debut disc *Out of the Cellar,* Hill knew how to turn loud guitars into hard cash. Unfortunately, he didn't turn them up loudly enough for Moore's liking. 'I thought, "Fuck it, I want my solos turning up!" Moore later told *Kerrang.* 'So, there was immediately some conflict over that.' Further mixed feelings arose when Hill reportedly didn't show quite enough enthusiasm either for Moore's playing, ('Too non-committal'), or one or two of his new tunes. 'They were probably too English [sounding] and wrong for him anyway,' Moore later grumbled. So, once Hill completed work with Moore and Hughes on the rather generic (and distinctly American-sounding) 'Out of My System' and 'Nothing to Lose', he was on a plane and heading back to the States.

Glenn Hughes wasn't far behind him. Though things took a temporary upturn when Andy Johns agreed to join the project, Moore's mood regarding Hughes' behaviours continued to darken the longer the singer/bassist stayed in London. Having 'gone through the fucking hoops' to ensure his involvement, Moore now felt that Hughes was demanding much but contributing little, his attentions focused less on writing music and more on partying. Suffice to say, there were words had and at considerable volume. Yet, given that Hughes remained in thrall to many of the same demons that plagued he and Moore's original partnership, mounting a creditable defence was always going to be difficult. 'Well, we were still great friends [during *Run for Cover*],' Hughes later told *Guitar World.* 'But I was drunk again and it wasn't an appropriate time to work with Gary because he was so against all that behaviour.' After contributing bass to three more tracks with Andy Johns at the helm, it was all over, including the shouting. 'I wasn't at my best then,' Hughes said. '[So] Gary had to let me go.'

The brilliant, if troubled Glenn Hughes wasn't the only one to come and go quickly. Over the course of four eventful months, Moore amassed an army of contributors to help him finally get his record across the finish line. In addition to touring band members Neil Carter, Paul Thompson and Bob Daisley, Moore roped in engineer James 'Jimbo'

Barton, top session drummers Charlie Morgan[7] and Gary Ferguson as well as an electronic Simmons floor kit to capture the right balance of human endeavour and inhuman sparkle. '[Originally,] I wasn't convinced about using drum machines or click tracks and sampling,' Moore said. 'But now I'm totally convinced that that's the way to do it.'

The man who convinced Moore that such modern marvels might work for him was producer Peter Collins. Then busy laying down the building blocks of what would become a notable career, Collins scored his first hit with rockabilly rebels Matchbox back in 1979 before joining forces with upcoming pop production guru Pete Waterman, who subsequently managed Collins' affairs for the next four years. After further singles success via mod revivalists The Lambrettas and cherubic reggae act Musical Youth, Collins struck out on his own in the mid-eighties. 'One of the reasons [Pete Waterman and I] parted company,' he later told *Sound on Sound*, 'was at that time I was getting more into adult-orientated rock music.' The more 'adult' sound Pete referred to was Gary Moore's 'Empty Rooms'.

Heartened by the positive response 'Empty Rooms' had elicited in concert-goers throughout the USA while on tour with Rush in 1984, Gary approached Collins to re-record the tune for a single release. One couldn't fault Moore's logic, really. Collins was a pop hitmaker who wanted to try his hand at rock. Moore was a rock guitar hero frantically looking for a way into the pop market. Nice symmetry, but it hadn't quite worked. As already detailed, 'Empty Rooms' disappointed in the States and barely scratched the Top 50 at home. That didn't matter to Rush, though: when they heard Collins' ultra-modern reworking of Moore's tune the Canadian trio snapped him up to oversee their next album, the synthesiser-heavy, multi-platinum selling *Power Windows*. That left Moore, who had hoped to use Collins for a good portion of his own LP, scrambling for a replacement producer, with Beau Hill and Andy Johns ultimately filling the vacuum. But when Moore heard Collins had a brief break in schedule, it was game on again.

---

7   Before aiding Moore, Charlie Morgan had contributed to recordings by artists such as Judie Tzuke, Nik Kershaw and Kate Bush. Following his stint with Moore, he would go on to work with Elton John for 13 years.

Still convinced that 'Empty Rooms' had what it took to put him over the top despite two previous attempts at getting it right, Moore, Neil Carter and Collins reconvened at Sarm East Studios in London's Ladbroke Road during the spring of 1985 to test the old adage 'third time's the charm'. Aided by 'Jimbo' Barton on sampled drums and Andy Richards on glistening keyboards (more of him in a minute), the quartet finally re-shaped 'Empty Rooms' into the hit 45 Gary always knew it was. Now all eighties synth-pads and breathy backing vocals, the song entered the UK singles charts at number twenty-three in August 1985, while also making it to a creditable number twelve in Ireland. By then though, Moore had already had a Top 5 success in both territories, and a good few other besides, with another Pete Collins-assisted production: the brilliant 'Out in the Fields'.

Buzzing around the back of his head like an angry bee for several months before recording for the new album commenced, Moore first brought the bones of 'Out in the Fields' to Beau Hill for consideration. Concerned the track was 'too frantic,' the Texan producer passed, and in so doing, probably hastened his exit from the project. Irritated by the perceived slight and surer than ever he was onto something, Moore continued to work up the tune and its lyrics, eventually settling on the story of a soldier facing his death on an unnamed battlefield for an unknown cause. Of course, given Moore's point of origin and recent return to Belfast after an absence of 10 years, it was easy to jump to the conclusion he had part-based his story on the Troubles. But Moore always denied the connection. 'I've written a lot of songs like [this] in the past with sort of anti-war, political lyrics,' he said at the time. 'But they're just observations, and just one aspect of my writing.' 'Out in the Fields', it seemed, represented a universal rather than local complaint.

As it was, the song might have stayed a catchy, if frenetically paced anti-war anthem with a fair chance of skimming the Top 20 on a quiet week. Yet, Moore's idea to involve Philip Lynott on vocals elevated it to the status of a classic. 'I decided to work with [Lynott] again simply because the song was suitable for his voice,' he later said. 'In fact, when I first wrote the song, it didn't occur to me that it was the kind of thing that Philip could sing well.' Moore was wrong on that one. Philip Lynott could sing 'Out in the Fields' very well indeed. It was everything else he seemed to be having trouble with.

Since Thin Lizzy ceased trading in September 1983, reasons for Lynott to celebrate had been few and far between. His new band Grand Slam briefly threatened to reactivate interest in the singer/songwriter, but the tunes were good rather than great and the concerts hit or miss. Worryingly, Lynott's reputation continued to be tarnished by well-founded rumours of drug addiction, leading record companies to steer clear of both him and his group. By early December 1984, just a matter of weeks before Lynott and Moore appeared together in Belfast and Dublin, Grand Slam had played their last shows.

On a personal level, Philip's circumstances were also less than ideal. While there was no doubt he loved his wife Caroline and their two children, marriage had come too late to save Lynott from himself. A serial philanderer nursing a serious heroin habit, Philip's inability to change his ways saw Caroline exit the relationship in mid-1984, both daughters in tow. Now left to his own devices, Lynott's elegant mansion on west London's Kew Road began to deteriorate at roughly the same rate as its owner, an increasing number of hangers-on, ne'er-do-wells and fellow addicts filling the space his family once did.

One visitor who bucked the trend was Gary Moore. 'I'd go round to [his] house at lunchtime when he'd just got out of bed, and he'd come down with a glass of whiskey in one hand and a spliff in the other,' Moore later told *The Independent*. Back in their Dublin days, Lynott had often cooked breakfast, cleaned several corners and written a song before Moore even emerged from beneath the blankets, so this was hardly progress. 'I knew he was in trouble, and you could tell he wasn't very happy.' Gary continued. 'But he couldn't admit he had a problem. As far as Philip was concerned, he could handle anything.'

Whether he chose to acknowledge it or not, Lynott was obviously in the trenches and Moore knew it. Yet, unlike many record companies at the time, Moore was still sure enough of his friend's gift to back him when it came to 'Out in the Fields'. After hearing a series of quick demos cut by the duo at Eel Pie Island Studios, so were Virgin, who signed off on the single with producer Pete Collins at the helm. Now, there was only the matter of Lynott's fee. Astoundingly, he asked for £5,000 in cash, a laughable sum that, had he allowed manager Chris Morrison to negotiate on his behalf, would have been tripled, and then some. 'He came in [afterwards] and asked if I could get him out of it,' Morrison said, 'but he had to swallow it.' Cynics later suggested Lynott was simply covering the cost of his drug bills. Though sad to admit, they were probably right.

Again recorded at Sarm East Studios, 'Out in the Fields' was approached with military precision. For a returning Don Airey, now back in Moore's good books after a brief period in the doghouse for missing a tour, this was all for the best. 'Well, Pete Collins banned drinking in the studio and asked that we got in at 11 each morning,' he later said. 'We'd work through until six and then go home. Usually, you'd arrive at two or three in the afternoon, have a couple of drinks . . . and finish about two in the morning. But Collins was good for Gary and for me, actually.' Less so for Lynott, who according to newcomer Andy Richards, had obviously found a way to get what he needed. 'Oh, Philip was a lovely man,' said Richards. 'I remember he was drinking whiskey, lots of it actually, and [at first] there was the thought that "This might not end well". But it turned out great. Philip was a true gentleman and he and Gary had a real shorthand.'

Brought in by Collins to provide some of the same 'magic dust' he had already sprinkled on several mega-hits the previous year, Andy Richards was the UK's go-to keyboard programmer at the time. A former classical organ scholar who had somehow negotiated a path from playing piano with folk rockers The Strawbs to working alongside producer-in-excelsis Trevor Horn, Richards' lush chords were a vital part of Frankie Goes to Hollywood mega-hits 'Relax' and 'Two Tribes'. In fact, if one included his contribution to George Michael's 'Careless Whisper', Richards' keyboard lines had spent 19 weeks at the top of the UK charts during 1984 alone.

Witty, self-effacing and one of the few people in Great Britain who then owned a Fairlight sampler – 'I think it cost more than I paid for my flat, but you know' – Richards added a variety of whizzing bullets, shattering glass and other battlefield noises to Moore's latest opus. 'When Gary hooked up with Peter Collins, it was obvious he was after a hit single,'

Richards recalled in 2020. 'But he was still playing with tremendous power. You could feel the energy coming off him.' This was frighteningly evident on Moore's solo for 'Out in the Fields'. Probably recorded on a brand-new white Hamer Special[8], he moved from whammy-bar-assisted legato to chunky palm muting in the space of seconds before scrambling up the guitar neck so fast and precisely, it almost beggared belief. Regarded as one of Moore's finest ever fretboard excursions, the metronome-scaring solo on 'Out in the Fields' continues to befuddle guitarists to this day. 'The solo on 'Out in the Fields'?' laughed Richards. 'Well, it's like "whoosh", isn't it? Gary sounds like a bloody aircraft taking off!'

With Philip Lynott trading vocals alongside Moore, Pete Collins and Andy Richards putting a thoroughly modern spin on things, and Moore channelling Concorde for the song's solo, 'Out in the Fields' was almost ready to go. However, there were still a couple more boxes to be ticked before the single could be let loose on the public. First up was the filming of an ambitious video, featuring Moore playing an array of six strings, including the short-lived, but then up-to-the-minute guitar/synthesiser interface 'the SynthAxe'.[9] The promo also featured the equally weapon-referencing 'Axe-cam', a 35mm camera attached to the head of Moore's guitar neck and then pointed downwards toward the fretboard, allowing viewers a chance to see those lightning fingers at ultra-close quarters.[10]

---

8 There is a possibility that Moore's landmark solo was cut with an Ibanez Roadstar II RS530, as featured in the video for 'Out in the Fields'. However, Gary later confirmed using his white Hamer Special for much of the album. A 22-fret, Dimarzio pick-up/Floyd Rose tremolo fitted beast, the guitar was made especially for him by Hamer. Somewhat greedily, Moore had an identical model made by the company, this time in black.

9 A 'fretted, guitar-like MIDI controller' that used synthesisers to produce its sound, the SynthAxe was created in the early eighties by Bill Aitken, Mike Dixon and Tony Sedivy in a joint enterprise funded by Virgin boss Richard Branson. But the instrument was expensive to produce and complicated to play, and manufacture ceased with fewer than 100 units made.

10 An entirely new way to film the mechanics of guitar heroism, 'Axe-cam' was an extension of camera techniques developed by the American National Football League. Spotted by Moore's manager Steve Barnett and used to great effect in *Emerald Aisles* and the promo for 'Out in the Fields', 'Axe-Cam' might now be considered old-hat, but it still makes Gary's fingers appear as if they're on fire.

But perhaps the simplest, and certainly cheapest, innovation was Philip Lynott's idea for he and Moore to dress in red military hussar jackets, thus enhancing the themes of combat resonating throughout 'Out in the Fields'. 'Even though the song was written long before Philip got involved, it was his packaging of the whole thing that made it,' Moore later told author Mark Putterford. 'The uniforms we wore during [the video] and [while] promoting the single were his idea. He had a gift for marketing . . . a great sense of how to sell something to an audience.'

Lynott also provided a suitably war-soaked B-side for 'Out in the Fields' in the shape of the hard rock/soul hybrid 'Military Man'. Possibly the best tune he had penned while fronting Grand Slam, 'Military Man' conveyed all the power and pathos of vintage 'dark' Thin Lizzy, its unsettling lyric detailing the fear and disillusionment felt by a young recruit as he walks towards his fate. Though a fine companion piece to 'Out in the Fields', as with 'Got to Give It Up' some five years before, it was all too easy to ask whether Lynott was exploring his own doubts and anxieties here, those myriad references to an early, pointless death making 'Military Man' an even more perturbing listen.[11]

Backed by a lively round of TV and radio appearances throughout April/May of 1985, 'Out in the Fields' did what no Gary Moore single had done before and put him into the UK Top 5. It didn't stop there, either. At the same time Moore was enjoying the spoils of war in Blighty, it hit number three in Ireland while stalling just one place short of the top spot in both Sweden and Norway. An emphatic step forward in establishing Moore as a hard-rocking 'crossover success', Philip Lynott was also a beneficiary of 'Out in the Fields'. Having previously been unable to secure a deal for Grand Slam, Polydor Records now stepped forward with a firm solo offer for the Dubliner. It wasn't ideal: they wanted singles first, he wanted to record an album. But it was a start, and Lynott again began talking up overcoming his addictions to anyone who would

---

11 Moore and Lynott also cut a new version of 'Still in Love With You' at these sessions, which appeared as the B-side of some single versions of 'Out in the Fields'. Though nicely produced by Moore, and featuring yet another quite lovely solo, it still lacks the raw charm of the original.

listen. 'He said to me, "Gary, I'm going to kick this fucking drug habit,'" Moore later told the author Graeme Thomson, '"and I'm going to kick all the booze."' But not just yet, of course. Lynott had a wedding to attend.

According to the author Harry Shapiro, Kerry Booth moved down to London from her home in east Lincolnshire to pursue a modelling career in 1981, or thereabouts. A brutal industry at the best of times, assignments were hard to get and she initially had few contacts to draw on. However, Booth persisted and found both work and a new social circle that included drummer Paul Thompson's wife (and fellow model), Susan. While out at a nightclub, Booth was introduced to Gary Moore, who asked her for a date. At first, she was unsure. After all, there was a fair age gap to consider. Booth was not yet 21. Moore was in his early thirties. Yet, he was persistent and charming with it. Something clicked. The two began dating and Booth found herself moving into Moore's flat in south Hampstead.

Indeed, right from the off, Gary had been keen to bring his new partner right into the heart of his life, with Booth often seen accompanying him on tour, including those hit-or-miss US jaunts of 1983/4. There were rapid house moves to negotiate as well, the always restless musician upping sticks from leafy Hampstead to a brand-new nest for he and Booth in west London's swish Maida Vale. It wouldn't be long before they moved on from there too. Of course, there was the odd tiff. But even when Philip Lynott reportedly made a drunken pass at Kerry one evening at a party, the emotional fireworks that had accompanied several of Moore's previous relationships now seemed under control. 'Ah, Lynott often did that when he'd had a drink,' laughed a friend of the Thin Lizzy man, 'and it wasn't the first time he'd tried it on with one of Gary's partners either!' By late 1984, Moore and Booth were engaged. By July 1985, they were heading up the aisle.

Over the years, Gary Moore and Kerry Booth's wedding day has slipped into the realms of Lincolnshire legend, the service and party afterwards generating stories so improbable among the local population, they might well be true. Held at the quiet, quaint parish church in the village of North Thoresby, the setting for the couple's nuptials wasn't far from where Kerry's parents lived. It was also only eight miles north of Grimsby Town FC, a club managed at the time by Kerry's father (and ex-Barnsley defender) Tony Booth. Yet no matter how picturesque the surroundings, the site of an already refreshed and very late Philip Lynott running up the church path bedecked in black dress jacket, straw boater and ultra-tight striped jeans must have been priceless. 'He'd actually bought a bloody suit,' Moore later said of Lynott's choice to wear 'rock star pants' to the wedding, 'but you probably couldn't see his knob.'

The tall stories continued when bride, groom and guests set out for the reception at the Mill House in nearby Covenham. Here, Moore supposedly declined the landlord's offer of a disco and instead set up his own band to provide the musical entertainment at ear-shattering volume, an articulated lorry full of amps parked outside the venue just in case more decibels were required. While Lynott cracked on to the female guests and several elderly relatives ducked for cover, Moore's latest drummer, Gary Ferguson, made his live debut. Taking over from a departing Paul Thompson, Ferguson had cut his teeth with female vocal powerhouses such Shirley Bassey, Etta James and Cher before contributing to Moore's latest LP. Now, he was playing sixties classic rock tunes for an audience of aunts, uncles and some very sozzled musicians. Running on well into the night, the festivities continued until the Mill House ran out of beer and Gary ran out of tunes. After waving the happy couple off on their new life together, Philip Lynott powdered his nose one last time and then reportedly left with one of the bridesmaids. 'Phil had an aura,' laughed Scott Gorham. 'If you walked in a room with him, no one was looking at you. You know when they talk about the "it" thing? Well, Phil had "it".' Or perhaps it was just the trousers.

Two months after the newlyweds exchanged vows, it was time for Virgin to land 'the mothership' and release Moore's fifth solo album, the much-anticipated *Run for Cover*. Even Moore sounded nervous. 'Well, it's difficult for me to be objective [about my music] because I'm in front of the notes, so to speak,' he told *Guitarist* in September 1985. '[But] I'm putting as much into it as the [fans are] receiving, I hope!' Ultimately, *Run for Cover* proved a solid enough effort, and thankfully one that displayed little of the uphill struggle it had been to make. Still, with one or two possible exceptions, if fans already had 'Out in the Fields' and 'Empty Rooms' in their collection, there was little more to get really excited about.

On the upside, the more commercial side of Moore's nature was well presented, with the smooth AOR tones of 'Once in a Lifetime' and John Waite-style balladeering of 'Listen to Your Heartbeat' aimed squarely at the American market. No great surprise really: both tunes were produced by Mike Stone, the man who led Journey to multi-platinum sales with 1981's masterful *Escape*. In fact, Stone had been specifically brought in to give *Run for Cover* a final 'spit and polish' after Beau Hill, Andy Johns and Pete Collins concluded work on the LP. 'I thought it was good to have different producers for certain styles of songs,' Moore told *International Musician*. 'Andy Johns [was there] for the heavier stuff, Pete Collins was the obvious choice for the singles and I used Mike Stone for some of the softer songs [and a few remixes] because I still wanted to keep a bit of uniformity on the album.'

While Stone had done a bang-up job on balancing *Run for Cover*'s overall sound, some of the disc's contents sat awkwardly alongside each other, with future-facing pop-rock gems like 'Out in the Fields' and 'Once in a Lifetime' dragged down by the dull thud of 'Nothing to Lose' and 'All Messed Up'. By having Glenn Hughes and Philip Lynott tackle lead vocals on several tunes, Moore also risked diluting his own brand after three years of progress in front of the microphone. Still, when one heard that guitar sailing into the heavens on 'Reach for the Sky' or how brilliantly Gary had incorporated the whammy bar into his playing style on the album's rollicking title track, it was easy to forgive such backsliding.

Specifically designed to take Moore into the upper echelons of the charts worldwide, *Run for Cover*'s synth-friendly, cyber metal sheen almost did the job. Though only returning Moore to number twelve in the UK, a spot he had previously occupied with *Victims of the Future*, the new album enjoyed a much longer shelf life, eventually earning its creator a gold disc by the Christmas of 1985. As well as his usual strong showing in Scandinavia, Moore charmed central and western Europe, with Germany and Holland both inviting Moore into their Top 30. Yet, while New Zealanders were happy to purchase the album in the thousands, the USA once again spurned Moore's advances, rewarding his latest effort with an anaemic number 146 in the Billboard Top 200. Sure that 'Empty Rooms' and its parent album would finally unlock the door Stateside, Moore did little to disguise his disappointment. 'It's stupid to go where you're not wanted,' he bristled. As good as his word, Moore would avoid America completely for the next two years.

If the States didn't quite get what he was bringing to the party, then at least Moore could still rely on his British fans to break out the bunting when he came to town. This point was emphatically made in the autumn of 1985 when Gary struck out on the road in support of *Run for Cover*. As ever, he brought tight musical support with him, as now regular bassist Bob Daisley and new drummer Gary Ferguson held down the backbeat while Neil Carter continued to take care of keyboards, second guitar and backing vocals stage left. However, at Manchester Apollo on 23 September and Hammersmith Odeon fours day later, Moore's faithful were given an additional treat when Philip Lynott joined him on stage for a two-song encore of 'Out in the Fields' and 'Parisienne Walkways'.

At first, Lynott had cheekily suggested doing two or three tunes a night for the entire tour, but Moore was having none of it. 'No pressure, no hard work . . . but plenty of limelight,' he laughed. 'I knew what he was up to!' Perhaps, but Lynott was back on stage at Hammersmith for a second bite of the cherry on 28 September, strumming and singing alongside Moore like it was 1979 all over again. Yet, while Moore appeared fit and raring to go despite performing a near two-hour set, Lynott looked tired from the minute he stepped under the lights. The grin was still infectious and the trademark charm still in place, but his movements were heavier, slower and those sharp, dark eyes were now red-rimmed and bleary. Even those in the cheap seats could see this was not a well man.

Those two concerts at Hammersmith Odeon turned out to be one last hurrah for Philip Lynott, who died on Saturday, 4 January 1986. He had fallen ill a week or so earlier, his mother Philomena discovering him shivering and half-delirious at the house in Kew. Not knowing the severity of her son's addictions, she called Philip's estranged wife Caroline for help. At first, an overdose was suspected and Lynott was taken to

Clouds House drug clinic. But when it became apparent other issues were at play, he was transferred to Salisbury General Infirmary.

For a while, the former Thin Lizzy frontman appeared to rally, with tales told of Philip cracking jokes with family, friends and nursing staff. But matters soon worsened. Lynott had been diagnosed with septicaemia, a bacterial infection that plays havoc with the body's blood and essential organs. A strong immune system is key to fighting it, though his was already compromised not only by years of drug addiction and alcohol abuse, but an earlier bout of hepatitis some contend he had never truly recovered from.[12] Weak, tired and now terribly ill, Lynott developed pneumonia, heart and liver problems, after which there was no way back. Though it felt like he had been around forever, Philip Lynott was only 36 when he passed away. 'Philip got caught,' said his old friend Paul Scully. 'I was surprised that he did, but that's what happened. He just got caught up in it all.'

Moore was on holiday in Tenerife with his wife when they heard the news. '[Kerry] was reading the Sunday paper and gasped,' he later told writer Harry Doherty. 'I knew right away what had happened. It was so upsetting it took a couple of days before I could actually cry.' Unable to face returning home for the funeral on 9 January, Moore stayed on in Tenerife, but there was no escape from what had happened. 'I went out for a drink and they started playing our songs,' he told the *Belfast Telegraph*. 'Then a guy came up to me and said, "I'm sorry about Philip." Well, I went home that night and fucking let rip. It was terrible.'

As the years pass, Philip Lynott's death seems more and more inevitable. The drink, the drugs, the countless little injuries sustained in a life lived at full pelt. Indeed, by his own admission, when 'Mr Thin Lizzy' had boarded the rock'n'roll train in 1970, he had no intention of ever getting off again. 'I was tired of hearing rock'n'roll stars saying how sorry they

---

12 Chalkie Davies tells of looking through some photos he had taken of Philip circa 1979 and thinking they had been damaged. 'Philip looked yellow,' he said. But on closer inspection, Davies found nothing wrong with the prints, leading him to believe Lynott might still be suffering the effects of hepatitis three years after he was first hospitalised with the condition. Several others believe Lynott never really recovered from it.

were for themselves, how they disliked fame,' Lynott once told an interviewer. 'Me, I jumped at it. I thought, "Great." The women were after me, people wanted to buy me drinks. I really went for it, hook, line and sinker.' Still, for Moore, who walked out of Thin Lizzy at the start of his friend's unravelling, there was always more to Philip Lynott than fame, women, pills and booze. In fact, behind all that chest-beating machismo, a songwriter of some genius and no little sensitivity had been hard at work. 'Philip was one of the first people to really bring that poetic, romantic Celtic style to rock music. He deserves great credit for that.' And Gary Moore was going to make damn sure Lynott got it.

CHAPTER NINETEEN

Black Rose (Slight Return)

As inevitable as Philip Lynott's tragic passing in January 1986 might have been, it still caused shockwaves among the rock music community. Though his recent troubles were something of an open secret, Thin Lizzy's frontman had remained a much-loved figure, and in some minds at least, an indestructible one. 'A lot of people thought Philip was fucking bulletproof,' said Scott Gorham. And for a time, he was. Like so many of his generation, Lynott's early experiences with drugs and drink appeared to be 'all promise and no threat'.[1] Then came Paris, *Black Rose* and delight slowly turned to delirium. 'Philip got caught,' his friend Paul Scully had said. Sadly, no one was able to free Philip Lynott.

One man who had tried reaching out a hand was Gary Moore. Briefly restoring Lynott to his rightful place near the top of the charts with 'Out in the Fields', Moore even brought his former bandmate home with him, the pair walking old roads together around Belfast and Dublin during the winter of 1984. In the end, it wasn't enough to turn the tide. But the friendship between Moore and Lynott had been re-established,

---

1   The phrase 'All promise and no threat' was coined by author Paul Du Noyer in an article he wrote about The Beatles for *Mojo* in September 2020. Said article can be found on Du Noyer's own website and is well worth a read.

and Gary was soon back in the city on the Liffey to honour it once again, this time for a charitable cause.

When Moore had lived in Dublin during the late sixties, Ireland was experiencing a rare period of economic growth, with prospects apparently at their best since gaining independence from the UK some 40 years before. It proved a false dawn. Strikes, bad loans and inflation soon put the country back in the financial doghouse, and by the early eighties, the Republic of Ireland had taken on the unenviable mantle of the sick man of Europe. With unemployment sky high and youth again leaving for foreign climes in their thousands, something needed to be done. Inspired by the success of 1985's Live Aid, a combination of media and union-affiliated figures pulled together Self Aid.[2] The brief was simplicity itself. Organise a benefit concert for the country's unemployed, transmit it live on Irish TV while running a simultaneous telethon and raise millions for a job creation trust fund.

Staged at Dublin's RDS Arena on 17 May 1986 in front of 30,000 fans, Self Aid brought together the cream of Ireland's musical crop with Rory Gallagher, Christy Moore and U2 nestling alongside Auto Da Fé, Moving Hearts and Clannad, among many, many others.[3] Of course, one of the city's most famous sons was now sadly missing from the action, but he was far from forgotten. 'There's one man who would have loved to be on this stage tonight,' the compere Dave Fanning told the gathered crowd at the climax of the show. 'But in a way, I think he probably is. Ladies and gentlemen, here's Philip Lynott's band, Thin Lizzy!' Upon which Scott Gorham, Brian Downey, Darren Wharton and Gary Moore stepped into the spotlight for a three-song reunion of sorts. Taking lead vocals, Moore led the group (with Bob Daisley on bass) through a sprightly 'Don't Believe a Word' before 'King Rat' – and the man behind Live Aid – Bob Geldof emerged from the wings to growl his way through 'Cowboy Song'. After that, everyone and their dog joined Lizzy on stage

2 Self Aid was founded by RTE producer Niall Mathews and his colleague Tony Bolland. Jim Aiken promoted the concert.
3 In addition to homegrown acts (including a solo spot from Skid Row's Brush Shiels), Belfast's Van Morrison and 'English-born, but Irish parents' performers such as Elvis Costello and Chris Rea also did their bit.

for a show-closing, floorboard-creaking, very lively rendition of 'Whiskey in the Jar'. As grand finales went, it wasn't the worst.

Even if Ireland's financial recovery was still years ahead, Self Aid was a success at the time, the event generating millions of pounds in donations and more than 1,000 concrete job pledges. For Gary Moore, the concert was also a largely positive experience. 'It became clear to me how much talent cities like Dublin and Belfast have produced,' he said, before adding, 'It really made me want to remember the music I'd grown up with.' Even so, there were one or two complexities to negotiate. Though Moore did a creditable enough job fronting Thin Lizzy on the night, certain members of the band and management were still smarting from the guitarist's abrupt departure seven years before. Hence, while it was all smiles for the crowd, behind the scenes the atmosphere was formal rather than friendly. Still, in the light of recent events, a now heroin-free Scott Gorham[4] was beginning to see Moore's actions of July 1979 in a slightly different light. 'Gary didn't do drugs,' the Californian later said. 'He thought heroin was a never-ending downwards spiral. And in the end, he was proven right. So, you've got to give it to him on that one.'

Offering not only the opportunity to lend his talents to a good cause, but also publicly acknowledge the loss of an old friend, Self Aid provided Gary Moore with one more benefit: a much-needed excuse to blow away a few cobwebs on stage after months of work on his new studio album. In fact, Moore had either been talking about or recording demos for his sixth solo disc since the start of the year. As usual, he was full of ideas. Having bonded with drum machines on *Run for Cover*, he now bought one of his own, using it to develop songs at home on an eight-track recorder. 'Programming drums and being able to trigger samples,'

---

4 A year before Philip Lynott's death, Gorham managed to kick his heroin habit using Dr Meg Patterson's 'black box' method. He then tried persuading Lynott to follow suit. 'I turned up at his house after taking the cure . . . and I'm glowing with health,' Gorham said in 2020. 'So, I'm telling Philip, and he's like, "Yeah, I can do it." But I knew there was no way. You see, Philip couldn't ask for help because that was a sign of weakness, and being strong was his whole thing. That whole alpha male shit. He was 36 years old when he died; 36 fucking years old. And it's such a shame because he could have been here now, and you'd be talking to him and not me!"

Moore explained to *Metal Rendezvous*. 'Well, it helps me get everything [closer] to the way I originally envisioned it."

When finally ready to make the leap from living room to studio, Gary enlisted the help of former Re-Flex drummer Roland Kerridge to transfer his original loops and beats to the new-fangled Linn 9000. Then the most advanced drum machine of its kind, the Linn would allow Moore total control of timekeeping as well as thousands of thunderous rhythms at the push of a button. 'I used to give drummers such a hard time in the studio,' he once said. Now, if he chose, he didn't have to use them at all.

If Moore had turned a corner when it came to hi-hats, cymbals and snares, getting the right producer on board for his new project still remained of vital importance. As ever, he had several favourites in mind, including the then white-hot Keith Forsey. A former percussionist, native Londoner Forsey had recently co-written or produced a series of multi-platinum sellers, including Irene Cara's 'Flashdance . . . What A Feeling', Simple Minds' 'Don't You (Forget About Me)' and crucially for Moore, Billy Idol's 1983 mega-selling album *Rebel Yell*. Combining pop metal smarts, cleverly programmed drums and the post-modern musings of lead guitarist Steve Stevens (one of the few guitarists capable of giving Moore a run for his money), *Rebel Yell* was precisely the type of future-facing album Moore was keen to make.

Yet, while *Rebel Yell* remained a major influence on the overall sound of Moore's next LP, he could not secure Forsey's services because of scheduling conflicts. Hence, a mad scramble for a suitable replacement began, with names as disparate as Steve 'U2' Lillywhite and Bill 'Rick Springfield' Drescher both under consideration. Ultimately, it would take three seasoned studio boffins to help Moore get his album up and running. Pete Smith, then basking in the success of Sting's million-selling *Dream of the Blue Turtles*, was first to arrive behind the production desk, beginning work on two tunes before James 'Jimbo' Barton took up arms for three more. Barton had already aided Gary on *Run for Cover*, so it made perfect sense that Pete 'Empty Rooms' Collins was also drafted in, his ability to turn loud guitars, advanced technology and emotive choruses into hit singles/albums an already established cornerstone in Moore's musical plan.

'I think rock bands have got to learn to move forward with their·
production, otherwise it's just going to go down the drain,' he told
International Musician. 'A lot of these heavy bands are just playing the
same way they did 10 years ago, and they're approaching the studio the
same. Until they go into the studio with a Mutt Lange or a Peter Collins,
or someone known for modern production, they won't be converted to
it. I was the same until I started working with Peter. I wasn't convinced
about using drum machines or click tracks and sampling. But now,' he
concluded, 'I'm totally sure that's the only way to do it.'

Perhaps so, but albums using such cutting-edge techniques cost proper
money to make, and Moore went back on the road to secure more of
it. Hitting the always lucrative summer festival circuit throughout June
and July of 1986, Gary and co. traipsed across Italy, Germany and England,
where the quartet appeared second on the bill to Genesis-loving prog-
revivalists Marillion at Milton Keynes Bowl on 28 June. Using the event
to trial several new songs, Moore also marked his appearance at central
England's biggest garden party by wearing a then very fashionable ankle
length linen coat, though it was soon discarded as temperature levels on
stage began to soar.

While in Sweden, Gary again found himself battling raised tempera-
tures when providing support for old mates Queen at Stockholm's
Råsunda Stadion. Since their barnstorming set at Live Aid a year earlier,
Freddie Mercury's quartet had all but become national treasures in the
UK. But the band's (deeply questionable) 1984 decision to appear at
South Africa's Sun City entertainment complex during the apartheid
regime still rankled with certain journalists. In some eyes, Moore's decision to now play alongside Queen made him guilty by association. Gary
was in no mood for any such guff. 'One listen to [the lyrics] of . . . 'Out
in the Fields', and you'll know how I feel about the whole South African
situation,' he curtly informed *Kerrang*, before adding, 'I wouldn't play
Sun City, but I will play Stockholm.' The concert passed without incident.

With his year neatly divided by Self Aid and those festival dates, Moore
returned to London's Marcus and Townhouse studios in the autumn of
1986 to complete work on the album, taking various producers, Neil Carter,
Bob Daisley and Linn programmer Roland Kerridge with him. One band

member who would not be coming back was drummer Gary Ferguson. Essentially redundant following Moore's choice to use digital percussion for the record, Ferguson had honoured his live obligations during the summer, before bowing out in the direction of session work soon after. 'Gary Ferguson was a great player and I think probably Gary's favourite of [all his] drummers,' Neil Carter later told rock journalist, Arend. Unfortunately, Moore's obsession with obtaining 'perfect time' meant saying au revoir to yet another sticksman.[5] There would be more goodbyes in due course.

Still, when lead-off single 'Over the Hills and Far Away' barged its way onto the nation's airwaves one could understand the method behind Moore's madness concerning the use of electronic percussion. Rumbling into earshot with an intense cannonade of digital snares and synthetic tom toms, the song's opening bars immediately put listeners on the front foot before the guitars really started flying.

Released in December 1986, 'Over the Hills and Far Away' was a prime slice of Celtic pop rock and as good an advert for Gary Moore's forthcoming album as one might hope to find. The tale of a man wrongly condemned to prison for theft – but unable to escape his fate without revealing he was in bed with his best friend's wife on the night in question[6], 'Over the Hills and Far Away' was originally conceived as a duet with Philip Lynott. Yet, Lynott's sad passing put paid to that idea, leaving Moore to tackle the song's storyline alone. That said, he did seek musical help elsewhere. Enlisting Ireland's premier instrumental folk band, The Chieftains[7], to bolster the song's distinctly Thin Lizzy-like riff, Moore's central guitar lines were soon aligned to the rousing sounds of tin whistles, fiddles, Uilleann pipes and bodhráns.

---

5 While Moore was committed to working with electronic drums on his new album, producer Peter Collins did bring in session drummer Charlie Morgan to help out on certain arrangements.

6 Moore may well have gained some lyrical inspiration from Danny Dill and Marijohn Wilkin's 1959 country tune 'Long Black Veil', which tells a similar story.

7 Formed in Dublin in 1962, The Chieftains' take on traditional music made them not only Ireland's pre-eminent instrumental folk group, but also a huge hit abroad. Led by Paddy Moloney until his death in 2021, The Chieftains were even given the honorary title 'Éire's Musical Ambassadors' by the Irish government for their work in popularising Celtic folk around the globe. Like Gary Moore, the group also appeared at Self Aid in May 1986.

An altogether glorious racket, the arrangement was overseen by a visiting Don Airey. 'God, they were funny, The Chieftains and Gary,' the keyboardist said of Moore's rock/folk interface. 'All the Irish getting together like that . . .' Funny and profitable. One of Gary's better singles, 'Over the Hills and Far Away' made it to number twenty in the UK, while also scoring Top 10 placings in Sweden, Norway, Finland and Ireland, where a memorable TV appearance on *The Gay Byrne Show* saw Moore, his band and The Chieftains hammering out the song's spinning riff at top volume to an audience of largely middle-aged (and rather amused-looking) Dubliners.

Within two months of 'Over the Hills and Far Away' charting, Virgin (via its '10' records imprint) delivered Gary Moore's sixth album. The cover presented our hero standing on a hilltop staring moodily into camera, his chest hair spilling out from beneath the buckskin collar of a fringed, Davy Crockett-style jacket. Held in Moore's clenched fists was a beautiful blonde Gibson L5, the very guitar he had purchased from Greg Lake seven years before, while in the background, a woman dressed head to toe in nineteenth-century, traditional Irish mourning-wear surveyed the fields below. God alone knows what it was all meant to mean, but John Swannell and Bill Smith's cleverly doctored sleeve design certainly captured the LP's title. 'Welcome,' chuckled one of Moore's friends, 'to the *Wild Frontier* . . .'

Popularly regarded as Moore's finest solo disc of the eighties, *Wild Frontier* ably blended Moore's love of classic rock, pure pop and Celtic folk while also maintaining his commitment to contemporary production techniques. As importantly, it also acted as a fitting homage to Moore's friendship with Philip Lynott, at least four tracks directly influenced by or paying tribute to the fallen Thin Lizzy man. 'Having gone back to Ireland [in 1984 and 1986], I decided to go back to my musical roots,' said Moore of *Wild Frontier*'s musical genesis, 'and Philip's death also inspired me to write in a very Celtic tradition. In a way,' he concluded, 'I see the whole album as a tribute to Philip.'

While Moore might have seen *Wild Frontier* as a eulogy of sorts to Lynott, there were four more tunes on the LP where it was harder to see an immediate join. 'Take a Little Time' could well have been a paean to the work of Billy Idol, its scuttling beat, whooped vocals and whizz-wheels solo instantly recalling the peroxide rocker's then recent best seller 'Rebel Yell'. 'Strangers in the Darkness' too, was an exercise in bang–up-to-date moody pop, with Moore and co-writer Neil Carter's story of lost youth falling between the cracks tying into the homelessness crisis then sweeping Great Britain. 'It tells the story of people who visit the promised city of London and are seduced into addiction,' Gary confirmed to *Guitar World* at the time. 'Some even turn to prostitution to support their habits.'

In comparison, Moore's cover of Australian garage rockers The Easybeats' 1966 classic 'Friday On My Mind' was lighter in touch, though still specifically designed to knock on the door of the pop charts. 'It's one of those songs I grew up listening to,' he said of the tune. '[But] I don't think there's much point doing a cover version unless you take it somewhere else.' Previously tackled by performers as disparate as The Shadows, David Bowie and the wonderfully weird Blue Oyster Cult, Moore's take on 'Friday On My Mind' remained in thrall to the original's 'live for the weekend' vibe, but with some clever additions. Aside from turning the guitars up to ten and peppering the tune with samples, Moore also threw a (faux) sitar in the works – the first time he had dabbled with the Indian stringed instrument since experimenting with a real one at Slattery's basement bar in sixties Dublin. 'Did Gary play sitar with us at Slattery's?' laughed Dr Strangely Strange's Tim Booth. 'Now I think about it, he probably did. I mean, we'd do anything down there.'

True or not, the sitar seemed to do the trick, as 'Friday On My Mind' popped into the UK Top 30 when released as a single in May 1987. Just as importantly, the song's authors also loved it. 'I spoke to Harry Vanda and George Young of The Easybeats about [musicians] covering their songs,' said rock critic Glenn A. Baker. 'I mean, Bowie had recorded 'Friday On My Mind'. But Harry said, "No, Gary Moore's [version] was the one'. He loved that version. So, when you can cover the great Australian working-class anthem to the satisfaction of the man who wrote it, you've done very, very well." As a reward, the Aussies (and New Zealanders) pushed Moore's cover high into their own charts, giving him his first real hit in the Antipodes outside Thin Lizzy's *Black Rose* for nearly a decade.

If 'Friday On My Mind' was a shout out to the music of Moore's youth, then 'The Loner' was an eight-fingered salute to 'the guitarist's guitar hero, Mr Jeff Beck'. Composed by Beck's Fender Rhodes-wielding keyboardist Max Middleton[8] as a sly nod to his then boss's musical style, 'The Loner' first appeared on drummer Cozy Powell's debut solo LP, 1979's *Over the Top*. A crotchety little instrumental full of unexpected twists and turns (a bit like Jeff himself), it was former Colosseum/Humble Pie guitarist David 'Clem' Clempson's job to bring Middleton's notes to life, and a bang-up job he did of it. So much so, that when Moore – who was also working on Powell's LP at the time – heard Clemson's 'mean as a snake' take on 'The Loner,' he regretted not persuading Middleton and Powell to let him have a crack at it too.

By 1986, Moore was ready for his turn. Once described as 'a squirrely theme tune to a downbeat detective series', Moore had transformed 'The Loner' into something much less menacing and considerably more grandiose, albeit at some cost. In fact, cutting the track proved 'a huge struggle between guitar and keyboards', as Moore, producer Peter Collins and Fairlight King Andy Richards fought to get the right balance between technical virtuosity and real emotion. '[The drum and bass sounds were created] on Andy's Fairlight . . . [with] guitar and violins laid over,' Moore later told *Guitar World*. 'That combination of natural instruments stirring up the emotions and more cold-sounding technology fascinates me.' For Richards, however, Moore's ability to summon the four winds with six strings was always going to win the day. 'Gary had such an attack, such a presence on guitar,' Richards remembered in 2020, 'that when he started to play, he just took you with him.'

Substantially re-working its middle eight to make the track better fit his signature style (and possibly get a writing credit in the process), Gary Moore's version of 'The Loner' didn't lack for power or conviction, the

---

8   A superbly talented player and genuinely lovely bloke too, Max Middleton brought class and chops to Beck's recorded output throughout the seventies, while also contributing several classic tunes, including 'Led Boots', 'Freeway Jam' and the glorious jazzy chords that frame 'Scatterbrain'.

Belfast man sustaining notes on the neck of his new Jackson Soloist guitar for what seemed like days. Obviously, his approach worked, as the slow-burning tune soon became an in-concert favourite among fans, with Moore often devoting 15 minutes or more of his set to it. But whether, as some believe, 'The Loner' actually lost something in its elevation from gnarly jazz oddity to rock's big league remains questionable. Moore didn't care either way. He was just happy to talk about the man who inspired it. 'Jeff is the only guitarist who can be flash, emotional…and dead subtle,' Gary had once said and many might agree. 'Jeff's beautiful. He's got so much control and he doesn't slog himself to death on the road. That's helped keep him fresh while also building [up his] mystique over the years. Jeff doesn't make an album until he's ready – or until he needs new parts for his car!'

Just as he had back in 1965, Gary Moore still loved Jeff Beck. But as he continued to intimate, *Wild Frontier* was first and foremost both tribute and eulogy to his friend Philip Lynott, and the album's remaining tracks confirmed it. Like 'Over the Hills and Far Away', Gary and Neil Carter's 'Thunder Rising' was another Lynott-inspired mini-epic in the vein of 'Emerald' and 'Massacre', its rattling electronic drums and scurrying, angry guitars perfectly complementing the song's title. Moore's lyrics were also full of mighty battles and fallen kings, his recent reading of an old Irish history book seeing him delve into the same mythology that helped inform Lynott's wordplay on 'Black Rose: A Rock Legend'. Keeping the tempo fast and the solos faster, 'Thunder Rising' sounded like it had fallen off the track listing of a long-lost Thin Lizzy LP. 'Well, Philip always said, "Try everything fast",' Moore confirmed at the time. 'He always thought fast songs were harder to write and he was right about that. He tried everything fast, even if it had a bluesy lyric.'

Following in the wake of the double-bass drum-assisted climax on Thunder Rising (all electronically rendered, of course), album closer 'Johnny Boy' was a much slower, even regal proposition. Written shortly after the death of Lynott in the style of a traditional Irish air, 'Johnny Boy' was all restraint both vocally and musically, with acoustic rather than electric instruments now taking the song's sad tale to its mournful, sun-setting conclusion. Moore summed 'Johnny Boy[9] up thus. 'It's very Celtic that tune, and it has a lot of memories [in the lyrics] of those early days with Philip and Skid Row [for me].'

Ultimately, it was left to *Wild Frontier*'s title track itself to truly bookend Moore's friendship with Philip Lynott. Inspired by his return to Belfast alongside Lynott in late 1984, 'Wild Frontier' was again a Celtic rock treat, its huge, melancholy riff setting the scene perfectly for Moore to tell of a city seemingly at war with itself.[10] 'It's a pretty political song,' he confirmed to *Guitar World*. 'It describes the fate of anyone who grew up in Belfast and returns to it after many years. It's shocking how much the city has changed.' It was also a song that directly addressed the loss of a man he had known for nearly 20 years.

'I could really hear Philip singing 'Wild Frontier',' he later said. 'You know, it's extraordinarily difficult to find a partner with whom the musical chemistry is so right as it was with him. That kind of thing doesn't happen twice.'

A strong collection of tunes exploring themes of friendship, loss, history and even hope, *Wild Frontier* at last presented Gary Moore as a mature artist confidently placed between the worlds of rock and pop. Mind you, it had taken some effort. To get the album to the standard he envisioned, Moore and his fellow musicians worked and reworked tunes within an inch of their life, not letting go until 'everything was exactly spot on'. In this, they were abetted by producers Pete Smith, Jimbo Barton and most especially Peter Collins, who pushed Moore's vocals to the absolute limit. Getting his charge to sing in a more pop-like way, Collins even

---

9 Irish folk troubadour Christy Moore covered 'Johnny Boy' on his 2021 album *Flying Into Mystery*, while 20 years earlier, Finnish symphonic metallers Nightwish cut a thunderous version of 'Over the Hills and Far Away'. For those seeking something a little more novel, Patty Gurdy's recent hurdy-gurdy driven take on 'Over the Hills and Far Away' might be worth a listen, though Japanese guitarist Shinji Tagawa's mega-emotional in-concert rendition of 'The Loner' (filmed in Tokyo during 2017) really is the bee's knees.

10 In a TV interview with Sky's Amanda Redington shortly before 1986's Self Aid, Moore revealed plans to record 'Wild Frontier' with Thin Lizzy's Scott Gorham and Brian Downey. For one reason or another, it didn't happen.

had Moore change song keys to create a more dramatic effect. Moore might have hated it, but the results were impressive. More surprisingly, Moore's guitar performances were also reined in, with solos shorter and more melodic, and less emphasis placed on obvious showmanship. Of course, Gary being Gary, there was still much blazing to be done, those liquid excursions on 'Take a Little Time' and 'Thunder Rising' coming immediately to mind. But as 'The Loner' showed, restraint was being observed here in pursuit of the greater good.

The gamble paid off. Released in March 1987, *Wild Frontier* barged into the charts across Scandinavia and Europe, taking Moore to number one in Finland and Norway, number two in Sweden and Spain, while scoring Top 20 placings in Austria, Switzerland, Germany and Holland. Closer to home, Moore reaped equal profit from his endeavours, the album almost taking the top spot in Ireland while landing at a very impressive number eight in the UK. These were big numbers and Moore was justly proud of them, even if he professed not to know exactly how he had managed it. 'Honestly, I don't think you can really sit down and deliberately write a hit song,' Moore confessed. 'It's down to the people to make it a hit song. That's their job, really.'

With a best-selling LP on his hands, Moore wasted no time taking his new songs on the road. It was to be quite the jaunt too as the guitarist had to avoid the UK for 10 months (or thereabouts) lest he face a huge bill from the Inland Revenue. Moore called the enforced detour 'a right pain in the arse,' but if handled right, the earnings made from record sales and concert receipts would set him up for life. As was the case with just about every tour Moore had undertaken, there was also another recruit to blood. Having lost Gary Ferguson when he decided to embrace electronic percussion making *Wild Frontier*, Moore was now a man down behind the kit. And while one suspects he might secretly have preferred bringing his beloved Linn drum along with him, the prospect of a small rectangular box placed where Ian Paice, Mark Nauseef or Simon Phillips once parked their posteriors was frankly ludicrous. It was time to bring in a human.

At first, Moore almost offered the job to Zak Starkey, the 21-year-old Londoner then showing the first real signs of following in his father Beatle Ringo Starr's illustrious footsteps. But when bassist Bob Daisley suggested Eric Singer, with whom he recently worked on Black Sabbath's 1986 LP *The Eternal Idol*, Moore's interest was piqued. A huge fan of John Bonham and Queen's Roger Taylor, Ohio-born Singer had already drawn praise while touring with rock/metal guitarist Lita Ford before making an unholy racket as part of Sabbath. The possessor of formidable chops, and crucially for Moore, metronome-like in his technique, Singer was potentially quite a catch and quickly called to audition. Within hours, he had the job. 'The one thing that always stood out for me was Gary's passion and intensity as a guitarist,' Singer later said. 'He played every note, every song like it was the last time he would play it. And while I admit he could be a bit tough on drummers, he only asked and expected [in return] what he gave to the music.'

Now with a full set of musicians in tow, Gary Moore arrived at Edinburgh Playhouse for concert number one in late March 1987 and was still entertaining crowds in Dortmund, Germany on 6 November, some 70 dates later. From Spain, Portugal and France to Japan, Belgium and Denmark, Moore played the lot. 'That whole 1985-1987 period was very exciting,' Moore's onstage lieutenant Neil Carter later confirmed on his website. 'Things were becoming successful and the band nucleus . . . was really solid.' So solid, in fact, that after ignoring the territory since 1984, Gary decided to return to the United States for another bite at the cherry.

There was to be no hero's welcome. Long used to appearing in arenas and concert halls with his name in lights outside, Moore now found himself back in many of the same-sized clubs he had visited three years before. That said, those who did manage to see him on his 28-date trawl across the USA were unlikely to forget it in a hurry. 'I saw Gary live . . . in [the summer of] 1987, during the era of 'the big hair' and he was just really fiery,' future guitar god Paul Gilbert later told *Brave Worlds*. 'Gary was . . . strong, masculine and really street! Even in a cape and goofy hair. You wouldn't want to mess with Gary Moore in an alley.'

In fact, as Moore's latest US expedition progressed, a breakthrough finally looked possible when 'Over the Hills and Far Away' elbowed its way into the *Billboard* Top 30. But then parent album *Wild Frontier* stalled at number 139, and any momentum was lost. Despite certain critics, various radio stations and a plethora of guitar/hard rock magazines championing his cause, Moore still remained a cult figure in America. For some, that would be enough. But Moore saw 'cult' as just another word for 'failure'. A stubborn sort of fellow, he would try yet again in due course.

If lack of success in the States felt like punch to his gut, at least Moore could take heart from the fact he had made considerable inroads elsewhere, as silver and gold discs continued to roll in from the UK, Japan, Europe and Scandinavia throughout 1987. Beyond the commercial and critical acclaim he received for *Wild Frontier*, he had even scored his first UK number one, albeit as part of a larger, charitable concern. Lending those famous fingers to a cover of The Beatles' 'Let it Be', Moore joined performers as varied as Paul McCartney, Kate Bush, Boy George and Edwin Starr to raise proceeds for families affected by the Zeebrugge ferry disaster of March 1987. With Dire Straits guitar legend Mark Knopfler providing the tune's softer solo passages, Moore was deployed to 'bring the rock,' his brief, but spectacular whammy bar-driven outburst cleansing the palette before an all-star chorus[11] sang 'Let it Be' home. Topping the British charts for three weeks and raising a fine sum for a good cause, Ferry Aid was yet another example of Moore's newfound position as 'the heavy metal guitar god' it was OK for pop fans to like too.

Yet, while he was more than happy to contribute on this occasion, behind the scenes Moore was beginning to have trouble with what being a 'heavy metal guitar god' actually meant. Having just honoured the memory of Philip Lynott and sold half a million records in the process, one might have thought this was a time to celebrate his victories rather than dwell on lazy artistic definitions. But the demons that had caused Moore to repeatedly change musical tack during the seventies were on

---

11 In addition to Moore, McCartney et al., a huge (and often surreal) supporting cast turned out to sing the iconic chorus of 'Let it Be', including members of Squeeze, Go West, Frankie Goes to Hollywood and Sham 69, as well as TV personalities, comedians and Page Three Girls. Moore only had eyes for Mark Knopfler. 'He's out there on his own,' enthused Moore, 'almost like an eighties Hank Marvin or Peter Green.'

the rise again and no amount of shiny gold discs or critical back-slapping seemed capable of keeping them at bay. 'I don't know,' Moore later told Q. 'The labels "Hard Rocker" or "Heavy Metal" just really began to get on my nerves. I felt like I wanted to break those chains.' The obvious questions, of course, were how and when he was going to do it.

CHAPTER TWENTY

Consider Me Gone

Even if he was becoming slowly allergic to his music being called 'hard rock' or (don't even say it) 'heavy metal', Gary Moore still had a hell of a 1987. Scoring a hit album, three hit singles, a number one charity record and a 73-date world tour playing to more than 100,000 thousand fans within the space of 12 months was impressive by anyone's standards. As usual, Moore avoided revelling in too much self-praise. Instead, he was busy planning his next, somewhat surprising move. 'Really, I should go into the studio with Tina Turner,' Moore said when asked 'where next?' 'But unfortunately, up to now something has always come between us. Still, the idea of making another record with someone else excites me.'

On this occasion, the excitement of teaming up with Turner would have to wait, as Moore finally caught up with life outside the recording studio. Like many a jobbing rock star before him, he had made the decision to move out of London soon after getting married, setting up a plush new home 40 miles west of the capital in Shiplake, near Henley-on-Thames. 'I said to myself, "When a tour is over, you should really finish it and get away",' he told journalists Harold Mac Wonderlea and Christine Rebmann. 'When you're living in London, the show just goes on. Now, my nearest neighbour is so far away I can really make a lot of noise and no one will complain!'

Joining Gary and wife Kerry among all the amplifiers was their newborn son, Jack Moore. In a manner of speaking, Jack had been on tour for several weeks before making an official debut, with his heavily pregnant mother accompanying Moore across the USA for a string of concert dates throughout the late summer. However, Kerry was long home by the time Jack arrived on 12 October 1987. Destined to be an eerily handsome composite of his respective parents, young Jack would eventually gravitate towards the tools of his father's trade, though it was a while yet before he picked up that first guitar.

Another addition to Moore's extended family around this time was former backline manager at John Henry's professional music services, Graham Lilley. Joining a retinue that already included Steve Barnett and Stewart Young at Part Rock, long-time business advisor Colin Newman and trusted guitar tech Keith Page, Lilley was the latest in line tasked with helping support Gary Moore's overall affairs. Over subsequent years, he would move from dealing with Moore's favourite axes and managing the stage to the position of media production director, and ultimately, close friend. 'Back in the seventies, Gary wasn't quite ready to be a group leader,' said Moore's former bandmate Neil Murray. 'He was still youthful . . . and needed figures like Jon Hiseman to mentor him.' Not anymore. By 1988, Moore had graduated from scruffy guitar hero-in-training to CEO of an ever-growing musical empire, and the likes of Graham Lilley were vital to make sure it ran as smoothly as possible.

While Moore's life was now defined as much by the responsibilities of commerce and fatherhood as it was by music, it would still take a well-aimed shot from an elephant gun to stop him playing guitar. Even with his band on sabbatical while he worked out his next move, he couldn't help himself, with any spare minute in the diary given to guest starring on someone's else's tune. Over recent years, Moore had already appeared on records as diverse and improbable as a 12" mix of Frankie Goes to Hollywood's 'Warriors of the Wasteland' (cut with producer Trevor Horn at Sarm East) and The Beach Boys self-titled 25th anniversary LP, on which he added a blast or two of the short-lived SynthAxe.

Elsewhere, there was some brief, but surprisingly good link-up play with Japanese rock/pop singer Minako Honda on the 1985 single 'Cancel'[1], and he also laid down a nifty lick or two for former Manfred Mann vocalist Chris Thompson's disc *Out of the Night*. Indeed, Moore even managed to reactivate his musical friendship with Johnny Duhan, providing several crisp lines for the Dubliner's latest album, *Oceans in Motion*. 'Oh, you heard that,' Duhan laughed in 2020. 'Yeah, it was great of Gary to do that record.'

Come 1988 and Moore was at it yet again. First up was his contribution to bassist Mo Foster's quite beautiful 'The Light in Your Eyes', with Moore's solo fair flying across the composition. A chance for the pair to work together for the first time since 1983's *Victims of the Future*, 'The Light in Your Eyes' and the more rocking 'Pump II' (on which Moore also provided a solo) soon turned up on Foster's 1989 LP *Bel Assis*. 'He was such a lovely guy, Gary,' Mo later told *Bass Player*. 'I remember doing a couple of charity shows where [guitarist] Ray Russell and . . . I had invited him to join us as a guest. I composed a fun announcement for him, saying to the audience, "Would you please welcome a dear friend of ours, and one of the finest guitarists in his price bracket."' After another lovely 12-bar flight around singer Vicki Brown's gentle 'If I Thought[2], Moore finished his latest round of guest spots at Sarm East Studios where he added a little fire and ice to Don Airey's debut solo disc *K2: Tales of Triumph and Tragedy*. His former Colosseum II colleague would pay the favour back within a year.

A part-time passion of Moore's, playing on other people's records not only gave him a chance to blow off steam but also avoid the more onerous demands associated with his own solo career. Still, with Virgin Records

---

1 Obviously a fan of Gary's, Honda also recorded a version of 'Crying in the Shadows', the B-side of 'Over the Hills and Far Away' as a single in October 1986. Re-titled 'The Cross (Ai No Jujika)', Moore contributed a fine solo to the recording, which went to number five in the Japanese charts.

2 A superb pop, rock and classical all-rounder, Vicki Brown had been on the music scene since the early seventies, working with bands, duos, as a solo artist and renowned backing vocalist. Married to English songwriter/guitarist Joe Brown – whose rhythm playing Moore admired greatly as a child – Brown sadly died two years after Gary appeared on her 1989 album *Lady of Time*.

seeking a new LP and an expanding business model to maintain, Moore couldn't hide in sessions forever. Tina Turner would have to wait.[3] Hence, in the early spring of 1988, Moore was back in Dublin on a songwriting sabbatical with bandmate Neil Carter. The reason for the duo's presence in Ireland (aside from Moore's ongoing tax situation) was to once again tap into the same Celtic spirit that had made *Wild Frontier* Moore's best seller yet.

By April 1988, tunes were written and Moore, Carter and prodigal bassist Bob Daisley, who had toured/recorded with both Ozzy Osbourne and Black Sabbath while Moore and Carter worked on songs, now moved their base of operations from Dublin to PUK Studios in Aarhus, Denmark. A musician-friendly space that had already played host to Elton John, George Michael and Depeche Mode, PUK's past life as a farmhouse belied the fact it was one of the most technologically advanced recording facilities in Europe. This fact alone surely delighted producer Peter Collins and keyboard whiz Andy Richards, who had once again been invited by Moore to join in the fun. Yet, unlike last time out, Moore had also extended an invitation to a drummer or two.

Moore's relationship with drummers was a complex one. As evidenced, several of them had come and gone at the drop of a (hi)-hat over recent years. Come late 1987, and Eric Singer was the latest to move on, throwing in his lot with new hard rock supergroup Badlands (and in due course, Kiss). But while Moore might have previously brushed off such a loss by again embracing Linn drums and Fairlight synthesisers, 1987's prolonged touring schedule seemed to re-activate a desire in him to use real people instead of computers. In fact, while writing in Dublin, Moore had asked former Thin Lizzy bandmate Brian Downey to consider joining his group. Not quite ready to return to the fray after the trials and tribulations of Thin Lizzy, Downey turned down the offer, at least for the time being.

With Brian Downey temporarily declining[4], Moore next called on Cozy Powell. A veteran of The Jeff Beck Group, Rainbow, Whitesnake, Michael

---

3   Frustratingly, Moore never recorded with Tina Turner, though his hero Jeff Beck did, providing two wonderful solos for her multi-platinum album, *Private Dancer*.

4   Though Downey declined Moore's offer of joining his group, the pair did record a new version of 'Emerald' together at around this time. It wasn't among either's best work.

Schenker Group and even a reconstituted ELP, Moore knew Powell well through guesting on several of his solo LPs. Then marketing himself as a 'gun-for-hire', Powell took little persuading to throw in his lot with Moore. On something of a roll, Moore also signed up 'human metronome' Charlie Morgan and 'session-man extraordinaire' Simon Phillips to provide assistance for the project too. Now in possession of power, precision and craft, Moore's woes in the drum department finally appeared behind him.

Unfortunately, the making of Moore's seventh solo album presented more problems than just drums and those hired to bash them. From the off, Moore seemed uncomfortable at PUK and reportedly soon removed their resident studio engineer from the project. He was replaced by Ian Taylor, then still fresh from working with Chicago pop-rockers Cheap Trick. An amiable, straightforward man with a fine ear for guitars and genuine love for warm analogue sounds (unusual at the time), Taylor hit it off immediately with Moore, the two cultivating a partnership destined to last many years.

Yet, while Moore and Taylor were busy forging new alliances, older associations were becoming occasionally bumpy. When recording 'Out in the Fields' and 'Empty Rooms', Moore had often deferred to Peter Collins' greater wisdom, the guitarist mindful of his producer's proven track record as a hitmaker. Now, however, Moore sought to exercise stronger control over the fate of his songs and guitar parts, and wasn't afraid to say so. 'Well, [by then,] Gary had a bit of an ego,' Andy Richards said in 2020. 'But no worries, I could live with that, and lest we forget, really, he was a nice guy. But I think by that record, Gary was more confident. He knew what he wanted and that might have started creating some small problems with Peter Collins. Still, it was nothing that couldn't be worked out.'

Perhaps the pressure of following up his best-selling LP thus far was getting to him. Perhaps that 'heavy metal' label he so detested was really beginning to bite. Whatever the case, Moore's deadly serious attitude to the task at hand followed him all the way back to London where work was finally completed on the record at AIR Studios. Here, Simon Phillips had hoped to take things up with Moore exactly where they had left off when they made 1978's *Back on the Streets*. But Moore was in no mood for joyous reunions. 'Hmm. Well, now,' laughed the drummer. 'To begin with, Gary wasn't actually there at the start. I was working with just Peter [Collins]. I also remember the sound wasn't great and the music was much more rock'n'roll sounding than *Back on the Streets*. But you know, [the tracks] were good and we finally got it done. Then Gary turned up. Now, I'd really been looking forward to seeing him. But he was very uncommunicative. I remembered him from the *Streets* . . . sessions, and he was like a kid [then], really friendly, lovely, you know. This time, I was like, "Wow. This really isn't the same Gary."'

Thankfully, Moore's new album wasn't quite as cheerless to listen to as it had sometimes been for him to make. But it was no great shakes, either. Released in January 1989, *After the War* found Moore once again flitting between musical themes, with the Celtic, hard rock and pop flavours that made *Wild Frontier* such an interesting collection all present and correct. Yet, unlike that LP, . . . *War* lacked for killer tunes, and served up several rather ordinary ones instead. Of course, Moore was far too committed to the cause to make a really bad record. But several times during *After the War*, his heart sounded elsewhere.

On the plus side, the album's title track rumbled along well enough, even if its resemblance to 1985's 'Out in the Fields' was a tad close for comfort. Still, Moore's obsession with nations turning their young into cannon fodder remained solidly in place, his lyrics more barbed than ever. Tied to Andy Richards' helicopter-aping Fairlight and with a suitably vexatious guitar solo, 'After the War' took Moore back into the Top 20 in Norway, Finland, Sweden and Ireland when released as a taster single for the forthcoming LP. But it stumbled in the UK at a disappointing number thirty-six, giving Moore a small taster of things to come.

Away from 'After the War', Moore's tribute to master blues guitarist Roy Buchanan, 'The Messiah Will Come Again', was a worthy addition to his distinguished catalogue of instrumentals. Recorded shortly after 48-year-old Buchanan took his own life in a police cell[5] following a

---

5 The verdict of suicide that marked Roy Buchanan's death on 14 August 1988 has been the matter of some dispute among his family and friends.

domestic disturbance, the stately pace and mournful tone of 'The Messiah Will Come Again' suited Moore well. Using volume swells, overbends and sustained notes to honour Buchanan's established techniques, Moore also threw in a number of his own, with one trademark scurry sounding like he was falling down a steep flight of stairs while simultaneously playing a solo. Aided by old mate Don Airey on keyboards and guesting jazz-fusion bassist Laurence Cottle, 'The Messiah Will Come Again' was one of *After the War*'s few real highlights. 'Roy Buchanan was a fantastic guitarist,' Moore later said, 'and it was great to be able to cover one of his tracks for the album.'

The tunes Moore and Neil Carter worked up in Ireland a year before were of some quality too. Its title honouring a ruined medieval fortress on Northern Ireland's rocky coast, 'Dunlace (Parts One & Two)' was yet another moody instrumental, though one that depended more on Celtic drones and bagpiping guitars than bluesy turnarounds to make its point. And as for 'Blood of Emeralds', the track picked up where *Wild Frontier* had left off two years before. Tracing Moore's story from his childhood origins in Belfast and time in Skid Row to the sad loss of Philip Lynott in 1986, this was autobiography put to music, or more specifically, very Irish-sounding music. Propelled along by Simon Phillips (who nearly did himself an injury creating its double-kick drum effect) and using the Gregorian monk-like pipes of Andrew 'Sisters of Mercy' Eldritch on deeper-than-deep backing vocals, 'Blood of Emeralds' represented no great artistic leap forward. But as the title suggested, it certainly roused the blood.

Elsewhere on *After the War* pickings were slimmer. Though Moore's playing throughout the album was exemplary, his deployment of various Jackson, Hamer and Heritage guitars[6] stirring and soothing as and when

6 Like many shredders at the time, Moore had begun using Jackson and Hamer guitars, their fast actions, high-output pick-ups and Floyd Rose/Kahler tremolos perfect for the creation of eighties hard rock. However, during the making of *After the War*, Moore found love with a Heritage H-150, its liquid tone recalling the very best vintage Gibson Les Pauls. Pictured cradling the guitar on the album's cover, Heritage later introduced a 'Gary Moore' signature model based on his specifications,

required, the remaining album tracks let him down. Both 'Speak for Yourself' and 'Running from the Storm' shamelessly recycled parts from *Wild Frontier*'s 'Take a Little Time' and 'Thunder Rising', while 'Livin' on Dreams' and 'This Thing Called Love' sounded like rejects from 1979's *G-Force*. Even the chugging boogie of 'Ready for Love' (essentially a re-write of ZZ Top's 'Legs') seemed tired and formulaic, the track saved only by another magnificent solo outburst from Moore.[7]

Last, and in some minds possibly least, was *After the War*'s opinion-splitting centrepiece 'Led Clones'. Pointing a finger at several acts then accused of nakedly stealing their sound and look from Led Zeppelin (Kingdom Come and David Coverdale's then recently resurrected Whitesnake were two probable targets), 'Led Clones' was not the first time Moore had turned his guns on the work of other artists. Since questioning Alvin Lee's taste back in 1970, there had been snipes in and out of the press, with Swedish hard rockers Europe the latest group to feel his ire. 'Europe? Spare me from Europe,' he growled to *Guitar World* in 1987. 'They are completely unoriginal.' Joey Tempest and co. didn't need to take Moore's remarks to heart. After all, they were in fine company. 'Eddie Van Halen's a great, exciting, flash guitarist, [but] he doesn't play anything melodic,' he told *International Musician* in 1985. 'The letters will all be coming now, but I don't care. I can't read.' Given Van Halen was supposedly Gary's friend at the time, one wondered what had been said when the microphone was turned off.[8]

Helping Gary pour acid on the 'Led Clones' was Ozzy Osbourne. Once Black Sabbath's resident banshee and now a superstar in his own right, Moore and Osbourne's friendship went back to the late seventies when the Brummie singer and his bandmates visited Moore during the recording of *Back on the Streets*. On that occasion, Sabbath drummer Bill Ward had reportedly thrown up in a bin after too much drink while Osbourne

---

7   In a nice little 'tying of the bow' Vicki Brown's daughter Sam – then forging a singing career of her own with 1988's hit 'Stop' – contributed backing vocals to Moore's 'Ready for love'. Released as a single in March 1989, it went to number fifty-six in the UK.

8   This wasn't Moore's first snipe at EVH. In previous years, he had espoused the opinion that Van Halen's output had gone 'downhill' since the band's second LP. 'I think everyone agrees with that, really.' Except for those who didn't.

repeatedly threw himself at the studio wall for a spot of fun. Matters darkened when Osbourne lost all feeling below the waist and was rushed to hospital. It turned out that the numbness was less to do with the sturdiness of the wall and more to do with the amount of cocaine he had allegedly snorted.

Given Moore's growing distaste for drink and drugs, and the fact that Ozzy circa 1978 was a poster boy for both, the smart money was on the duo leaving it there. But when Moore parachuted out of Thin Lizzy in 1979, he and Osbourne's paths crossed again and an unlikely confederation was formed. Both using Los Angeles as a base to put together new bands, Moore and his G-Force colleagues lent Ozzy a hand when auditioning prospective musicians. When Osbourne suggested combining their talents, Moore turned him down flat, leaving Ozzy a tad miffed. 'Gary Moore is an arsehole,' he railed to *Kerrang* at the time. 'A great guitarist, but the kiss of death in rock'n'roll and you can print that.'

The spat proved temporary. The two were soon friends again and in new lead guitarist Randy Rhoads, Osbourne had found someone that impressed even Gary Moore. 'I met Randy when he first came to London with Ozzy Osbourne [in 1980] and really, really liked [him],' Moore later told *Louder*'s Dave Ling. 'He was just so humble.' Like Moore, Rhoads was also truly obsessive about guitar. A devoted music student who continued to take lessons even after scoring one of hard rock's most coveted jobs, Rhoads brought discipline, flair and a neo-classical[9] edge to Osbourne's group. 'Randy came to a gig of mine at The Marquee with Ozzy [and my then manager] Sharon, and he loved 'Parisienne Walkways',' Moore confirmed. 'He kept telling Sharon I should release it as a single, even though I already had, and it was a hit!' Tragically, while aiding Ozzy's return to the limelight, Rhoads was killed in a plane crash, his bright future cut criminally

---

9 Possessing a superb technique that combined EVH-like tremolo dive-bombs and tapping with complex variations on the augmented/diminished scale, Randy Rhoads was one of the founding members of metal's neo-classical guitar school. As such, his influence can be heard on the likes of Paul Gilbert, 'Dimebag' Darrell (R.I.P.) and John Petrucci, among many others.

short at the age of 25. 'Terrible loss, that, just terrible,' Moore later said.[10]

Though profoundly shaken by the loss of Randy Rhoads, Ozzy Osbourne soldiered on, and by the late eighties had rebuilt his career as 'heavy metal's leading terrorist', marrying Sharon Arden in the process. Now, he was in London lending a hand to Moore's lyrical evisceration of Led Zep's more obvious copyists. Aligned to a distinctly 'Kashmir' style rhythm, Osbourne's Robert Plant-referencing moans and several blasts of very Jimmy Page-like guitar, 'Led Clones' Whitesnake/Kingdom Come-baiting wordplay was amusing enough. Yet, it was difficult to understand why so much time and effort had been put into what amounted to little more than an industry in-joke. 'Oh, the song was just great fun,' said Ozzy by way of explanation, 'and it was an absolute honour to record with Gary. He's an unbelievable guitar player and a lovely man.' No doubt he was, but neither Osborne nor Moore were likely to get a Christmas card from David Coverdale in the immediate future.

If 'Led Clones' confirmed Moore's lack of fear in speaking his mind either on record or in print, it couldn't save him from others doing the same about his latest effort. '*After the War* suffers from a lack of memorable songs or a cohesive direction,' opined *Kerrang*, before declaring the disc 'Moore's weakest effort to date'. *Melody Maker* were even more succinct. 'Forgettable.' The general view that *After the War* had missed the mark was also reflected in the album's overall sales. Though breaking into the Top 5 in Moore's stronger markets (Scandinavia and Northern Europe), the LP stalled at number twenty-three in the UK and number sixteen in Japan. Not bad numbers per se, but no real improvement on the success of *Wild Frontier*.

Knowing the most reliable way to drive up units sold was to hit the road, Moore and his management began preparations for a tour, but the curse of the drummer struck again. Soon after rehearsals commenced, Cozy Powell and Moore started to butt heads. Ever the perfectionist, Moore asked Powell to stick to the exact patterns he performed on the

---

10 It wasn't just a terrible loss for Gary Moore. Bassist Bob Daisley had worked with Rhoads on both Blizzard Of Ozz albums, while Don Airey was on the road with Osbourne and Randy when he died, the keyboardist even witnessing the plane crash.

album. Powell, on the other hand, did not need to be told what or how to play. He was, in all fairness, Cozy Powell. One week before the group were due to begin touring, Powell walked, taking his drums with him.

His replacement was Chris Slade. A fine drummer, Slade's work with Pink Floyd's Dave Gilmour and Jimmy Page's post-Led Zeppelin quartet The Firm spoke for itself. Yet, even a musician of his calibre would have trouble learning a full set list in a matter of days, especially to Moore's exacting standards. Consequently, two of the opening dates were cancelled to let everyone bed in properly. In so doing so, Moore and co. walked straight into back-to-back dates at Dublin's St Francis Xavier Hall (or as it was better known, the 'SFX') and Belfast's King's Hall on 8/9 March 1989.

While these concerts were in front of some of the most partisan crowds Moore would face, his perfectionist nature made for a tense atmosphere backstage. In the end, quality won out and his latest homecoming was rewarded with several encores, the likes of 'Out in the Fields', 'Over the Hills and Far Away' and 'Blood of Emeralds' carrying particular resonance both artist, audience and Moore's father Bobby, who had come to see the show. But despite all the cheers and paternal confirmation, Moore still fretted. 'Chris Slade came in and learnt the set very quickly, but it was a stressful time,' Neil Carter later said, 'and [looking back], I never quite felt we hit the mark with him on stage.'

Though an element of close, but no cigar hung over the band's performances behind the scenes, one would have been hard pressed to notice it as the tour unfolded through the spring of 1989. Following a high-profile appearance at London's cavernous Wembley Arena on 12 March, it was onwards and more or less upwards. A long-established star in Germany, Belgium and Scandinavia, Moore spent much of March and April travelling to Hamburg, Berlin, Brussels and Copenhagen before again heading east for Japan. Once, Moore had courted Deep Purple's Ian Paice to help raise his profile in the country. As packed houses at Tokyo's Nakano Sun Plaza and Nagoya-shi Kōkaidō Hall now confirmed, he no longer required such assistance. 'Japan loves great guitar players,' ran the saying, and rest assured, Gary Moore was a great guitar player.

In fact, such was the level of devotion accorded Moore in the land of the rising sun, he had even been given a nickname by some of his fans: 'Guitar Face', in honour of the 'glorious derangement' his facial muscles underwent when soloing. Moore wasn't the only six-stringer whose features transformed while chasing around the fretboard. Journey's Neal Schon, for instance, inhaled and exhaled like a professional runner when tackling tricky riffs, while Rush's Alex Lifeson's gurns and sly winks to the crowd put one in mind of a nightclub comedian. There were Jimi and EVH's beatific smiles. The pained grimaces of Carlos Santana and Michael Schenker. All of them were at it, but no one could do it quite like Gary. 'Moore,' author Geoff Nicholson once said, 'is a face puller of international class.'

Thankfully, Moore found it all quite funny. 'It's almost a sexual thing,' he later laughed to the *Belfast Telegraph*'s Peter Robinson. 'You could take a picture of that person from the neck up and ask someone else what that person is doing. The answer wouldn't always be, "They're playing the guitar." It could be pain or pleasure. People make fun of me for doing that, but it's really not contrived. When I'm playing, I get completely lost in it and I'm not even aware of what I'm doing with my face. I'm just playing.'

And play he certainly did. By the time Moore's trek across Europe concluded on 26 May 1989 at Edinburgh's always boisterous Playhouse, the band had put 39 dates under their collective belt. None of them, however, were in the USA. For the briefest of moments, it looked like 'Over the Hills and Far Away' might finally provide Moore with the keys to the kingdom, Stateside. But despite a blink-or-you'll-miss-it on *Billboard*'s Top 30, everything soon returned to normal when *After the War* proved another commercial disappointment. Skulking into the charts at number 114 for a week in March 1987, it was on the way down again just a week later. With the Americans continuing to more or less ignore him, Moore chose to more or less ignore them too. Having seen little or no gain from his last US club tour of 1987, Moore chose to concentrate his in-concert efforts exclusively on the UK, Europe and Japan.

Yet, despite his bullish stance, Gary's continuing failure to make inroads in the United States was now beginning to exasperate not only the guitarist, but his management and record company too. 'Brand Moore' had been a resolute success in European and north-east Asian territories, with Moore capable of packing them in from Oslo to Kawasaki. Similarly, he could confidently expect to shift more than half a million units per album, plus singles sales. But without cracking America, the business model remained static, and as Part Rock, Virgin and Moore himself knew all too well, sales were likely to decline the older he got. With his hard rock competitors almost a decade younger than him, simply pretending the USA didn't exist or matter made little economic sense. Still, Moore wasn't for turning. 'They'll have to take me as they find me,' he said of his US situation, 'or not at all.'

Of course, there were matters other than America on Moore's mind. Now nearly 40 years old, he had watched rock music transform from young blues disciples playing in smoke-filled basements to a billion-dollar industry driven by concert receipts, CD sales and the 'crash, bang, wallop of heavy fucking metal'. No harm there, really. After all, aside from a small dip in numbers for *After The War*, Moore had profited rather well from that journey thus far. But the circus was beginning to tire him. 'It wasn't just the music,' he later told writer Dave Ling. 'Before each tour you'd spend more time with the fucking set designer than playing with the band, and it got really stupid. It was a model of Stonehenge or Andy Pandy's fucking playset. We were playing these huge venues and it seemed like things were going really well, but I'd be in the dressing room playing blues licks to myself.'

And there you had it. While thousands of adoring fans waited expectantly for their hero to emerge from the wings all guns a blazing, Moore was tucked away backstage playing Clapton, Green and B.B. King riffs for his own amusement. '[The tour] had gone all right, you know,' he later told *Classic Rock*'s Mick Wall, 'Good crowds, the usual thing. But towards the end, I used to look at myself in the mirror, all dolled up like some guy in Def Leppard, and think . . . "Who do you think you are? You look like a cunt."' It wasn't just about the leather trousers. 'I didn't know who'd made these albums,' he continued, 'and I didn't recognise myself in them anymore. I thought "Fuck it, I've got to do something about this."'

Less temporary slough of despond, more full-blown existential crisis, Moore had come to the end of his tether with the Sturm and Drang of the rock/metal scene, and his part in it. But whereas 12 months before, he sounded unsure of how to proceed, a stray conversation between Moore and bass player Bob Daisley now offered a way out. 'One night, I was playing blues [backstage] and Bob . . . came in,' Moore later recounted. 'He said, "You know, Gary, you should make a blues album next. It might be the biggest thing you ever did." I just laughed. He laughed too. But I did, and he was right. It was.'

PART FOUR:

1990 – 2011: Blues Run The Game

'Whatever I did, at least I meant it . . .'
Gary Moore

CHAPTER TWENTY-ONE

Less Is Moore

There was no real eureka moment when Gary Moore decided to abandon hard rock and return to the blues. In fact, Brian Downey had spoken with Moore about the possibility in the mid-eighties. 'Yeah, we'd had a conversation a few years before when Gary said he was getting sick of playing heavy music and wanted to branch away,' said the Thin Lizzy drummer. 'I said "Ah Gary, you need to go back to the blues." He looked straight at me and said "You know, that's what I might do." I was only kidding, but a couple of years later, there he was.' Producer Tony Platt too, was one of the first and strongest advocates for Moore taking the plunge and returning to his roots. 'Well, after *Emerald Aisles*, I actually said to him, "You know, we should make a simple blues album, a blistering three-piece set-up, you know?"' Platt confirmed in 2020. 'But his management weren't wholly interested in doing that. They were on course to turn him into a pop star. To be honest, that didn't feel like Gary to me.' Two years later, Moore was talking blues again with former Thin Lizzy guitarist Eric Bell, though this time also pouring cold water on the whole 'guitar hero' scene. '[Gary was] saying it's "Widdle, widdle, widdle, up and down the neck as fast as possible",' Bell laughed. '"It's a load of fucking bollocks, Eric!"'

Given his previous form, such a statement was a bit rich coming from 'lightning fingers' Moore. After all, he had spent his career committed to producing 'the most exciting guitar playing' he could, much of which relied on passages of blinding speed. However, Gary had long drawn a distinction in his mind between the glorious noise produced by original progressive blues players such as Clapton, Beck and Hendrix and the post-Van Halen school of 'neo-classicists' or 'shredders' who came to dominate the eighties rock/metal scene. For him, playing complex scales at incredible pace to impress one's peers not only compromised the sheer joy of making music, it also negated the ability of the musician to make an emotional connection with those listening. 'If you're doing it just to show everyone how fast you are, if you're not reaching people, then it's rubbish,' Moore had said back in 1984. Evidently, he had seen or heard nothing to change his mind since.

Moore's viewpoint was, of course, debatable. One might argue that players the calibre of Yngwie Malmsteen, Steve Vai, Joe Satriani and Nuno Bettencourt were actually introducing a new form of dialogue for guitar, their technical expertise expanding the instrument's possibilities far beyond what was deemed previously possible. Latter-day Paganinis fusing often astounding dexterity with a stage magician's flair for the theatrical, these 'shredders' really were the next generation of guitar gods. What's more, from the number of platinum discs adorning the walls of their respective mansions, they had no trouble connecting with a new generation of guitar fans, either emotionally or financially. Moore remained unconvinced. 'If you miss out on the blues, well . . .'

If Moore could take or leave (though mostly leave) 'Generation Shred', there was no fear of him missing out on a return to the blues, even if that meant substantially altering his supporting cast of musicians to do so. In the case of the recently acquired Chris Slade, that was no great problem. Employed for the 1989 tour, Slade was now let go to pursue his own interests, which turned out to be taking up the recently vacated drum seat in rock leviathans AC/DC. As for bassist Bob Daisley, the situation was a little more delicate. A solid part of Moore's band for the best part of a decade, it was Daisley who most recently suggested Moore might try doing a blues album. He had also spent many a soundcheck in 'blues jamathons' with his boss, and even pointed him in the direction of Albert King's 'Oh Pretty Woman' as a possible cover. Now, it appeared Moore was at last ready to embrace the idea, but unfortunately mostly without Daisley, who found himself returning to Ozzy Osbourne's band.

The greatest surprise, however, was the departure of Neil Carter. Moore's unofficial right-hand man, Carter had toured, recorded, sung and even written with him, the pair penning 'Thunder Rising', 'Blood of Emeralds' and the sad-eyed 'Empty Rooms' since joining the group in 1983. Yet, Carter long had an inkling that this might not be his 'forever home'. 'Well, I think after all those years it was inevitable Gary would move on, [though] I really wasn't aware how disenchanted he was with rock music,' Neil later told *Let It Rock*. Faced with Moore's decision to re-embrace the twelve-bar life, Carter immediately knew his future lay elsewhere. 'Blues was never an option for me,' he continued. 'My era was glam and the bands I loved wrote diverse songs with less noodling. [So, blues] wasn't something I'd choose to play myself.' Like Bob Daisley, Carter was now a free man, though just like the Aussie bassist, he wasn't finished working with Gary Moore quite yet.

Previous group disbanded, Moore immediately set to work pulling together a new, more bluesy one. At first, a dream list of names was compiled, the likes of Mick Fleetwood and Cream's Jack Bruce mentioned as contenders for the rhythm section. When it became clear that such a team-up was unlikely, Moore cast his net in a different direction. Brian Downey was again called to help his former Thin Lizzy colleague with prospective songs while a flattered Bruce also dipped in and out on bass, solo commitments permitting.[1]

But it was when Moore received a tip-off regarding bassist Andy Pyle that things started to really motor. Once a prospective member of Colosseum II who ended up temporarily joining Moore for 1980's *Live at The Marquee* LP before Wishbone Ash came calling, Pyle was a rock solid four-stringer. Crucially, he also knew to keep it simple when Gary went into all-out solo mode. With Pyle eventually came journeyman drummer Graham

---

1   While Bruce was happy to lend a hand, he had recently signed a solo deal with Epic Records.

Walker[2] and later Mick Weaver, whose expertise on Hammond organ had made him a go-to guy for blues sessions since the late sixties.

Having created his core quartet for a series of demos, Moore now started putting the cherries on top. One of the first musicians that came to mind was saxophonist/harmonica player Frank Mead, whom Moore met when performing at various charity gigs during the late eighties. Like Pyle, Mead knew his onions from years on the funk and R&B circuit, and had even dipped a toe in live Irish traditional music, which further endeared him to Gary. Pulling together a brass section on Moore's behalf, Frank added Raoul D'Oliveira, Nick Pentelow and Nick Payn on trumpet, tenor and baritone saxes, respectively, and in so doing, opened up further possibilities for Gary to explore as part of his new sound.[3] Another wise addition was pianist Nicky Hopkins. Dubbed 'rock's greatest session musician', Hopkins had played with everyone in his time, from The Beatles and Rolling Stones to The Kinks, The Who and The Jeff Beck Group. Eventually sprinkling his magic on three tracks, Hopkins' presence further underlined the seriousness with which Moore was taking the project.

That said, arguably the most important keyboardist Moore invited to join his new venture was Don Airey. Once the pair had staged some of the most spectacular musical dogfights in jazz rock as part of Colosseum II. Now, they were again joining forces, though this time to enable Moore to return to the sound of his teenage years. In fact, even before Airey arrived at rehearsals, en route from recording with metal gods Judas Priest, no less, he had already been an important enabler in Moore's plans. 'Well, I'd mentioned to Gary that I'd recently done a gig with The Hawks . . . at my local pub, featuring the twin guitar work of Mick Grabham,' and Ray Minhinnett,'[4] Airey told writer Jeb Wright. 'I said how impressed I was not only with their playing, but also the whole

---

2 Pyle originally suggested ex-Blodwyn Pig bandmate Clive Bunker for the drummer's chair, but that didn't quite work out, leaving the way open for Pyle's then current rhythm partner Graham Walker to step in.

3 In addition to those mentioned above, trumpeter Stuart Brooks and tenor saxophonist Andrew Hamilton also contributed to Moore's new project.

4 An old school friend of Airey's, Mick Grabham spent much of the seventies playing guitar with Procul Harum, while The Hawks' other guitarist Ray Minhinnett had been an early contender to replace Gary Moore in Thin Lizzy.

measured blues feel of the band. So, Gary got hold of their bass player, Andy Pyle, and [then their] drummer Graham Walker.' One imagines Grabham and Minhinnett were thrilled.

With Don Airey bringing his keyboard, arrangement and conducting skills to bear, a *Who's Who* of session musicians and distinguished guests also in train, it was down to Moore to find an ideal producer for the album. Predictably, Moore's thoughts turned to Peter Collins. But as enticing a prospect as melding traditional blues tunes to up-to-the-minute digital technology was, Moore had different ideas this time around. Having enjoyed a fruitful working relationship with engineer Ian Taylor on *After the War*, Moore suggested the pair share a co-production credit for his new disc. The offer was gratefully accepted.

When he first mooted the idea several months before, there had been little real excitement about Gary Moore doing a blues album. One couldn't blame either Part Rock or Virgin Records for thinking this might be just a temporary aberration on Moore's part before he once again returned to the serious business of making hard rock/pop records. But then the demos came in. Impressing everyone who heard them, including manager Steve Barnett and Virgin's A&R department, further recording sessions were booked and rumours began to circulate that Moore had a potential monster hit on his hands. What began as 'a daft vanity project' to be released on a subsidiary label was now gaining serious traction. The time had come to throw some money at it. 'But obviously not too much time or too much money,' Moore later quipped.

Budgets set tight and clock already ticking, London's Sarm East was secured for several weeks over the late autumn of 1989, with Moore, his band, Ian Taylor and Don Airey keeping tight business hours to get the job done. As ever, Sarm East was there to help them. It had a solid hardwood floor, four comfortable rooms for recording, including an extra-large one for drums, and additional space to relax on those rare occasions Gary actually put his guitar down. Suffice to say, Moore felt right at home. 'The studio was really fresh-sounding,' he later said, 'and that's exactly what I was going for.'

Obviously, Sarm East's convivial atmosphere did the trick. Freed from the chains of digital drum programming, Gary and co. cut most tracks live, including many guitar solos, with only horns, orchestration and vocals added later. Setting the bar at three or four takes per song, if something wasn't working, the group just moved on to something else instead. An old practice used by blues icons such as Muddy Waters, Howlin' Wolf and Buddy Guy, by keeping the pace hot, a song's natural energy was caught on disc rather than lost in endless rehashing. 'It was always there at the back of my mind,' Moore said, 'the idea of going back to the blues.' Now he was doing it for real.

Yet, there was one area where little or nothing was left to chance. To wit, the guitars. Knowing that Moore's playing would be at the very heart of the album, both artist and producer Ian Taylor pulled out all the stops to get it right, though in comparison to previous studio visits, Gary's equipment set-up was trimmed down considerably. Using a Marshall JTM45 as his main amplifier (very Clapton-period Blues Breakers), Moore supplemented his tones with a high-gain Soldano head for extra grit and a 1963 Fender Twin Blackface, when things needed dialling down a decibel or 10.

As far as actual guitars were concerned, gone were the Floyd Rose-equipped Superstrats and Hamers that marked Moore's progress throughout the eighties. Instead, Moore's trusty 'Greeny' Les Paul was now back in favour, while that recently acquired Heritage 150 – 'very sweet and sustaining' – also remained close to hand. Elsewhere, he employed a fetching 1962 Fender Stratocaster to provide 'twang and gristle' on one or two tracks, while a vintage Ibanez Tube Screamer and brand-new Marshall Guv'nor overdrive pedal allowed him to put the burners on all axes and amps when required. Meanwhile, waiting patiently to make its entrance was a distinguished, if unprepossessing 1959 flame top Gibson Les Paul Standard purchased by right-hand man Graham Lilley on Moore's behalf a year or so before.[5] Thus far, the guitar – or 'Stripe' as it was

---

5 'Stripe' was purchased from guitar player/collector Phil Harris by Moore via Lilley in 1988. Harris, who had known Moore since the early seventies, originally brought two Les Pauls along for Moore's consideration. One a worn, light burst LP 'with a lot of flame' the other considerably darker. Moore much preferred the lighter model and bought it. However, aside from giving his new axe a brief spin on *After the War*, Stripe had more or less remained in its case until 1990.

known – hadn't been used much by its new owner. But it would make its presence felt (and then some) over the coming months.

With most of the recording concluded by the end of the year, 'Project Blues' moved to the next stage of its development: the reimagining of Gary Moore. While Moore could probably live with his latest disc being a commercial failure, the prospect of spending the next ten years dressed in leather and spandex was simply beyond him. 'I just thought "Fuck this,"' he told author Mick Wall about his heavy metal-leaning wardrobe. 'I wanted to look like how I felt – a grown bloody man.' Still, image changes could be very tricky things. Done right, and an artist and group could reposition themselves perfectly within the market place, retaining old fans while also bringing a new audience to their work. Go too far or too fast, however, and all was lost, leaving one's core support angry or resentful, and prospective punters just plain confused.

The man brought in to help smooth Gary Moore's transition from hairy rocker to hairy bluesman was photographer Gered Mankowitz. Son of famed author/playwright/screenwriter Cyril 'Wolf' Mankowitz, Gered began taking photographic assignments in the early sixties. But a move from the world of fashion to the blossoming music scene of swinging London proved immensely wise. Soon working with The Rolling Stones and Marianne Faithfull, Mankowitz found himself surrounded by some of the most enduring icons of the late-twentieth century. Not that he knew it at the time.

'When I started, I didn't know I was "making history",' he laughed. 'I wasn't even making a living! Nobody knew, really. These artists, as wonderful as they were, didn't even know if they'd get a chance to make another album. To give you an example, The Stones' Bill Wyman once told me the reason he became the band's archivist. He started a scrapbook for his infant son Stephen so that years later, when he'd gone back to his ordinary job as a plumber or whatever, he could say, "Hey, I was more than just a plumber, you know. For a brief moment in the sixties, I was a pop star." The fact that The Stones are still around 60 years later would have been frankly incomprehensible back then.'

Though he quickly became known for capturing The Stones in their youthful pomp, it was another photo session with an unassuming young

American guitarist in February 1967 that cemented Gered Mankowitz's status. Meeting a pre-fame Jimi Hendrix at his studio in central London's Mason's Yard, Mankowitz's subsequent images of the guitar legend, hands on hips, short Hussar's jacket, looking straight to camera, have travelled down the ages for all to see.

'Jimi was gentle, humble, modest, quiet, funny and just a pleasure to work with,' Mankowitz said in 2020. 'I got him at the most fantastic moment in his career. 'Hey Joe' was just about to be released and he was really pleased with the way it had turned out. Jimi was suddenly in a space that he wanted to be, and he had a wonderful future in front of him. Nobody had told him what to wear or how to behave. This was an excited, confident and optimistic man, looking forward to what was going to happen. That's the Jimi I got on [on film], and what you saw was 100 per cent the real Jimi. But within weeks, things changed. He didn't look as good. He'd lost that natural, spontaneous wildness as people began to style him.'

Though Gered went on to take several hundred more iconic photos, including shots of Free, Slade, Elton John, Kate Bush, David Bowie and Marc Bolan, it was his photograph of Jimi Hendrix that remained seared in Gary Moore's mind. 'Oh, Gary was a massive fan of Hendrix,' said Mankowitz. 'And I think it was originally suggested to him that as I'd photographed Jimi, how he might feel about [us working together].' Very happy indeed, as it turned out. Super keen to join forces with the man who shot his hero, Moore handed over responsibility for his album cover to Mankowitz. '[By then], I'd done around 500 covers, though,' he said. 'That little square's a great format.'

Loosely based on a concept Mankowitz had used many years before[6], the front cover shoot for Moore's new disc featured a dark-haired young boy huddled over a guitar in his bedroom, album sleeves strewn all around him. At the boy's feet was a Dansette record player and a Marshall Blues Breaker amp. On the wall above was Mankowitz's image of Jimi Hendrix, all wild hair and shy smiles. 'Well, they knew I was quite geared up to

---

6 "There was an image I did many, many years ago, as part of the story of rock'n'roll for Sire records [where] I'd photographed a kid teaching himself to play guitar in a late fifties [bed]room," Mankowitz said of his inspiration for Moore's album cover.

building photographic sets in my studio,' Gered recalled, '[and I had] this concept of having 'the young Gary' in his little bedroom teaching himself guitar. Also, that kid had a look to him that just worked. No relation to Gary, though!'

Brilliantly capturing the pinpoint dedication of a 'young genius' at work, Mankowitz's grey-tinted image was certainly eye-catching. But the album's back cover wasn't too shabby either. Fast-forwarding the previous scene three decades, Gary Moore was now pictured sitting alone upon a bed, guitar in hand, CDs tossed casually around him. On the floor was a Marshall Blues Breaker amp, while outside his window, a neon 'Hotel' sign burned brightly in the night. Above Moore's head, neatly typed in bold white letters, was the album's title: *Still Got the Blues*. 'Gary was very cooperative, laid back and took direction very well,' Mankowitz said of the two-day shoot. 'He knew what we were trying to do, so was very supportive of it. He was [also] pretty chuffed at the set and made sugges-tions about what props we might use for the period. Together, we brought the whole thing to life.'[7]

There was one more task Mankowitz had to perform. With Moore adamant his days as a heavy metal scarecrow were behind him, a set of photographs presenting the 'new Gary' were needed. Again, Mankowitz delivered, with a dark-suited, guitar-cradling Moore caught stepping into a shaft of white light as shadows and smoke danced around him. 'That was in my studio, with Bill Smith responsible for the design,' Mankowitz confirmed. 'Again, a simple idea . . . [but] capturing a shaft of light can be quite difficult, as . . . smoke doesn't often do what you want it to. It dissipates. Yet that particular shaft of light really worked. Gary looked confident and I love the way he's holding the guitar like it's his baby.'

For Mankowitz, the 'suit shots' were an important factor in contrib-uting to all that came next. 'Well, it was exactly the sort of the project I wanted to be involved in,' he confirmed. 'Evolving as an artist [in terms of image] can be terribly difficult, and it's often done in a ham-fisted way. So, creating an image . . . that allows the artist to move forward – to

---

7   Though Mankowitz and Moore worked together on bringing the images to life, Moore is actually credited for 'Cover Concept' in the liner notes of the album.

evolve, to mature – well, it's a great challenge, but one worth pursuing.' As for Moore, it was the first time in years he could look at a photo of himself without wanting to laugh or cry. 'The reason I put on a suit . . . was that I wanted to send a very clear message to rock fans . . . [that] this was something else, something new,' he later told *Classic Rock*. 'I wanted to start with a clean slate and the suit seemed a good way of getting that message across.'

Cover sleeve in place and new image confirmed, all that was left to do was release the album. On 26 March 1990, *Still Got the Blues* landed in shops with a gentle bump and a disclaimer of sorts from its creator. 'I didn't make this album for the fans,' Moore told *Guitar Magazine* at the time, 'I made it for me. Of course, I hope they like it, but you know, if they don't, that's just the way it is.' Despite Moore's now customary bluntness, there was little for fans not to like. Brushing away the more obvious metallic textures he had come to despise, *Still Got the Blues* was the sound of an artist reclaiming the past while also angling for a new musical future.

'When I heard *Still Got the Blues*, I thought, "Jesus Christ, Gary's finally got the message!"' said his friend and former manager Ted Carroll. 'I mean, what an album. Peter Green, Eric Clapton and Jimi Hendrix were all his idols when he was growing up, and Gary could really play the shit out of the blues. So, when he finally did it [on record], when he realised "Less is more" and put his own spin on things, well, I was delighted. *Still Got the Blues* was the moment when it all really made sense.'

As the contents of the album confirmed, Moore's spin on the blues proved surprisingly widescreen. In addition to drawing on old standards, new torch songs and youthful favourites, Moore dropped downtown Chicago and authentic roadhouse flavours in there too, while also peppering the disc with the odd jaw-dropper. 'This record's very special to me,' he told *Guitare et Claviers* at the time. 'It's also a very honest record, and one I wanted to make. It's not often you get this sort of chance, and you know, it really sounds like me . . . at least my version of the blues.' As one might expect, there was no dearth of rocking tunes, with album opener 'Moving On' coming out of the traps at a greyhound's pace. In its writer's own words, 'My attempt at a kind of country blues,' (albeit of the very loud variety), the scuttling rhythm in 'Moving On' was consolidated by another rare foray into the world of slide guitar. Never a favourite tool of Moore's, ('I'm sloppy with it,' he repeatedly grumbled), he nevertheless did a fine job of mimicking a pedal steel, his note-blurring slurs and swells adding precisely the kind of countrified feel he was looking for. 'I was trying to do some things I hadn't really done before, and 'Moving On' was one of them.'

'Texas Strut' also bopped along at a fair old clip, though the inspiration here was more Southern boogie than Nashville twang. A love letter to the music of the Lone Star state, replete with namechecks for ZZ Top's peerless Billy Gibbons and Stratocaster King Stevie Ray Vaughan (more of him later), 'Texas Strut' even featured Moore mimicking a line from ZZ's own ode to illegal love shacks, 'La Grange', while a guesting Brian Downey beat the living daylights out of his drum kit in the background. 'Now, that's a great track,' said the former Lizzy man.

If 'Moving On' and 'Texas Strut' were on the boisterous side, then 'Walking By Myself' was full-blown blues rock. By far the closet *Still Got the Blues* came to Moore's previous life, it wouldn't have been too out of place on either *Run for Cover* or *After the War*, with Moore's overdriven, high-speed solo leaning more to metal than blues. However, according to Moore, it was all part of the bigger plan. 'I'd played rock for a long time and then I made *Still Got the Blues* in 1990,' he later told *Guitar Player*'s Shawn Hammond. 'I started off [playing] very quietly [in rehearsals], and going back to the early Fleetwood Mac kind of [sound]. But then I realised, "Man, if I play like this, everyone is going to think I'm faking it. It's not going to sound like me." So, I decided to keep more of the rock guitar sound. I tried to get a modern, less high-gain version of that natural sound that Eric Clapton had in the sixties.' In fact, according to some sources, Moore felt that since ending Cream in November 1968, Clapton had completely lost the power and intensity of his earlier playing, and Gary was determined to now re-light some of that original spirit on *Still Got the Blues*.

That said, he had not forgotten the fire Eric Clapton's work with John Mayall had lit within him either. Hence, Moore treated listeners to a propulsive, if faithful cover of one of the cornerstones of his own youthful record collection. "All My Love' was the first track I heard on *Blues Breakers* . . . the song made a huge impact on me and so it just had to be on the album,' he later re-confirmed to *Guitar Magazine*. 'It was done as a cross between John and Eric's take on the song and the original version written by Otis Rush.'

Another debt repaid by Moore on *Still Got the Blues* was to Peter Green. Aware that the former Fleetwood Mac man was still dealing with the mental health issues that saw him leave the group two decades before, Moore not only dedicated the LP to Green, but recorded one of his most famous tunes too. Augmented by the good-time bounce of Mick Weaver's barrelhouse piano, Moore's treatment of 'Stop Messin' Around' was as faithful to Peter and Clifford Davis's 1968 foot-stomper as an old Labrador.

Green was also the clear inspiration behind two more of *Still Got the Blues'* finer tracks. Recalling the almost mystical nature of Peter's work with Mac, Moore's 'Midnight Blues' was deathly slow and full of angst, his reverb-drenched guitar calling out to the night in the same way Green's Gibson Les Paul had on 'The Supernatural', three years before he gifted it to Moore for a song. Written by 'Peppermint' Harris for the super-smooth Fenton Robinson back in 1959, Moore's version of 'As the Years Go Passing By' was also soulful, stately and sincere, and again more than a little indebted to Green's gossamer style.

Benefiting from the piano genius of Nicky Hopkins – 'Just an incredible player,' Moore later confirmed – 'As the Years Go Passing By' not only featured Moore's best vocal on *Still Got the Blues*, but also a blistering performance from his new horn section. Fluttering in and out of the song like mournful nightingales, Frank Mead's crack squad of saxophonists and trumpeters made a huge difference to 'As the Years Go Passing By', and indeed, the album as a whole. 'I think the horns were a missing ingredient for me,' Moore later told *Guitar World*. 'It made the whole thing more of a departure than it would have been otherwise.'

A real highlight of *Still Got the Blues*, Gary Moore's super-sad take on 'As the Years Go Passing By' was but the latest reading of a song already covered by artists as diverse as The Animals, Boz Scaggs and

Santana. For many people, the definitive version could be found on Albert King's 1967 LP *Born Under a Bad Sign*, a fact the Mississippi-born singer/guitarist was surely aware of when he agreed to guest Moore's LP. A real coup for Moore, Albert King's appearance on *Still Got the Blues* conferred the type of legitimacy money couldn't buy. A proper legend who had lived almost as long as the music itself, King was blues royalty, and what's more, he knew it. Huge in physical stature, silken of voice and stinging on guitar, King had been an abiding influence on all who heard him.

'You wouldn't have had Hendrix play the way he did if it wasn't for Albert King,' Moore told writer Harold Steinblatt. 'All those long bends . . . the white guys didn't get hold of that until the mid-sixties. When you hear the solo on Cream's 'Strange Brew', it's totally Albert King's licks. Hendrix's 'Red House' [too], it's all totally Albert.' And now Albert King was going to sing and play 'Oh, Pretty Woman' with Moore.

There were easier sessions. Invited to London by Moore, 66-year-old King arrived at Metropolis Studios in Chiswick with little clue as to his host's identity or the music he made. 'He didn't know me from Adam,' said Moore, 'he came over for the money.' Worse, when Moore was running through 'Oh Pretty Woman', a song Albert made his own some 25 years before, he fluffed one of the lines, leading to a prolonged lecture from the elder statesman on the importance of getting things right. A perfectionist by both nature and design, Moore repeatedly bit his tongue. Hard.

Gary also revealed, with recording soon to begin, it became apparent Albert's guitar was tuned to his own ear rather than traditional concert pitch. Though not an uncommon practice among blues and rock players, King's more cavalier approach to 'A above middle C' would surely have rankled the ever-fastidious Moore. But then the mood changed. After pacing around each other like a pair of barnyard dogs, the two just started playing. Soon enough, King found himself mightily impressed. 'That boy can play,' he later told writer Steve Newton, 'I guarantee it!'.

In the end, the result of King and Moore's studio liaison was likeable enough, if no true meeting of musical minds. On the plus side, Gary had made every effort to emulate the Stax horn sound that put Albert

King on the map, with Frank Mead's brass section working overtime to get things swinging. Moore's vocal was also impressive, moving through the octaves in sympathy with all those roving saxes and trumpets. But that white-hot, super-overdriven guitar all but cauterised the reedier tones of King's trademark Flying V, creating a somewhat jarring effect on the ears.

Still, the duo's brief association provided Gary with some important pluses. In addition to getting a thumbs up from a true blues original, Moore also drew enough inspiration from the oak-tall American to write a tune in his honour: 'King of the Blues'. Referencing King's eventful life through the lyrics of his best-known songs, its retinue of crosscut saw-wielding hunters, two-timing Laundromat women and ever faithful six-string 'Lucy' often eclipsed their combined efforts on 'Oh Pretty Woman' itself.[8]

Moore's solo, all slow, stretched notes and nail-biting tension, was in itself another form of tribute to Albert King. 'When he was leaving the studio on the last day,' Moore later told *Vintage Guitar*, 'Albert said, "Gary, play every other lick." That's such a profound thing – *play every other lick*. Those four little words meant the world to me. It took a long time to really take it in, but he was absolutely right. If you leave that space . . . and you play expressively, you can make people really *feel* your guitar and they won't be able to wait for the next note.'

If Albert King took his time warming to Moore, one couldn't say the same of another of Moore's guests on *Still Got the Blues*. 'I've had the privilege of seeing Gary Moore play quietly in a little room and he's incredible,' said George Harrison. 'It's not just the speed, either. He's got a great sense of melody and pitch, and when he bends those strings, he goes straight to the note. No flapping about! There's more to Gary than a big stack of Marshall amplifiers, you know.' Back in November 1963, Moore watched mouth agape as The Beatles tore through 'She Loves You' on stage at Belfast's Ritz Cinema. Now, one of their number was a friend. 'George was a character . . . a very charismatic person,' Moore

---

8 A rollicking tune in its own right, 'King of the Blues' bore more than one or two similarities to Albert King's own 'I'll Play the Blues for You'.

later told writer Brian D. Holland. 'He was kind . . . and very funny [and] had what we call a wicked sense of humour – quite . . . naughty. He'd make you laugh, like a naughty school boy with a glint in his eye.'

Moore first met George Harrison shortly after moving to his new home in Shiplake. Unofficial leader (though he would probably have balked at such a description) of 'the Henley-on-Thames set', Harrison had been resident in the area since he bought his monumental, 62-acre neo-gothic mansion Friar Park in 1970. Within a decade, Deep Purple's Ian Paice, Traffic's Jim Capaldi, Joe Brown and Bad Company's Mick Ralphs had all moved close by, making Henley a safe haven for rich musicians escaping the clutches of the city.

With rules and customs all their own, Gary and his wife Kerry were reportedly treated with a degree of trepidation by the gathered tribe upon their arrival. But one party invite from fellow Thames-side resident Alvin Lee later, and Moore found himself face to face not only with the Henley set, but his boyhood idol too. 'I met George at a party soon after moving to Henley-on-Thames,' Moore later confirmed to the author Harry Shapiro. 'He said, "I really like your playing, it's neat, tidy."' Inevitably, the guitars were pulled out, with Moore's finger skills soon startling the guests. So far, so good. Yet, when Moore asked whether Harrison was playing the intro to 'A Hard Day's Night'[9] correctly, a chill wind threatened to descend upon the Thames. 'Yes, Gary,' came the slow, sure reply, 'it's right.' As Moore fought to regain his composure, Harrison burst out laughing. Upon such stuff are friendships made.

Following their party antics, Moore and Harrison grew closer in subsequent months, with Harrison even popping along to watch Moore from the wings during his 1989 *After the War* tour. Bigger compliments were to come. About to record his occasional supergroup The Traveling Wilburys' second album, Harrison asked Moore whether he might

---

9 A topic of some debate among musicians, the ringing chord that introduces 'A Hard Day's Night' was heavily treated during the production process, with various instruments added by producer George Martin. Hence Moore's honest, if ham-fisted enquiry to Harrison. However, after years of being asked about it, Harrison tried to finally clear up the mystery in 2001. 'It's F with a G on top (on the 12-string guitar),' he told *The Beatles Bible*. 'But you'll have to ask Paul about the bass note to get the proper story.'

contribute a solo. Stoked at the prospect of adding his name to a roll call that already included Bob Dylan, ELO's Jeff Lynne and Tom Petty, Moore leapt at the chance, his scurrying outburst to be heard on *The Traveling Wilburys Vol. 3*'s 'She's My Baby'. 'It took him just five minutes,' laughed Harrison, 'Unbelievable, really.' Billed as 'Ken Wilbury', Moore was beside himself with pride at being an honorary member of the band.

Still Got the Blues gave Moore the chance to go even further. When he heard that Gary was revisiting his musical roots on a new album, Harrison said he might have just the song for him. A jaunty little tune previously demoed by Moore's other teenage hero Eric Clapton for a Romanian charity LP[10], 'My Kind of Woman' wasn't strictly blues, but it was catchy. 'I didn't think Eric did a great job, if I'm honest,' Moore said, but he felt it was worth taking a shot at the song – if Harrison lent a hand too. When Harrison agreed, Moore was back in his happy place.

'Well, I recorded my vocal at George's house and he played slide guitar and did some backing vocals, so that was a great thrill,' Moore later told *Vintage Guitar*'s John Heidt. 'God, I loved going to his house because he had all the Beatles guitars there. He'd let me get them down off the wall. He had everything, you know, the painted Strat from *Magical Mystery Tour*, the Gibson acoustics, the Rickenbacker he played on 'A Hard Day's Night'. It was an amazing room. It was sort of like meeting all your old friends that you saw in the movies when you were a kid.' Chugging along on the combined charm of Harrison's glistening guitar lines, a set of bopping horns and a (now) guesting Bob Daisley's rock-solid bass[11], 'My Kind of Woman' probably wasn't the best track on *Still Got the Blues*, but it was the only one featuring a Beatle. 'Ah, George was truly special,' Moore later said, 'and I had some genuinely great times with him.'

---

10 Clapton's version of 'That Kind of Woman' was released on *Nobody's Child*, a 1990 charity LP benefitting Romanian children made orphans following the fall of communism in their country. The project was put together by George Harrison and his wife Olivia, and featured contributions from Stevie Wonder, Paul Simon and Guns N' Roses, among others.

11 After his tenure with Moore, Daisley briefly returned to Ozzy Osbourne's band in 1990 before returning again to . . . Gary Moore.

While 'My Kind of Woman' was more consummation of musical friendship than enduring masterpiece, the title track of Gary Moore's eighth studio album was something altogether different. A bold, beautiful statement of intent, 'Still Got the Blues' married the weeping guitar sound of 'Parisienne Walkways' to sweeping strings (led by Gavin Wright), suitably traumatised vocals from Moore and, in the words of one critic, 'A proper bloody melody.'[12]

Spotted as a real contender early in the project, 'Still Got the Blues' was responsible for opening the purse strings of Virgin Records, and as was now clear, worth every penny of their investment. Picked up by radio as soon as the LP was released, it quickly became the flag under which Moore's new marketing campaign would be fought. Part love song, part guitar showcase, it repositioned Moore perfectly, ending his reign as a 'small metal god' and beginning his tenure as a born-again bluesman. Better not tell Moore, though. 'I didn't think about the bloody market or how many it was going to sell,' he protested at the time. 'This was just something I wanted to do.'

One aspect of 'Still Got the Blues' that Moore was unlikely to argue about was the quality of its solo. Evolving from the song's signature melody line, he had cut the part not on his trademark 'Greeny', but on 'Stripe', the very same Les Paul he had used to create merry hell with on 'Oh Pretty Woman'. This time around, however, Moore and his new favourite axe were in a more evocative mood, re-shaping the A minor pentatonic scale (with a couple of inversions) into arguably the most heart-rending solo flight of his illustrious career.[13] Voted number seventeen in the 'Fifty Greatest Ever Guitar Solos' by *Guitar World* readers in 2021, Moore's Herculean effort was made even more impressive by the

---

12 According to Don Airey, Moore almost forgot the melody to 'Still Got the Blues'. 'Gary said, "What was that thing we came up with on Wednesday?" I said, "What, the kind of slow tune?" He said, "Yeah, I can't remember what it was." So, I played it to him and he said, "Oh, yeah". But for me writing that down (at the previous session), I don't think 'Still Got the Blues' would have existed.'

13 As with much of the album, Moore used a Marshall JTM45 amp, Guv'nor overdrive pedal and Alesis Quadra Verb unit to enhance Stripe's pre-existing qualities on 'Still Got the Blues', while also switching between neck and treble pick-ups during the solo for added emotional impact.

fact it was cut mostly live. 'Yes,' Graham Lilley later confirmed to *Music Radar*, 'it was a one-take, first-take solo.'[14]

As with any classic in the making, from The Beatles' 'Yesterday' to Pet Shop Boys' 'It's a Sin', 'Still Got the Blues'' haunting guitar line had a sense of familiarity about it, as if the both the melody and supporting chords had been around forever. In fact, that was precisely what Moore was after. 'I went for really melodic songs – *actual songs* – on this album,' he told *Guitar Magazine*. 'As opposed to just shuffles and standard 12-bars.'

However, some eager-eared types found more than occasional similarities between 'Still Got the Blues' and several existing tunes. The dancing strings from Gustav Holst's 'Mercury'. Little snippets from Alan Silvestri's outstanding film score for 1985's *Back to the Future*. 'Stop' by Sam Brown. 'Europa' by Santana. Eric Clapton's smouldering take on 'Autumn Leaves'. Even Moore's own 'Parisienne Walkways'. The list went on. Yet, for Don Airey, who scored and arranged the strings on 'Still Got the Blues', such things were par for the course when it came to the songwriting process. "Still Got the Blues' was like a lot of things,' he said. "Autumn Leaves', [is] a bit like Lionel Richie. But Gary made it his own.' In time, others would disagree.

For now at least, all such troubles were lost in the rush to lavish praise on *Still Got the Blues*, as both album and song began garnering some of the best reviews of Moore's musical life. 'No Celtic strains or Euro-metal stylings here,' said an ebullient Bill Milkowski for *Guitar World*. 'This one strictly deals with the purely American sound of the blues, with an emphasis on the Texas and Chicago approaches to the genre. More, *Still Got the Blues* is no idle whim, no shrewd marketing ploy. Moore's phrasing and bent-string abandon make it apparent that the blues was bred into this boy's bones at an early age, and he may find this to be the right album in the right place at the right time.'

That he did. For years, blues, especially the British variety, had been out of fashion. Once the province of super-hip young things like The Stones, The Yardbirds and Fleetwood Mac, such bands had bust nails and

---

14 According to co-producer Ian Taylor, because of tuning problems, two notes of the solo were later fixed. The other 10,000, however, appeared to be just fine.

strings in an effort to copy the work of old masters like Son House, Skip James and Big Bill Broonzy. But when the form morphed into 'progressive blues' and later 'blues rock', the desire to create new sounds replaced the wish to emulate old ones. As a consequence, it was left to the likes of first-wave performers such as Alexis Korner to fly the flag for 'trad blues' on late-night TV, while punks flicked V-signs from the wings. Obviously, there were exceptions. The whippet-lean punch of Dr Feelgood. The good-natured charm of Paul Jones's Blues Band, and latterly, the high-energy jinx of Nine Below Zero. Fine groups all. But by the mid-eighties, blues had largely been consigned to the local pub, where once-aspiring guitar heroes dusted down youthful dreams in front of an audience of their now middle-aged peers.

However, as the decade faded, change was in the air. After years of being soothed by the glistening, if pristine sounds of synthesisers and digital drums, music fans began seeking something more 'real'. Cometh the hour, cometh the blues. Again. Always seen as an authentic art form (even when people were mostly ignoring it), a resurgence of interest had been brewing awhile, with Bonnie Raitt, Lonnie Brooks and Stevie Ray Vaughan all making sizeable inroads into the American market. But when the triple whammy of Eric Clapton's lavish *Crossroads* box-set collection, John Lee Hooker's guest-star strewn *The Healer* and Delta Blues' original shining star Robert Johnson's *Complete Recordings* arrived in stores to extremely healthy sales, the cat was out of the bag worldwide. Robben Ford's *Talk To Your Daughter*. Jeff Healey's *See the Light*. Robert Cray's *Don't Be Afraid of the Dark*. Even U2 had a go with 'When Love Comes to Town'. Blues was back and Gary Moore evidently still had his in spades. 'For me, it's not so much a case of "still got the blues",' he laughed to author Mick Wall, 'as the blues has still got me.'

Cynics might suggest that being no fool, Moore had spotted this renewed interest in the blues and pursued it with vigour. After all, he had been shaken by the thought of becoming an ageing rock guitar hero, 'all leather fucking trousers and ever-tightening waistbands', and with no dignified end in sight, putting on an older, more comfortable suit made sense. Yet, the truth was probably a lot less complicated. While Gary could have banked the hard rock/heavy metal shilling for a while longer, he was tired of playing dress-up, both sartorially and musically. It was time to follow his heart. 'In the eighties, if you were a guitarist, rock was what you played,' Moore later told VH1. 'But I don't think I ever felt that comfortable with it, so I just went back to the blues. The blues,' he concluded, 'allows me to tell the truth.'

And there was no better place to do so than the concert hall, to which Moore returned with his new band in the late spring of 1990. Of course, there was an element of risk here. As with the release of *Still Got The Blues*, Moore was asking his existing audience to walk with him into unknown territories, while hoping to pick up a few converts on the way. There would be no 'Out in the Fields' or 'After the War' to cheer for the old faithful, nor even 'Parisienne Walkways' to soothe the collective brow. Instead, his set list was based heavily in favour of the latest album, with a spray of covers to fill any remaining gaps. What's more, as well as Andy Pyle and Graham Walker on bass/drums, and unofficial musical director Don Airey covering the keys, Moore was also bringing a very un-heavy metal horn section with him, once again led by Frank Mead.[15] No fancy backdrops, banks of Marshalls or back-combed hair here. Just Moore, a crisp suit and his Midnight Blues Band.

After a couple of low-key warm-up dates in Scandinavia, the official opening night of the tour at Cardiff's St David's Hall on 6 May was an unnerving experience. 'Yeah, people were shouting, "Where's the real Gary Moore?"' he later told *Louder*'s Dave Ling. 'I was like, "Fuck, is this what it's going to be like?"' Yet, as dates progressed, Moore began to win over the doubters. While 'Moving On', 'All My Love' and Moore's rendition of Freddie King's own nimble-fingered 'The Stumble' were unlikely to strip paint or remove eyebrows, they carried a different type of punch. Less visceral, more expressive, the set was designed to take punters on an emotional journey, with horn driven belters giving way to sad, slow torch songs before the tempo picked up again for a long ride home.

Plus, Moore had help from one of the finer bluesmen in the business. Hailing from Leona, Texas, veteran guitarist/singer Albert 'The Iceman' Collins was completely unknown to Moore until alerted to his existence

---

15 In addition to Frank Mead, Nick Pentelow, Nick Payn and Martin Drover provided tenor, baritone saxophone and trumpet support for the tour.

by John Wooler, then head of Virgin's A&R department. A week later, Collins was in the studio with Moore trading licks on Johnny 'Guitar' Watson's rowdy ode to exhaustion, 'Too Tired' for inclusion on *Still Got the Blues*. In fact, Gary got on so well with Collins that he took him out on the road, Collins' snappy Telecaster lines warming up audiences at the start of the evening before he joined Gary on stage at the show's climax for a trio of classic blues standards: 'Too Tired', T-Bone Walker's scratchy, horn-infested 'Cold, Cold Feeling' and Bobby Bland's gambolling 'Further On Up the Road'.

With Collins an always welcome guest, Albert King reprising his performance of 'Oh Pretty Woman'[16] at Hammersmith Odeon and Moore himself storming the Montreux Festival for the first time on 21 June 1990[17] (he would soon make it a habit), what started off in Cardiff as a shaky first night in April had become a huge success within the space of six months. Gigging his way across the UK and Europe then back again, Moore's Back to the Blues tour took in 50 dates, from Danish festivals topping 250,000 attendees to an intimate fan-club type date at London's Town & Country Club in front of just hundreds. Moore even managed to squeeze in a few dates supporting his beloved Tina Turner, though once again, there would be no studio date to seal their musical union.

But he could probably live with that. At the start of 1990, when asked what the follow-up to *Still Got the Blues* might be, Moore brushed the question off with a joke. 'The next album?' he smiled to *Guitare et Claviers*, 'God, I haven't got a clue. You tell me. Maybe it'll be a jazz, bebop, acid, cèilidh rock record. Depends on how this one does, I suppose.' Now he had his answer. Bolstered by touring, talked up by critics and driven by radio play and single releases[18], Moore's 'little blues LP' had taken the number one spot in Finland and the Netherlands. That was just the start.

---

16 Key players on *Still Got the Blues*, Albert King and Albert Collins both sadly died within three years of appearing on the album, in 1992 and 1993, respectively.

17 Moore's appearance at the legendary Montreux Jazz & Blues Festival was released on video under the title *Gary Moore & The Midnight Blues Band – Live at Montreux 1990*. A DVD update featuring three bonus tracks from a later performance followed 14 years later.

18 Four singles were released internationally from *Still Got the Blues*, including 'Oh Pretty Woman', 'Walking By Myself, 'Too Tired' and the title track itself.

Still Got the Blues had also sold 200,000 copies in Sweden, with 250,000 more in Germany and a further 112,000 in Japan. When one added platinum and gold discs from Australia, New Zealand and Spain, things were looking very peachy indeed.

Yet, these were not the biggest numbers. Back in Blighty, Moore was to smash his previous record to pieces by shifting 300,000 units, allowing him to join the UK's prestigious platinum sales club. But the real shock came from America. Somehow, *Still Got the Blues* was well on its way to selling 200,000 copies. All Moore had to do, it seemed, was set sail across the Atlantic and it was his for the taking. Still, as the saying goes, 'It isn't the mountain ahead that wears you out, it's the grain of sand in your shoe.' In Moore's case, however, it was less about sand in his size nines and more about the buzzing in his ears.

CHAPTER TWENTY-TWO

Don't Forget To Bring The Trumpet

O n 27 August 1990, Stevie Ray Vaughan died. Perhaps the most naturally gifted blues guitarist of his generation, the 35-year-old Texan's last disc – 1989's *In Step* – had sold more than two million copies in the USA alone and won him a Grammy for best contemporary blues album. Coming to prominence via his liquid lead lines on David Bowie's 1983's megahit 'Let's Dance', Vaughan had overcome alcoholism, drug addiction and a turbulent love life to become American blues' most celebrated superstar. But his death in a helicopter crash after a performance in East Troy, Wisconsin, brought it all to a horribly premature end. Like nature, however, the music business abhors a vacuum, and soon enough, nets were being cast wide to find a successor to Vaughan's crown as the king of modern blues. Though well placed to stake a claim, it wasn't going to be Gary Moore.

Make no mistake, Moore had admired Stevie Ray Vaughan from afar for some time, going as far as to send a shout his way on *Still Got the Blues'* raucous 'Texas Strut'. They also shared a mutual friend in Jeff Beck with whom Vaughan previously toured, and there was even talk of Moore and Vaughan playing dates together in the autumn of 1990. When news of Vaughan's passing reached him, Moore dedicated an emotionally charged take on Elmore James's 'The Sky Is Crying' to the cowboy-hatted bluesman on stage in Essen, Germany.[1] However, the more some pockets of the music press talked up Gary as the obvious heir apparent to Vaughan – particularly in the American market – the less Moore appeared interested in the vacancy.

There were reasons for Moore's position, though one had to dig a little to find them. A shock to its maker though a delight to his record company and management, Moore's *Still Got the Blues* had already sailed past the million sales mark when news broke of Vaughan's death. 'It's ironic that when I go back to playing songs that I've been playing since I was 14, I get my first real international success,' he said. Come the end of 1990, and those sales were on the way to two million, with the USA now responsible for a decent percentage of all CDs purchased. When Moore performed 'Still Got the Blues' on NBC TV's influential talk show *Late Night With David Letterman* in early February 1991, sales spiked even further, as single and album reached number ninety-seven and number eighty-three, respectively.[2] Whichever way one did the maths, Moore was perhaps looking at 500,000 units in the States alone. With the American blues scene in search of a new star and Moore's musical background ensuring further crossover appeal with rock and pop audiences, should Moore hit the road Stateside as part of the right tour package, he might push sales of *Still Got the Blues* up by another million. These were big, big numbers.

But Moore was going nowhere. While gigging in Europe, he had been struck down with a variety of physical maladies, from influenza and sore fingers to persistent ear canal infections. These were wars fought by many

---

1   Like Moore, Vaughan loved Elmore James's 1959 standard 'The Sky Is Crying' and recorded it for his LP, 1984's *Couldn't Stand the Weather*. In concert, Stevie Ray would often dedicate the song to old friend Albert King, who in turn, had first covered 'The Sky Is Crying' in 1969 on the album *Years Go By*. Tying up a neat bow, the mighty King often referred to Moore and Vaughan as his 'godsons', which never failed to make Moore laugh.
2   The UK album and single release of 'Still Got the Blues' reached number thirteen and number thirty-one in the UK charts in March and May 1990.

touring musicians, life on the road leading to weakened immune systems, injured digits and God knows what else. In fact, Moore had long soaked his fingers in white spirit to toughen the calluses for a bruising night's work ahead. However, ear infections and the ringing that accompanied them were more perturbing. Well known for playing at maximum volume (even in rehearsals) the inability to shake off his auditory problems had unnerved Moore and made him wary of permanently damaging his hearing, even if getting him to turn down the 'bloody amp' was some-times a lost cause. Unfortunately, his difficulties were accompanied by a growing dislike of flying, the prospect of air travel making him anxious on top of his pre-existing ailments.

When Moore dispensed with his European touring obligations, the prospect of doing it all over again in the States, no matter how high the stakes or commercial gain, held no appeal. Sick, tired and according to some sources, 'just fucking over it', Moore dug his heels in. A one-off late-night TV appearance, perhaps. But beyond that, no can do. For those that knew him, while his stance was incredibly frustrating, it was also no great surprise. 'He could be very moody,' Don Airey later told the author Mick Wall. 'The trouble with Gary was that he wasn't really in control of what was coming through him. As soon as he put on that guitar . . . it would pour out of him. He couldn't stop it. He was a genius really, and I suppose that sort of thing comes at a price.'

Moore's refusal to tour the USA in late 1990/early 1991 was made all the more galling because he was residing there at the time. Now well on the way to being properly wealthy, if he had returned to the UK for more than two months he would face yet another punitive tax bill, thus stripping away much of the income his recent jaunt across Europe had generated. 'It seems to me they want to punish everyone in this country that does well. What's the point of that?' he grumbled.

As a result, Moore, his wife Kerry and now three-year-old son Jack temporarily upped sticks across the Atlantic to the fecund surrounds of Greenwich, Connecticut, then, as now, one of the most desirous locations in the USA. With America's West Coast only a matter of hours away by plane and the likes of New Orleans, Chicago and Houston at a similar distance, Moore could have technically navigated his way around the

States for a series of one-off dates easily enough. But even this was off-limits. Seemingly. Instead, Moore shut the door, took the phone off the hook and went to ground.

Unsurprisingly, his sabbatical didn't last. Before long, Gary had demoed two new compositions at Sountec Studios, the home recording facility of Deep Purple bassist (and fellow Greenwich resident) Roger Glover, who also produced and played on the sessions. At least another three songs were tried on for size at BearTracks Studios in Rockland County, New York, with The Midnight Blues Band's Andy Pyle and Graham Walker, but the results proved 'inconclusive'. However, things soon took an upward turn. Hugely impressed by the rhythm section that backed him on *Late Night With David Letterman,* Moore temporarily commandeered bassist Will Lee and percussionist Anton Fig[3] to help formulate several tunes at Carriage House Studios in Stamford, a matter of miles from where he was then living. While there, Moore's new buddy Albert Collins[4] also joined the party, with the pair cutting a thoroughly upbeat cover of Little Milton's 'The Blues Is Alright', for inclusion on Gary's next LP.

By now, Moore's head was once again full of ideas. Having successfully incorporated a brass section into the sound of *Still Got the Blues*, he was now keen to take things to the next level. Inspired by the funky riffs of The Memphis Horns on Albert King's landmark *Born Under a Bad Sign,* Moore decided to go straight to the source and commission the legendary duo for a studio session all his own. Hence, Wayne Jackson and Andrew Love now brought the same trumpet and sax that graced Otis Redding's '(Sittin' On) The Dock of the Bay' and Elvis's 'Suspicious Minds' to bear on Moore's increasingly melodic vision of the blues. 'Well, writing melodies is easier for me,' he said, by way of explanation. 'Having been a guitarist for so long, I find it easier to do that. But I do tend to leave writing lyrics to the last moment. I find it harder.' Yet, while Moore's

---

3 Anton Fig was no stranger to the United States' third smallest state, having appeared on Kiss guitarist Ace Frehley's first self-titled solo LP, in turn recorded at Frehley's home studio Ace in the Hole in Wilton, Connecticut, during the summer of 1978.

4 At around this time, Moore and Collins also shot a humorous promo for the single release of 'Too Tired'. It reached number seventy-one in the UK charts on 15 December 1990.

acquisition of Memphis's finest added a real element of melody and sass to his latest songs, there would be no abandonment of guitar heroics either. If his tone was less supercharged than before, Moore would still meet every brass blast or sax break with equal force, six strings and a feisty amp.

By the summer of 1991, Moore and his family were back in Britain and he was back in the studio, or more precisely, two of them. Moore's first stop had been Sarm's Hook End Manor in Oxfordshire, where producer Ian Taylor was patiently waiting to press 'record', with Frank Mead and the Midnight Horns also on call should the need arise. But when Gary's tax exile status again forced him to leave the UK for a time, things moved onto Paris where the guitarist and a core trio of Andy Pyle, Graham Walker and Tommy Eyre conspired to get the album done at Guillaume Tell studios on the banks of the Seine.[5] With additional strings/brass and backing vocals bolted at Abbey Road studios, and a black-and-white cover image of Moore beatifically lost in his own guitar musings (courtesy of photographer John Swannell), Moore's latest was finally ready to go.

Released on 10 March 1992, *After Hours* was in some ways a more cohesive effort than the album that preceded it. By following his desire to fuse Stax-like horns to classic blues in all its various forms, Moore had established a unified theme throughout the record, with ballads, rockers, tear-jerkers and foot-stompers enhanced by the presence of some pretty serious brass. Whether putting the swing into Moore's impish take on Hudson Whittaker's 'Don't You Lie to Me (I Get Evil)' or helping Moore mourn the death of yet another relationship on 'Separate Ways', horns were the glue holding *After Hours* together. This was especially pronounced on the none-more-doleful 'Story of the Blues', where saxes and trumpets eked out every ounce of emotion as Moore sang his sad tale of lost love using stock lines from a number of beloved blues tunes.

'Yes,' he later said, "Story Of The Blues' has that very Stax-y type horn line . . . and lyrically it's made up of little snippets of famous blues

---

5   Though Andy Pyle remained a key component of Moore's sound during recording, Moore also used bassists Mo Foster, Johnny B. Gaydon, Will Lee and old mucker Bod Daisley on at least one other tune for the album.

songs all tied together. Little quotes from songs that I grew up [with] really, and some that very personally . . . relate to me.'

Another clever enabler on *After Hours* was the judicious use of strings. Providing class and elegance to both 'Story of the Blues' and Moore's sublime cover of Duster Bennett/Fleetwood Mac's 1968 classic 'Jumping at Shadows', the violins and cellos were there again propping up 'Nothing's the Same'. With its fluttering oboe line (courtesy of Richard Morgan) and hesitant flamenco-like melody, it sounded more like a stray Sting single than soul-infused blues ballad. Yet, thanks to the presence of Gavin Wright's classical quartet (and some clever keys from Tommy Eyre), what might have been the musical orphan of *After Hours* actually ended up closing the record in some style.

Of course, with Gary Moore's name on the album cover, a good number people who bought *After Hours* were there for the guitars. As usual, he delivered, even if there were some real changes to his signature style and tone. Obviously taking Albert King's advice to 'play every other lick' to heart, Moore's performance throughout *After Hours* was less frenetic and more considered, his guitar also sounding cleaner, clearer and lighter.[6] This nuanced approach suited material such as 'Jumping at Shadows', 'Separate Ways' and the moody 'The Hurt Inside'. But when Moore wanted to turn on the fireworks, he still could. Both 'Only Fool in Town' and Moore's frenetic version of the Blues Breakers' 'Key to Love', a tune he 'played the hell out of' in his Belfast days, displayed white-knuckle levels of soloing, while lead-off single 'Cold Day in Hell' (originally cut with Deep Purple Roger Glover) also traded in scorching volume and crunching power chords as much as brass stabs and saxophone breaks. 'This is the sort of record I secretly wished Eric Clapton would make,' Moore laughed to *Q* in another EC-related barb, 'so, I decided to do it for him!'

A satisfying, rounded collection of songs with Moore in strong voice

---

6 Keen to branch out from the Marshall-heavy blues rock tones that ruled parts of *Still Got the Blues* (and probably give those ears a bit of a rest), Moore used a variety of smaller amps while making *After Hours*, including Fender Bassman, Tremolux and Princeton models. He also added a rather nice 1952 Twin Reverb to his armoury at around this point, too.

throughout, *After Hours* was another silver star in Gary's proverbial school report. Yet it also had the unenviable task of following up *Still Got the Blues*, a record that despite Moore's refusal to tour it in the States, had still amassed nearly three million sales. To give *After Hours* a fighting chance, Virgin put together an advertising campaign, with flyers and posters popping on city walls, while promo CDs landed on the desks of DJs, promoters and journalists. The biggest coup, however, was the album's launch party, held smack in the middle of London's Covent Garden at the Hard Rock Café. Here, in front of a crowd that included visiting rock dignitaries (and Travelling Wilburys) George Harrison, Tom Petty and ELO's Jeff Lynne, Moore performed a brief set before bringing on stage the man many called the true monarch of the blues: Riley 'B.B.' King.

Armed with his beloved black Gibson ES-335 guitar 'Lucille'[7], King was there on the night to perform two tracks with Moore. The first, 'The Thrill Is Gone' was B.B.'s signature tune, his version of Roy Hawkins and Rick Darnell's tear-jerking masterpiece having earned him both blues immortality and a Grammy upon its release in 1970. 'Really, it's the perfect sad blues love song,' Moore once noted, 'and B.B.'s the master of that style.' The second number on the agenda, Gary's own 'Since I Met You Baby', was considerably more cheery and a good deal newer. But King was already familiar with it. After all, he had recorded the version that appeared on *After Hours* with Moore only two or so months before.

'B.B.'s one of my absolute heroes but he contacted us first, though that sounds a bit conceited,' Gary told *Q*. 'Apparently, he'd bought *Still Got the Blues* and wanted to do a whole album together.' When that idea proved unfeasible, King 'flew in on Concorde one night [in December 1991], came in the next day, did his bits [for 'Since I Met You Baby'] and then then flew back,' leaving Moore in awe. 'He's the nicest guy I've ever worked with and so professional. He did all his guitars in an hour and his vocals in an hour and a half. He didn't mind doing things over

---

7   There was more than one version of 'Lucille' over the years, with King giving that name to each guitar he played. But his Gibson ES-335s (or subtle variations thereof) remain the instrument most people associate with 'Lucille'. How he came up with the name, however, is a tale too long for a footnote.

again. There was no ego trip. It's just inspiring to be around people like that. He actually said to me, 'I'd do this for nothing if I had to.' B.B. lives for music.' A bouncy castle of a song that played into King and Moore's lighter side, 'Since I Met You Baby' worked wonderfully both on *After Hours* and as a whoop-inducing crowd-pleaser at the Hard Rock Café on 2 March 1992.

With Virgin pushing hard to make the record a success and B.B. King even flying back to London to help Moore promote it, *After Hours* was in little danger of being ignored. Indeed, the disc made a strong showing in its first week of release, landing at number four in the UK and thereby giving the guitarist his highest ever album chart placing after Thin Lizzy's *Black Rose*. Numbers were also high elsewhere, with *After Hours* hitting the top spot or thereabouts across Europe, the Antipodes and Japan. Unlike its predecessor, however, sales proved immediate rather than sustained and the album was soon heading down the Top 30. In reality, no one was expecting a repeat of Moore's golden year, least of all him ('A bit unrealistic, don't you think?'). But it did underline the fact that unless the stars realigned and the gods of the Delta (Thames or Mississippi branch) smiled again from on high, there was never going to be another *Still Got the Blues*.

Still, tours push records, and Moore once again took to the road. This time out, there was an addition to his Midnight Blues Band with Carroll Thompson and Candy McKenzie[8] joining the ranks as backing singers. Lending a new level of tunefulness to Moore's onstage arsenal, the introduction of Thompson and McKenzie also brought the show one step closer to an old-fashioned blues/soul revue, with horns, pianos and three-part vocal harmonies all now available to the boss. It was this line-up then, that flew to the States to mark *After Hours'* release with two shows on each side of the country: one at the Universal Amphitheatre in Los Angeles on 16 May, the other seven days later at New York's Beacon Theater. Grossing approximately $130,000 per concert, these gigs were profitable enough, and the resultant publicity did help push *After Hours*

---

8 Wonderful singers both, Thompson and McKenzie had worked with Michael Jackson, Sting, Whitney Houston and Diana Ross among others, as well as releasing several albums in their own right.

into the US charts at number 145, with approximately 200,000 units sold on the way. But beyond that, there was to be no sustained effort on Moore's part to crack music's potentially most profitable territory. When done, Moore left America and returned to the UK. He would never perform in the USA again.

While his managers and record company keenly examined the factors behind Moore's lax attitude towards cracking the States, he just kept on trucking. First, there were two nights at Hammersmith Odeon in early June to attend to before a trio of shows brought Moore to Rotterdam and Paris later the same month. Then it was back to Hammy, where Moore and The Midnight Blues Band joined Otis Rush, Buddy Guy, Jimmie Rogers and three quarters of The Rolling Stones[9] for National Music Day's Celebration of the blues on 28 June.

As a teenager in Belfast, Moore wasn't known as a huge fan of Mick Jagger and co., preferring the mind-bending blues exotica provided by Jeff Beck-period Yardbirds. Moore wasn't really interested in Buddy Guy at that time either, his love of Eric Clapton and Peter Green causing him to bypass one of the true geniuses of the original Chicago blues scene in favour of Cream and Fleetwood Mac. But time can bring wisdom, and so it was with Moore, who now loved every minute of jamming with Guy, Jagger, Charlie Watts, Ronnie Wood and Otis Rush (who, to be fair, he had always loved). 'Yeah, I did a short set with Gary and his band,' Mick Jagger later said. 'We did numbers by Sonny Boy Williamson, Z.Z. Hill, and 'Who Do You Love' by Bo Diddley. A really good evening. I hadn't done anything like that for a while.' Nor had Moore.

The rest of the summer wasn't quite as magical. By late July, Moore's record company announced his ear problems were back, and tour dates were being cancelled or rescheduled as a result. By mid-September Moore had rallied sufficiently to perform a spray of dates in Germany, before headlining back-to-back concerts at the Royal Albert Hall on 4/5 October. Then came a special one-off appearance at north London's

---

9   Though Mick Jagger, Charlie Watts and Ronnie Wood were in attendance, Stones guitarist and 'human riff' Keith Richards couldn't make the party as he was recording his second solo LP, *Main Offender* in New York at the time.

White Knuckles

intimate Town & Country Club, where a visiting B.B. King and Moore renewed their acquaintance over 'Since I Met You Baby' and a genuinely shivery version of 'The Thrill Is Gone'.[10]

With promotional activities coming to a close at the Town & Country Club on 11 November 1992, Moore returned home to Shiplake to be with his family and look at the numbers. Though by no means repeating the runaway success of *Still Got the Blues*, *After Hours* hadn't done bad business, with sales closing in on 700,000 units. That number was consolidated by the healthy chart interest accorded the album that closely followed it. Released just six months after Moore's latest tour concluded, *Blues Alive* was a surprisingly rough and ready document of the 1992 shows, its contents mainly drawn from concerts in Los Angeles and London's Hammersmith/Royal Albert Hall.

Alongside the no-nonsense sound of *Blues Alive*, its cover sleeve also featured Moore caught in full-on grimace mode, his body hunched over, his face not pretty. Yet, to the man who had taken the photograph, this was Moore at his very best. 'Gary was actually quite difficult to photograph on stage,' said Gered Mankowitz. 'There was quite a lot of blue light, which created a low key [vibe]. He also made some extraordinary faces. [Those] grimaces, and all those violent movements. But because sustain was such a key part of his [guitar] style, you could capture him then as he stood still while finding the note.'

Yet, it was not Moore in stately repose that made the final cut. 'Oh, I got a lot of pictures with Gary throwing his head back and things, but they seemed such a cliché,' Mankowitz continued. 'What I especially liked was that intense 'hunchback' thing that he did. It seemed unusual, especially for a front cover. So, [we worked on that] and then [sleeve designer] Bill Smith had the idea of repeating the same picture on the sleeve. A very clever idea that, and one that really worked.' Featuring the best bits from *Still Got the Blues* and *After Hours* with a few surprises thrown in for good measure[11],

---

10 The Town and Country Club concert on 11 November 1992 was filmed and later released on video as *Blues Alive*.

11 Drawing the majority of its contents from Moore's previous two studio albums, *Blues Alive* also featured Moore's hyper-ventilating take on 'The Sky Is Crying' and 'Further On Up the Road', as well as a searing version of his own 'Parisienne Walkways'. The latter was re-released as a single in June 1993, reaching number thirty-two in the UK.

Blues Alive reached an extremely credible number eight in the UK charts on 22 May 1993.

If Moore's latest concert memento allowed him to stay in the public eye while planning his future from the leafy banks of the Thames, it wasn't the only recent(ish) release bearing the guitarist's name. Bassist Mo Foster's album *Southern Reunion* had Moore dusting off his jazz-rock credentials for the slow, but moody 'Gil' while ex-Free/Bad Company vocalist Paul Rodgers also put Moore's talents to good use on his 1993 collection *Muddy Water Blues*. A tribute to the Mississippi/Chicago legend, *Muddy Water Blues* found Rodgers singing the likes of 'I Can't Be Satisfied', 'Hoochie Coochie Man' and 'Good Morning Little Schoolgirl' while various famous guitar players soloed enthusiastically behind him.

With Jeff Beck, Guns N' Roses's Slash and Queen's Brian May (among others[12]) determined to make their mark, competition was fierce. But as always, Moore gave a good account of himself, dusting off his now little seen Fiesta Red Fender Stratocaster to add some sparks to Muddy's 1951 gem 'She Moves Me'. 'I had a quick run through and when Paul came in, I seriously started going for it,' he told *Guitar Player*'s Chris Gill. 'It didn't take long at all. A couple of quick passes, some lunch, we came back, had a listen, fixed a couple of bits and that was it.' However speedy the session, 'She Moves Me' allowed him to repay a debt he had carried since covering Free's 'Wishing Well' 10 or so years before. 'I was always a big fan of Paul Rodgers. As far as I'm concerned, he's the best singer to have come out of England. This new record is the best he's sung in years. To take any Muddy Waters song, and do it justice, well, you'd better be good.'[13]

★

---

12 Quite the gathering of axemen, *Muddy Water Blues* also featured Stray Cat Brian Setzer, Journey's Neal Schon, Bon Jovi's Richie Sambora, Steve Miller and Yes's ever-underrated Trevor Rabin. But honestly, Jeff Beck's contributions knocked everyone else's into a cocked hat.

13 Another six-stringer making an appearance on *Muddy Water Blues* was Pink Floyd's David Gilmour, whom Moore had shared space with on actor-turned-singer Jimmy Nail's 1992 debut CD *Growing Up in Public*. A surprisingly serviceable effort from a man better known for playing Geordie bricklayer Oz in Brit cult comedy drama *Auf Wiedersehen, Pet*, Nail was also a keen guitarist, which might explain the presence of Gilmour, Steely Dan's Elliott Randall, Moore and George Harrison on his album.

While completists pored over the concert souvenirs, jazz–inflected side-projects and various guest appearances, Gary Moore spent the early part of 1993 at home by the river Thames reflecting on past events and future moves. With his career compass successfully reset by re-embracing the blues, and millions of CD sales confirming the wisdom of that decision, the easy option for the guitarist was to produce more of the same. Indeed, even if *After Hours* hadn't quite scaled the heady peaks of its illustrious predecessor, the album's sturdy chart performance proved the public were still not tired of hearing Moore dust his proverbial broom. Given the circumstances, some would have shrugged their shoulders, banged out a new disc's worth of old Delta standards and just enjoyed the ride. Not so Gary, though. In yet another display of the musical restlessness that had come to define him, Moore again cast his net wide around for inspiration. This time he found it in the 'Tales of Brave Ulysses' . . .

CHAPTER TWENTY-THREE

Set The Controls For 1966

Cream were inducted into the Rock and Roll Hall of Fame on 12 January 1993 at Los Angeles' Century Plaza Hotel. Joining a cast that included The Doors, Creedence Clearwater Revival and the 'Queen of R&B' Ruth Brown, the trio played three songs to mark the occasion. 'Sunshine of Your Love', 'Crossroads' and 'Born Under a Bad Sign', the latter a tune they had never performed in concert before. Indeed, in his acceptance speech on behalf of the band, Eric Clapton confirmed that until the day before, they hadn't actually played anything in concert together for more than 25 years.

Yet, minutes after Cream left the stage the rumours started, with some seeing the group's appearance in LA as the precursor to a full-blown reunion; tours, records . . . perhaps even a moon landing. Ignited by one 20-minute performance, everything now seemed possible. But despite bassist/singer Jack Bruce and drummer Ginger Baker's reported willingness to reunite the group some say invented rock music, Eric Clapton wasn't so keen. A superstar in his own right for over two decades, the guitarist could afford to turn down such offers, and politely declined the idea. Truth be told, he probably hadn't forgotten what happened the last time all of them were in a room together for more than half an hour.

Possibly Belfast's biggest Cream fan in his youth, Gary Moore had long put things in perspective concerning Jack Bruce, Ginger Baker and EC. Firm friends with Bruce since the late seventies, the pair sang together on Moore's apocalyptic 1982 banger 'The End of the World' before spending the next ten or so years meeting up for the occasional drink or late-night jam. Bruce was also there when Moore needed a solid ear while prepping material for *Still Got the Blues*. So, when the guitarist in Bruce's own band, tousled-haired super-shredder Blues Saraceno, set off in the direction of American glam-rockers Poison, it was Moore whom he turned to for help. Down one guitarist for two solo gigs in southern Germany, Jack put in a call to Shiplake and Gary was there in time for the second night. In retrospect, Moore's dash to Esslingen on 15 August 1993 was the opening gambit in a much larger, if wholly unexpected, chess game destined to play out over the next year.

Moore had enjoyed striking up the band again with Jack Bruce, even if it wasn't his own. Still unsure of how to proceed after the horns, strings and sass of *After Hours*, a night of playing old Cream riffs had done Moore 'the world of good', as well as acting as a reminder of how much he loved the energy generated by a classic rock song. Obviously inspired, Moore asked Bruce whether he might like to hear some of the ideas he had been working on, and by late autumn, the pair were ensconced at Moore's home doing just that. 'There was no great plan or corporate strategy behind it,' Moore later told DJ Robin Ross. 'It just sort of fell together naturally.'

The next stage in Moore and Bruce's inexorable advance towards forming a group was Jack's 50th birthday concert at Cologne's E-Werk hall on 2/3 November 1993. Pulling together a list of mates and previous colleagues to help him celebrate his sixth decade on Planet Earth, Bruce invited Colosseum guitarist Clem 'The Loner' Clempson, Funkadelic keyboardist Bernie Worrell, Cream lyricist Pete Brown and cult saxophonist Dick Heckstall-Smith, with whom Bruce worked in both Blues Incorporated and The Graham Bond Organisation. There were also drummers, and lots of them. In addition to Bruce's regular sticksman Gary Husband, another former band member was there to pay his respects and bash some skins. 'Jack's 50th?' laughed Simon Phillips, 'Oh yes, I was there. But there were a lot of people there!'

Gary Moore was there too, though. His long-established habit of seeking as much privacy as possible before a show meant there were few obvious displays of camaraderie with his fellow performers. 'I don't really remember saying much to him,' Phillips continued. 'Just "Hello," really. I was kind of like, "Well, if you're going to be like that, whatever." Again, I felt he was a bit . . . isolated.' Not on stage, though. Stepping under the lights in Cologne, Moore joined Phillips and Bruce to make short work of the bassist's vinegary 'Life on Earth' before Simon struck up the beat of a salty sixties classic, 'N.S.U.'. This time, Phillips wasn't the only man with a pair of drumsticks in his hands. 'Obviously, I was with Jack (and Gary), but then Ginger came on and we played double drums on a couple of songs. God, he was so funny.'

When the mischievous, giggling form that was Ginger Baker placed his lanky frame behind the kit, Moore found himself in the preposterous situation of co-fronting a new, mutated version of Cream. Yet, as footage of the gig confirms, he was up to the task. With Phillips soon withdrawing to the wings, Moore, Bruce and Baker proceeded to make a quite wonderful racket, rattling their way through a set that included classic rock staples 'Spoonful', 'Politician' and 'White Room', each song sewn into the very fabric of Moore's youth. Even if he was well over being starstruck around his teenage heroes, this must have been a truly surreal 40 minutes.

Inspired by the events in Cologne, Moore and Bruce returned to England to continue work on Moore's next album. With the guitarist now increasingly committed to exploring beyond the blues base that informed his previous two records, it made sense to get Bruce fully involved in an official capacity. With Bruce came the possibility of using his own drummer Gary Husband, another outstanding player whose CV included spots with jazz-rock guitar magus Allan Holdsworth and pop funk maestros Level 42. But by the time Moore was finally ready to enter the studio, Husband was committed to another project. To solve the issue, Bruce suggested they get Ginger Baker involved.

So much has been written about the relationship between Jack Bruce and Ginger Baker, it seems almost pointless to add to it here. The arguments. The threats. The physical violence. Suffice to say, their time together in Cream can only be described as volatile, and was surely a contributing factor in bringing one of the planet's more promising bands to an abrupt end after just 18 months. Yet, here was Bruce – the same Bruce, in fact, that Baker had allegedly pulled a knife on back in 1965 – now extolling the virtues of his former nemesis in rhythm. Not unreasonably, Moore asked the obvious question. 'Are you sure?' Apparently, Bruce was. 'Ginger and I played [together] for five years before "that band" happened,' he said of their time with Blues Incorporated and Graham Bond. 'And you know what . . . I always enjoyed playing with Ginger.' A call was made. Baker locked the doors of his home in Parker, Colorado, said goodbye to his beloved polo ponies and flew to London.

Bruce was spot on about the benefits of inviting Baker to the party. Once described as 'Satan behind a drum kit', Baker's legendary temper seemed likely to scupper things before they even began. But the man who arrived at Berkshire's Hook End Studios appeared calm, measured and precise, though some of that serenity might have been down to what he was reportedly smoking. 'By the time I worked with Ginger,' Moore later told journalist Pete Makowski, 'he wasn't such a fiery character. He just used to smoke spliff all day just to keep himself even.' It appeared to do the trick. Picking up where he left off in Cologne some months before, Baker immediately provided Moore and Bruce with what they had been seeking: the greatest living backbeat in rock music. Still, best not tell Baker. 'Fuck off! I'm not a fucking "rock" drummer,' he once hissed. 'I'm a fucking jazz drummer.' And few would argue.

With Ian Taylor sitting in the co-producer's chair alongside Moore and the band taking well to Hook End's residential atmosphere, recording was quick and mostly trouble free.[1] The very definition of seasoned pros, Moore, Bruce and Baker cut many songs live, with Moore's solos often first takes. Now right in the midst of it all, Moore was also able to glean how Eric Clapton might have approached playing alongside such forces of nature. 'With Jack and Ginger, I began to realise why Eric played the way he did. The whole thing – the song, the mood, the dynamics – shifts

---

1 When Baker experienced issues bonding with a click track on the tune 'Where in the World', Moore's obsession with perfect time-keeping kicked in and veteran Welsh percussionist Arran Ahmun was hired to complete the song.

all the time.' Another revelation for the guitarist was how the relationship between rock's 'terrible two' was a lot less combustible than he previously thought. 'No, it wasn't what I thought at all,' Moore later told Robin Ross. 'They weren't at each other's throats. In fact, I think Jack looks up to Ginger a bit. They were just like brothers, winding each other up.'

If the notion of Bruce and Baker being more like blood brothers than mortal enemies represented a challenge to existing canon, what remained carved in stone was their place among the founding fathers of rock music, even if Baker hated the term. So, while Jack Bruce guesting on a Gary Moore solo record was one thing, two former members of Cream taking up arms alongside a world-class guitarist for an album's worth of original material was quite another. In short, this was no longer Moore's follow-up to *After Hours*, but a whole new band with a whole new slew of marketing possibilities. Keen to own part of the spoils, Virgin Records brokered a deal that allowed the group to exist outside the terms of Moore's existing solo contract.

With an agreement in place, the trio now needed a name. An attempt to find one was made over a few drinks, with Ticklers and Herbal Remedy (possibly one of Baker's) both given brief consideration. In the end, they went with a safer option. 'Well, it was actually a 'Gary Moore' album and Jack and Ginger ended up playing on it . . . [but] it didn't seem right to just call it ['Gary Moore'],' Moore later explained to *Vintage Guitar*'s Lisa Sharken. 'So, we had one of those meetings to think of a name, but everybody was just laughing and joking around. The names just got worse and worse. I mean, Ginger wanted to call the band 'Beyond Repair.' That was . . . a funny night. Anyway, we ended up just using our initials – *BBM* – and being really boring.'

The same couldn't be said for the image chosen for the cover of BBM's album. Taken as part of a set of group/individual portraits by photographer David Scheinmann, the picture presented the normally demonic-looking Ginger Baker as a black-clad, cigarette-chomping angel, a pair of huge white wings placed just so behind his back. 'When it was time for Ginger's portrait . . . he stood there lost in his cigarette,' Scheinman later told *Hypergallery*. '[Then] Jack and Gary had a moment of rock'n'roll mischief. They wheeled an old studio prop [of angel wings] behind him without him even noticing, [and] I scrambled to take the picture as quickly as possible. The flash went off and Ginger was awoken from his reverie. He looked round, saw the wings and said, "I'm not standing in front of these fucking things."' Too late.[2]

Released on 26 May 1994, with Baker forever cast as a fallen angel on its sleeve, the contents of BBM's *Around the Next Dream* weren't quite as lauded as David Scheinmann's soon-to-be iconic photograph. That said, there were moments of delight and occasional surprise. 'Where in the World' had the makings of a proper epic, with Moore and Bruce trading vocals and licks over a series of suitably confounding key changes. 'Can't Fool the Blues' on the other hand, sounded like a bullish escapee from one of Moore's recent solo albums, with horny guitars now replacing boisterous horn sections. Moore's own 'Naked Flame' sat well among the album's highlights, a guesting Tommy Eyre's keyboards providing soulful padding as Moore channelled his inner Jimi Hendrix for an extended lead break. But perhaps the biggest shock was 'Wrong Side of Town'. A proper jazz ballad with all the trimmings, and featuring a gorgeous, reedy vocal from Bruce, it was quite unlike anything else on the record. 'Wrong Side of Town' was written a long time before we got together,' Moore later confirmed. 'It took its lyrical slant from conversations about Charlie Parker and that whole drug scene. To me, it's the sound of heroin, as if the drug is singing to you.'

However, though parts *Around the Next Dream* motored along nicely, there were other elements that felt overly familiar. When prepping for the album, Moore had spoken of deliberately crafting songs with his guests in mind. 'Yes, I was very conscious of writing for Jack's voice and Ginger's style, he told the BBC. 'It was quite refreshing, actually.' Unfortunately, he was so good at it, that parts of *Around the Next Dream* sounded exactly like a Cream record. 'Waiting in the Wings' was 'White Room' by any other name, 'Glory Days' a musical doppelgänger for 'Badge', and as for 'City of Gold', the band's old signature cover 'Crossroads' was born again, but this time wearing bovver boots. Still, with Bruce

---

2 The defining image of one of music's more colourful drummers, Baker actually ended up using David Scheinmann's photograph for the cover of his 2010 autobiography, *Hellraiser*.

co-authoring or singing many of the tunes and Baker's signature stomp all over the album, the chances of *Around the Next Dream* sounding like anything other than a Cream LP was remote.

Despite some harumphs from certain quarters of the music press, *Around the Next Dream* proved there was still a market for sixties-themed power trios by entering the UK charts at an extremely solid number nine. But for Jack Bruce, while albums were worthy enough documents, the songs they contained gained a true second life on stage. 'Jack always said Cream were two bands,' Moore confirmed. 'The studio one and the live one.' Unfortunately, the aspiration of giving new life to their songs meant they would have to perform them together in concert. That wasn't always going to be easy.

From the off, there was trouble. Two warm-up gigs in Holland and Germany were mysteriously cancelled. Then the band's performance at London's Marquee on 19 May 1994 saw Moore visibly bridling at Bruce because his bass stack was drowning out the guitarist's own amplification. There was no encore. Luckily, things improved over subsequent dates in Denmark and Sweden, though just like 1966 all over again, it was now Baker who was telling Bruce to turn his amp down while on stage. Obviously getting clever in his old age, Baker tried to avoid further conflicts by disappearing promptly after a show leaving Bruce and Moore with the task of being interviewed by visiting music journalists, radio DJs and other media types. But there continued to be tantrums here and there from all three members, with each outburst chipping away at the veneer of collective peace.

A brace of concerts across Spain showed fans what the trio could really do, as 'City of Gold' and 'Can't Fool the Blues' rubbed shoulders with fiery covers of Muddy Waters' 'Rollin' and Tumblin'' and Cream's own 'Tales of Brave Ulysses'. Here, improvisation met mad-eyed invention head on and Moore got the chance to silence any doubters that he was no more than 'A cut-price Clapton', according to naysayer fans of the latter. But BBM's revelries were brief. By the time the tour hit France in late June, dates had already been cancelled due to a recurrence of Moore's ear and throat problems. The possibility of a US jaunt once under serious discussion now went unmentioned, and following the band's appearance at the Berlin Festival on 3 July, it really was all over. One album, one single[3], 12 official concerts and then 'Time gentlemen, please'.

As Jack Bruce returned to his wife in nearby Esslingen and Ginger Baker his beloved ponies back in Colorado, Gary Moore tried to explain where things had gone wrong. As ever, one had to be careful not to drown in his honesty. 'There were a couple of good songs on the album,' he told writer Lisa Sharken, 'but we just had so much going on around us. I mean, can you imagine trying to go on the road with the people involved in that?' For Moore, a combination of unrealistic expectations and occasional press sniping had started the rot. 'The media perception at the time was that [Jack and Ginger] had tried to get Cream together but Eric wouldn't do it so they got me. That wasn't the case; I actually formed the band.' But in the end, it was egos that did for BBM. 'We used to have our fights because everyone in the group had their own bands [before]. That was the real problem.' In a band of leaders, it seemed, nobody was interested in following anyone else. Still, it wasn't all bad. 'Yes, the shame of the whole thing was that it was a bloody good band!' Moore later told *Guitarist*. 'It was a great musical experience to work with Jack on a more permanent basis, and with Ginger, who's the finest drummer I've ever played with.'

Great things had been expected for BBM, not least by the marketing department at Virgin Records. But the band's premature end now meant that Moore had to be re-established in the public eye as a solo artist, and quickly. The easiest option was a greatest hits package, which duly arrived just in time for Christmas 1994.[4] In line with Moore's wishes, some real thought had been put into the CD. Instead of offering a cynically gathered collection of pre-existing singles, *Ballads and Blues 1982-1994* focused on the more dewy-eyed aspects of his back catalogue,

3 The august-sounding 'Where in the World' reached number fifty-seven in the UK singles chart upon its release in August 1994.

4 At around the same time Moore's compilation was hitting stores, ex-Thin Lizzy guitarist Snowy White released his latest solo album *Highway to the Sun*, to which Moore had contributed a feisty, if odd solo on the track 'Keep on Working'. Pink Floyd's David Gilmour, Geordie slide guitar guru Chris Rea and Ace vocalist Paul Carrack also guested on the LP.

its track listing bringing together 'Falling in Love With You', 'Empty Rooms' and 'Still Got the Blues' alongside several unreleased tracks. Of these, the acoustic-leaning 'With Love (Remember)' sounded like a stray Bond theme attempted by Colosseum II, while the moody 'Blues for Narada' also brought Moore back to his jazz-rock routes, pyrotechnic guitars and all. A pleasing, if non-essential package featuring recent BBM outtake 'One Day', *Ballads and Blues* reached number thirty-three in the UK charts.

Commercial holding pattern established, Moore was once again free to unpack the drawing board and figure out which direction he was headed in next. For the first time in more than a decade, that decision would be taken without the full input of Steve Barnett. One of the most respected managers on the rock scene with a client list that now included AC/DC and Foreigner, Barnett had moved to the States some years before with the intention of further expanding Part Rock's business into the American market. That resulted in the birth of Hard To Handle Management, with Barnett acting as president.

Unfortunately, while Barnett's new geographical location gave Moore a firm foothold in the USA should he want it (though he very often didn't), it also meant that he wasn't around to help with Moore's UK-based affairs (of which there were many). A fix of sorts was put in place when Barnett's British-based business partner Stewart Young offered his support. But that didn't quite gel, and Moore's newest tour manager, Ian Martin, found himself fast-tracked into handling Moore's affairs. That promotion more or less coincided with the birth and dissolution of BBM, so it must have been a hell of a ride. With the advent of Ian Martin came two more new faces: replacement tour manager and former soldier Ian Robertson and soon-to-be personal assistant Darren Main, who like Graham Lilley, was destined to become a crucial cog in the wheels of Moore's day-to-day operations.

While the management team around him might have been new, Moore's latest direction wasn't. In fact, it could be construed as the musical equivalent of drawing a warm blanket around his knees. Blossoming at Belfast's Club Rado in the spring of 1967 and nurtured ever since, Gary's love of Peter Green was enduring and heartfelt. When

Moore once again turned to the blues at the start of the 1990s, his intention had been to record an LP in the vein of early Fleetwood Mac, perhaps even using certain members of the band to enable it. In the end, Moore had to be content with covering Green's 'Stop Messin' Around' while dedicating the album to his old friend. But the idea of creating a more substantial edifice in Green's honour had never left him. At last, he was ready to do it, though Gary being Gary, it had to be done just right. 'This is not a "tribute",' he said. 'It's a celebration of Peter's music . . . a big thank you for everything he's given us, not just me, but all the inspiration he's provided over the years for people everywhere.'

Moore's vision for his pet project was as exacting as one might expect. Assembling the old gang of Andy Pyle and Graham Walker on bass/drums, he augmented his trusty rhythm section with the equally trusty Tommy Eyre on keyboards and Nicks Payn and Pentelow on saxophones. To keep order and get those guitars exactly on point, Ian Taylor was also brought back to co-produce the album. But whereas before, emphasis was placed on exploring every sonic possibility available to the band, this time around Moore was chasing the original sound and spirit of Green-period Mac. That meant studying the original recordings in meticulous detail with the hope of recapturing the clear-toned alchemy contained therein.

'When I did *Still Got the Blues*, I actually started off (much more low key [sound-wise],' he told *Guitarist*. 'But by the time the album came out and we went on the road, the whole thing had got bigger and bigger, and it became like a rock thing again. I ended up playing very loud with a big distorted guitar sound and . . . lost the essence of it. It was very successful and everything, but that's not the point. Musically, this [album] is more where it started off. I've gone right back to that very bare feeling . . . very dry and very pure.'

Of course, Moore had a piece of kit that made that aim considerably easier. Now with him for nearly quarter of a century, the 'Greeny' Les Paul may recently have been put aside in favour of his newer (and less valuable) 'Stripe' for road work, but it was now back in a big way for the new record. 'It's the best guitar I've ever owned,' he reiterated at the time. 'It has a magic and a sound all its own and I've used it all the way through this album.' For Moore, the 'Greeny' remained less an instrument and more a sacred relic.

Given the tools to hand and the effort involved, it was no great surprise that *Blues for Greeny* was at times almost spooky in summoning the tone and timbre of one of the great British bands and their formidable, former leader. From the horn-assisted push of *Mr Wonderful*'s 'If You Be My Baby' and funky 'Long Grey Mare' to the spare, tearful blues of 'Merry Go Round' and 'Love That Burns', Moore and co.'s painstaking recreation of vintage Fleetwood Mac was spot on in almost every detail. Moore had even captured Green's brief tenure with John Mayall on 1967's *A Hard Road* to near-perfection, his covers of 'The Same Way'[5] and 'The Supernatural' sending shivers to the same parts of the spine that the originals had 28 years before.

Still, *Blues for Greeny* wasn't just some slavish, if well-intentioned copy. Though Moore was hell-bent on shining a proper light on Green's version of the blues, as the rowdier flavours of 'Driftin'' and 'Looking for Somebody' confirmed, Moore hadn't forgotten where to locate the grit in the oyster. 'I didn't want to just clone it and do everything exactly the same as he did,' Moore told writer David Mead. 'Yes, I've tried to be faithful to the original songs, but put a bit of myself in there as well.'

With its pining, string-drenched lead-off single 'Need Your Love So Bad'[6] reaching number forty-eight in the UK, and the album itself hitting a creditable number eighteen, *Blues for Greeny* could be deemed a success. But as Moore was at pains to point out, this was as much about giving kudos to his youthful idol as it was about chart positions. 'I don't really like to use the word "tribute album" because Peter Green's not dead. People may say it's a tribute album but for me it's a "thank you" album.' That sentiment was not only emotional, but financial too. In a show of great decency, Moore had deliberately chosen songs that listed Green as

---

5   Moore had been playing 'The Same Way' since his days with The Gary Moore Band in 1973.

6   Written/recorded by Little Willie John and Mertis John Jr. in 1955 and covered by Green and co. 13 years later, it had reportedly been manager Mike Vernon's idea to add strings to Mac's version of 'Need Your Love So Bad'. Moore was happy to follow suit for his own take on the tune.

their sole author, ensuring he received the lion's share of songwriting royalties.[7]

But surely the real benefit of *Blues for Greeny* was that it brought teacher and pupil together again. Though Moore and Green were close in the early seventies, circumstances had seen the two drift apart. There was the odd exception here and there. While recording 'Don't Believe a Word' with Philip Lynott for *Back in the Streets*, Moore was surprised to find Green in the studio bar downstairs. 'Hey Gary,' Green said on hearing the track, 'that sounds like something Fleetwood Mac would have done.' However, when their paths reportedly crossed again a year or so later, conversation flowed less easily. Still beset by the psychiatric problems that had plagued him on and off since leaving Mac, Green's moods could be capricious, his attention span sporadic.

Fortunately, by the time of *Blues for Greeny*'s release, Green was on the up. Improvements in the balance of his medication and a renewed interest in music found him in considerably better health and spirits. That said, according to Moore, Green's memory could still play tricks, even when it came to the Gibson Les Paul he once owned. 'I had this idea for the cover [of the album] where I'd take [the 'Greeny'] along, go and meet him and take a picture where we both had our hands on it,' Moore told writer Pete Makowski. 'But [when] he picked up the Les Paul, he said, "Aw, I sold mine." I said, "*That is yours.*" He goes, "No, no, that can't be mine. It's got too old." I said, "Well, I bought it a long time ago, Peter." Then he looked down and said, "Yeah, actually it does look like mine," played a chord and said, "Success!" Then we both put our hands on the guitar. But yeah, he'd totally forgotten that he'd sold it to me.' Thankfully, Peter Green was there in person to witness Moore not only playing his old axe, but also performing a concert in his honour at London's Shepherd's Bush Empire on 27 April 1995. Opening up with Mac's 'The World Keep on Turning' and finishing on a sublime 'Jumping at Shadows' some 90 minutes later, Moore was even lucky enough to have the great man himself emerge

---

7   There were three exceptions here: As above, 'Need Your Love So Bad' was written by Little Willie John and Mertis John Jr. while Green shared co-writing credits on 'If You Be My Baby' and 'Love That Burns' with his former manager Clifford Davis.

sheepishly from the wings to take a now rare bow in front of a suitably appreciative crowd.[8]

Delightfully, both Gary Moore's album and accompanying gig seemed to galvanise something in Peter Green. After two decades of only the faintest of musical activity, he decided to return to the fray with a new band, The Splinter Group, coincidentally featuring previous Moore/ Whitesnake associates drummer Cozy Powell and bassist Neil Murray. 'Well, as you know, Gary and I parted amicably, and had remained friends,' Murray said in 2020. 'In fact, I appeared with him [and The Chieftains] on *RTÉ's The Late Late Show* in 1987 [for 'Over the Hills and Far Away']. Then we ended up jamming at Peter's manager's wedding.' For Moore himself, Green coming back to music in the wake of a record named for him had a wonderful symmetry to it. 'It was lovely Peter came out on stage with us at Shepherd's Bush that night, and even better that he went back to playing music soon after,' he later said. 'That was just brilliant.'

In the wake of Moore's appearance at Shepherd's Bush, there were a few more stray dates, including yet another tear up fronting The Midnight Blues Band at 1995's Montreux Jazz Festival. But as with BBM, Moore didn't seem in the mood for any major road work. Much to everyone's surprise, he even turned down a series of summer gigs supporting The Rolling Stones. Still, there were extenuating circumstances. For while his past two albums had paid off debts both professional and personal, things on the home front were becoming somewhat complicated. 'It's a lovely part of the world, Shiplake,' said one of Moore's friends. '[But] the Shiplake years ended for Gary when his wife caught him with the babysitter . . .'

---

8   The *Blues for Greeny* Concert was filmed and released on video on 22 May 1996. Though there has been no DVD re-release, footage of the gig can be found on YouTube.

CHAPTER TWENTY-FOUR

The Mind Is Its Own Place

Up to late 1993, Gary Moore had avoided the worst excesses of being in the public eye. Several good reasons for that. Moore's profile was built on the back on engagement with the serious music press, and beyond the occasional push into *Top of the Pops* or 'youth TV'.[1] earlier in his career, his appeal had always remained well within the purview of the rock community. Further, unlike say Ozzy Osbourne, Gary hadn't bitten the head off dove nor bat, while his days of falling out of pubs and nightclubs drunk and insensible were also long over. Mostly. In fact, aside from the odd reference to a sometimes-testy manner with journalists and the exact nature of how he got that scar, Moore's public persona was a manageable combination of jobbing guitar god, occasional rock star and latterly, born-again Belfast bluesman. However, in late November 1993, he found himself dragged from the pages of *Q*, *Melody Maker* and *Guitarist* into the potentially more hazardous world

---

1 Moore's more notable TV spots from around this time included an appearance on BBC1's *French & Saunders*, where he joined Lemmy, Mark Knopfler, David Gilmour, Ralph McTell and Level 42's Mark King for a Pythonesque skit revolving around the merits of correct guitar tablature. Yep. Moore was also a guest on the love it or hate it cult BBC2 music show *Never Mind the Buzzcocks*.

of the 'red tops' when an affair with his son's former nanny hit the headlines of *The Sun*.

Some five years after the birth of first-born Jack, Kerry Moore gave birth to another boy, christened Gus. When she and Gary sought additional help with the infant's care, an advertisement was placed in a local paper and Camilla Harding-Saunders was taken on as a nanny. Harding-Saunders stayed with the family until it became clear she wasn't really needed and then moved on again. Sometime later, Moore happened upon her in Henley-on-Thames and they began an affair, only to be reportedly discovered by her boyfriend, who in turn confronted at the guitarist at his Shiplake mansion. At first, Moore denied it. Then he simply drove away in his car. He did not return.

However sad the circumstances, unions are injured or broken every day. Yet the results seldom end up splattered across the pages of *The Daily Mirror* and *The Sun*. That said, Gary Moore was – or at least used to be – a long-haired, guitar-toting type. He was also a man in his early forties, while Harding-Saunders was only 23 when they met. Ticking boxes in the salacious trinity of 'sex, drugs and rock'n'roll', it was only a matter of time before a private matter became a public mess. Someone told the papers. Tick, tick, boom. All of a sudden, Moore was facing trial by tabloid. In the end, he got lucky. No sooner had the story broken than it quietened again as readers turned their attention to a new emotional bonfire. Still, there was a considerable amount of tidying up to do.

As with most all his former romantic partners, Moore fell hard for Harding-Saunders. Fine wines, flowers and jewellery were surely bought and promises no doubt made over moonlit dinners in reassuringly expensive restaurants. In keeping with how he did things, there would also be no return to the house at Shiplake. Calling an end to eight years of marriage, Moore had his belongings moved elsewhere and their former home was put up for sale. In time, Moore bought a new one, with Harding-Saunders moving in thereafter. But while his marriage was over, Moore's role as a father was not. Determined to play an active part in the lives of his two sons, he stayed close to his former family even after divorce, flitting between Henley-on-Thames, nearby Marlow, west

London and wherever else Kerry and the boys were. This would be the way of things from now on.

Looking back, it must have been an extraordinary time for Moore: a near-decade long marriage upended by an affair soon after the birth of his second son, a new relationship with a woman almost 20 years his junior, sides being taken, judgements being made, press intrusion, a divorce, then the inevitable financial settlement. Given the circumstances, it was a wonder he wasn't howling at the moon.

Unfortunately, just as this period of terror and exhilaration began to stabilise, Moore received terrible news. A matter of weeks after saluting his teen hero Peter Green at the Shepherd's Bush Empire, he found out his old friend Rory Gallagher had died. Just 47, Gallagher had been in ill-health for some time, his death on 14 June 1995 was the result of complications arising from a recent liver transplant. 'I saw him at Self-Aid in Dublin about ten years ago and he didn't seem very happy [or] look too well,' Moore told *Hot Press* at the time. 'I sat next to him on the plane back. He was very nervous and didn't like flying very much.'

Though their lives often took them in different directions, the pair had kept in touch, with Moore meeting Gallagher at Chelsea's Conrad Hotel in the spring of 1994 to play him the new BBM album. But when the pair talked again a year later, Gary knew something was seriously amiss. 'Rory sounded so beaten down,' said Moore. 'He'd had a row with some promoter who had treated him badly . . . and it really did his confidence. He told me he hadn't been out of the house since the New Year . . . and this was March or April.' Weeks later, Rory passed away.

'The weird thing,' Moore again confirmed to *Hot Press*, 'was that while I'd been driving around the night before he died, I passed the hospital where he was and thought of dropping in. But then, it was too late.' For Moore, Gallagher was a one-off. 'What tells you more than anything about Rory was [when I spoke to him], he didn't say anything about his problems. He was more interested in my problems. Apart from [being] a great player . . . Rory never compromised himself musically. He would never do something that was, for him, below a certain level of integrity. All came to light for me at the funeral. It wasn't like a rock'n'roll circus [where] . . . people were there to be seen. There was just so much respect. Rory had earned that. He was a purist.'

Back in sixties Belfast, Rory Gallagher and Gary Moore were both purists of a sort. Bonding over Teles and Strats, broken strings and Jimi Hendrix, the two had been among Ireland's most promising guitarists north or south of the border, their primary inspiration drawn from the blues. But while Gallagher remained wedded to the music of the Mississippi Delta to the very last, Moore had later struck out for destinations unknown. From the space-rocking antics of Skid Row and Colosseum II to the reels and airs of *Black Rose* and *Wild Frontier*, Gary was never afraid of taking a jackhammer to his then current path when the situation called for it. Yet of late, he had once again come to rest in the blues, or at least thereabouts. Indeed, for five years, Moore's path had seldom strayed far from the sounds that informed his youth. 'Still Got the Blues'. 'Story of the Blues'. 'Can't Fool the Blues'. *Blues for Greeny*. The clue was in the titles. But by 1996 the restlessness that had recently set fire to Moore's personal life now found its way into his professional career. For the umpteenth time, Moore was ready to change musical course, and on this occasion, it involved break beats.

To enable his new frame of mind, he broke with the recent past. That meant saying goodbye to The Midnight Blues Band and hello to drummer Gary Husband and bassist Guy Pratt instead. Moore knew Husband well through their shared association with Jack Bruce, and was now delighted to work alongside the percussionist on a project all their own. However, Pratt was a novel and inspired addition to the team. Known throughout the business as an 'all round good hang', Pratt thus far numbered Michael Jackson, Madonna, Jimmy Page and Pink Floyd among his musical playmates while also co-writing Jimmy Nail's 1992 number one UK hit 'Ain't No Doubt'. A fine bass player as well as occasional stand-up comedian[2], Pratt brought both levity and four-string expertise to Gary's latest enterprise. He was quite the fan of his latest employer too. 'Oh

---

2 Aside from playing bass with a *Who's Who* of the rock and pop scene while also co-writing several hit songs/TV theme tunes of his own, Pratt occasionally acted. His one-man music/comedy show *My Bass and Other Animals* was later performed at the Edinburgh Festival (2005) as well as turned into a book of the same name (2007).

God, I adored Gary,' Pratt later told *Talking Bass*, 'and he was a fucking brilliant guitarist.'

Latest rhythm section in place, Moore was eager to get recording. Yet, in a continuing effort to avoid the taxman's attentions, his time in Britain remained strictly limited, leading to enforced bi-weekly trips between the dependable Hook End Studios in Oxfordshire and luxuriant, if unfamiliar grounds of Château Miraval in the Var region of southern France. Once owned by composer/pianist Jacques Loussier, who made his fortune retooling the works of classical composers such as Bach for a jazz audience, Miraval had long been a go-to destination for successful rock star types. Set in the grounds of an expansive estate, the complex was terracotta in colour, surrounded by (some rather fine) vineyards and boasted its own working farm.[3] Once inside, visitors were greeted with a large recording hall overlooked by an exquisite oval window around which one previous visitor (Yes's Jon Anderson) had reportedly painted a swirling, multi-coloured mural. But the cherry on top for Moore was not connected to the fine arts. Instead, he was there for Miraval's Solid State Logic (or 'SSL') recording console, seen by some as the holy grail of modern studio technology.

The man behind the console, at least for the majority of the project, was Chris Tsangarides. Joining Moore in the co-producer's chair for the first time since 1978's *Back on the Streets*, Tsangarides had remained friends with Moore ever since, their respective families even holidaying together. Now Tsangarides had been brought in to replace Ian 'Still Got the Blues' Taylor, helping facilitate Moore's pursuit of 'something very different'. For a while, that goal appeared mutually achievable, as Moore, Tsangarides, Husband and Pratt made short work of Gary's new songs. Yet, following a short break in recording, Moore switched tactics and parted with Chris Tsangarides, turning to new face Andy Bradfield in an effort to complete the album the way he originally envisaged it.

A graduate of London's prestigious Olympic Studios and general hot

---

3 Used by the likes of Pink Floyd, AC/DC, Sting and Sade, Château Miraval studios and its grounds were purchased by Hollywood power couple Brad Pitt and Angelina Jolie in 2011. Though they later divorced and Jolie sold her share in the property, Pitt still retains a sizeable interest in the domaine.

ticket item following his mixing work on Everything but the Girl's platinum-selling *Walking Wounded*, Bradfield had full command of the cuts, beats, bumps and bleeps then defining modern electronic dance music. He also knew his way around an SSL recording desk like nobody's business. These were all qualities Moore was hell-bent on using for his own ends, and Bradfield was flown to southern France to join him in the autumn of 1996.

Accompanying Bradfield was Magnus Fiennes. Part of the distinguished Fiennes clan that included brothers Ralph and Joseph (actors), sisters Martha and Sophie (filmmakers) and Sir Ranulph (explorer, third cousin, once removed), Magnus was a gifted composer in his own right. Like Bradfield, he was also extremely adept at keyboard programming and loop building. Over subsequent months and several trips to London, Miami and the perhaps less glamorous Reading, the trio (aided by Def Leppard/Bryan Adams keyboard whiz Phil Nicholas) pressed on until Moore had his record.

Released on 26 May 1997, *Dark Days in Paradise* was a valiant attempt on Moore's part to fashion a creditable and contemporary-sounding AOR/pop album. It was also the most lyrically honest work of his career, with themes of love, betrayal and emotional recrimination almost embarrassing to hear given his recent relationship travails. Still, he wasn't ducking it on that front. 'These are all very personal songs,' he said in a press kit interview of the time, 'and I tell the truth when I write. I can't make things up.' Yet, however brave Moore had been in exposing what some might deem a mid-life crisis over the course of 11 songs, *Dark Days . . .* lacked the authenticity and cohesion of more recent releases. Unfortunately, by modernising his output, he also risked alienating a core following blissfully happy to support his role as a latter-day bluesman.

Still, there were some clever moments. 'I Have Found My Love in You' had a timeless quality to it, combining nu-soul atmospherics with some gorgeous, lilting guitar work. 'One Good Reason', 'One Fine Day' and 'Afraid of Tomorrow' were also distinguished in their own way, allowing Moore a rare opportunity to indulge his love of Beatles chording with the same Indian-like melody lines George Harrison introduced to the group back in 1966. This exploration of Asian textures was present on the Nitin Sawhney-influenced electronica of 'Always There for You' too, Magnus Fiennes's programmed tabla-like drums connecting wonderfully well with Gary Husband's oh-so subtle backbeat. On 'Like Angels', it was Guy Pratt's chance to properly introduce himself to listeners, the bassist negotiating the various twists and turns in Moore's lush ballad with real aplomb.

Yet, where there were peaks, there were also troughs. On 'Like Angels', the limits of Moore's vocal style were cruelly exposed, his falsetto simply not up to the task of carrying a slow soul-pop tune.[4] Contrastingly, while there was little wrong with Moore's singing on 'What Are We Here For?', the song's lyrical message could be construed as naive, his questions about humanity's place in the universe always a potentially dangerous area for multi-millionaire musicians to pontificate on in a post-punk world. Still, as Moore sailed across the stars with only a bottleneck slide for company, the impulse to forgive became palpable. That couldn't be said for 'Cold Wind Blows'. Bolting Canned Heat-style sixties trance blues to nineties digital programming, one got the distinct impression Moore had simply warmed up an unused tune from *Still Got the Blues* in the hope it could bear a contemporary spin.

Where Gary Moore did manage to successfully align melody, lyric and intention was the album's (official) closing track, 'Business As Usual'. A near relative to *After the War*'s 'Blood of Emeralds', but far more confessional in its storytelling, the song tracked Moore's life, warts and all, over the course of 32 lines, four choruses included. Indeed, with Gary's lyrics covering everything from parental discord and childhood truancy to his recent affair and subsequent divorce, no detail had been spared. At times, when recounting his adventures with Rory Gallagher, Dr Strangely Strange, Brush Shiels and the one and only Philip Lynott, he could sound happy. However, when recalling first love with Sylvia Keogh and the heartache it eventually led to, the tone was much more wistful. Yet, as Moore sang his heart out over

---

4 Wisely, Moore had backing vocalists Chyna Gordon and Dee Lewis (sister of singer Linda) to help him out on several of *Dark Days in Paradise*'s poppier or more soulful tracks.

a swaying, slow-building Celtic anthem[5], it all pointed in one direction: gut-wrenching honesty.

In the early nineties Gary Moore re-embraced the blues, and in doing so, neatly avoided being part of the hard rock/hair metal bonfire that followed in the wake of grunge. Given the low opinion he held of most of the acts put to the torch by the rise of Nirvana, Pearl Jam and their like, Moore probably warmed his hands in the ashes. By consolidating the success of *Still Got the Blues* with *After Hours* and BBM, he had also remained impervious to the demise of grunge at the hands of Britpop while bopping around the UK Top 10 throughout. Indeed, whether by accident or design, Moore had avoided any real damage from the sea of changes in rock and pop over the previous half-decade. Yet, the release of *Dark Days in Paradise* brought all that to a swift end. 'Too pop for the rockers, too rock for the poppers' and with a distinct lack of guitar solos for the faithful, *Dark Days in Paradise* lived up to its ominous title. Entering the British charts at a lowly number forty-three in mid-June 1997, the album fell out again soon after. With numbers only slightly better in Europe, this was real cause for concern – not only for Moore, but Virgin Records, too.

Strangely, Moore appeared unfazed by the album's poor reception. In fact, aside from the occasional radio interview and a pre-booked 30-minute VH1 live TV special in which he, Guy Pratt, Magnus Fiennes and Gary Husband performed several tunes from the record[6], Moore seemed uninterested in taking his latest songs live. In the end he relented, bringing his new band with him on a 26-date European tour that included a third spot at the Montreux Jazz Festival on 9 July 1997 and according to Fiennes's official website, a 'Hells Angel festival near Lyon, France' where the keyboardist dislocated his shoulder during a particularly strident flourish. 'All very Spinal Tap,' he quipped. After further concerts (though no further injuries) in Germany, Austria, Spain and an

---

5 Moore's extended solo on 'Business as Usual' strongly recalls his work on Dr Strangely Strange's 1970 tune 'Sign on My Mind', leading one to believe he was referencing a solo cut 26 years before in Dublin.

6 In addition to several choices from *Dark Days in Paradise*, Moore augmented his VH1 set with heavily modified versions of 'Still Got the Blues' and Otis Rush's 'All My Love'.

eye-catching appearance at a military base in Hell, Norway, the band were home by mid-October.

For Moore however, 'home' now no longer included the presence of Camilla Harding-Saunders. Having dated his ex-babysitter for a year or so after their initial affair ended Moore's marriage, the relationship seemed to peter out completely, with Harding-Saunders fading from his life story almost as quickly as she had entered it. Houses were sold, and others bought with Moore on the move again for the fourth time in as many years. Yet, he was not alone for long.

While prepping *Dark Days in Paradise*, Moore was introduced to a 28-year-old conceptual art student named Jo-Anne (or 'Jo') Rendle, then dividing her time between a degree course at London's Guildhall, helping design film sets for the likes of director Julien 'Absolute Beginners' Temple and a PR job at Moore's management headquarters in south west London. Suffice to say, the two hit it off immediately, and were soon both a couple and working team, with Rendle handling various media, promotional and touring responsibilities for Moore and his band. Having reportedly spent her early childhood on an army base in Singapore, Jo Rendle was clear-headed, well-liked by Gary's friends – 'Jo was a lovely person,' said The Strangelies' Tim Booth – and also had crucial, first-hand experience of the demands Moore faced as a professional musician. Henceforth, she would keep him in safe harbours for much of the next decade.

If Jo Rendle represented new romantic possibilities for Moore, the events of recent years illustrated the value of old friends too. In fact, when the wheels came off his personal life in 1993, several were struck just how isolated Gary appeared to be, with most of his inner circle comprised of purely professional contacts rather than anyone from beyond the business. In the music industry, especially its upper tiers, this was not uncommon. An often-closed world where security and discretion were crucial, doors were hard to prise open from the outside. But even so, it was not unusual to find the odd childhood mate or teenage drinking buddy still knocking about on the inside, their friendship established over years rather than through business contracts. Yet, with Philip Lynott seven years gone and Rory Gallagher recently departed, links to Moore's life before rock stardom were now few and far between. So, when the opportunity to reacquaint himself with a newly reformed Dr Strangely Strange arose, Moore leapt at it.

The Strangelies had never officially disbanded: they simply ceased operations from a while. Following two critically acclaimed, if commercially unsuccessful LPs at the turn of the seventies, the multi-instrumentalist folkies first downed tools in 1972. Following his muse, Tim Goulding retreated to a Buddhist monastery before becoming a successful fine artist while Tim Booth pursued an equally notable career as a graphic designer/film animator. For the hell of it, Ivan Pawle ran a launderette for a while before transforming himself into a successful vintner alongside his wife, Mary.

By 1982 (or thereabouts), however, the good doctors were back providing music for one of Booth's film projects[7], only to disappear soon after. But a reunion gig at an Incredible String Band convention in 1994 again fanned the flames and a new album was discussed. The man they asked to produce it was former Skid Row roadie and now venerable sound engineer, Dubliner Paul Scully, his previous 10 years or so spent in the eye of the storm touring alongside The Pogues. When Scully said yes, the game was back on and on 18 November 1997, Dr Strangely Strange's third disc, *Alternative Medicine*, arrived in stores.

Recorded at Tadhg Kelleher's studio in Ballyvourney, Cork, a few months before, Moore had come over for 'just a couple of days', to help out with the record, docking at the nearby Mills Inn Hotel for the duration of his stay. 'We made sure he had a nice bottle of Sancerre [on arrival],' said Ivan Pawle, while also offering to cover Moore's costs. But Moore wasn't there for the money or the wine. 'You know, he paid 100 per cent of his own way,' Paul Scully confirmed in 2020. 'Never asked for a penny. I mean he even brought us out to dinner! But then, Gary always had a heartfelt connection with The Strangelies and this [record] renewed it.'

That it did. Relaxing into the task at hand, Moore cut three tunes for *Alternative Medicine*, adding some bluesy twang to the countrified

---

7   The film was called *The Prisoner*, and while visiting Dublin, Moore added some guitars to the soundtrack.

reggae of 'The Heat Came Down' and 'Hard As Nails', while also providing a wonderfully mournful solo on the organ-driven 'Whatever Happened to the Blues'. 'Yes, Gary really liked 'Whatever Happened to the Blues',' said Tim Goulding. 'In fact, he said, "You must come and play that with me if I do Glastonbury next year." I said, "Of course." Nothing came of it, though. Just as well really, as I'd have been shitting bricks! Still, to see a master at work . . . well, it was always jaw-dropping.'

In sixties Dublin, Moore had been known by The Strangelies as a skilled comedian as well as master guitarist. On this visit, he was determined not to disappoint on either front. 'Well, Goulding was trying to add a little bit of keyboard to a track,' Tim Booth remembered in 2020, 'and he left his sunglasses on the side of the Roland [synth]. So, Gary slips out for a moment and comes back in with a reel of black thread. He then says, "Can you distract Tim for a moment?" So, I do, during which time Gary wraps the thread around the corner of Goulding's sunglasses and rolls it back to where he's standing on the other side of the studio. Now, every time Tim starts to play the keyboard part, the sunglasses twitch. After a while, this really starts to unnerve Goulding. We'd say, "What's wrong, why aren't you getting the part?" And he'd say, "Sorry, I thought I just saw my sunglasses move . . ." So, he'd try again, and sure enough, Gary would pull the thread again. This went on for about 10 minutes before we all collapsed with laughter and told Tim what we were doing. The funniest, sweetest man was Gary. And a real prankster too . . .'

Moore's visit to southern Cork had been 'an absolute delight', allowing him to not only re-affirm bonds put in place with The Strangelies over two decades before, but also dust off those blues roots at the same time.[8] 'Yes,' said Tim Goulding, 'it had been a real joy to see the return of the bluesman.' Yet, the sessions did nothing to alter Moore from his then musical course. Though *Dark Days in Paradise* became his worst selling album since the start of the eighties, he was determined to proceed along similar lines for his next project. Virgin

---

8 When Moore arrived for The Strangelies sessions he didn't have a guitar with him, leading to a frantic scramble around the music shops. 'Gary ended up buying a Strat,' Booth confirmed, 'and after recording, he gave it to a teenagers' charity in Killarney.'

Records, however, were not. Having put the crack marketing duo of Mick Garbutt and Tony Barker behind the project, the label was expecting a far better chart placing for *Dark Days in Paradise* than an anaemic number forty-three. Probably fearing this was the start of an ever more slippery slope, they made the decision to let Moore go, leaving him without a deal for the first time in 16 years. Given Moore's manager Ian Martin had reportedly quit at the end of 1996 following a series of financial disagreements, his position coming into 1998 could only be described as sub-optimal.

As was Gary's style, he pressed on, cutting a series of demos at Kensington's Marcus Studios on his own dime in the hope of finding a new label. (To save more time and costs, Moore also played bass and synth parts on several tracks.) Re-enlisting Gary Husband behind the kit[9] and Phil Nicholas behind the buttons for three tracks, Moore also reached out to a new face in Roger King, the north Londoner sessioneer's keyboard, programming and re-mixing skills allowing Moore to branch out into even more unpredictable musical areas than those exhibited on *Dark Days in Paradise*. 'I was really shitting myself, wondering what they were all going to think,' he later told *Record Collector*. 'But they loved it'. To complete the team, co-producer Ian Taylor also received a recall, Moore hoping the strong working relationship they enjoyed on *Still Got the Blues* and *After Hours* could be replicated on his latest musical endeavours.

After a long gestation period, Moore presented the tracks to several record labels, with some showing genuine interest. But it was former album re-issue specialists Castle Music that eventually stepped forward with the readies: the company agreed to finance the release of Gary's new record in mid-1999. 'I gave [this project] a lot of thought and production time, and I'm so happy with it,' Moore told the *Belfast Telegraph*. 'I tell you, this album is going to surprise and energise the listeners.'

On 26 September, listeners finally got to make up their own minds,

---

9   At around the same time Moore and Husband were working on Moore's new album, the duo appeared with their former bandmate Jack Bruce on *The Cream of Cream*, an instructional video the Scots bassist had put together featuring Moore, Husband and Bruce performing old Cream classics while also telling stories about their construction.

though Moore wasn't greatly exaggerating about the album's contents. In fact, if *Dark Days in Paradise* had been a mid-life crisis set to music, then Moore's twelfth solo disc, *A Different Beat*, was the sound of a man trying to write himself out of it by taking things even further. Now fully committed to the programmed loops and beats he had introduced on his previous record, *A Different Beat* was awash with samples, scratches and other drum and bass production techniques. 'Actually, I call it "Drum & Blues"!' Moore laughed to VH1.

In places, it was precisely that. 'Worry No More' sounded not unlike a John Lee Hooker-style one chord vamp being dragged along by an electronic rhythm box while 'Bring My Baby Back' married artificial kick drums and shivery synths to Delta-referencing acoustic box-tops. Elsewhere, Moore threw in a few of those long-promised surprises. 'Fatboy' was a sincere and lively tribute to the work of DJ Norman 'Fatboy Slim' Cook, then the UK's biggest-selling exponent of 'big beat'. 'Yeah, it has those modern beats and dance rhythms,' said Moore, 'and it's a departure from my usual thing.' As was 'Can't Help Myself'. All semi-robotic snares and industrial thumping, the only things that really connected it to Moore's previous work were the presence of a giant-slaying guitar riff and several shards of ear-eating feedback.

Still, Moore hadn't completely abandoned his former life. A combustible take on Jimi Hendrix's ageless 'Fire' proved an inspired idea, the song's jittery drum pattern seamlessly fitting in with all those cuts and beats elsewhere. 'Fire''s got a jungle-y rhythm,' he said. 'When Jimi made *Electric Ladyland*, it had a house beat and flashing lights . . . like a rave! I tell you, if Jimi was around today, he'd be into dance.' On the moody 'House Full of Blues', there was yet more looking back, with Moore's acetic lyrics seeming to point at the relationship troubles he had faced in recent years before settling into a new life with Jo Rendle.

While no classic, *A Different Beat* was certainly a more cohesive release than the brave, but grim *Dark Days in Paradise*. Energetic and experimental, but with emphasis still on melodies rather than just clever loops, the album also returned Moore's trademark guitar heroics to the fore, the Belfast man sounding as if he were no longer embarrassed to take a solo on one of his own tunes (the elegant, languorous break on 'Lost in Your Love' confirmed that). 'Well, you can refine your playing and adapt to your setting,' he told writer Alan Paul, 'but you'll never abandon your favourite licks or your basic feel.'

Still, despite these improvements, several additional re-mixes courtesy of drum and bass duo E-Z Rollers and a dozen or so live dates to promote the album before an injured finger brought things to a temporary halt[10], *A Different Beat* could not repair the damage done to Moore's brand by his recent, radical change of direction. Overlooked by the mainstream music press and largely ignored by fans, the record failed to chart in Britain, with only small gains made in Europe and Scandinavia. Moore's sole chart position of note in the UK during 1999 came with Virgin's advance-recouping greatest hits collection *Out in the Fields*, which limped into the Top 100 at a middling number fifty-four in October of that year.

In 1997, David Bowie tried drum and bass with *Earthling*. Some months later, Jeff Beck had a crack at techno with *Who Else!*. Neither were particularly bad records. But both were either largely critical or commercial disappointments for their creators. If two of the more established and forward-thinking musicians of the later twentieth century couldn't persuade their respective fanbases to join them on an electronic dance/rock odyssey, then Moore stood even less chance. 'I don't know,' he told VH1. 'If you want to get [modern] sounds, you just have to go into the technology. There's no way around it. To me, I'm just playing "Gary Moore" music.' The problem was that, for the moment at least, fewer people were listening.

---

10 As with *Dark Days in Paradise*, Moore was initially reluctant to tour *A Different Beat*, only to enjoy it when he did. 'I was worried about taking the songs live,' he told VH1. 'But it's actually worked out well.' Moore performed 19 dates in all, including a fourth visit to Montreux and several other European festivals in the late summer/ autumn of 1999. His then new touring band will be dealt with in the next chapter.

CHAPTER TWENTY-FIVE

Postcards From The Past

Come midnight on 31 December 1999, the world would enter a new millennium. For some, that heralded the astrological Age of Aquarius, a time when humankind might finally take control of its destiny and expand into hitherto uncharted realms. For others, the first moments of the new century would bring nothing but fear as the Y2K computer bug threatened to topple the banks, stop the clocks and bring planes crashing from the sky. Having spent much of the nineties dodging his own series of personal and professional potholes, Gary Moore probably wasn't fussed either way.

Bad jokes aside, while Moore's previous decade had certainly been marked by profound change, there were signs that things were beginning to steady themselves again. Despite the manner in which Gary's marriage to Kerry Booth had ended, the two were still on equitable terms as he continued to keep regular contact with sons Jack and Gus, now about twelve and seven, respectively. '[I live close] to my ex-wife Kerry,' he told the *Belfast Telegraph*, 'so that I can spend as much time as possible with the boys.' By now, Moore had also considerably strengthened ties with his eldest daughter Saoirse, the two gradually rebuilding their relationship following Gary's split with Sylvia Keogh years before.

As well as the ongoing connection he enjoyed with his children, Moore was also busy consolidating ties with his own parents and siblings. Over the years, he had remained close to his mother Winnie, sisters Maggie, Patricia and Michelle, and younger brother Cliff – by now a gifted guitarist in his own right. But as evidenced, Moore's bond with his father Bobby had been less sure at times. Still, recent events seemed to find the pair on better terms, as circumstances also brought the two men closer together. In mid-1997, Bobby's own dad Robert had died at the age of 87, with Gary reportedly travelling back to Belfast to attend the funeral. By then well on its way to the signing of 1998's historic Good Friday Agreement, a political accord that would bring peace to the province after decades of unrest, Northern Ireland might not have been Moore's home any longer. But that's not to say he didn't miss it. 'I still have a real affection for the place,' he told the *Belfast Telegraph*'s Eddie McIlwaine at the time, 'even though I haven't been a resident since I was 16.'

Of course, Bobby Moore had remained in Belfast through thick and thin, though a previous move had taken him from Castleview Road and the grounds outside Stormont to Sydenham, further east of the city. Still, as relations improved between Moore Sr. and Jr. over the years, the head of the family had visited Gary more frequently (and vice versa). Indeed, by 3 September 1998, Bobby had another familial call to make when Jo Rendle gave birth to the latest addition to the Moore clan: Gary's second daughter Lily. 'Born singing,' Lily's arrival prompted her father to put down even stronger roots, the guitarist now purchasing a luxury flat overlooking west London's Chelsea Harbour.

If Gary Moore's life outside the music business had stabilised, there was still much to be done on the inside. Beginning the nineties on a high with the three million-plus sales of *Still Got the Blues*, Moore's last album, 1999's *A Different Beat*, had failed to chart even at home. Inevitably, there were theories concerning Moore's recent commercial descent. In joining the multi-platinum club, ran one argument, Moore had no worlds left to conquer. Free to do what he wanted, he did precisely that, treading on expectations by releasing a highly experimental dance/pop/rock album and losing much of his established blues audience as a result. Conversely,

377

another proposition found Moore and his management team realising blues had become a shrinking market compared with its early nineties heyday and prompt measures were needed to reset the guitarist's commercial path. Too old for pop. Too clever for his own good. From mid-life crisis to 'wackadoodle', when it came to Moore's career path, there was a protractor to measure every angle.

Yet, if one examined Moore's artistic history, it was littered with volte-faces and changes of direction: prog, jazz rock, metal, Celtic, even French chanson. *Dark Days in Paradise* and *A Different Beat* were just the latest examples of Moore's ever-itchy musical feet. He had even predicted both discs were likely to meet a sticky end, the use of break beats a step too far for the blues heads, his songs too guitar-focused for the techno kids. 'Turns out nobody wants to hear a fucking guitar solo over drum and bass,' Moore's hero Jeff Beck once said. Turns out he was right. Still, divorce settlements, growing families and swish apartments did not come cheap. A plan of action was required. It was time to go back to the blues.

Moore's 1999 tour had already laid the foundations for a metaphorical return to the Delta, with the majority of his set list dwelling less on the songs of *A Different Beat* and more on old favourites drawn from *Still Got the Blues* and *After Hours*. When Moore again picked up the concert trail in 2000 (including a series of rescheduled festival dates following an injured digit) this pattern was repeated, the likes of 'Oh Pretty Woman', 'Too Tired' and 'Further On Up the Road' his go-to tunes on the night. That said, it was no longer Gary Husband, Guy Pratt and Magnus Fiennes accompanying Moore under the lights. Instead, in the umpteenth overhaul of his backing musicians, Moore had recently installed three new faces to support him, their appointments a mix of old-fashioned serendipity and rigorous examination.

In Pete Rees's case, the happy accident occurred when Moore spotted him gigging at a private party in late 1998. A rock-solid, well-respected session bassist who knew the value of keeping it simple as the guitar pyrotechnics went off all around him, Rees had impressed Moore, who was quick to make him an offer. For Rees, this was quite a leap, his previous musical life with hardy blues rockers The Papa George Band

and former Jeff Beck vocalist Bobby Tench on London's busy pub circuit a far cry from the packed arenas and glamorous French recording complexes Moore regularly inhabited. But talent will out and Rees obviously had it. On Rees's suggestion, Moore also commandeered Vic Martin to his cause. A friend of Rees and an excellent keyboardist whose credits included time served with Eurythmics and the Average White Band, Martin's soulful style was supplemented by a somewhat philosophical sense of humour. 'Musicians,' he once posited, 'should be entitled to free beer for life.'

The final soldier to join Gary Moore's reconstituted blues army was then-relatively unknown drummer, Darrin Mooney. Only 22 years old, Mooney's CV up to meeting Moore had been select though eclectic, his stickwork appearing on releases by former Jethro Tull guitarist Martin Barre, ex-Zombies singer Colin Blunstone and Bristol trip-hoppers Massive Attack. That said, word had already got around concerning Mooney's talents and Scottish rock experimentalists Primal Scream were keen to secure him. Yet, when Gary Husband chose to move on pending Moore's decision to reinvestigate the blues, Mooney was at the subsequent auditions, ready to give it a go. Within minutes he had the gig, should he want it, that is. He did, though he was also quite interested in joining up with Primal Scream.

In the end, an agreement was brokered, and in a musical menage à trois of sorts, Mooney was free to shuttle between both Moore and The Primals, recording/tour diaries permitting. Though like most every percussionist before him, he occasionally locked horns with Moore over arrangements and phrasing, Mooney would eventually earn the distinction of being Moore's longest-serving percussionist. 'A lot of people said Gary was hard on drummers,' Thin Lizzy's Brian Downey confirmed, 'But he wasn't really. He just had a particular sound in mind. In fact, he'd have made a great blues drummer if he'd put his mind to it. You see, when you listen to old blues songs, it was about nailing down the beat. John Mayall once said that the problem he had with drummers was that they were too busy. That they overplayed. And Gary saw that and spoke to me about it. Well, we totally agreed with John. It was about the beat, not the fills. That's what Gary was after. Keeping the beat straightforward. You don't need the flourishes in blues, no over-elaborate displays, thanks. And don't forget, it was his band, and really, it was about the guitar!'

With a new group comprised of equal parts youth and experience, Moore must have felt quietly confident re-entering London's Waterloo Sunset Studios in the autumn of 2000 to cut his thirteenth solo album. Making the journey with him was Chris Tsangarides, now back on board as co-producer after he and Moore went their separate ways towards the end of the previous year's ill-fated *Dark Days in Paradise*. However, whereas before Moore was obsessed with making the most up-to-date record possible, the onus on this occasion was capturing a genuinely live feel. Minimal overdubs, no fancy tricks. Just Gary, his group 'and 10 tunes ready for baking'. For Tsangarides, who had begun his career fulfilling precisely such briefs, this was *Back on the Streets* all over again.

Another former associate making a timely return for Moore's latest album was photographer Gered Mankowitz. For this cover sleeve, Mankowitz went right back to basics, picturing a slightly gnarled Moore seated on an empty railway platform, guitar close to hand. Yet, while the image looked as if the sunglasses-wearing Moore was somewhere in America's deep south, the actual location was somewhat less exciting: Therapia Lane tram depot in sunny Croydon. 'It's very effective though, isn't it?' Mankowitz laughed in 2020. 'It does look like St Louis or somewhere like that. It's a bit of a cliché, I suppose, but I never steered away from clichés! I always think if you get the balance right, it can be a lovely thing to do.'

Though it had been nearly a decade since the two had worked together, during which Moore's life had undergone many twists and turns, Mankowitz found his subject essentially unchanged. 'Yes, he was very much the same,' he confirmed. 'Gary was a very stoic, rooted individual, though I believe his family life had [recently] been pretty chaotic and emotional. But then, he was always very easy to work with. Pliable, malleable, in many ways. If you said, "Go and lean against that pillar," there'd be no "I don't want to do that. It might ruin my jacket." He'd just go over and lean against the pillar. There were no moods on set. Like any performer, he did have a degree of vanity to him. But Gary also acknowledged the passing of time with that cover. Ten years had gone by and he wasn't afraid to show that in the image.'

Released on 12 March 2001, Moore's new album *Back to the Blues* was just that, with the guitarist seeking to find his way home musically after a period of creatively fertile, if commercially barren experimentation. And a solid effort it was; the disc's ten tracks allowed Moore to stretch his own version of the blues in several rather entertaining directions. For those seeking bang (and a bit of crash and wallop) for their buck, he provided it with 'Enough of the Blues', 'Looking Back' and 'How Many Lies', all three tunes the type of hardened rocker that sat well with the more ornery side of his previous output. 'You Upset Me Baby' was also vintage Moore, though this time the barrelling presence of the Midnight Horns meant the mood was more *After Hours* than *Still Got the Blues*. Always a fan of 'a good ballad,' Moore gave us three on this album with the forlorn-sounding 'Picture of the Moon', the finger wringing histrionics of old blues chestnut 'Stormy Monday' and Peter Green-like flutterings of 'Drowning in Tears' each twanging at emotions in their own special way.

Possibly smarting from criticism that his last two albums lacked the wild guitar solos for which he was justly celebrated, Moore didn't hold back on *Back to the Blues*. A mean, scratchy cover of Calvin Carter's 'I Ain't Got You' found Moore grinding his strings to paste, Gary's delightfully askew note choices surely mirroring Jeff Beck's take on the same tune when he was a jobbing member of The Yardbirds. Moore was also on flying form during 'Cold Black Night', his whistling run ending in a wah-assisted blast reminiscent of a small mortar attack.

But it was on 'The Prophet' that Moore truly excelled. A slow-moving, Arabian-sounding instrumental that again drew clear inspiration from the work of Roy Buchanan, 'The Prophet' had Moore approaching the tune with a surgeon's hand, using quarter notes, overbends and violin swells to convey a sense of lingering melancholy. Propped up by some wonderfully simple, yet sympathetic backing courtesy of Pete Rees, Darrin Mooney and Vic Martin, Moore's aching lines on 'The Prophet' were a balm for the ear. Like most tracks on *Back to the Blues*, 'The Prophet' was probably recorded using Moore's favourite new guitar, a gorgeous 1963 Gibson ES-335 semi-acoustic. Bought from former Horslips axeman Johnny Fean, the instrument's distinct cherry red colour and eye-catching square inlays had seen it take pride of place on the cover of *Back to the Blues*, with Moore clutching the Gibson's neck as if his life depended on it. Central to Moore's desire for a cleaner, more 'hollowed out' tone, the ES 335's presence was felt at many a show over the coming years.[1]

With its in-your-face production style, diverse moods and expressive guitar work, Gary Moore's latest album picked things up roughly where he had let them drop in the mid-nineties. This must have delighted Moore's new label Sanctuary – which, having acquired the musician's recording contract along with Castle Communications back in 2000 – was not only keen to get Moore back to the blues, but back into the charts too. And return he did, although not quite as spectacularly as either Sanctuary[2] or Moore might have liked. Reaching number fifty-three in the UK and placing reasonably in Germany, Austria and Scandinavia during the spring of 2001, *Back to the Blues* could not be deemed an outright failure. Yet, nor could it be considered a real success. If Moore was intent on making up ground lost at the turn of the previous decade, re-establishing 'Brand Blues' was key.

Moore did what made most sense and hit the road, taking his music back to the halls and arenas of the UK and Europe in an effort to reconnect with a fanbase severely tested by the drum and bass shenanigans of *Dark Days in Paradise* and *A Different Beat*. However, now nearly 50 years old and with two children under the age of 10 to care for, this would be no Bacchanalian jaunt across the Alps. Tour legs were to run for weeks rather than months and Moore was to have plenty of time off to see his family and maintain his health. Hence the 39-date run through France, Holland, Switzerland (featuring yet another appear-

1 Though a real beauty, Moore's choice to be photographed with the ES 335 on the cover of *Back to the Blues* was odd given that he had recently put his name to a signature Gibson Les Paul also worthy of genuine promotion. Based on a 1959 standard, but designed to Moore's specifications, the guitar was finished in amber burst, featured a pair of Burstbucker pick-ups and played extremely well.
2 When Sanctuary hit hard times in 2004/05, Gary secured a new deal with Eagle Records.

ance at Montreux), Germany and England was more 'relaxed than raucous'.

Still, old habits were hard to break, and when Moore found himself at a loss for something to do, there was always the odd guest appearance to help pass the time. At regular intervals throughout 2000/2001, Gary contributed to albums by his Blues Breaking teenage hero John Mayall, ex-Traffic singer/fellow Henley-on-Thames resident Jim Capaldi and the ever-present, but always welcome Jack Bruce. For Mayall, Moore went dark, his solo pass on the slow, rumbling 'If I Don't Get Home' one of the genuine highlights of Mayall's LP *Along for the Ride*. Moore's work on Capaldi's 'Heart of Stone' from 2001's *Living on the Outside* was in a similar vein, those gentle note choices sitting dolorously atop a bed of keyboard chords.

As usual, it was Jack Bruce who got the best out of Moore. Aside from chipping in an inspired flurry or two for Bruce's latest solo disc, *Shadows in the Air*, Moore also joined Bruce and drummer Gary Husband on the star-studded John Lee Hooker tribute album *From Clarksdale to Heaven*[3], his chilling performances on 'I'm in the Mood' and 'It Serve You Right to Suffer' (a song Gary used to cover with his own band in the early seventies) absolutely nailing the spirit of Hooker's mournful ode to a lost lover. 'I felt teardrops in my eyes singing "serves me right",' John Lee once said of a song so blue it caused him to start wearing shades on stage, '[so] I put sunglasses on to keep people from seeing me crying.' Hooker was still wearing them right up to his death in June 2001.

For Gary Moore, each of these sessions was another personal ambition fulfilled, allowing the kid in him to climb out and play alongside his former idols. Yet, by befriending so many of these heroes, Moore also ran the risk of losing them. The reality of that dilemma was brought home to Gary on 29 November 2001 when, only months after his friend

---

3 One of the better blues tribute albums out there, *From Clarksdale to Heaven* also featured performances from Jeff Beck, an ever-rejuvenating Peter Green, former Rolling Stone Mick Taylor and John Lee himself. Mind you, John Mayall and Jim Capaldi's own discs didn't lack for guest stars, with Moore, ZZ Top's Billy Gibbons, Mick Fleetwood and Peter Green (once again) contributing to the former while George Harrison, Ian Paice, Steve Winwood and Paul Weller popped up alongside Moore on the latter.

and former keyboard player Tommy Eyre succumbed to cancer[4], George Harrison passed away from the disease. A monumental influence on Moore, both musically and personally, Harrison had not only shared songs, guitar tips and life lessons with Gary, but a similar, impish sense of humour too.

Moore found this out when appearing alongside Harrison at a benefit concert for the Natural Law Party[5] on 6 April 1992. One of an exceedingly select number of live appearances Harrison made following the break-up of The Beatles, Moore was 'absolutely floored' when asked by Harrison to join him on stage at the Royal Albert Hall for a performance of 'While My Guitar Gently Weeps'. Determined to get it right, Moore practised for days, learning every nuance of Eric Clapton's original solo[6] while adding a few choice notes of his own. Arriving at rehearsals in ebullient mood, Moore blazed through the song with customary intensity before coming to rest several minutes later before a stunned backing band. Without losing a beat, Harrison strolled up to his friend and said, 'Gary, it's called 'While My Guitar *Gently* Weeps' before pealing into laughter. An amusing tale, and one he was always keen to tell, the RAH story neatly summed up Moore's good-natured bond with the man they called 'the quiet Beatle'. 'George was a giant for me,' Moore later said, 'a giant who became a really good friend.'

With Gary Moore's tour in support of *Back to the Blues* concluding in late 2001, expectation dictated he would take a break, gather some tunes and then return to the studio to record them for a new album. Sticking to script, Moore did precisely that. But he also flew in the face of expectations by once again stepping away from the blues in favour of

---

4   One of the great session keyboardists/arrangers, Tommy Eyre's work can be heard on Wham's 'Wake Me Up Before You Go-Go' Joe Cocker's version of The Beatles 'With a Little Help From my Friends' and Gerry Rafferty's 'Baker Street', among countless other tunes. A sad loss.

5   Founded in 1992, Natural Law are a transnational party based on the teachings of Maharishi Mahesh Yogi and committed to the practice of transcendental meditation.

6   Written by Harrison in 1968 and appearing on The Beatles' *White Album*, 'While My Guitar Gently Weeps' featured a solo from Harrison's friend and occasional musical collaborator Eric Clapton. For those seeking to learn more about said friendship, the 2021 biography *All Things Must Pass Away* by Kenneth Womack and Jason Kruppa might be of use.

a new musical journey. In a move that probably exasperated both his management and record company, Moore had decided to explore fusing classic sixties power riffs with the alt-rock sensibilities of current acts such as Radiohead, Rage Against the Machine and Queens of the Stone Age. And while the services of drummer Darrin Mooney were to be retained for the project, bassist Pete Rees would not be joining them for the adventure. 'And here we go again . . .' laughed one of Gary's mates in 2020.

In the rear-view mirror, Moore's decision to again park the blues after so quickly re-embracing them appeared foolhardy. Given the reception accorded *A Different Beat*, one might even say crackers. However, like all the best musicians, new sounds genuinely excited Gary's ear and he appeared powerless to resist them. Whether it was Andy Richards' miraculous Fairlight synthesiser or Studio Miraval's time-bending SSL recording desk, Moore was drawn to the shock of the new like a moth to a flame. Therefore, it was no great surprise that when he heard the likes of RATM's 'Bulls on Parade' or QOTSA's 'Feel Good Hit of the Summer', he wanted to join in. If Moore played his cards right, he might even be able to have the best of both worlds, balancing vintage blues releases with contemporary rock. It was a nice idea. Unfortunately, it was also extremely unlikely.

Joining Gary Moore and Darrin Mooney on what would turn out to be an honourable, if short-lived enterprise was bassist Richard 'Cass' Lewis. A fine, inventive player, Lewis had begun his climb up the musical ladder in the mid-eighties alongside Amos Pizzey in synth-pop/rap duo Dark City. When that didn't quite work, Cass hitched his skills to those of superstar-in-waiting Terence Trent D'Arby, only to watch the brilliant American rock and soul performer confound audiences with a series of baffling musical turns before later rebirthing himself as the singer Sananda Francesco Maitreya. Not to be put off, Lewis became a founding member of politicised alt-rockers Skunk Anansie, who sustained success throughout the nineties before coming to a sudden halt in 2001. Still, alternative rock's loss was to be Gary Moore's gain. 'Darrin Mooney suggested that Gary take a look at Cass,' ran Sanctuary's press release '[and] when they all got together to play for the first time, it was perfect. Everything just

385

clicked. It was immediately obvious to Moore that this was going to be the ultimate line-up.' Again.

Raring to go after a brief period of rehearsal, Moore, Mooney and Lewis entered west London's Sarm West Studios alongside returning co-producer Chris Tsangarides to work up Gary's songs into an album. With further recording taking place at Sarm's sister complex in Brick Lane (the cleverly named 'Sarm East'), things were almost ready to go. However, adamant that this was not to be another 'Gary Moore' record, and with Cass Lewis and Darrin Mooney bringing fanbases of their own via Skunk Anansie and Primal Scream, a band name was required. Improbably, they settled on Scars, no one seeming to connect their choice of moniker with the facial disfigurement Moore had lived with since the early summer of 1974.

Released in early September 2002 wrapped in a cover sleeve more akin to a Nine Inch Nails album than a traditional GM record, Scars was something of a disappointment. Groove-orientated as much as song-based, red raw in terms of production style and exhibiting all the strengths and weaknesses that came with using a power trio format, the disc appeared to be a bold attempt by Moore to frame the sound and spirit of The Jimi Hendrix Experience in a modern rock setting. Sometimes, as with 'Stand Up', this approach worked well enough, Mooney and Lewis's contemporary styles providing able contrast to Moore's more overt Jimi-like musings. The utterly bizarre, if lyrically entertaining 'Wasn't Born in Chicago' even managed to meld funked-up drums and squelching synth bass to passages of the most ferocious blues rock.

But elsewhere, as with the 'Jimi does Nirvana' composite 'When the Sun Goes Down' or the soul/grunge stew of 'Just Can't Let You Go' (essentially Radiohead's 'Creep' with added Otis Redding), the experiment fell between two widely spaced posts. Still, even if Moore and Scars couldn't quite land the overall idea, the guitarist sounded like he was having an absolute ball channelling his inner Hendrix, the extended solos on 'Rectify' and 'World of Confusion' making full use of Moore's super-powered 1961 Fiesta Red Fender Stratocaster, the guitar's vibrant tones given their most substantial airing since *Corridors of Power* back in 1982.

Like Moore's last two forays into the world of modern rock/pop, Scars faltered at the proverbial box office, with audiences as confused by his attempt to create a new form of 'future blues' as they were when he began bolting guitar riffs to break beats. Still, a financially attractive deal had already been struck with ZZ Top for Scars to provide support on the Texan trio's European tour of autumn 2002, so on they went. However, adjustments were made. Savvy enough not to confound punters every night with a set list of brand-new tunes, Moore, Mooney and Lewis incorporated several tracks from Moore's blues back catalogue into their slot, with 'Walking By Myself' and 'Since I Met You Baby' rubbing shoulders alongside 'Ball and Chain' and 'World of Confusion'. If there was a number that showed off what they were truly capable of, it was Scars' take on Jimi Hendrix's 'Fire'. First lit up by Moore in 1999, the version performed by Moore, Mooney and Lewis was simply incendiary, each musician bringing their own brand of power and potency to a classic now 35 years old.

No matter how fine their take on 'Fire', by the late spring of 2003, Scars' future was at best uncertain, though that didn't necessarily mean the group had broken up. In a move perhaps even more surprising than Moore's recent flits between electronica and blues, the guitarist now accepted a personal invitation from David Coverdale to step out with Whitesnake and San Francisco pop metal veterans Y&T on a 'Monsters of Rock' tour package. What's more, Mooney and Lewis were accompanying him. To further confound matters, Moore would be drawing on nearly every period of his musical life for the set list, including old chestnuts such as 'Out in the Fields', 'Don't Believe a Word' and 'Shapes of Things'. 'Christ on a bike,' said one fan on hearing Moore's choice of tunes, 'he's even playing 'White Knuckles'!'

Given that Moore had publicly rubbished the majority of his eighties hard rock/metal output and many of the acts still working in that genre (including Whitesnake on 1989's 'Led Clones'), this was news indeed. However, with his usual brand of paint-stripping candour, he explained the decision in full. '[Scars] were writing songs when the offer came in [and] I said to the guys, "It's a bit fucking dinosaur, but do you want to do it?"' he told *Classic Rock*'s Dave Ling. 'Darrin and Cass are from a totally different era, but I sold it to them on the basis that we could play

387

to lots of people, have some laughs and also do some of our stuff. The money was good as well.'

With the opportunity to re-visit his back catalogue, give several Scars tunes a proper run out and make a packet while he was at it, Moore and co. struck out on a 10-date trawl around some of the UK's biggest sheds throughout May 2003. It wasn't his finest hour. While the band were tight as tuppence and audiences mostly appreciative, the set list felt uneven, the likes of a frantic (and keyboard-less) 'Out in the Fields' butting heads with 'Wishing Well', which in turn sat uneasily alongside Scars' very shouty 'Rectify'. To further upset the general mood, pockets of the crowd kept yelling for some proper blues tunes, causing Moore to paraphrase George Harrison's remarks to him a decade before 'The tour's called 'Monsters of *Rock*' you know.' A live album/DVD drawn from the group's performance at Glasgow's SECC on 22 May 2003 entitled *Gary Moore: Live at Monsters of Rock* was quietly released later that year. But by then Cass Lewis had moved on[7] and Moore was again circling back in the general direction of the Mississippi. As oftentimes before, he would settle in one of its noisier neighbourhoods.

---

7   By 2008, Cass Lewis was back in the ranks of a reformed Skunk Anansie, with whom he continues to perform today (2022).

CHAPTER TWENTY-SIX

Tributes And Tribulations

Though financially lucrative, Gary Moore's involvement in with 2003's chest-beating, ear-scalding, if still entertaining Monsters of Rock package felt like a misstep. He knew it too. '[I thought] I'd left all that behind in the eighties,' Gary told *Guitar & Bass* a year after the event, 'and I didn't want to get lumped in with it again.' That said, the opportunity to crank up the Marshalls, stomp on the overdrive pedal and go hog wild all over the fretboard did have its charms, even for a man now in his sixth decade. 'Yeah,' he laughed to writer Robert Silverstein, 'it's nice to turn up and let rip a bit!' Keen to follow his own advice, Moore did just that for his next album.

Obviously, he was not seeking to remake *Corridors of Power* or *Victims of the Future*. Those ships had long sailed. Moreover, having seen the Hendrix-leaning alt-rock of Scars roundly ignored by his own fans, there was no stomach nor commercial impetus to re-examine that sound. Instead, Moore's vision was another return to the blues, but this time with added firepower. 'The thinking behind it,' he told *20th Century Guitar*, 'was a very raw, very aggressive blues album, or as you say, a proper "blues rock" album.' That drummer Darrin Mooney would be a part of his plans was never in doubt. Now in their fourth year as bandmates (at least of a sort), Moore knew Mooney could handle anything he threw at him. But with Cass Lewis on his way back to Skunk Anansie, Moore now had to find another bassist, and one equally adept at rocking it up as he was holding things down. For Moore, there was really only one choice. After an absence of over a decade, Bob Daisley was recalled from his home in Australia to re-join the ranks.

Moore, Mooney and Daisley made short work of what would become Gary's fourteenth solo disc, approaching the recording sessions with urgency and precision. No longer able to command the huge budgets that propped up the making of *After Hours* and *A Different Beat*, songs were cut in hours rather than months, with co-producer Chris Tsangarides again manning the desk, this time at south London's Sphere Studios, to make sure nothing went astray from fretboard to console. Taking up a role he had fulfilled in Ozzy Osbourne's group, Daisley found himself contributing song ideas to Moore, with he and Mooney eventually credited on as co-writers on the album's fast-slow-fast-fast-slow title track and the jack-booted stomp of 'Getaway Blues'. 'The three of us were in the same room,' Moore said, 'and it was all done kind of live, with little in the way of separation.'

Released on 22 June 2004, *Power of the Blues* not only carried this sense of musical intimacy, but was Moore's most impressive collection of songs since *After Hours*. From the blood and thunder of tracks such as 'There's a Hole' to a growling cover of Willie Dixon and Howlin' Wolf's 'Evil', Moore had found 11 on the amp's volume setting and stayed there, his guitar almost breathing in one's ear. This aural hooliganism was even more pronounced on 'Tell Me Woman'. Surely influenced by Jeff Beck's wah-wah masterclass on 1968's 'I Ain't Superstitious', 'Tell Me Woman' found Moore adding extra bottleneck as well as added bite, the results as slippery as they were loud. Of course, there were corners of quiet to enjoy. 'That's Why I Play the Blues' was the type of well-judged mid-tempo ballad B.B. King had been specialising in since the early seventies, while 'Torn Inside' found Moore revisiting his fascination with the spookier side of Peter Green.

But as Moore's quite astounding take on Willie Dixon's 'I Can't Quit You Baby' confirmed, *Power of the Blues*' primary focus was all about shaking the walls. Seemingly intent on pushing Led Zeppelin's better-known version of Dixon's tune off a short plank, Moore threw everything he had at 'I Can't Quit You Baby', those vocal hollers, thumping power chords and finger-knotting solos as intense as anything he had committed to vinyl in his days as a hard rocker. 'Ah, I could do a whole album's worth of Willie Dixon covers,' he said of his inspiration to *20th Century Guitar*'s Robert Silverstein. 'Willie Dixon was like the Lennon and McCartney of the blues world.'

A thumping effort loaded with potent tunes and a real sense of immediacy in its grooves, *Power of the Blues* seemed specifically designed to kick on from Moore's recent return to 'classic rock' and hoist him back into the UK Top 30. Instead, the record failed to chart. If looking for excuses, one might have blamed the cover sleeve, its graffiti-style design perhaps more suited to a hip-hop or dance release than a rowdy blues rock album. Another bone of contention was the lack of an obvious single, Moore's latest batch of songs more heavy duty than 'heavy rotation'. Yet, as before, these theories hid a more brutal truth. At 52 years old, Moore was now past his commercial peak and to compound things further, had spent the best part of the previous decade testing his audience's patience riding a musical merry-go-round. Gary had often said there had really never been a plan. When sailing on the back of multi-platinum success, that was fine. But as events were about to make plain, it made for a harder road when things went against you.

In October 2003, Moore had joined an all-star cast led by The Who's Roger Daltrey and Procol Harum's Gary Brooker at Ronnie Scott's Jazz Club in London's Soho to perform a concert in aid of the Teenage Cancer Trust. Quite the night, the 250-strong audience had paid £500 per ticket, meaning that with extra donations, Daltrey (who had organised the gig) was on course to raise more than £350,000 for the charity. Always one to support a good cause and knowing that his old mate Greg Lake was also due to attend, Moore was mad keen to appear. But a nagging hand problem threatened to skew his involvement. A pain-numbing injection apparently worked wonders and Moore played a blinder, his renditions of 'Oh Pretty Woman' and 'Parisienne Walkways' raising the roof of Ronnie's before gently setting it down again. But his health problems were noticed. 'I was sure there wouldn't be any stress, so we went for . . . Gary, who said he'd be happy to play 'Parisienne Walkways'' Roger Daltrey later confirmed, before adding, 'Even with his arthritis, he was still one of the most powerful players going.'

Whatever the exact cause of his malady, Moore's hand appeared to improve in subsequent months, allowing him to summon the furies on *Power of the Blues* while also committing to a tour in support of the album. But before an appearance at the Pistoia Blues Festival in Tuscany, Italy, on 4 May 2004, his problems returned.

First the gig was cancelled, then all remaining dates. Of course, Moore had been down the cancellation route before, either through illness, or in the case of Scars, due to slow ticket sales. But this time it was very different. Because his hand problems were deemed a pre-existing condition, the tour insurers refused to pay out. With everything from crew costs to plane tickets affected, that came to a pretty penny. If he was sitting on another *Still Got the Blues* or 'Out in the Fields', such sums would have been of lesser consequence. But the last time Moore bothered the UK singles charts was with 1997's 'I Have Found My Love in You', and that had had only reached number ninety. In short, this was going to hurt. 'Basically, I injured my hand . . . and the insurance didn't pay up,' he later told *Vintage Guitar*. 'I cancelled shows and had to cover the costs with my own money. Because I didn't get paid for any of those shows, I ended up with debt.' Though he didn't know it at the time, the ramifications of that debt problem would have profound consequences.

Like anyone might in his position, Moore retreated from public view for much of 2004, using the time to sort out his finances while also trying to find a cure for his ailment. For a while, his predicament looked genuinely grim, his future as a guitarist in some peril. However, rest and recuperation provided respite from the pain, and Moore's condition began to improve after minor surgery. Indeed, by 24 September he was back at London's Wembley Arena to perform Jimi Hendrix's 'Red House' as part of The Strat Pack, a glittery, star-packed night celebrating 50 years of the Fender Stratocaster guitar. With such fellow Strat devotees as David Gilmour, The Eagles' Joe Walsh and Moore's childhood hero Hank Marvin also in attendance, the pressure Moore put on himself before stepping on stage must have been immense. But armed with his trusty 1961 Fiesta Red and a set of reasonably-gauged strings rather than the 'hellion's innards' that normally adorned his axes, Moore's rendition of Hendrix's most famous slow blues was pretty much faultless.

Following Gary's Strat Pack appearance, the trail again went more or less cold for a while, though he did contribute a fine solo to master Indian percussionist Trilok Gurtu's album *Broken Rhythms*.[1] New territory for the guitarist – and given his recent output, that really was saying something – Moore's collaboration with Gurtu came about via old mate Martin Levan, whom Colosseum II had worked with all those years ago on Andrew Lloyd Webber's bestseller *Variations*. 'I was [producing] Trilok Gurtu on *Broken Rhythms*,' Levan remembered in 2020, 'and I believe Carlos Santana and Jeff Beck were going to contribute to the album, but for whatever reason neither could make it. So, I said "Well, maybe I can get Gary to play on it." The sound file was sent over to Chris Tsangarides and . . .'

Moore's contribution to the track 'Kabir' also gave Levan the chance to ponder all that had happened to the guitarist since their first meeting in 1977. 'Well, his solo success was a bit of a surprise,' reasoned the producer. 'But not because he wasn't talented. Because he was phenomenally talented! No, it was more the fact that he was so readily embraced by the pop world. And also, the vocal side of it, you know, him singing [as a pop artist]. But the stuff he did was so good, it just worked out.'

Though sightings of Gary Moore had been few over the previous 12 months, he was present at London's Royal Albert Hall on 2 May 2005, where for the first time in more than 37 years Eric Clapton, Jack Bruce and Ginger Baker were reuniting as Cream for a series of four concerts. Given the band had chosen the RAH as the site to end their original artistic union back in November 1968, these dates were pregnant with significance, and fans were falling over themselves in an effort to witness

---

1 During the same period, Moore also provided guitar for One World Project's 'Grief Never Grows Old', a charity record written by DJ Mike Read in support of the 2004 Indian Ocean earthquake and tsunami disaster. With other contributors including The Bee Gees, Beach Boy Brian Wilson, Rolling Stone Bill Wyman and Yes's Rick Wakeman, the tune reached number four in the UK charts in February 2005.

the return of their heroes. For Moore (who was on the guest list), he had seen most if it before, and up close and personal too. Long-term friend to Jack Bruce and one third of BBM, Gary knew more than most what made the original members of Cream tick. He was also aware how tricky sustaining any such reunion might be. But like everyone else, the prospect of seeing Bruce and Baker playing 'Crossroads', 'Spoonful' and 'Outside Woman Blues' with Clapton one more time must have set Moore's pulse racing.

Sadly, great expectations were let down by harsh reality. 'Actually, I think [Jack, Ginger and I] kind of sounded more like Cream than they did on the reunion tour,' Moore told *Vintage Guitar* after the event. 'I saw them at the Royal Albert Hall . . . reunion, and to be honest, it wasn't like what it was in the sixties. Jack's voice was amazing, but Ginger Baker was playing a different way and Eric was kind of doing his usual thing. They'd all kind of moved on, so it wasn't the same three guys being put back together. It was just three different guys who were older, and . . . all so different from what they were like back in those days.'

If Moore's honesty concerning Cream's return was refreshing (if a tad harsh[2]), 20 August 2005 brought about another reunion much closer to home, when the guitarist fronted a memorial show in honour of Philip Lynott at Dublin's Point Theatre. Timed to coincide with Lynott's 56th birthday, the concert was made all the more poignant by the ceremony that proceeded it earlier that afternoon. In a touching display of respect to a much-missed son, the city of Dublin had chosen to remember Lynott by erecting a life-sized statue of the singer/songwriter on Harry Street.[3] Joining fellow artistic Dublin legends Oscar Wilde and James Joyce by

---

2 In fairness to Cream, for the opening RAH dates, Ginger Baker was experiencing back problems and Eric Clapton had the flu. However, these maladies couldn't be blamed for the brevity of the reunion. After three more shows at New York's Madison Square Garden in October 2005, familiar grudges resurfaced and Cream finally called it a day.

3 A relatively quiet location just off the busy shopping thoroughfare of Grafton Street, Harry Street was well known to Philip Lynott. As a member of both Skid Row and Thin Lizzy, he often played Bruxelles (formerly Mooney's), a famed music pub and firm fixture of Harry Street since 1886. Incidentally, Lynott's statue was funded by the Róisín Dubh trust, a foundation set up by Philip's mother, Philomena.

having his features cast in bronze, this was quite the honour for the boy from Crumlin, even if Moore thought he would have found it all quite surreal. 'Philip would probably approve of the fact that his songs are being kept alive,' Moore said, '[But] he'd also probably think it was pretty funny that there's a statue of him!'

For Moore, his friendship with Philip Lynott had always first and foremost been about the music, and it was this abiding connection that ultimately inspired the idea for a concert to 'serenade' the statue's unveiling. Indeed, the whole event had a cyclical aspect to it. Having utilised a classic 'power blues' set up as part of his last project, Moore had spent the subsequent months waiting for his hand to heal while also trying to figure out where he might venture next musically. By early 2005, and with his hand now properly on the mend, Moore settled on the idea of returning to Celtic music for new inspiration, even going as far to demo several tunes in that vein. However, when Moore learned of Dublin's plans to commemorate Lynott, the penny dropped. Instead of pursuing another album in the style of *Wild Frontier*, he settled on the notion of a gig in Lynott's honour; one that celebrated his memory in song while also bringing together on stage the former members of Lynott's beloved band, Thin Lizzy.

To test the notion, he phoned the group's drummer. 'Yes, that was all Gary's idea,' Brian Downey confirmed in 2020. 'And you know, it shows you that despite the fact he had left Lizzy [the way he did] all those years before, really, he was still behind the band, the songs and Phil.' Downey was interested and voiced his support in principle. Yet, he was not willing to get involved until Moore had conquered the logistics of such a huge undertaking. Gary was not to be put off. 'He called everyone to get their buy-in,' Downey continued. 'He got the finances and record company working [behind it], and lo and behold . . .'

In reality, 'lo and behold' took considerable work. Moore was long outside the Thin Lizzy bubble, with some 26 years having passed since his astounding contributions to *Black Rose*. Further, while Moore remained close with guitarist Eric Bell and on nodding terms with Brian 'Robbo' Robertson, Philip Lynott's long-serving lieutenant Scott Gorham was still smarting from Gary exiting the band mid-tour back in 1979. Moreover, alongside former guitar partner John 'Thunder and Lightning' Sykes, the Californian had reactivated Thin Lizzy as a touring proposition in recent years, with Downey wielding sticks and bassist/singer Marco Mendoza stepping in for an absent Lynott.⁴ In short, the skies looked grey.

But after an initially terse phone conversation between he and Moore, Gorham saw a way forward. 'No, I still hadn't forgiven Gary at that point,' Scott said. 'But I couldn't let him get up there and do it on his own either. Especially given the fact he was thinking about doing songs he hadn't even been involved in. I said "Well, that's not gonna fucking happen." I thought, "You were out of order . . . for throwing us in the shit like that, but I've got to represent [Lizzy] right here." So, yeah, I agreed to do it. And you know, I'm glad I did.'

On the night, so was everyone else. Originally billed as 'The Boy Is Back in Town' until someone had the good sense to rename it 'One Night in Dublin', the Point gig of 20 August 2005 was a strange but ultimately uplifting composite of Gary Moore solo concert, Philip Lynott tribute and Thin Lizzy reunion, albeit one where the original master of ceremonies was sadly in absentia. Taking to the stage with Brian Downey on drums and new face/ex-Jethro Tull bassist Jonathan Noyce covering four strings, Moore set the pace and tone for what was to follow by opening with 'Walking By Myself'. Determined to make sure that the gathered hordes knew this was essentially a Gary Moore show, albeit one with several heavy-duty friends, 'Walking By Myself' quickly deflated the notion that the guitarist was just here to hijack Philip Lynott's memorial event for the sake of a quick buck.

That said, this was a concert in part celebrating a Dublin icon, so it wasn't long before Moore deviated sharply into Lizzy territory with a rollicking 'Jailbreak'. Following that up with the Lynott-approved blues version of 'Don't Believe a Word', Moore then took the stabilisers off the bike by introducing Brian Robertson from the wings. Greeted with some of the loudest cheers of the night, the Glaswegian contributed a

---

4 In a neat turn of the wheel, old Gary Moore cohort Guy Pratt covered on bass for the reformed Thin Lizzy in 2003.

solo or two to 'Emerald' before he and Moore traded licks on the slow-burning masterpiece 'Still in Love With You'. Uncharacteristically, however, Robbo's heart didn't seem to be in it, his contributions understated, his interest seemingly elsewhere.

With Robertson curiously quiet, there was little left to do but call in Scott Gorham. Thankfully, 'Great Scott' was in the mood for sport, the American providing fireworks aplenty on 'Black Rose' (as ever, Moore covered the middle bit), 'Cowboy Song' and 'The Boys Are Back in Town'. 'Doing 'Black Rose' with Scott gave me a real shiver,' Moore later told *Louder*. 'I realised just how good those songs were.' After Moore and Gorham's blast from the past, Eric Bell almost stole the show with a neatly understated performance of 'Whiskey in the Jar' before Moore closed proceedings with he and Lynott's timeless chanson 'Parisienne Walkways', those gathered in the hall singing every line as if they'd personally written it.

Post gig, Moore and most everybody else congregated at the Westbury Hotel on Balfe Street for a drink, the location but seconds away from Lynott's newly erected statue. Here, Robbo 'sat with his lot', while Moore was among his own family and friends. However, over the course of the night, Gary and Scott Gorham found themselves deep in conversation, burying hatchets as they went. 'At the gig, and afterwards, we finally reconciled,' Gorham confirmed. 'He apologised to me. He said, "I can't tell you how sorry I was, I am, for doing what I did to you guys. I fucked up." And he really meant it. What are you going to say? "Yeah, you fucked up, but Jesus I still love your playing!" You know, just watch the video of that night.[5] Gary and I are smoking. Playing-wise, song-wise, we were locked in. That,' he concluded, 'was a really cool show.'

With the cheers of One Night in Dublin still ringing in his ears, the idea that Gary Moore would pick up those Celtic-themed demos where he recently dropped them and charge towards the recording studio probably seemed a given. But though Dublin had provided him a huge

5 Filmed by Eagle Vision, *Gary Moore: One Night in Dublin (A Tribute to Phil Lynott)* was released on video and DVD on 4 April 2006, the occasion of Moore's 54th birthday. A fine record of an even finer night, the only thing missing is the brief solo set Skid Row's Brush Shiels performed before Moore and friends took the stage.

thumbs up and his hand was now 100 per cent better, there were to be no new high-speed jigs or reels. Instead, in keeping with his contrary musical nature, Moore now abandoned plans for an Irish-themed album and once again walked slowly towards the blues. Still, given the contents of his 2006 disc, *Old New Ballads Blues*, it wasn't his worse notion.

Conceived as a concept LP of sorts, *Old New Ballads Blues* found Moore mixing and matching tunes that had been hanging around for a while with newer compositions and selected covers, the guitarist also updating two songs from his recent back catalogue. Recorded in a blitz of activity at the ever-familiar Sarm West Studios (with some extra noodling done at Sphere), Moore's choice of personnel for the project was as varied as his choice of tracks. Marking his fifth year with Moore, Darrin Mooney was back in the drum seat, though he now partnered Jonathan Noyce on bass rather than Pete Rees or Cass Lewis. But while Mooney was in, after co-producing three of Moore's recent releases, Chris Tsangarides was sitting this one out, his place taken by a returning Ian Taylor. 'I hadn't worked with Ian for seven or eight years [actually six],' Moore told *Blues In Britain* at the time, 'so it's nice to have him back on board again.'

As it was with Don Airey. Missing in action since the salad days of *Still Got the Blues*, the keyboardist had never fallen out with Moore. In fact, it was Airey that recommended Mooney to the guitarist after hearing him in session. But time and tide had taken them in different directions since 1992, with opportunities to work together few and far between. No more, however. After bumping into each other at a gig, Moore made a mental note to reactivate their partnership. *Old New Ballads Blues* gave him the chance.

Released on 2 May 2006, Moore's fifteenth solo album presented almost every facet of Gary's unique take on the blues: from big-boned bruisers such as 'Done Somebody Wrong' and slashing instrumentals like 'Cut It Out' to the teary R&B of 'Gonna Rain Today' and Roy Buchanan-style wails of 'No Reason to Cry', it was all there at the press of a button. Even where Moore had gone back to make improvements on two of *Still Got the Blues*' already distinguished moments, the thinking behind his decision was clear. In 1992, Moore's take on Otis Rush's 'All My

Love' had been all fire and brimstone, the Belfast man almost landing punches with his Gibson Les Paul at the beginning of each verse. Now, 'All My Love' was slower and more serious, the drop in tempo giving Moore's keening vocal a new solemnity, his guitar work a new power. 'Midnight Blues (2006)' was much the same, with Moore's application of the rhythmic brake allowing the saxes and trumpets of Nick Pentelow, Frank Mead and Sid Gauld to weave in and out of the beat rather than just drive its progress.

Ballads Blues also illustrated how much Moore had become a scholar of his chosen form. Back in 1966, Moore learned directly from Mayall and Clapton, Beck, Hendrix and Green, seldom seeking out where they had drawn their original inspiration. Forty years later, however, and Moore was drinking straight from the source. Now steeped in the work of Willie Dixon, Moore's cover of the legendary bluesman's 1960 tune 'You Know My Love' was probably the best thing on *Old New Ballads Blues*, Moore's expansive solo as emotionally wrenching as it was technically accomplished.

This respect for the old masters was also apparent on 'Done Somebody Wrong', as Moore looked beyond the fruit on the tree to find the roots beneath. 'I first heard 'Done Somebody Wrong' on The Allman Brothers' *Live at the Fillmore*,' Moore said of a band he supported (and worshipped) while a member of Skid Row in 1971. 'But then, then I heard Elmore James's version . . .' Cannily updating James's classic train blues for a post-millennial audience, Moore even found himself enjoying playing the slide guitar part that drove the track. 'Well, I enjoy [playing slide] in the studio more than I do live,' he said of a device he had always endured rather than embraced. '[But then,] tell me, how can you do an Elmore James song without playing slide?' No doubt about it, *Old New Ballads Blues* had something for everyone. But while it was a good enough collection, it was also Gary's third album in a row not to trouble the UK charts.

Unfortunately, Moore's reduced album sales coupled with the insurance debacle around his 2004 tour and lack of recent shows meant that the guitarist's finances remained precarious. And while his hand was better and he could soon properly return to the live arena, he still had to deal with the here and now: mortgages, children, alimony, staff . . . It all added up and until the figures could be balanced, something had to give. That something turned out to be the 'Greeny'. In reality, Moore had considered selling his prized Gibson Les Paul several times over the years. Though obviously his favourite axe, Greeny's value alone meant taking it on tour was always a risky business and even the idea of bringing it to the studio created problems of logistics and security. Further, having been in the wars with him for over 35 years, the guitar's specs were now considerably altered, with various parts replaced or repaired. Yet, Moore believed the Les Paul to be imbued with something truly special and had strongly resisted the urge to let it go.

For the reasons outlined above, that changed in 2005 when discreet feelers were put out about finding it a suitable home.[6] As Moore wanted the instrument to go to a genuine collector and have little or no publicity generated around its sale, this took time. But when guitar dealer Phil Winfield at North Carolina's Maverick Music stepped forward with a potential (unnamed) buyer, a deal appeared in sight. To clarify his position, Moore had an agreement drawn up, allegedly stating Winfield was to act only as an intermediary for the third-party buyer and not seek to sell the guitar as an individual or via Maverick's website. Moore was then paid a sum between $500,000 and $1.2 million, though somewhere near the lower figure is much more likely, and the transaction brought to a close in March 2006.

Except, of course, it didn't quite end there. At some point after Greeny left for the States, the instrument reportedly turned up at a Dallas guitar festival with a price tag considerably higher than the one Moore had been paid. 'It was here, there and everywhere,' grumbled Gary, 'being paraded around like a bearded lady.' Winfield later explained that the anonymous buyer on whose behalf he acted had become unnerved by adverse publicity surrounding the sale. Hence, Greeny was acquired by Maverick Music in July 2006, with the company paying another $50,000 on top to secure it. On hearing that the Les Paul was now in the hands of Maverick, Moore

---

6   Though Moore wanted to handle the sale of Greeny himself, he approached London guitar dealer Rick Zsigmond for advice/assistance.

cried foul on the terms of their original agreement.[7] 'I don't really want to talk about that because it was supposed to be a very discreet sale,' he confirmed to *Classic Rock*'s Dave Ling, 'and now it's all over the web. I'm really unhappy because I didn't want to part with it in the first place.'

Inevitably, the fate of Greeny and Moore's reasons for selling it soon became a matter of fierce debate among the guitar community, with the whole sorry saga finding its way onto the internet. Some took Moore's side, asking who exactly the mystery buyer was and why they had chosen to remain anonymous. Others felt that, even if Peter Green himself made no official comment about the sale[8], the whole thing had an aspect of karma to it. Despite money changing hands back in 1972, went the argument, the charmed Gibson Les Paul was really a gift from Green to Gary Moore and therefore never truly his to sell.

Moore didn't see it that way. '[Greeny] was a very special instrument, obviously,' he told *Vintage Guitar*'s Lisa Sharken. 'But it got to the point where I couldn't take it anywhere. I didn't want to sell it. I had to sell it . . . mainly because I injured my hand a few years ago and the insurance didn't pay up. It was a financial thing, and [selling the guitar] was the quickest way to do anything about it. That guitar was played by Jimi Hendrix and Jeff Beck. Rory Gallagher played it, I played it! I mean,' he asked, not unreasonably, 'why would I want to bloody sell it?'

As the arguments around its sale continued and Greeny began its journey around the guitar cosmos looking for a suitable owner, Gary Moore again found himself counting out from a large bag of mixed blessings. Financially better off for his decision, but battered by all that came with

---

7   When Phil Winfield signed the agreement confirming him as an intermediary for a third-party purchase, a buyer was reportedly in place. More, Winfield claims to have documentation proving at time of sale (March 2006), funds came from a source other than he or Maverick Music. Further reports suggest that when Moore went public with his dissatisfactions (Gary really was quite vitriolic in his criticisms), Winfield took this as a breach of their contract, and thereby put Greeny up for sale directly via Maverick. The tale was subsequently covered in full detail in the pages of September 2006's *Guitar & Bass* magazine (the article was called 'Deal or No Deal') and later by Harry Shapiro in his 2017 book *I Can't Wait Until Tomorrow*.

8   At the time of the guitar's sale, Moore had not spoken to Peter Green in several years, believing the former Fleetwood Mac man to be living in Sweden.

it – 'It was a bad experience' – Moore's recent travails seemed emblematic of a much larger game, the previous decade of his life full of wins,
losses, leaps and stumbles. In short, the plot of one of those blues tunes
he was so fond of singing. Still, the none-more-grim prospect of never
be able to play again had been emphatically laid to rest on a Dublin
stage in August 2005. What he needed to do now was get back out there
and make some new music. Over the next five years, Gary would put
every effort into doing both, each step moving him slowly closer to
staking a claim for a statue of his very own.

CHAPTER TWENTY-SEVEN

Gotta Keep A Runnin'

If the choices Gary Moore made in his musical life after 1995's *Blues for Greeny* had led to reduced sales and some knotted brows among fans and critics, he at least appeared to make better progress when out of the spotlight. In fact, after the emotional bangs and crashes of the mid-nineties where affairs began, marriages ended and he appeared to change address every other month, 2006 found the guitarist happily settled by the coast, his neighbours now mainly seagulls.

Surprising some within his circle, Moore had left behind the flowing waters and clanking masts of Henley-on-Thames and Chelsea Harbour in 2003, purchasing a five-bedroomed house in the reassuringly sedate seaside resort of Hove, East Sussex. Nestled roughly equidistant between shingle beach and high street, the location of Moore's home was not just about the pursuit of peace and quiet. Nor was he intent on recreating those idyllic summers he enjoyed as a child in Millisle or Donaghadee (though frankly, who could blame him). Instead, the move to Hove accorded Gary easy access to sons Jack and Gus who were now living/ studying in nearby, and considerably livelier, Brighton.

With partner Jo and daughter Lily in situ, elder daughter Saoirse making the occasional trip down from London and old friends/associates such as Eric Bell and Gered Mankowitz dropping by when they could, Moore had a strong, stable base from which to operate for the first time in years. As pub owners would come to learn, he was able to sniff out a 'blues night' from several miles away too, turning up guitar in hand at local taverns such as The Neptune, The Ranelagh and The Horse & Groom for a beer and an occasional jam with local musicians.[1]

Yet, however inviting the beach huts, lawns, promenades and pubs of Hove must have seemed, Moore was eager to get back to basics. With the exception of Dublin's Point experience, The Strat Pack and a brief spot at a tribute concert honouring the late, great saxophonist Dick Heckstall-Smith in June 2005, Gary had not really been on stage for two years. Given his hand was now fixed, and with *Old New Ballads Blues*, there was another disc's worth of songs from which to draw, an extensive tour seemed to make artistic and financial sense (even if the sale of 'Greeny' would also provide additional funds).

Indeed, given the drop off Moore had experienced in album sales over recent years, extending that tour's perimeters to include Japan and even the States might be prudent as well as profitable. Unfortunately, Gary's continued fear of flying meant that wasn't really on the cards, though he was (just about) content to extend his plane journeys into Europe and Russia. Still, Europe – or thereabouts – was a pretty big place, and even if his CD sales had dipped since 1990's *Still Got the Blues*, Moore remained a formidable draw on the concert circuit. Hence, he would spend a reasonable chunk of the next few years exploring its various nooks and crannies: from Norway and Estonia to Spain and Bulgaria.

Moore's latest journey began at Sheffield's Hallam Arena on 29 March 2006, where he had the pleasure of appearing on a 'Once in a Lifetime Double Bill' with the great B.B. King. Promoted in some quarters as B.B.'s last ever UK dates (he was 80 at the time[2]), Moore was lined up

---

1 As well as regularly communing with Brighton & Hove-based musicians, Moore also became enamoured of other local artists, basing the cover of his 2004 album *Power of the Blues* on the graffiti he observed while walking in the city.

2 These dates were not quite the last time King appeared in the UK, with B. B. making it back to London's Royal Albert Hall in on 28 June 2011 for a star-studded

for five shows in all, culminating with an appearance at London's Wembley Arena on 4 April. Though falling on the occasion of Moore's 54th birthday, there were to be no repeats of those glorious duets at the Hard Rock Café or Town & Country Club, as both men focused on their own sets. But at least Gary could take heart from sharing a stage with the man who introduced him to King's crying guitar in the first place. After renewing their musical vows at the Point in Dublin, Brian Downey had agreed to step out with Moore not only for his 2006 tour, but an album too. 'Well, I was delighted when he went back to the blues, said the drummer in 2020. 'I only wish he did it a couple of years earlier!'

Firm friends since bonding over John Mayall and Cream as teenagers at Sammy Houston's bar in Belfast, Downey had not cut all ties with Moore after his untimely departure from Thin Lizzy. Unlike his bandmate Scott Gorham, there appeared to be no simmering anger in Downey concerning Moore's actions of 1979, just a sense of regret at opportunities lost. That said, words were exchanged. 'Well, I'd said to him, "You know Gary, professional musicians don't do that. They just don't." But he looked straight at me and said, "I'm being honest here. The pressure came to a head. With all the pressure on me, all the things I was dealing with, I just could not do it anymore. Just couldn't." And you know, when your mind starts down that path, you know you're in trouble. So, I understood it. Fair enough.'

Meeting regularly over the years, and with Downey even appearing on 1990's *Still Got the Blues*, it really was only a matter of 'when' rather than 'if' before the two again joined forces. 'Yes, I don't have a personality that holds against people in that way,' Downey confirmed. 'I knew Gary as a friend first and a musician second. And thank God, through it all, that friendship never waned.' Joining fellow returnees Vic Martin and Peter Rees on bass and keyboards, Downey would keep the beat with Gary Moore for a while yet.

If Downey represented a friendly face from the past for Moore, then Otis Taylor was definitely one for the future. The Chicago-born son of

---

concert featuring Rolling Stone Ronnie Wood, Guns N' Roses' Slash and the quite brilliant slide guitarist Derek Trucks. The great man passed aged 89 in 2015.

a jazz-loving parents – 'I was raised by be-boppers, baby! – Taylor was first drawn to banjo as a child in the fifties. But on hearing the instrument's original African origins had been hi-jacked by black-face minstrels during the late-nineteenth century, he switched to guitar and harmonica instead. A professional musician throughout rock's first and second waves, which included a spell with brilliant, if troubled guitarist Tommy Bolin in the pre-Deep Purple act T&O Short Line, Taylor left the business behind in the late seventies, only to return again (banjo now back in hand) for 1996's solo LP, *Blue-Eyed Monster*. More discs followed, and with them several honours, from the prestigious W.C. Handy prize for 'Best New Artist' to various gongs from *Downbeat*, *Living Blues* and the Blues Music Awards.

By 2006, Taylor had six records to his name, each inching closer to a sound one critic described as 'terribly old, but shockingly new'. Potent, politically charged and lyrically reflective of everyday issues affecting the black community, Taylor's music was as complex as his wordplay, incorporating occasional washes of soul and post-psychedelic guitar with trance-like passages of the deepest blues. Having attempted something broadly similar on bits of the ill-fated *A Different Beat* (albeit with added drum loops), it was no surprise that Gary Moore was delighted and also probably a little envious when he came across Taylor performing at a small Brighton club in October 2006. Yet, when Gary approached Otis at the end of the gig to offer his congratulations, the American was clueless as to Moore's identity. 'He told me he loved [the concert], gave me his telephone number, then disappeared out the exit door with a big crash,' Taylor laughed. 'I didn't know who he was. Later, they told me, "That was Gary Moore. He's a star." So, I called him up the next day and said, "I hear you're fucking famous." He just laughed and said, "Do you want to play?" And that was the start.'

Quickly forming a mutual appreciation society, Moore added some wonderfully anarchic fills to 'Black Betty' and 'Something in Your Back Pocket' for Taylor's next release, *Definition of a Circle*, before scooping Otis up as his support act for a forthcoming tour. Now, it was Taylor's turn to be impressed. 'Gary could play it all,' he confirmed. 'Irish music, jazz, rock, blues, country. If it was music and it had strings, Gary could figure it out. Fast and clean, Gary. But even though he knew music – understood it intellectually – with him, the playing still came from an emotional place. That's how he was.'

A generous host, 'Gary took care of me. From the moment I was on the road with him, I was part of the family', Moore was also on hand to teach Taylor some little-known secrets of road life, including how to procure the best possible hotel room. 'Ha! Yes, Gary was always trying to get an upgrade,' he laughed. 'One time, he even got a place that was two rooms with a piano. A fucking piano. He wanted perfection.' Obviously meant for each other, Taylor was to work with Moore for several more years, not only providing touring support for him, but also enjoying another recorded collaboration on Taylor's 2009 album *Pentatonic Wars and Love Songs*. 'Man, Gary loved playing,' Taylor said of his friend. 'I mean, he'd do two, three encores. Me, I just wanted to get off the stage! But you know, we had a good connection and Gary really helped my career. Plus, he taught me how to be a [hotel] prima donna!'[3]

With Taylor on hand to provide able assistance, Moore's return to the road was always destined to be pleasurable rather than onerous. But tours run on new product as well as old favourites, and Moore's were no exception. Hence, in January 2007, he, Brian Downey, Peter Rees and Vic Martin entered Sarm Hook End Studios in Hampshire with producer Ian Taylor to record his next album.[4] Despite Moore's furiously itchy musical spirit and the presence of Downey behind the drums, there was no talk of 'Wild Frontier Part Two' or 'Black Rose: The Return'. Having fast-tracked *Old New Ballads Blues* just in time for his dates with B.B. King, Moore seemed to have parked his recent

---

3 Joking aside, Otis Taylor enjoyed touring with Gary Moore so much, he missed the chance to perform for Barack Obama's presidential campaign due to a clash of dates in Brighton on 9 June 2007. 'Yep, I turned down playing for Obama to make that last Brighton gig,' he said. 'It was a little tough but it was the right thing to do.'
4 Later the same month, Moore appeared at a memorial concert in honour of old friend and fellow Henley-on-Thames resident, Jim Capaldi, who had died of cancer aged just 60. Billed as 'Dear Mr Fantasy: A Celebration for Jim Capaldi', and held at London's Roundhouse on 21 January 2007, Moore's contribution on the night was a sublime version of 'Evil Love'. Said concert was released on CD/DVD a year later.

Celtic fixations until further notice. This was to be a pure blues set: hard in places, soft in others, but blues all the same.

Moore had set himself a high bar in several places, including the guitar side of things. In addition to cutting all solos live without resorting to overdubs, ('It's always tempting to say, "I'll go back and fix that bit," so I had to make sure I didn't do that',) there would be no effects either. 'No, I didn't want to use any pedals,' he later told *Guitarist*. 'I wanted the tones to be as immediate and in-your-face as possible, and the best way to do that is to eliminate anything extra in the signal path between the guitar and amp.'[5]

Another area Moore had shaken up considerably was his approach to lyrics. An always tricky part of the creative process for him, he often left writing them to the last minute, sometimes leading to decidedly mixed results. Yet, the introduction of a simple notebook in which he could capture ideas, snippets and turns of phrase had worked wonders, and Moore was now ahead of the curve in his wordplay rather than lagging behind. 'I got sick of putting backing tracks down and not having words for them,' he told *Guitarist*. 'You can never write good lyrics under that sort of pressure.'

One of the first successes of this new regime was the moody 'Trouble at Home'. Wrapping a spare musical arrangement around the despondent tale of an unravelling marriage, 'Trouble at Home' had Gary's protagonist worrying about the fate of his children as things slowly fell apart all around them. Given Moore had recently wed long-term partner Jo Rendle and appeared genuinely content with his domestic lot, ('I like to live a quiet, normal life as much as I can with my family when I'm away from the stage,' he confirmed in 2007), this seemed an unusual topic to cover. Yet, given where things were soon heading, one had to ask if there was also an element of foreboding to Moore's latest midnight ballad.

Recorded off the floor in just eight days and with 'Trouble at Home' one

---

5 Though Moore had forsworn effects, that didn't stop him using a variety of axes, with a 1959 Gibson Les Paul, a 1957 Gibson Goldtop, a vintage Fender Telecaster and a Burns Sonic ES-335 all making an appearance. On the amp front, Moore favoured them small and deadly this time around, employing a Fender Vibroverb and 'pretty vicious' Orange Tiny Terror, among others.

of its undoubted highlights, Moore's new LP *Close As You Get* turned out
to be another strong set. Alternating between the tender and tough, and
with an even distribution of covers and originals, Moore threw the net a
little wider than usual by introducing a variety of tones/colours largely
absent from previous releases. For fans of Moore's more melancholic side,
the jazz-inflected 'Nowhere Fast' and slow, sorrowful 'I Had a Dream' were
both fine exemplars, with Gary on particularly thrilling form throughout
the latter. "I Had a Dream' is almost country [in places],' he confirmed.
'I played it on a Telecaster . . . [and had] been listening to a lot of Roy
Buchanan there, I think.' Moore was also at his best when taking on John
Mayall's 1966 tearjerker 'Have You Heard'. However, though he knew
the tune inside out from studying *Blues Breakers* . . . in his youth, Moore
remained determined to put his own spin on Eric Clapton's landmark
guitar part. 'Well, there was no point trying to clone what he'd done,'
Moore laughed, 'because no one's ever going to do it as good!'

Conversely, for those seeking Moore's harder side, again he appeared
happy to oblige. A thumping cover of Chuck Berry's 'Thirty Days' had
Moore spitting rockabilly licks here, there and everywhere while his own
'Hard Times' came on like a long-lost Howlin' Wolf track. Featuring a
bruising, ill-tempered solo from Moore, 'Hard Times' also benefited from
the blazing harmonica of Nine Below Zero's Mark Feltham. 'Mark played
harp on the record,' said Moore, 'and he was bloody brilliant.'

Once the harp man for Rory Gallagher, though now a special guest
on Moore's new LP, Feltham's seismic blasts could be heard on Moore's
version of 'Checkin' Up on My Baby' too, a song written by vintage
country bluesman Sonny Boy Williamson and now beefed up for *Close
As You Get*. Williamson was also the source behind Moore's salty take on
'Eyesight to the Blind', though this time, it was Brian Downey's turn to
hog the spotlight with some deft stickwork. 'Brian brought a real blues
vibe to [the record], because he grew up listening to the same records
as I did,' Moore confirmed. 'It's also great having a friend in the band,
because that's what I've got with Brian Downey. We've known each
other for ever.'

Downey was also behind one of the more left-field choices on *Close
As You Get*: a captivating study of Royce Swain's 'Evenin", made famous

White Knuckles

by jump blues legend Jimmy Witherspoon. 'We used to do 'Evenin'' with Sugar Shack . . . and Gary would always ask, "Who's that song by?"' confirmed the drummer. 'Anyway, come 2007, we're recording *Close As You Get* and Gary wants to do 'I Put a Spell On You' by Nina Simone. "Great song," says I, "but I think it's been done to death." Then out of nowhere, Gary says, "What was that song you used to do with Sugar Shack that I loved?" So, I went through a few of them, B.B. and Freddie King, you know, the usual suspects. But he said, "No, it was quite jazzy . . ." and I said, "Ah, Jimmy Witherspoon!"' A languorous, almost sultry tune with a similar chord structure to Moore's original choice, 'I Put a Spell On You', 'Evenin'' found Moore approaching his vocals in a completely different way. 'Yeah, I had to learn a new way of singing almost, for that one,' he later said. 'It's kind of like a Billie Holiday jazz approach, where the vocal's dragging behind the beat. It's not something I'd done before, so there was a real challenge there.' If there were a tune on *Close As You Get* that saw Gary Moore moving in an entirely uncharted direction, it was 'Sundown'. Authored by one of founding fathers of country blues, Moore had come across Eddie 'Son' House's wondrous song while building playlists for *Blues Power*, a series of six shows offered to him by Planet Rock radio in late 2006. Acting as DJ, host, tutor and fan, Moore's brief was to spin some of his favourite songs, talk about what they meant to him, and wherever possible, embroider the originals with a burst or two of guitar.[6] 'I'd take the guitar and demonstrate licks in different styles,' he later confirmed. 'Peter Green . . . Carlos Santana, Billy Gibbons [and others].'

Of course, there was no doubt that many of Moore's choices would err towards the likes of John Mayall, Eric Clapton, Fleetwood Mac and Cream. After all, he had named the programme in part-honour of Mayall's 1999 LP *Blues Power*. But in recent years Moore's ears had also opened wide to fifties Chicago legends Muddy Waters, Howlin' Wolf and Willie Dixon. In addition to these electric pioneers, Moore had tracked right back to the source itself, his investigations now centring on Delta

---

6 Transmitted in 2007, *Blues Power* was a surprisingly good listen, with Moore's playlist including everyone from Carlos Santana and ZZ Top to Sister Rosetta Tharpe. 'Taking listeners on a personal journey through the blues,' Moore's efforts were rewarded when he and Planet Rock won a New York Radio Award the following year.

410

blues cornerstones Robert Johnson, Skip James, and for some, the best of all – Son House.

'I suppose I've saved up [listening to country blues] until now,' he told *Guitarist* in 2007, 'which is lovely in a way, because you're getting back to the roots of the music later in life. These guys,' Moore continued, 'came from the humblest of backgrounds, but they were so eloquent. Some of those blues lyrics are like poetry, and with Son House, when you hear his voice, you believe every word the guy's singing.' To give him his due, Moore's cover of 'Sundown' was as sincere as the original. Cut after a few relaxing pints at the local pub, 'Out of respect, you understand', Moore sat himself down on the studio couch with an Ozark acoustic resonator guitar and fair sang his heart out.

According to its maker 'The most relaxed record I've ever made,' and preceded by a fan-club-only gig at west London's Bush Hall where Moore ended the show with 'Sundown' to the delight of 400 gathered invitees, *Close As You Get* was released on 21 May 2007. To help promote it, Gary struck out with Otis Taylor in tow for the latest in a lengthy procession of dates around the UK, Scandinavia and outer reaches of eastern Europe. On this occasion, Moore was even able to get back home, with gigs in Dublin's Vicar Street and Belfast's Waterfront Hall allowing him not only to play to the faithful but also visit old haunts with his new family. 'I had a beautiful time in Ireland,' he later told the *Belfast Telegraph*. 'I had a few days off either end of my gigs [there], and I took my partner Jo and our daughter Lily on a bit of a nostalgia trip around the places where I used to live.'

However, before doubling back to Britain for a second round of dates in late autumn, Moore put himself forward for one of the sterner tests of his musical career. To celebrate the 40th anniversary of Jimi Hendrix's legendary performance at 1967's Monterey Pop Festival, a new, enhanced version of the guitarist's set was being released on DVD/CD. To mark its passage into shops, London's Hippodrome club was screening the film to a select gathering of Jimi's devotees, friends and journalists, followed by a live set from a Hendrix tribute act. Of course, this was to be no mere cover group. Instead, Gary Moore would be fronting it, with special guest appearances from Jimi Hendrix Experience drummer Mitch Mitchell and Band Of Gypsys bassist Billy Cox.

As with his tenure alongside Jack Bruce and Ginger Baker in BBM, Moore had been preparing for this moment for over four decades. A huge fan since seeing Hendrix incinerate Belfast's Whitla Hall on 27 November 1967, Moore's admiration only grew in subsequent decades, the guitarist's devotion to Jimi perhaps only surpassed by his fealty to Peter Green. Hence, Moore took the Hippodrome show with almost comical seriousness, chasing down the same effects pedals Hendrix had used back in the sixties while also dusting off his own 1961 Fiesta Red Fender Strat[7] and Marshall stack in an effort to capture every facet of Jimi's sound.

Accompanied for most of the set by a returning Darrin Mooney and former Eric Clapton four-stringer Dave Bronze, Gary Moore's 11-song performance at the Hippodrome on 25 October 2007 was genuinely monumental. Finally given a platform to indulge one of his favourite obsessions on the concert stage, Moore's takes on 'Manic Depression', 'Angel' and 'I Don't Live Today' stepped beyond the bounds of mere mimicry and sailed close to actually channelling the great man himself. This spooky vibe was enhanced when Mitch Mitchell and Billy Cox joined him for a three-song medley of 'Red House', 'Stone Free' and 'Hey Joe'. Though only playing together for the first time the previous evening[8], the trio absolutely nailed the spirit of Hendrix's originals, even if song arrangements occasionally strayed due a lack of rehearsal. Still, when Moore put the hammer down at encore time for a cover of 'Voodoo Chile (Slight Return)', any rough edges were submerged in steady waves of shrieking feedback.

With the success of 'Blues For Jimi' providing him with fresh momentum, Moore continued to tour into 2008, each concert replenishing his finances while also providing funds for the inevitable next album. That

7 In 2017, Fender Custom Shop master builder John Cruz created a limited run of Stratocasters based on the exact specifications of Moore's iconic 1961 Fiesta Red. The results were spookily close to Moore's original guitar.
8 Flying in from New York for the gig, Mitchell and Cox had recently been on tour together as part of 'Experience Hendrix', performing old Jimi tunes with the likes of The Doors' Robby Krieger, former Rolling Stone Mick Taylor and the peerless Buddy Guy.

came soon enough, with Moore again entering Sarm West/Sphere Studios in mid-summer. While Vic Martin and Pete Rees were there to cover keys and bass, a sudden virus precluded Brian Downey's involvement, leading Moore to secure the talents of Jamaican jazz, blues and boogie specialist Sam Kelly on drums. Additionally, neither Chris Tsangarides[9] nor Ian Taylor were given a call back on this occasion, as Moore handed engineering/co-production reins to Greg Jackman. 'We went with Greg as [co-]producer,' Gary later confirmed. 'He'd worked with Status Quo of all people, and I'd already worked with him [as an engineer] during the nineties. He's fantastic at getting good sounds.'

This time bashed out in just five days ('I wanted to get in as soon as possible to keep up that energy,' said Moore), *Bad for you Baby* took up precisely where *Close As You Get* left off a year or so before. Again providing a perfectly serviceable mix of covers and self-penned tunes, the album offered up two Muddy Waters specials, 'Walkin' Thru the Park' and 'Someday Baby', one bottleneck stomper in J.B. Lenoir's 'Mojo Boogie' and a sad-eyed lament courtesy of Al Kooper's 'I Love You More Than You'll Ever Know'. Of Moore's own compositions, both the title track and 'Umbrella Man' saw him getting back in touch with his inner riff monster, while 'Down the Line' was country blues played on a hot-wired Telecaster and put through a very loud amp.

Consolidating his and Moore's friendship once more, Otis Taylor and his magical banjo made an appearance on the stop/starting 'Preacher Man Blues'[10] while the duo were joined by Taylor's daughter Cassie on backing vocals, a task she happily performed on the soul-leaning 'Holding On' too. It was then left to 'Trouble Ain't Far Behind' to close proceedings, the ballad's somnambulant pace and Santo & Johnny-like lead lines ending the record on a dreamy high, as Moore flew above the clouds with another lilting solo.

---

9 Sadly, 2004's *Power of the Blues* would be the last time Chris Tsangarides worked with Moore. A long-time friend of the guitarist as well as a great talent in his own right, Tsangarides passed away in January 2018 aged just 61.

10 'Preacher Man Blues' was recorded using a red Gibson Firebird Moore bought in Finland the previous year. 'A great guitar with a real twang to it,' he said. In addition to the Firebird, Moore also used various Les Pauls, vintage Telecasters and a 1963 ES 335 while making the album. A Fender Vibroverb, Dual Showman and several hand-wired Marshall amps (including a fifty-watt JCM800) were also on display throughout.

Not his best perhaps, but by no means his worst either, *Bad for you Baby* was released on 22 September 2008[11], though once again to only moderate sales. That said, the critics remained on side, concentrating their praise not just on Moore's guitar playing, but also his singing voice, with Classic Rock commenting favourably on Gary's ever-improving vocal range, while VintageRock.com's Ralph Greco Jr. pointed to Gary's 'dynamic . . . rock solid vocals'. For a man who had to be dragged screaming to the microphone back in the early eighties, this was worthy of celebration. Moore was quick to point towards his abandonment of hard rock for the improvement. 'I hated singing rock,' he said. 'It wasn't until I discovered the blues that I really started to enjoy singing. I brought the song keys down a bit, and I didn't play rhythm guitar through every song, so I was kind of answering myself with the guitar. That made it a lot more interesting.'

A part of Moore's melodic arsenal grown considerably stronger since his days as a metal god, the praise accorded Gary's vocals on *Bad for you Baby* should have at least lifted his spirits. Unfortunately, he was too busy putting out fires elsewhere to pay it proper mind. After 11 years together, Moore's time with Jo Rendle had come to a sudden end in the autumn of 2008 when he became involved with a 33-year-old German woman called Petra Nioduschewski while on promotional duties for his new album. A genuine shock to those around him, at first Gary reportedly denied the seriousness of the affair. But as the months wore on, it became apparent that Moore had not brought things with Nioduschewski to an end.

Suffice to say, by the start of 2009, Moore had moved out of the family home in Hove and moved into another one nearby with Nioduschewski soon joining him there. As was the case with sons Jack and Gus following his divorce from Kerry Booth, he was keen to stay in close proximity to his youngest daughter, Lily, while also remaining on reasonable terms with his now estranged wife. Yet the combination of another failed relationship, the challenges involved in establishing a new one and once again becoming a visiting rather than live-in father this time seemed to weigh heavily upon

---

11 On the same day *Bad for you Baby* was released, Moore appeared at Dublin's Olympia Theatre for a tribute concert in honour of the late, great Irish guitarist Jimmy Faulkner. Fellow attendees included Brian Downey, Christy Moore and Moore's old buddies from Skid Row Brush Shiels and Noel Bridgeman.

Moore. Indeed, it could also have been a factor in the marked change in his physical appearance over the coming months.

Away from the upheavals of his private life, there were more troubles for Gary (or more specifically his lawyer) to contend with. On 3 December 2008 a court in Munich ordered the guitarist to pay damages after ruling the solo from his 1990 hit single 'Still Got the Blues' had been plagiarised from an instrumental tune written some 16 years before. According to Reuters, the solo 'was too similar to the one in 'Nordrach' by the [Offenbach progressive rock] band Jud's Gallery not to have been copied, even though the German song was not available on record at the time.' While Moore denied knowing of 'Nordrach' for precisely that reason, the court pointed to the fact he might have heard it on the radio or in a concert setting.[12] 'Moore and his record label,' Reuters continued, '[were] to pay damages to [Jud's Gallery] band leader Juergen Winter, who brought the case. The amount,' they concluded, 'was yet to be fixed.'

Just months after the events of Munich, Ronnie Montrose, all-round American axe hero and the man behind seventies hard rock game-changers Montrose, also stepped forward claiming Moore was in possession of a 'rare 1959 Gibson Les Paul' stolen from him at an Edgar Winter concert in October 1972. When private detectives hired to find it at the time had no success, Montrose thought the instrument lost forever. Until that is, he saw an article in UK magazine *Guitar Buyer* focusing on Moore's collection, one of which Montrose became convinced was his Les Paul, now probably worth in the region of $500,000. The guitar in question, Gary's beloved 'Stripe' (serial number 9-2227), had a rich history all its own to Moore, and one that he immortalised on the solo section of 'Still Got the Blues.'[13] However, when Gary reportedly failed to respond to Ronnie's efforts to contact him, Montrose filed a lawsuit at the US

---

12 The court also reportedly stated that '[though] there was no evidence that the guitar solo was lifted from 'Nordrach' copyright infringement does not depend on outright theft'.

13 A year before interest in 'Stripe' was renewed, Gibson released a new, mid-budget Gary Moore signature model called the 'BFG'. Lightweight (the body was chambered), usually 'Lemon Burst' in colour and equipped with a Burstbucker pick-up at the bridge and P90 pick at the neck, the BFG was manufactured between 2008 and 2012. Moore reportedly used a prototype for his slide parts on *Bad for you Baby*.

District Court in San Francisco on 9 June 2009. This time, the matter was quickly dismissed due to jurisdictional issues.[14] 'I've had that guitar for more than twenty years,' an aggrieved Moore told *Marin Independent Journal*, 'The whole thing is a sham.'

Battered by matters legal and personal, many would have pulled up a rock and crawled under it. Gary Moore chose to keep on trucking, and for much of 2009 toured his way around the UK, Scandinavia and several far corners of Europe.[15] With new drummer (and old friend of bassist Pete Rees) Steve Dixon now replacing Sam Kelly, concerts were played, festivals blitzed and crowds from Moscow to Cardiff sated, as the band played 62 dates over the course of eight months. Whether Moore was simply intent on restocking his financial reserves after the 'Still Got the Blues' court case or as likely seeking to avoid the any difficulties caused by his actions at home remains unclear. But despite appearing tired and 'out of sorts' at several gigs, he seemed in no mood to come off the road for very long.

Even when Gary did finally return to Hove at the end of the year, he could not easily settle, those still itchy fingers leading him towards several local pub jams and an appearance five miles up the road at Shoreham-on-Sea's small but perfectly formed Ropetackle Centre on 29 November. Here, Moore joined US blues guitarist Buddy Whittington, until recently the latest player to fill Eric Clapton's spot in John Mayall's Blues Breakers, but now a year or so into his own solo career. A fluid, clever soloist whom Moore first met and jammed with in 2006 when he was still a part of Mayall's set-up, Whittington had been the subject of Moore's praises ever since. 'I love Buddy,' Moore told *Guitarist*. 'He's really original and . . . just walks across the strings. John tried to get a little duel going between us, [and] I tell you what. If he lived over here, I'd play with him all the time!'[16]

14 A brilliant musician, Ronnie Montrose sadly passed away on 3 March 2012.
15 While not on tour, Moore still found ways to play, appearing with old friend/bassist Mo Foster and much underrated six-stringer Ray Russell at Vibes from the Vines, an open-air festival held on 8 August 2009 at Horam Vineyards in aid of Cancer Research UK. Foster and Russell had written the instrumental 'So Far Away', which Moore continued to occasionally play live right up to 2010.
16 Delivering on the spirit of that promise, Moore and Whittington performed Otis

Following several further impromptu drop-ins at various Brighton blues venues[17] over the winter/early spring of 2009/10, Moore was back at the coal face by April, leading his group out to Russia for the third time in as many years. A country he enjoyed visiting, Moore was set to perform first in in St Petersburg before a 'glamour date' at Moscow's 7,300-seater Crocus Hall mid-month. However, the man who arrived for the press conference publicising these events appeared to have little interest in fashion, frippery, or more worryingly, his physique.

Dressed in a heavy black wind-breaker drawn close to his body, Moore looked wan, tired and paunchy. Once upon a time, of course, he had stuck out like a sore thumb among guitar gods, appearing more like a promising middle-weight boxer than the stick-thin waifs then wielding hefty Les Pauls upon the stage. Now, however, Moore's general demeanour seemed to confirm rumours that since the breakdown of his marriage, he had been eating and (perhaps of greater concern) drinking more than usual, thereby losing his previous sharpness as a result. However, there were enough flashes of the old Moore left to suggest otherwise. 'Clapton?' he quipped to the assembled press corps. 'Boring. I don't like his music any more. When he played with the Blues Breakers, he was . . . brilliant. But since then,' Moore giggled, 'Well, he's just gone downhill. . .'

Out of shape perhaps, but not necessarily out of the game, Gary continued on the road throughout April, his progress even bringing him back to Japan after an absence of nearly two decades. A destination once struck from the touring diary because of Moore's fear of flying, recent monetary issues might have forced a rethink, as he now made the near 10-hour trip from Moscow to Tokyo. Visiting Nagoya and Osaka as well as the country's capital, Moore took advantage of his location by journeying even further to South Korea, bringing a classic blues set to Seoul's Olympic Gymnasium on 30 April 2010.

Then came another surprise. Having seriously explored the possibility

---

Rush's 'All My Love' and Albert King's 'Crosscut Saw' to 350 gathered fans in Shoreham-on-Sea.

17 In addition to popping into his local pub – The Neptune – for a quick jam or two, Moore also performed at Hove's Little Fish Market for another charity gig in early April 2010.

of a Celtic rock-themed tour/album in 2005 before being distracted by a series of concert dates with B.B. King, Moore once again resurrected the idea. Placing his current band to one side with the assurance he would pick things up again further on up the road, Gary set about assembling a new troupe more in keeping with the demands of rock rather than creating shades of blue. Out went old dependables Pete Rees, Vic Martin and Steve Dixon, to be replaced by equally experienced, but slightly noisier dependables Darrin Mooney and Jonathan Noyce on drums and bass.

In a clever move that pointed at exactly what he had in mind for the project, Moore also reached out across the decades to Neil Carter, his right-hand man during the melodic, if hairy days of *After the War* and *Wild Frontier*. As it turned out, he didn't need to reach out that far at all. Following his tenure with Moore in 1990, Carter had become increasingly drawn to classical music and soon found himself studying it. That led to a teaching qualification which then blossomed into a delightful second career, with Carter becoming head of woodwind and brass at Brighton College – an independent school where Moore's sons Jack and Gus and youngest daughter Lily were all at one time or another pupils. Given the circumstances, it was no surprise that Moore and Carter had become reacquainted, though Gary's subsequent offer of a job back in his band still came as a shock. 'I had always said firmly I would never "go back",' Carter wrote on his website, 'but he caught me on a bad day at school and I said, "Why not?"'

Christened 'Trondheim Rocks' (at least the word 'Monsters' was absent on this occasion), Moore, Carter, Mooney and Noyce took the experiment live on stage at Norway's premier festival on 22 May 2010. A city where the fire for Gary's music in all its forms continued to burn bright, Trondheim was the perfect place for the guitarist to test rewinding the clock in front of a sympathetic audience. Mercifully, things went well, with Moore digging out 'Over the Hills and Far Away', 'Blood of Emeralds' and 'Empty Rooms' to the delight of those who had first heard them in concert back in the eighties. There were three new tracks on offer too, all redolent of the type of material that made *Wild Frontier* such a solid seller before the blues again came calling for Moore in 1990. Whether summoning the boisterous spirit of Thin Lizzy on 'Days of Heroes' and

'Oh Wild One' or seeking the arms of a former lover in the bittersweet (and perhaps emotionally prescient) 'Where Are You Now?' Moore could obviously still write a good rock song when the mood took him.

Unfortunately, not every gig was as satisfying as the one in Trondheim. On 6 July, Moore and the group appeared at the Montreux Jazz Festival, a town he had always loved and an event at which he had always excelled. Although fellow performers Billy Idol, Missy Elliot, Phil Collins and John McLaughlin all handed in fine sets, Moore was not at the races. In a rare duff performance, notes were fluffed, vocals sub-par and (astoundingly) his timing occasionally wobbly. Moore rallied twice, first making quick work of the scurrying solo for 'Out in the Fields' before stretching out beautifully on a tune he had written with Philip Lynott over 30 years before. Indeed, when Gary reached for the endlessly sustaining note that signalled the climax of 'Parisienne Walkways', both he and the crowd were visibly off their feet. A night of few wins, but sadly of more losses, some said Moore sounded as if he had been drinking while on stage at Montreux. Perhaps. Perhaps not.[18] But he was certainly disappointing.

This pattern of hit or miss continued over several subsequent concerts, with Gary receiving either brilliant or patchy notices when gigging across the UK and Europe before recapturing his old, more reliable form in Russia later that autumn. Of course, even when Moore was having an off night, with musicians the calibre of Carter, Mooney and Noyce supporting him, concerts were never really in jeopardy. Equally, there was little real fear backstage, where Moore continued to be buoyed by one of the most loyal and professional support teams in the industry, the likes of Graham Lilley, Darren Main, new tour manager Dick Meredith and others[19] ensuring he could do his job whatever life, the elements or

---

18 As we shall see in the final chapter, there may have been other, health-associated reasons for Gary's sub-par performance at Montreux and elsewhere on his 2010 European tour.

19 In addition to those named above, over the years Moore also enjoyed the loyal support of tour managers such as Steve Croxford and Andy Crookston, sound engineers like Chris Hedge and Mike Warren, and his agent and promoter/bookers Barry Dickins, Prue Almond and Simon Moran. Happy to offer praise, Gary frequently thanked his team and crew in album credits. Unfortunately, for reasons of space, not everyone who worked with Gary can be listed here.

architecture threw at him. Yet, when the last chord rattled the chandeliers of Moscow's Kremlin Palace on 30 October 2010, thus calling time on seven months of sporadic, if intense activity, one sensed everyone was looking forward to a break from the road.

Touring responsibilities dispatched, Moore wound down the rest of the year at home in west Hove, reportedly choosing to spend the Christmas holidays with girlfriend Petra Nioduschewski, his daughter Lily close by. Of course, there were always other options. As he had done many times in the past, Moore could have journeyed west to Somerset to see his mother Winnie, taking the opportunity to catch up with his brother and sisters while there. Alternatively, his children Saoirse, Jack and Gus might have come visit from London or elsewhere, each bringing fresh news with them. On one occasion, the story went, Gary had even spent Boxing Day alone at an old Dublin inn, though given his wish to be among both family and friends over the festive season, that sounds highly unlikely.[20] Still, for whatever reason, come Christmas 2010 and Moore could again be found by the sea, his thoughts his own, his guitar, as ever, close to hand.

If any new songs were written, however, they would remain unheard.

---

20 Though Moore's solo visit to Dublin's Brazen Head for a meal on Boxing Day, 1991, sounds extremely far-fetched, one Hove resident does recall seeing him 'bombing along' the promenade on a bitterly cold Christmas Eve morning back in 2010. The author Harry Shapiro also places him by the sea during this time.

CHAPTER TWENTY-EIGHT

If I Don't Get Home . . .

Gary Moore died on 6 February 2011, just two months shy of his 59th birthday.

Following the Christmas break, he had resumed work on his long-percolating Celtic rock album. With proof of concept established by a series of spirited, if occasionally haphazard shows over the summer/autumn of 2010, Moore now knew there was still an audience out there for the likes of 'Wild Frontier' and 'Over the Hills and Far Away'. Further, with album sales long reflecting his status as middle-aged blues artist rather than some fresh-faced pop ingenue, the prospect of even a moderately successful rock crossover record and the touring opportunities it might generate was surely tempting. Yet, though such ideas must have run through his mind, they were unlikely to be the key driver. As time had come to show, if Moore fancied changing musical direction at will, he did just that, dropping hats and damning torpedoes as he went.

Rehearsals for the Celtic project had officially begun in London during mid-January. Returning on bass was the ever-dependable Jonathan Noyce, though due to work commitments, Neil Carter would be joining he and Gary a week or so later. Another absentee was Darrin Mooney, now locked out of the band due to pre-existing commitments with

Primal Scream. That meant Moore was back in the market for a new drummer. The solution came via his ex-wife Kerry Booth's partner, Rob Green.

A strong pocket player who put groove ahead of flash, Green rose to prominence in the late nineties with million-selling pop-rockers Toploader. However, he had come to know Gary via his connection to Booth. Given the circumstances, things might have been awkward between them. Yet, both men hit it off almost immediately and when Darrin Mooney couldn't commit, Rob got the call. 'I'd played with a lot of musicians,' Green later told *DrumsWise*, 'but I've never played next to someone who was such a force as a player. When you were next to those two Marshalls stacks and Gary got going, your face was literally pushed back. Just an incredible, incredible player. For me, sitting in that hotseat was pretty scary and I had to have my shit together. But yeah, it was a phenomenal experience.'

Preliminary rehearsals concluded to everyone's satisfaction, things were again parked for another few weeks. This would give Neil Carter time to step back in to the band while also allowing Moore the opportunity for a short holiday with girlfriend Petra Nioduschewski. Their destination was the Hotel Kempinski, a luxury resort on Spain's Costa del Sol, its location close to Estepona beach allowing guests to see the coast of Morocco on a sunny day, of which there were many. The couple arrived in the late afternoon of Saturday, 5 February, following a 45-mile drive from Malaga airport. After check-in, Moore and Nioduschewski went for a walk before making their way to the hotel's bar/restaurant for some food. While Gary had been looking after himself more of late, drink was taken, though exactly how much still remains a bone of contention. Their meal finished, Nioduschewski returned to their room first with Moore following soon after at around 11.00 p.m. Before leaving the restaurant, he signed autographs for several staff.

By around four the next morning, Gary Moore had passed away. According to reports, Nioduschewski awoke to find Moore unresponsive and, after failing to resuscitate him, called a security guard for help. Doctors were contacted, though by that time it was certainly too late. After receiving the news, Gary's brother Cliff (accompanied by Graham

Lilley and Darren Main) flew to Spain the next morning to meet with authorities and begin the process of bringing Moore's body back to the UK. Petra Nioduschewski appears not to have accompanied on the subsequent trip home, and aside for a statement later given to health officials in relation to Gary's death, now faded from view.

Inevitably, the cause and circumstances around Moore's passing activated the interest of the media, with the majority of reportage tying into rumours that Gary's drinking had increased in recent times. The *Belfast Telegraph* wrote that Moore had 'binge[d] on enough alcohol to put him nearly five times over the [UK] drink-drive limit' on the night he died. And while no illegal drugs were present in his system, the newspaper stated other 'tests revealed [Moore] . . . had abused alcohol for years.' The *Daily Mail* and *Irish Independent* both went with similar angles, though the latter upped the drink/driving ratio by nearly three whole notches, albeit by using European rather than UK legal limits.

With an initial post mortem in Spain seeming to indicate an alcohol-related heart attack, it was left to Her Majesty's Coroner's Office for Brighton & Hove to confirm the exact circumstances around Gary's death. That Moore had been drinking at the Hotel Kempinski was never in doubt, the guitarist enjoying both Champagne and brandy over the course of his final evening. But this was not the sole reason behind what happened. As detailed by Gary's official biographer Harry Shapiro, according to the authorities, Moore had a long undiagnosed heart condition[1] as well as an enlarged liver. By drinking a substantial amount after reducing his alcohol intake in previous months, both organs would have difficulty dealing with a sudden increase in what were in effect 'toxic substances'. Hence, the Coroner's Office reported the official cause of Moore's death to be of natural causes, albeit hastened 'by an episode of acute toxicity from alcohol.'

Away from the hard facts behind Gary's passing was the sense of grief surrounding it. As is the case with any unexpected death, Moore's

---

1 According to the author Harry Shapiro, those around Gary had noticed he was not his usual self in the months leading up to his death, the guitarist exhibiting several signs of ill health that, with hindsight, may have been emblematic of a worsening heart condition.

family were left shocked and bewildered by their loss – the impact drawing them closer together, their resulting silence to be respected. Gary's former colleagues and friends were also stunned, with band members and admirers both past and present offering tributes to the guitarist. In addition to the likes of Black Sabbath's Ozzy Osbourne and Tony Iommi, Rush's Alex Lifeson, Queen's Brian May and Deep Purple's Roger Glover, old faces such as Brian Downey, Don Airey, Glenn Hughes and Bob Daisley were all keen to remember their friend.

'Gary Moore was the most ferocious, innovative guitar player ever,' said Hughes. 'His melodies were off the charts, he was a great friend and we made our pact toward the end of his life, becoming friends again.'[2] Daisley concurred. 'Gary was one of the greatest guitar players ever and a nice bloke with it . . . Rest in peace, we'll miss you mate.' From Skid Row's Brush Shiels, 'We had the best years of our lives, Noel[3] and I playing with Gary' to Neil Carter, 'I hesitate to use the word 'genius' but there was something otherworldly about Gary . . . I shall miss him a lot', musicians queued up to pay their respects.

On 18 February 2011, Gary Moore was laid to rest at St Margaret's Church in the picturesque village of Rottingdean, some six miles east of his home in Hove. A striking building, part of which dated back to the thirteenth century, and overlooking Rottingdean's peaceful green, St Margaret's suited the occasion well, with ninety or so mourners coming to pay their respects, including nearly all of Moore's family. Sadly, the only absentee was Gary's dad Bobby who reportedly stayed in Belfast due to illness. Among the relatives, former wives and partners were also a number of friends and bandmates from most every period of Moore's life, including Neil Carter, Jack Bruce, John Hiseman and Dr Strangely Strange's Ivan Pawle and his wife Mary.

---

2 One of rock music's great comeback stories, Glenn Hughes overcame his addictions in the early nineties, with the singer/bassist returning to the charts as part of KLF, Black Country Communion, The Dead Daisies and also as a solo artist. To his fans, Hughes remains 'The Voice of Rock'.

3 Called 'One of Dublin's greatest ever musicians,' Noel Bridgeman passed away on 23 March 2021. He was 74 years old.

The service itself was conducted by Fr Martin Morgan who raised a knowing chuckle early on when he described Gary as 'the kind of musician who would play anywhere if someone lent him an amp,' before talking more seriously of his achievements and frequent charitable endeavours. Other tributes included a verse chosen by his daughter Saoirse (and read by Ivan Pawle[4]) and a touching speech from Gary's youngest child Lily who spoke of her father's humour, childlike qualities and taste in 'colourful shirts'. In another tremendously fitting moment, Moore's brother Cliff and eldest son Jack brought out the guitars, their rendition of the ballad 'Danny Boy/ Londonderry Air' being particularly affecting. Of course, as events have come to show, the service at St Margaret's Church was by no means the end of Gary Moore's story.

Indeed, since his passing in 2011, barely a day goes by without some mention of Gary or his music. As these things do, it started in a small way. Only a matter of weeks after Moore's death, Eric Bell and Brian Downey staged 'A Gig for Gary', the intimate tribute concert honouring their friend taking place at Whelan's bar in Dublin[5] on 18 April. In July of the same year, American blues rock master Joe Bonamassa invited Moore's son Jack onto the stage of London's Royal Albert Hall for a poignant reading of 'Midnight Blues'. Both able confirmation of Jack's now established skills as a guitarist[6] as well as a fitting opportunity for Joe to publicly acknowledge his own debt to Moore, the duo's performance rightly received a standing ovation. 'Whereas the US had Stevie Ray Vaughan, Europe had Gary Moore,' Bonamassa later confirmed. 'Gary was

---

4   Ivan's wife Mary was originally asked if she might read the verse (entitled 'Guitar Poem'), but for the best of reasons, turned down the request. 'They asked me to read a piece Saoirse had chosen at the funeral, but I couldn't,' she confirmed. 'I'd have cried for Ireland. So, Ivan very manfully stood in.'
5   Though the Whelan's gig was pulled together fast, it wasn't actually the first Moore tribute gig. That honour went to a 'Gary Moore Night' held at Duff's bar in Brooklyn, New York, on 12 March 2011.
6   One of the first things Jack had done live was playing guitar alongside Gary on 'The Blues Is Alright' at Brighton Dome in 2007. '[My dad] said "Take the first solo – I'll give you a nod . . ." he laughed to *Andertons Music TV*. As word spread of Moore's skills as a guitarist in the wake of his father's death, Jack also joined Thin Lizzy and Deep Purple as an onstage guest.

this bull in a china shop playing blues songs on an old Les Paul through a couple of Marshalls. I'll give you one guess where I got that playbook!'

By 2012, Moore's life was the subject of an exhibition at Belfast's Music Centre, his father Bobby now well enough to travel into the heart of the city to see Gary properly acknowledged as one of Northern Ireland's more famous sons. 'We've all grieved for a year,' BBC Ulster's Stuart Bailie said to those gathered on what would have been Moore's 60th birthday, 'and now it's important to remember how great he was.' A decade on, and Moore remains a prominent fixture at the BMC, his story told using rare photos, guitars and items of clothing (other NI luminaries honoured at the BMC include Van Morrison and The Undertones).

Back in 2013 and another old friend was also remembering Gary, though this time in song, with Johnny Duhan's lyric to 'Rising with the Sun' from his album *Winter* offering a fond portrait of the months he spent living with Moore and Philp Lynott in sixties Dublin. 'We lived together in Donnybrook for about a year . . . and I still have great memories of that time,' Duhan told the *Galway Advertiser*. 'I was walking around the park . . . when word came to me that Gary had died. It hit me like a brick.'

Alongside the exhibitions and songs came news that Gary Moore's beloved 'Greeny' had finally found a lasting home with another guitar hero of note: Metallica's Kirk Hammett. While visiting London in mid-2014, Hammett was contacted by specialist dealer Richard Henry who let it be known he had a truly wonderful axe in his possession. When the case was opened, Hammett immediately knew what he was looking at. 'Well, the pick-up screws were inverted, so . . . ' he told *Guitar World*. Things got better after trying it out. 'It sounded like an incredible Les Paul in the bridge position and in the neck position, but when you put it in the middle position it kind of sounded like a Strat through a 100-watt Marshall stack. Then I got it. I really got it. I understood completely what Greeny was all about.' After a friendly shove from Led Zeppelin's Jimmy Page – 'I remember that guitar,' Page said, 'you should absolutely buy it!' – Kirk became Greeny's latest custodian, his purchase of the instrument[7] bringing to an end a long, bumpy journey from 'Mac to Moore to the arms of Metallica.'[8]

2017 brought yet more homages and testimonials. In one of his last projects before passing away a year later, Colosseum II leader Jon Hiseman recorded the album *Heroes*, a tribute of sorts to the 'musical giants' who had departed before him, including Ollie Halsall, Allan Holdsworth, Cream's inestimable Jack Bruce (who sadly died in 2014), and of course, Gary Moore.

Elsewhere, one of Moore's favourite bassists recorded a whole CD's worth of tunes in his former boss's honour. Entitled *Moore Blues for Gary*, Bob Daisley's 2018 disc featured 13 songs either written or inspired by the titular hero. With Thin Lizzy's John Sykes and Damon Johnson, Deep Purple's Steve Morse and seasoned Moore veterans, including Brush Shiels, Don Airey, Darrin Mooney and Neil Carter also making an appearance, *Blues for Gary* really was a mighty gathering of the rock star tribes.[9] The album also concluded on a high note with 'This One's for You', a rocking little number written by Bob (with Dennis Wilson) and calling upon the services of Gary's sons Jack and Gus, who provided six strings and lead vocals, respectively.[10]

Confirmation of the Moore clan's abiding musicality kept coming throughout the decade, with Gary's younger sibling Cliff releasing his third

---

7 As of March 2023, the price Hammett paid for Greeny remains undisclosed, though it was reported to be less than two million dollars. In honour of both Gary and the guitar, Gibson had manufactured a limited run 'Gary Moore Les Paul Standard' in 2013, its sound closely mirroring Greeny's liquid tone.

8 'Totally blown away by the sound' of 'Still Got the Blues', long-standing Moore fan Kirk Hammett 'wrote a couple riffs just based on [that song].' These ended up being used in spaghetti metal gem 'The Unforgiven' on Metallica's masterful *Black Album* of 1991. 'The opening lick of 'Master of Puppets'' guitar solo is also a variation on a lick that Gary played a lot,' Hammett said of another of the band's classic tracks.

9 Various other CDs have been released honouring Moore's memory including Henrik Freischlader's *Blues for Gary* (featuring old Moore cohorts Vic Martin and Pete Rees) and Siggi Schwarz's *A Tribute to Gary Moore* (with Neil Murray and long-time Moore admirer Steve Lukather both contributing). Guitarist Billy Merziotis and 'The Gary Moore Band' (again with Vic Martin, Pete Rees and drummer Graham Walker) have also amassed a strong live following covering tracks from all points in Gary's career.

10 Several months before, the brothers had teamed up for the release of 'Wolfy the Fifth', a wacky eighties-style tune accompanied by a suitably strange, Michael Jackson-referencing video.

solo collection *Blues Brother* in 2017. A pleasing mix of well-chosen covers and sprightly originals, *Blues Brother* joined previous releases *Cut* (2006) and *Afraid of the Dark* (2008) in providing proof that Cliff Moore was a wickedly inventive guitarist in his own right. Gary's sister Patricia also continued to make her presence felt as a singer on the blues, folk and rock circuit, fronting either her own group or guesting with one of the several Gary Moore tribute acts that popped up since his passing in 2011.

Back in the late nineties/early noughties, Gary's eldest daughter Saoirse had provided fine, distinctive vocals for a number of the trip-hop influenced acts, including Auralux and the underrated Children Of Dub. Come 2018, and Moore's youngest child, Lily, was also making her debut with the first in a series of well-received singles. Just a teenager when her father passed, Lily was now a forceful singer in her own right, her soulful tones put to good use on the likes of R&B gems 'Nothing on You' and 'Not That Special'. When one factored in Jack Moore's promising new trio, the eclectic dream-popping 'Smith, Lyle & Moore', and Jack's brother Gus's occasional, gravel-voiced forays into rock, Gary's musical legacy appeared in altogether safe hands. 'My dad never forced me into playing guitar and I didn't really pick it up until I was 16,' Jack told *Andertons Music TV* of his own adventures in sound. 'So . . . I had a lot of catching up to do. But [having Gary as a father], I guess I had an advantage.'

While siblings, sons and daughters were making bold new music of their own, Gary Moore's old record company continued to issue product bearing his name. Some of these albums, such as the concert sets *Live at Bush Hall 2007* and *Blues for Jimi* were appropriate reminders of Moore's onstage talent, his guitar blazing brightly at a fan-club gig for just 400 or melting the faces of those gathered to honour Hendrix at London's Hippodrome the same year. Others, like *Live at Montreux 2010* only served as a reminder of Gary's travails at that time, the gig's inferior quality begging the question why it had been issued at all.[11]

---

11 Presumably *Live at Montreux 2010* saw light of day because it gave fans a chance to hear Gary performing three (unreleased) Celtic rock-themed tunes then headed for his next studio album. However, for those seeking the best of Moore at Switzerland's preeminent music festival, 2009's five-CD set *Essential Montreux* might be a better purchase.

Still, it was hard to find anything bad to say about 2017's four-CD box set *Blues and Beyond*. A thoughtfully curated gathering of Moore's best bluesy moments both live and in the studio, *Blues and Beyond* also contained several items of memorabilia including a fully authorised biography on Gary named *I Can't Wait Until Tomorrow* written by the much-respected author Harry Shapiro.[12] In April 2021, *Blues and Beyond* was joined by another notable collection in *How Blue Can You Get*, the album's eight previously unreleased tracks including Moore's raucous version of Freddie King's 'I'm Tore Down' and a hard-to-beat take on B.B. King's aching 'Love Can Make a Fool of You'. Reportedly pulled 'deep from within the family archives' (and it has to be said, of variable sound quality), it seems likely *How Blue Can You Get* is but the latest disc in what promises to be a continuing series of posthumous releases.[13]

In the meantime, plans proceed apace to give Gary a much more permanent footing in the place of his birth. Following the example of Skånevik, the Norwegian village where residents erected a large metal likeness of Moore in 2012 to recognise his contribution to their annual blues festival (Gary played there on several occasions), the 'Wild Frontier Memorial Project' has its own designs on modelling something equally impressive in Belfast. Founded in 2018 and 'led by members of Gary's family and fans,' the 'WFMP' hopes to raise £75,000 for a memorial statue in Moore's honour at the centre of a city he loved. 'I know Gary is an idol to many . . . all over the world,' Moore's sister Patricia explained to *The Irish News* back in 2021, '[but] he loved his city and though his career would take him everywhere, his music was always influenced by the nature and beauty of Belfast.' With regular 'Gigs for Gary' raising money for the project, an ongoing pledge fund and Belfast's Green and Alliance parties also backing the idea, one imagines Moore will someday

---

12 Harry Shapiro's biography *I Can't Wait Until Tomorrow* was later released in its own right by Jawbone Press during the autumn of 2022.

13 Gary has returned to the UK charts three times since his death, with *Blues For Jimi* making number eighty in 2012, *Live From London* (a 2009 concert set recorded at Islington Academy) reaching number seventy in 2020 and *How Blue Can You Get* coming in at number fifty-four a year later.

soon be joining Philip Lynott and Rory Gallagher in having his features immortalised for the ages.[14]

Yet, before the marble is chosen, the bronze cast or the sculptors turn him into stone, it's worth taking a moment or two to remember Gary Moore as both a man and a musician.

That Moore had his faults is obvious. A passionate soul who saw the world in almost Manichean terms, he could be quick to temper and sometimes argued with those around him as a result. As a youth, that had unfortunately led to physical scars. His perfectionist streak was also the stuff of legend. A nervy performer, Gary demanded so much from himself that one fluffed solo under the lights could send him into the blackest mood for hours afterwards. This relentless pursuit of excellence extended elsewhere, with Moore demanding similar standards from those around him. Especially drummers, it seems. Yet, when not drilling his band in rehearsals or on tour, Gary enjoyed his creature comforts too, the guitarist's almost comical pursuit of the finest hotel rooms known to man a cause of some hilarity among his friends. Still, he was paying . . .

Away from these cast iron rules of the road, Moore's bluntness was renowned. Whether correcting journalists about some obscure point of guitar lore or offering scalding assessments of his own musical competition, Moore's frank turn of phrase could be immensely entertaining – unless, of course, you were on the receiving end of it. And then there was his romantic side. When in love, Gary's commitment was total, his intensity unwavering. Unfortunately, that intensity sometimes came with a jealous streak and it didn't seem to cure his roving eye either: passion, perfectionism, insecurity, infidelity. These were all recurring themes throughout his life.

But scratch beneath the surface of even our most revered musical icons, David Bowie, Bob Dylan, Jimi Hendrix, John Lennon, and one

---

14 In addition to Philip Lynott's graven image in Dublin, a memorial honouring Rory Gallagher was erected in his hometown of Cork in 1997. Thirteen years later, a statue marking Gallagher's place of birth was also unveiled in Ballyshannon, Donegal, with plans to honour Rory's association with Belfast approved in 2016. Not to be outdone even in death, Lynott was immortalised by the Irish postal authority (An Post) in 2019, with Jim Fitzpatrick's portrait of Philip and his album cover design for *Black Rose* both turned into stamps to mark Thin Lizzy's 50th anniversary. A coin celebrating Lynott's 70th birthday was issued in the same year.

will find uncomfortable stories and unfortunate behaviours. In this respect, like the rest of us, Moore was only human. He was also very funny, quick-witted and genuinely good company, with dozens of tales confirming a sharp sense of humour[15] and a keen mind unafraid of taking risks where others might hesitate. The canny, questing change of artistic course that led to *Still Got the Blues* was proof of that. 'Gary Moore was a racked, impassioned and sometimes troubled individual,' wrote the much-missed writer Gavin Martin in 2017. 'But it's our good fortune that much of his inner turmoil found release in his music.'

Here, Martin was surely correct. One can think of few if any other guitarists who could match Gary Moore for sheer fervour, commitment or all-out attack, with every note he played seemingly torn straight from his insides. And over the course of a lifetime, there were many, many notes. Sometimes they came at you like fighter planes speeding past the ear. Others were so gentle you were hard-pressed to hear them at all. But Gary gave each one absolutely everything he had. 'All the true guitar greats, you can tell it's them after a few seconds,' said Paul Scully of Moore's gift. 'Clapton, Hendrix, B.B. King. They all had a signature style. And so did Gary. You only need to hear a couple of notes and you know it's Gary Moore. The melodic phrasing, the power, the speed, all those little lines and tells. In a second or two, you just know it's Gary.'

Of course, as with his personal life, Moore's myriad switches of musical direction could be frustrating, his habit of embracing one style before rapidly embarking on another leading to befuddled fans and several commercial wobbles. There is also the room-sized elephant of Thin Lizzy

---

15 'The last time I saw Gary,' said The Strangelies' Tim Booth, 'We had a great night . . . playing songs [over] a good bottle of wine. Anyway, my partner Doris and I were then living in Dublin and she ran an ironing service called "Iron Maidens". That name really tickled Gary. Later that evening, Doris had to deliver the ironing to her clients. That included Mark, who ran the local chemists. In fact, I'd once taken some photos [of Gary] which he'd processed. As he was handing them back, Mark said "Is that Gary Moore? It is? God, he's a fantastic guitarist, I'd love to meet him." Of course, Mark was a guitar player too. So, before Doris does the delivery, she says to Gary "Would you do me a great favour and deliver these shirts to Mark?" Gary loved this idea. So, just as Mark was closing up, Gary walks in carrying five or six shirts and says "Here's your ironing, Sir." Mark looks up, realises who it is and nearly falls over.'

to contend with. Having made a huge contribution to *Black Rose* and with America seemingly within the band's grasp, Gary rode off into the LA sunset, leaving Lizzy in peril and his old pal Philip Lynott contemplating murder. There were reasons behind Moore's decision, and good ones too. But even so, his leaving at such a crucial juncture was not only deemed unprofessional, it also denied us all the opportunity of hearing where the group might have taken things next. Still, when Philip found himself drowning in the eighties, unlike many, Gary was there to offer a helping hand. Another chance. Another hit. Another throw of the dice. Tragically, it was too late to make a difference. But this time at least, Moore couldn't be faulted for his actions.

If Gary Moore's intricate attachment to Philip Lynott (and vice versa) sometimes stretched the adage 'Friendship is an act of bravery', then his abiding connection to Peter Green was much easier to fathom. Though Gary would pay frequent homage to teenage heroes like Eric Clapton, Jeff Beck and Jimi Hendrix, even going as far as to occasionally reform their bands, Moore seemed to hold Green in particularly high esteem. 'Peter's style of playing is just as important as Eric's or Jeff's,' he once said. 'But because he wasn't around to promote himself, he was forgotten. Yet, the restraint and the emotional content [Green displayed] was far above anything else at that time.' In fact, Peter's playing seemed to unlock something deep within Gary – allowing him to truly access the blues, and in so doing, enable his eventual success as a musician. 'Blues comes from inside,' Moore told *Guitare Et Claviers*. 'Look at Peter Green for the proof. He was a 21-year-old Jewish kid from London, [but] for me at least, he could blow B.B. King off the stage with his guitar. Green wasn't black. He wasn't from the States. But that doesn't matter. He had a gift. You either have it or you don't.'[16]

In the same way that Peter Green was a profound influence on Gary, so it is that each new generation of players continue to be beguiled by Moore. Regularly appearing near the top of various 'Greatest Ever Guitarists' polls, Gary has acted as an inspiration to established axe icons

---

16 Surely one of the better guitarists, singers and songwriters of the last six decades, Peter Green passed away on 25 July 2020, aged 73.

from Doug Aldrich, Vivian Campbell and Steve Vai to John Norum, John Petrucci and Zakk Wylde, to name but a few.

The list doesn't end there. More recently, other successful blues and rock artists such as Kris Barras, Kirk Fletcher, Eric Gales and Joanne Shaw Taylor have all been quick to champion Gary's cause, while hundreds more come to his music each day with fresh ears and dropped jaws. Just visit YouTube for the proof. There for all to see are dozens, if not hundreds of young players covering Moore's back catalogue, each putting their own spin on his songs and solos. He would surely have loved it.

A complex, mercurial but genuinely gifted man, Gary Moore was so in love with music 'you had to drag him off the bloody stage' to stop him from playing it. He had been that way since singing 'Sugartime' as a six-year-old at the Queen's Hall back in 1958, and if you visit his final resting place at St Margaret's Church in Rottingdean, that's precisely what you'll find written on part of his headstone. 'Robert William Gary Moore, Musician.'[17] Indeed, if there is a secret to unlocking the life and songs of Gary Moore, it might be just that. For while the guitar was his chosen means of expression, it was the music itself that really drove him. 'Yes, music ran through Gary's veins,' said The Strangelies' Tim Goulding. 'Not blood, but music. He was really one of the great blues players and truly one of the great musicians. That's where Gary started. The music. And he always, always went back to it.'

Some years before he passed, Moore was asked how he would like to be remembered. Curiously, he did not mention guitars or even music directly, but instead spoke of honesty. 'How would I like people to remember me?' he laughed to the *Belfast Telegraph*'s Peter Robertson, 'Oh fuck, I don't know. However they want!' But then, Moore became serious. 'As somebody that didn't bullshit,' he said. 'Whatever I did, at least I meant it. That's all I can say really, because I usually do mean it. I'm not full of shit like a lot of people. Whatever I do, whether it sells or not, at least I mean it at the time and I'm honest about it. I think,' he concluded, 'that's the only way to be . . .'

No argument there.

---

17 The complete dedication on Gary's headstone reads 'Robert William Gary Moore, 4th April 1952 - 6th February 2011, Musician, Loved Beyond The Stars'.

Gary Moore –
A Selected Discography

What follows is a selected discography covering Gary Moore's recorded career from 1970-2010. It concentrates on Moore's work both as a solo artist and band member, though many of his guest/session appearances with other performers and groups are also detailed here. While no means complete, the discography does track the majority of Moore's musical output over the course of five decades.

Unless stated otherwise, catalogue numbers below refer to UK releases only. From 1970-1984, these catalogue numbers refer to LPs. From 1985 onwards, they refer to CDs. For brevity's sake, Moore's single releases, 'greatest hits' packages and compilation sets are not detailed in this discography.

Albums:
As a band leader and solo artist:

The Gary Moore Band

Grinding Stone

Grinding Stone/Time to Heal/Sail Across the Mountain/The Energy
  Dance/Spirit/Boogie My Way Back Home
CBS S 65527 LP May 1973

Gary Moore

Back on the Streets

Back on the Streets/Don't Believe a Word/Fanatical Fascists/Flight of the Snow Moose/Hurricane/Song for Donna/What Would You Rather Bee or a Wasp/Parisienne Walkways
MCA MCF 2853 LP September 1978

G-Force

You/White Knuckles/Rockin' and Rollin'/She's Got You/I Look at You/Because of Your Love/You Kissed Me Sweetly/Hot Gossip/The Woman's in Love/Dancin'
Jet LP 229 LP May 1980

Gary Moore

Corridors of Power

Don't Take Me for a Loser/Always Gonna Love You/Wishing Well/Gonna Break My Heart Again/Falling in Love With You/End of the World/Rockin' Every Night/Cold Hearted/I Can't Wait Until Tomorrow
Virgin V2245 LP September 1982

Rockin' Every Night

Rockin' Every Night/Wishing Well/I Can't Wait Until Tomorrow/Nuclear Attack/White Knuckles/Rockin' and Rollin'/Back on the Streets/Sunset
Virgin VIL-6039 (Japan) LP May 1983

Gary Moore Live at The Marquee

Back on the Streets/Run to Your Mama/Dancin'/She's Got You/Parisienne Walkways/You/Nuclear Attack/Dallas Warhead
Jet 25AP 2677 (Japan) LP September 1983

Victims of the Future

Victims of the Future/Teenage Idol/Shapes of Things/Empty Rooms/
    Murder in the Skies/All I Want/Hold on to Love/Law of the Jungle
Virgin/10 DIX 2 LP December 1983

Dirty Fingers

Hiroshima/Dirty Fingers/Bad News/Don't Let Me Be Misunderstood/
    Run to Your Mama/Nuclear Attack/Kidnapped/Really Gonna Rock/
    Lonely Nights/Rest in Peace
Jet JETLP 241 LP July 1984

We Want Moore!

Murder in the Skies/Shapes of Things/Victims of the Future/Cold
    Hearted/End of the World/Back on the Streets/So Far Away/Empty
    Rooms/Don't Take Me for a Loser/Rockin' and Rollin'
Virgin/10 302 469-370 LP October 1984

Run for Cover

Run for Cover/Reach for the Sky/Military Man/Empty Rooms/Out
    in the Fields/Nothing to Lose/Once in a Lifetime/All Messed Up/
    Listen to Your Heartbeat
Virgin/10 DIX CD 16 CD September 1985

Wild Frontier

Over the Hills and Far Away/Wild Frontier/Take a Little Time/The
    Loner/Friday On My Mind/Strangers in the Darkness/Thunder
    Rising/Johnny Boy
Virgin/10 DIXCD 56 CD March 1987

After the War

Dunluce (Part 1)/After the War/Speak for Yourself/Livin' on Dreams/
    Led Clones/Running from the Storm/This Thing Called Love/Ready
    for Love/Blood of Emeralds/Dunluce (Part 2)
Virgin CDV 2575 CD January 1989

Still Got the Blues

Moving On/Oh Pretty Woman/Walking By Myself/Still Got the Blues
  (For You)/Texas Strut/Too Tired/King of the Blues/As the Years Go
  Passing By/Midnight Blues/That Kind of Woman/All Your Love/Stop
  Messin' Around
Virgin CDV 2612 CD March 1990

After Hours

Cold Day in Hell/Don't Lie to Me (I Get Evil)/Story of the Blues/
  Since I Met You Baby/Separate Ways/Only Fool in Town/Key to
  Love/Jumpin' at Shadows/The Blues Is All Right/The Hurt Inside/
  Nothing's the Same
Virgin CDV 2684 262 558 CD March 1992

Blues Alive

Cold Day in Hell/Walking By Myself/Story of the Blues/Oh Pretty
  Woman/Separate Ways/Too Tired/Still Got the Blues/Since I Met
  You Baby/The Sky Is Crying/Further On Up the Road/King of the
  Blues/Parisienne Walkways/Jumpin' at Shadows
Virgin CDVX 2716 CD September 1993

Blues for Greeny

If You Be My Baby/Long Grey Mare/Merry Go Round/I Loved Another
  Woman/Need Your Love So Bad/The Same Way/The Supernatural/
  Driftin'/Showbiz Blues/Love That Burns/Looking for Somebody
Virgin CDV 2784 CD May 1995

Dark Days in Paradise

One Good Reason/Cold Wind Blows/I Have Found My Love in You/
  One Fine Day/Like Angels/What Are We Here For?/Always There
  For You/Afraid of Tomorrow/Where Did We Go Wrong?/Business as
  Usual/Dark Days in Paradise (hidden track)
Virgin CDV 2826 CD May 1997

A Different Beat

Go On Home/Lost in Your Love/Worry No More/Fire/Surrender/
House Full of Blues/Bring My Baby Back/Can't Help Myself/Fatboy/
We Want Love/Can't Help Myself (E-Z Rollers Remix)/Surrender
(reprise)
Castle RAW CD 142 CD September 1999

Back to the Blues

Enough of the Blues/You Upset Me Baby/Cold Black Night/Stormy
Monday/Ain't Got You/Picture of the Moon/Looking Back/The
Prophet/How Many Lies/Drowning In Tears
Sanctuary SAN CD 072 CD March 2001

Live at Monsters of Rock

Shapes of Things/Wishing Well/Rectify/Guitar Intro/Stand Up/Just
Can't Let You Go/Walking By Myself/Don't Believe a Word/Out in
the Fields/Parisienne Walkways
Sanctuary SAN CD 215 CD September 2003

Power of the Blues

Power of the Blues/There's a Hole/Tell Me Woman/I Can't Quit You
Baby/Evil/Getaway Blues/Memory Pain/Can't Find My Baby/Torn
Inside
Sanctuary SAN CD 267CD June 2004

Old New Ballads Blues

Done Somebody Wrong/You Know My Love/Midnight Blues (2006)/
Ain't Nobody/Gonna Rain Today/All My Love (2006)/Flesh & Blood/
Cut It Out/No Reason to Cry/I'll Play the Blues for You
Eagle EAG CD 314 CD May 2006

Close As You Get

If the Devil Made Whisky/Trouble at Home/Thirty Days/Hard Times/
Have You Heard/Eyesight to the blind/Evenin'/Nowhere Fast/

Checkin' Up on My Baby/I Had a Dream/Sundown
Eagle EAG CD 346 CD May 2007

Bad for you Baby

Bad for you Baby/Down the line/Umbrella Man/Holding On/Walkin'
  Thru the Park/I Love You More Than You'll Ever Know/Mojo Boogie/
  Somebody Baby/Did You Ever Feel Lonely?/Preacher Man Blues/
  Trouble Ain't Far Behind
Eagle EAG CD 379 CD September 2008

Live at Montreux 2010

Over the Hills and Far Away/Military Man/Days of Heroes/Where Are
  You Now?/So Far Away/Empty Rooms/Oh Wild One/Blood of
  Emeralds/Out in the Fields/Walking By Myself/Johnny Boy/Parisienne
  Walkways
Eagle EAG CD 434 CD September 2011

Blues for Jimi

Purple Haze/Manic Depression/Foxey Lady/The Wind Cries Mary/I
  Don't Live Today/My Angel/Angel/Fire/Red House/Stone Free/Hey
  Joe/Voodoo Child (Slight Return)
Eagle EAGDV 034 CD September 2012

Live at Bush Hall 2007

If The Devil Made Whisky/Thirty Days/Trouble at Home/Hard Times/
  Eyesight to the Blind/I Had a Dream/Too Tired/Gary's Blues 1/Don't
  Believe a Word/Still Got the Blues/Walking By Myself/The Blues Is
  All Right/Sundown
Eagle EAG CD 535 CD September 2014

Blues and Beyond

Disc One: Enough of the Blues/Tell Me Woman/Stormy Monday/That's
  Why I Play the Blues/Power of the Blues/Ball and Chain/Looking
  Back/Surrender/Cold Black Night/There's a Hole/Getaway Blues/
  We Want Love/Memory Pain/The Prophet

Disc Two: You Upset Me Baby/Bring My Baby Back/I Can't Quit You Baby/World of Confusion/Picture of the Moon/Can't Find My Baby/Drowning in Tears/Evil/My Baby (She's So Good to Me)/I Ain't Got You/Just Can't Let You Go/How Many Lies/Torn Inside/Parisienne Walkways (Live)

Disc Three: Walking By Myself (Live)/Oh Pretty Woman (Live)/Need Your Love So Bad (Live)/Since I Met You Baby (Live)/Surrender (Live)/Cold Black Night (Live)/All Your Love (Live)/Still Got the Blues (Live)

Disc Four: Too Tired (Live)/The Sky Is Crying (Live)/Further On Up the Road (Live)/Fire (Live)/The Blues Is Alright (Live)/Enough of the Blues (Live)/The Prophet (Live)

BMG/Sanctuary BMG CAT 105BOX 4 CD Box Set November 2017 (A truncated, two-CD version of this set is also available: BMGCAT 105DCD)

Live from London

Oh, Pretty Woman/Bad for You Baby/Down the Line/Since I Met You Baby/Have You Heard/All Your Love/Mojo Boogie/I Love You More Than You'll Ever Know/Too Tired /Gary's Blues/Still Got the Blues/Walking By Myself/The Blues Is Alright/Parisienne Walkways

Provogue PRD 7605 CD January 2020

How Blue Can You Get

I'm Tore Down/Steppin' Out/In My Dreams/How Blue Can You Get/Looking at Your Picture/Love Can Make a Fool of You/Done Somebody Wrong/Living With the Blues

Provogue PRD 7646 5 CD April 2021

As a band member

Skid Row

Skid

Mad Dog Woman/Virgo's Daughter/Heading Home Again/An Awful

441

Lot of Woman/Unco-Up Showband Blues/For Those Who Do/After
I'm Gone/The Man Who Never Was/Felicity
CBS S 63965 LP October 1970

34 Hours

Night of the Warm Witch (inc. The Following Morning)/First Thing in
the Morning (inc. Last Thing at Night)/Mar/Go, I'm Never Gonna
Let You Part 1 (inc. Go, I'm Never Gonna Let You Part 2)/Lonesome
Still/The Love Story (Parts 1-4)
CBS 64411 LP September 1971

Skid Row: Gary Moore/Brush Shiels/Noel Bridgeman

Benedicts Cherry Wine/Saturday Morning Man/Crystal Ball/Mr
De-Luxe/Girl Called Winter/Morning Star Avenue/Silver Bird
Castle CLA CD 343 CD October 1990

Colosseum II

Strange New Flesh

Dark Side of the Moog/Down to You/Gemini and Leo/Secret Places/
On Second Thoughts/Winds
Bronze ILPS 9356 LP April 1976

Electric Savage

Put it this Way/All Skin & Bone/Rivers/The Scorch/Lament (Trad)/
Desperado/Am I/Intergalactic Strut
MCA MCF 2800 LP June 1977

War Dance

War Dance/Major Keys/Put it this Way/Castles/Fighting Talk/The
Inquisition/Star Maiden/Mysterioso/Quasar/Last Exit
MCA MCF 2817 LP November 1977

Thin Lizzy

Black Rose (A Rock Legend)

Do Anything You Want to Do/Toughest Street In Town/S&M/Waiting for an Alibi/Sarah/Got to Give It Up/Get Out of Here/With Love/ Róisín Dubh (Black Rose, A Rock Legend: Parts 1 to 4: Shenandoah/ Will You Go Lassie Go/Danny Boy/The Mason's Apron)
Vertigo 9102 032 LP April 1979

BBM

Around the Next Dream

Waiting in the Wings/City of Gold/ Where in the World/Can't Fool the Blues/High Cost of Loving/Glory Days/Why Does Love (Have to Go Wrong)?/Naked Flame/I Wonder Why (Are You So Mean to Me?)/Wrong Side of Town/Danger Zone (Bonus)/World Keeps on Turning (Bonus)/Sitting on Top of the World (Live)/I Wonder Why . . . (Live)
Virgin MOORE CDV 2745 CD May 1994

Scars

When the Sun Goes Down/Rectify/Wasn't Born in Chicago/Stand Up/ Just Can't Let You Go/My Baby (She's So Good to Me)/World of Confusion/Ball and Chain/World Keeps Turnin' Round/Who Knows (What Tomorrow May Bring)?
Sanctuary SAN CD 120 CD August 2002

Sessions And Guest Appearances

Gary Moore loved nothing more than to play guitar, and when he couldn't do that with his own band, he found other musicians to do it with instead. Hence, Moore's recorded appearances as a session musician or special guest are numerous and extremely varied. What follows here are the highlights, with Moore's contributions ranging from one short, sharp solo burst on a 1987 charity record to an album's worth of work

443

with the likes of Greg Lake and Jack Lancaster. Some of these appearances are also mentioned within the chapters of this book.

1970
Dr Strangely Strange – *Heavy Petting*
Granny's Intentions – *Honest Injun*

1973
Jonathan Kelly – *Wait Till They Change the Backdrop*

1974
Thin Lizzy – *Nightlife*

1975
Jack Lancaster and Robin Lumley – *The Rock Peter and the Wolf*
Eddie Howell – *The Eddie Howell Gramophone Record*

1977
Gary Boyle – The Dancer

1978
Andrew Lloyd Webber – *Variations*
Gary Boyle – *Electric Glide*
Rod Argent – *Moving Home*

1979
Cozy Powell – *Over the Top*

1980
Jack Lancaster – *Skinningrove Bay*

1981
Greg Lake – *Greg Lake*
Cozy Powell – *Tilt*

1982

Johnny Duhan – *'Molly' / 'Oceans of Motion'*

1983

Greg Lake – *Manoeuvres*

Cozy Powell – *Octopuss*

Chris Thompson – *Out of the Night*

Thin Lizzy – *Life*

1985

Frankie Goes To Hollywood – 'Warriors of the Wasteland' 12" mix

The Beach Boys – *The Beach Boys*

Minako Honda – *Cancel*

1987

Ferry Aid – 'Let It Be'

1988

Mo Foster – *Bel Assis*

Don Airey – *K2: Tales of Triumph and Tragedy*

1989

Vicki Brown – *Lady of Time*

1990

Vicki Brown – *About Love and Life*

Travelling Wilburys – *Vol. 3*

1991

Mo Foster – *Southern Reunion*

1992

Jimmy Nail – *Growing Up in Public*

1993
Paul Rodgers – *Muddy Water Blues*
Jack Bruce – *Golden Years: Jack Bruce's 50th Birthday Concert*

1994
Snowy White – *Highway to the Sun*

2001
John Mayall & Friends – *Along for the Ride*
Jim Capaldi – *Living on the Outside*
Jack Bruce – *Shadows in the Air*

2002
Various Artists – *From Clarksdale To Heaven: Remembering John Lee Hooker*

2004
Trilok Gurtu – *Broken Rhythms*

2005
One World Project – 'Grief Never Gets Old'

2006
Otis Taylor – *Definition of a Circle*

2007
Various Artists – *Dear Mr Fantasy – A Celebration for Jim Capaldi*

2009
Otis Taylor – *Pentatonic Wars and Love Songs*

DVDs/Videos
Like many successful performers, Gary Moore was no stranger to the business of concert and promotional films, with several video and DVD releases marking his commercial progress over the years. What follows below are the most notable of these packages, from a scorching

concert set in Sydney, Australia with Thin Lizzy in 1978 to his final, Celtic-themed Montreux Festival appearance of 2010.

Thin Lizzy – The Boys Are Back in Town

Jailbreak/Bad Reputation/Cowboy Song/The Boys Are Back in Town/ Waiting for an Alibi/Are You Ready/Me and the Boys/Baby Drives Me Crazy

Eagle Vision ERE DV035 DVD 2003

Gary Moore – Emerald Aisles. Live in Ireland

Virgin Video B000057M1F Video 1985

Gary Moore – The Definitive Montreux Collection

Disc One: (1990) Midnight Blues/Texas Strut/Moving On/Cold, Cold Feeling/Stop Messin' Around/The Blues Is All Right/The Messiah Will Come Again

Disc Two: (1995) If You Be My Baby/Long Grey Mare/Merry-Go-Round/The Stumble/You Don't Love Me/Key to Love/All Your Love/Still Got the Blues/Since I Met You Baby/The Sky Is Crying/ Jumpin' at Shadows

Disc Three: (1997) One Fine Day/Cold Wind Blows/I've Found My Love/In You/Always There for You/Business As Usual/Out in the Fields

Disc Four: (1999) Oh Pretty Woman/Need Your Love So Bad/Torn Down/I Loved Another Woman/Too Tired/Further On Up the Road/ Parisienne Walkways

Disc Five: (2001) You Upset Me Baby/Cold Black Night/Stormy Monday/Walking By Myself/How Many Lies/Fire/Enough of the Blues/The Prophet

Eagle Rock B000 TM0298 DVD 2008

Gary Moore & Friends – One Night In Dublin: A Tribute To Phil Lynott

Walking By Myself/Jailbreak/Don't Believe a Word/Emerald/Still in Love With You/Black Rose: A Rock Legend/Cowboy Song/The Boys Are Back in Town/Whiskey in the Jar/Old Town (Excerpt)/Parisienne Walkways/Bonus Feature: Interviews

Eagle Vision ERE DV 559 DVD 2005

Gary Moore – Live at Montreux 2010

Over the Hills and Far Away/Military Man/Days of Heroes/Where Are

You Now?/So Far Away/Empty Rooms/Oh Wild One/Blood of Emeralds/Out in the Fields/Walking By Myself/Johnny Boy/Parisienne Walkways

Eagle EAG 434 DVD 2011

Blues for Jimi

Purple Haze/Manic Depression/Foxey Lady/The Wind Cries Mary/I Don't Live Today/My Angel/Angel/Fire/Red House/Stone Free/Hey Joe/Voodoo Child (Slight Return)

Eagle EAGDV 034 DVD September 2012

Acknowledgements and Source Notes

There are many people to thank. So, here goes . . .

In the course of writing this book, I consulted the following magazines, newspapers, periodicals, radio & television networks, websites and weeklies – several of which have ceased publication. In some cases, I extracted previously published or broadcast material. For these extracts, I remain extremely grateful to: *20th Century Guitar Magazine, AllMusic.com, All Out Guitar, Andertons, Bass Player, BBC, The Beatles Bible, The Belfast Forum, Belfast Telegraph, Blabbermouth.net, Blues In Britain, Blues GR, Brave Worlds.com, Bridgwater Mercury, Brighton Argus, Brush Shiels' 'Brushfire', The Neil Carter Homepage, Classic Rock, Classic Rock Revisited, Culture Northern Ireland, Daily Express, Deep Purple Forever, Detroit Bass, Discogs, Discover Music, DrumWise, DTS, Eagle Vision, Edgehill Productions, Electric Ballroom, EV Classics, Fender.com, MagnusFiennes.com, The Fishy, Fly Guitars, Galway Advertiser, The Georgia Straight, Ground Guitar, Grumberf Warcraft, The Guardian, Guitar & Bass, Guitar Music, Guitare Et Claviers, Guitarist, Guitar Player, Guitar Presents . . ., The Guitar Show, Guitar World, Heavy Profile, The Highway Star, Hit Channel, Hot Press, Hypergallery, The Independent* and *International Musician & Recording World*.

And there's more.

The Irish Examiner, The Irish News, The Irish Times, Irish Rock Org, IrishShowbands.com, John Peel Wiki, Kayo Kyoku Plus, Kerrang, The Les Paul Forum, Let It Rock, Louder, SteveLukather.com, Marin Independent Journal, Marshall, Melody Maker, Mercury Records, Metal Express Radio, Metal Rendezvous, MetalReviews.com, Mojo, The Gary Moore Discography (The GM Bible), Moshcam, Mulatschag TV, Music Radar, Music UK, The Musician's

Olympus, *MusicToyz.com*, *Music UK*, *My Global Mind*, *NME*, *Norwich News*, *Notes from NI Lincs*, *One Two Testing*, *Planet Rock*, *Q*, *Radio Ulster*, *Record Collector*, *Rock & Blues Muse*, *Rock Candy*, *Rockline*, *Rock'n'roll Garage*, *RodCollins.com*, *Rolling Stone*, *Sea Of Tranquillity*, *The Slade Discography Website*, *EricSinger.com*, *Sol Musica*, *Something Else*, *Songfacts*, *Sounds*, *Sounds' Guitar Heroes*, *Sound On Sound*, *The South Bank Show*, *Spotlight*, *The Telegraph*, *Thalia.com*, *The ThinLizzy Guide.com*, *Travellers in Time. com*, *Uncut*, *Ultimate Guitar*, *Universal*, *Universal Wheels*, *VH1*, *Vintage Guitar*, *VintageRock.com*, *WHE*, *Wikipedia*, *YLETV* and *YouTube* (including Elena77960 and Ovidiu Buzdugan Romcea's excellent Gary Moore pages).

For providing additional source material, I would like to offer my sincere thanks to the following writers, journalists, authors, fans and musicians: René Aagaard, Anna Maria (from the *RoryGallagher.com* forum), Andy Aledort, Bimpe Archer, Arend, Tony Bacon, Stuart Bailie, Liz Barnes, Geoff Barton, Glenn A. Baker, Mark Beaumont, Max Bell, Johnny Black, Dante Bonutto, Brian Boyd, Mick Burgess, Alan Byrne, Jonathan Byrne, Lee 'The Captain' Anderton, Rod Collins, Steve Cooney, Mark Dean, Sean De Beer, Nick Deriso, Harry Doherty (R.I.P.), Malcolm Dome (R.I.P.), Ciaran Donnelly, Ben Edmonds, Paul Elliot, Martine Ehrenclou, Graham Fieldhouse, Damian Fenelli, Robert Forster, Darrin Fox, Rob Garratt, Chris Gill, Ronnie B. Goode, Ralph Greco Jr., Stuart Grundy, Shawn Hammond, Michael Hann, Colin Harper, Dermott Hayes, Hendy at the *Belfast Forum*, Bob Hewitt, Gary Hill, Brian D. Holland, Hal Horowitz and Johnny Hyland.

More sincere thanks to Kevin J. Julie, 'Metal Marty', Max Kay, B.B. King, Michael Leonard, Michael Limnios, Ivan Little, Nick Logan, Eddie McIlwaine, Phil Mann, James McNair, Pete Makowski (R.I.P.), Richard Mann, Neville Marten, Bill Milkowski, Scott Munro, Willie Moseley, Tom Mulhern, Peter Nielson, Steve Newton, Geoff Nicholson, Mike O'Cull, Daragh O'Halloran, Colm O'Hare, John O'Regan, Fintan O'Toole, Pete Pardo, Alan Paul, John Peel, Pierre Perrone, Rafael Polcaro, Martin Popoff, Peter Powell, the mighty Mark Putterford (R.I.P.), David Quantick, Christine Rebmann, Ryan Reed, Alan Robinson, Peter Robinson, Robin Ross, Chris Salewicz, Christopher Scapelliti, Paul Sexton, Amit Sharma,

Sidekick at the *LP Forum*, Rod Silverstein, George Simpson, Richard Skinner, Andy Smith, Peter Smyth, Mat Snow, Harold Steinblatt, John Stix, Dermot Stokes, Phil Sutcliffe, Adam Sweeting, Aπó Thodoris, Dave Thompson, John Tobler, Tom at *DrumWise*, Trinkelbonker, Eddie Trunk, Richard Walmsley, Ivan 'Big Ive' Williams, Harold Mac Wonderlea, Kit Woolven (R.I.P.), Jeb Wright, Zoli at *GaryMooreFC.com* and anyone else I might have missed.

Now, a few special mentions.

First and foremost, I must offer genuine thanks to Harry Shapiro, whose sterling work on Gary's Moore's official biography – 2017's *I Can't Wait Until Tomorrow* – surely acts as a foundation stone for those exploring Gary's life and times. Indeed, when travel restrictions during 2020/21 made journeying to Belfast difficult, Harry's book was particularly helpful while researching Gary's formative years. It also acted as a valuable source of information elsewhere, from confirming facts, studio dates and managerial changes to several short interview quotes and background details on certain of Moore's romantic partners. Additionally, Harry's account of Gary's last months provided both context and insight into the circumstances of that time. Once again, a sincere thanks to you, Mr Shapiro.

A hearty thanks must also be extended to Graeme Thompson, whose insightful Philip Lynott biography – 2016's *Cowboy Song* – was extremely useful when it came to getting the facts right about Thin Lizzy's much-missed frontman, as well as providing the odd quote. Much appreciated, Graeme.

As ever, a grateful nod to Steve Rosen, whose previous interviews with Gary Moore provided several quotes within the pages of this book. Steve, the more I write about guitars and the people that play them, the more I realise what an outstanding contribution you've made to the subject. From *Hot Wired Guitar* and *No Quarter* to *White Knuckles*, thank you!

Also, a mighty thumbs up to Neil Jeffries, Dave Ling, Lisa Sharken and Mick Wall whose interviews with Gary for *Classic Rock*, *Kerrang!*, *Louder* and *Vintage Guitar* were all tremendously helpful, and again, provided several quotes for this book.

To the *Belfast Telegraph*'s Linda Stewart. When I came across your 2016 piece – 'Belfast Blitz: Recalling the fear, death and horror of nights Nazi warplanes bombed city' – and read Alec Murray's evocative phrase 'Like fairyland,' I knew I had an opening line for the book. Genuine thanks then, for both a great article and some much-needed inspiration. Bless you too, Mr Murray.

I must also make mention of the website/Facebook page 'Lord Of The Strings' who have been providing reams of information for Gary's fans online from Budapest over the course of the years. Thank you.

Additionally, many thanks to the good people who compiled the 'Gary Moore Discography' or 'GM Bible', the contents of which proved helpful when researching the chapter about *After Hours* (again, Harry Shapiro's account of Moore's studio movements around this time was useful here).

Another shout must go out to Colin and Philomena Muinzer of the Ulster quartet Cruella de Ville, whose marvellous 1983 single 'Gypsy Girl' – and its spinning lyric 'Faster, faster, faster, faster' - provided the title for chapter five of this book. For those seeking a cult guitar hero to add to their collection, look no further than Colin Muinzer.

Elsewhere, I must offer thanks to Green Gartside, whose 1999 tune 'Brushed With Oil, Dusted With Powder' provides chapter 13 with its title. A candle lit for The Godz' Eric Moore too, whose 1978 gonzoid anthem 'Gotta Keep a Runnin'' is used as the title of chapter 27 of *White Knuckles*. R.I.P. Eric. I also raise a glass to the sadly departed Jackson C. Frank, whose 1966 tune 'Blues Run the Game' gives part four of this book its name. Wonderful singer, wonderful song and well worth a listen.

Last but certainly not least, a heartfelt thank you to everyone who kindly gave up their time and thoughts to help with this project: Tim Booth, Larry Canavan, Ted Carroll, Charlie Colton, Martin Davenport, Chalkie Davies, Brian Downey, Chris Dreja, Johnny Duhan, Jane Ebdon, Steve Galeazzi, Christine Gorham, Scott Gorham, Tim Goulding, John Hawken, Martin Levan, Catriona Lister, Gered Mankowitz, Dave Mattacks, Neil at Ace Records, Neil Murray, Adam Parsons, Ivan and Mary Pawle, Simon Phillips, Tony Platt, Andy Richards, Jan Schelhaas, Paul Scully, Nick Tauber, Otis Taylor, Ace Trump, Adrian Whittaker and the much-missed Steve York. For those who wished to keep their contributions 'behind the scenes', I also remain extremely grateful.

Several honourable mentions. A huge thank you to David Barraclough for both his patience and sage advice. David, I owe you several drinks and a Harry Dean Stanton biography. I must also sing the praises of Mark Smith and Claire Browne, whose fine editing skills have helped make this a much more readable book. And as ever, a bow and a curtsey to Chris Charlesworth, without whom, etc.

A short, but important point. While I was researching this book, Skid Row drummer Noel Bridgeman sadly passed away, succumbing to cancer on 23 March 2021. Because of the circumstances, it felt inappropriate to approach Noel's old friend Brush Shiels for an interview at that time. So, I instead used pre-existing quotes from both Noel and Brush to flesh out the story of Skid Row and Gary's Dublin years, with additional contributions coming from Tim Carroll, Brian Downey, Johnny Duhan, Paul Scully and the members of Dr Strangely Strange. Mr Shiels, I've tried hard to get all the facts right. But if there are any inaccuracies, please let me know and I'll ensure they're corrected.

Now, for some personal doffing of the cap: to John Constantine, 35 forever. That's quite the trick. You must show me how you do it. To Monica and Bianca Anderson, thanks for bringing the word 'Doovalacky' to my attention. Couldn't quite get it in this book on this occasion, but maybe next time. To Anthony Cutler, Ben Davis, David Kelly, Stephen Joseph and Andrew Robinson – gentlemen, as ever, thanks for listening. To absent friends, AKA The Deadpan Duke. Nice Telecaster collection, Maestro. Last – but certainly not least – to Trish. Seven-thirty and a small salad, please.

Of course, there remains one huge debt of gratitude. Bless you Gary, for letting us all hear what impossible sounds like.

Additional Sources

In addition to the sources named above, the following list of magazine articles, books, sleeve notes and DVDs/videos presented were particularly helpful when gathering information and quotes for this biography. I remain thankful to these authors, editors, journalists and publishers for all their endeavours.

Magazines, Periodicals, Newspapers, & Other Publications

'Gary Moore: When I'm Playing I Get Totally Lost In It', Peter Robinson, *Belfast Telegraph*, 2011

Gary Moore: Various Articles, Mick Wall, *Classic Rock*, 2004, 2014, 2021

'Listen: Ever Meet Hendrix? Glenn Hughes Interviewed', Geoff Barton, *Classic Rock*, November 2007

'Jumping At Shadows', Geoff Barton, *Classic Rock*, October 2014

'Gary Moore: leaving Thin Lizzy, the story of G-Force, and the terror of success', *Classic Rock*, Harry Shapiro, October 2022.

'How Van Halen's Debut Changed The Game', Unnamed author, *Classic Rock* 2018

'Gary Moore', *Guitarist Presents 100 Guitar Heroes*, 2009

'Moore The Merrier', Max Kay, Sounds' *Guitar Heroes* No.10, June 1983

'Roaring Back With Shapes Of Things To Come', Tom Mulhern, *Guitar Player*, October 1984

'The History Of Bruce, Baker And Moore', Ramon Goose, *The Guitar Show*, 2018

'Guitar On A Rampage', Steve Rosen, *Guitar World*, November 1984

'Gary Moore: The Wild Frontier', Harold Mac Wonderlea and Christine Rebmann, *Guitar World*, September 1987

'Flying In A Blues Dream', Bill Milkowski, *Guitar World*, July 1990

'Moore Better Blues', Harold Steinblatt, *Guitar World*, November 1990

'Gary Moore: After Hours Interview', Paul Sexton, CD Promo, 1992

Gary Moore: 'I jumped on the Blues bandwagon? I was the bandwagon!' Sian Llewellyn, *Classic Rock Presents Blues Rock*, 2007

'Gimme (Gary) Moore', Dave Ling, *Louder*, May 2006

'"We're not Cream!" How Gary Moore, Jack Bruce And Ginger Baker Made An Album', Harry Shapiro, *Louder*, 2017

'The Boy Who Thought He Was Bullet Proof', Dermott Hayes, *Mojo*, December 1993

'Whatever Guitar I Pick Up I Can Make Sound A Certain Way', Steve Rosen, *Ultimate Guitar*, 2011

'Still Got The Blues Again!', Lisa Sharken, *Vintage Guitar*, 2010

Books

The Guitar Greats by John Tobler and Stuart Grundy (BBC, 1983)

Gary Moore by Chris Welch (Bobcat Books, 1986)

Irish Rock: Roots, Personalities, Directions by Mark Prendergast (O'Brien Press Ltd., 1987)

Big Noises: Rock Guitar In The 1990s by Geoff Nicholson (Quartet, 1991)

Electric Eden: Unearthing Britain's Visionary Music by Rob Young (Faber & Faber, 2011)

Phil Lynott: The Rocker by Mark Putterford (Castle Communications/ Omnibus Press, 1994)

The Ballad Of The Thin Man: The Authorised Biography Of Phil Lynott by Stuart Bailie (Boxtree, 1997)

Guitar Presents: In The Listening Room compiled by John Stix (Cherry Lane, 2000)

1968: The Year That Rocked The World by Mark Kurlansky (Phoenix Press, 2004)

Irish Folk, Trad And Blues: A Secret History by Colin Harper and Trevor Hodgett (Cherry Red, 2005)

Green Beat: The Forgotten Era Of Irish Rock by Daragh O'Halloran (The Brehon Press, 2006)

The Boys Are Back In Town by Scott Gorham and Harry Doherty (Omnibus Press, 2012)

Cowboy Song: The Authorised Biography of Phil Lynott by Graeme Thompson (Constable, 2016)

Gary Moore: I Can't Wait Until Tomorrow – The Official Biography by Harry Shapiro (BMG, 2017)

Dr Strangely Strange: Fitting Pieces Into The Puzzle by Adrian Whittaker (Ozymandias Press, 2019)

DVDs/Videos/TV/Radio

Gary Moore: Emerald Aisles. Live in Ireland (Virgin, 1985)

Gary Moore & The Midnight Blues Band: Live At Montreux 1990 (EV Classics/Universal, 2004)

Thin Lizzy: The Boys Are Back In Town (Eagle Vision, 2003)

'Inside Thin Lizzy, 1971–1983: An Independent Critical Review' (Classic Rock Productions, 2003)

'Gary Moore And Friends: One Night In Dublin: A Tribute To Phil Lynott' (DTS, 2006)

'Outlawed: Thin Lizzy & The Real Phil Lynott' (WHE International, 2006)

'Rock Milestones: Thin Lizzy's Live And Dangerous' (Edgehill Productions, 2006)

Thin Lizzy: Live And Dangerous (Mercury/Universal, 2007)

Still Got The Blues (BBC, Stuart Bailie, 2011)

Sleeve Notes

The sleeve notes for reissued versions of Skid Row's *Self-Titled/34 Hours*, Thin Lizzy's *Nightlife*, *Fighting* and *Black Rose*, Greg Lake's *Self-Titled/Manoeuvres* and various Gary Moore releases (from *Grinding Stone* to *How Blue Can You Get*) were particularly helpful when researching *White Knuckles*, and provided several additional quotes throughout the pages of this book.